FUNCTIONAL CURRICULUM FOR ELEMENTARY, MIDDLE, AND SECONDARY AGE STUDENTS WITH SPECIAL NEEDS

FUNCTIONAL CURRICULUM FOR ELEMENTARY, MIDDLE, AND SECONDARY AGE STUDENTS WITH SPECIAL NEEDS

SECOND EDITION

Edited by
Paul Wehman
and
John Kregel

pro·ed
An International Publisher

8700 Shoal Creek Boulevard
Austin, Texas 78757-6897
800/897-3202   Fax 800/397-7633
www.proedinc.com

© 1997, 2004 by PRO-ED, Inc.
8700 Shoal Creek Boulevard
Austin, Texas 78757-6897
800/897-3202   Fax 800/397-7633
www.proedinc.com

Library of Congress Cataloging-in-Publication Data

Functional curriculum for elementary, middle, and secondary age students with special
needs / edited by Paul Wehman, John Kregel.—2nd ed.
    p. cm.
    Includes bibliographical references and index.
    ISBN 0-89079-956-3
    1. Special education—United States—Curricula.   2. Students with disabilities—
Education—United States—Curricula.   3. Curriculum planning—United States.
I. Wehman, Paul.   II. Kregel, John, Ed.D.

LC3981.F85   2003
371.9'0973—dc21

2002031907

This book is designed in New Century Schoolbook and Melior.

Printed in the United States of America

1 2 3 4 5 6 7 8 9 10   07 06 05 04 03

Contents

Preface

In this second edition of *Functional Curriculum for Elementary, Middle, and Secondary Age Students with Special Needs,* we have expanded our framework for a functional and longitudinal curriculum for children and adolescents with disabilities and other special needs. There is a stronger demand than ever to provide functional curriculum for students, that is, curriculum with everyday usefulness and value in making the student more competent and independent. In addition to the focus on functional curriculum in this book, there is a strong emphasis on showing how to link curriculum from the elementary to the middle school, and on up into the secondary school and adulthood. We believe that not enough attention has been paid to connecting the different curriculum levels so that there is a continuity of educational service for students and their families. We also believe that transitions for middle school to high school and high school to adulthood are more important than ever.

Youth with disabilities are significantly unemployed or underemployed compared to their nondisabled peers and tend to drop out of school more and go to college less. Increased concerns about the dropout problem are now emerging because of state and local education agency experiences with high-stakes accountability in the context of standards-based reform. States and school districts have identified what students should know and be able to do and have implemented assessments to ensure that students have attained the identified knowledge and skills. Large numbers of students, however, are not faring well on these assessments. For youth with disabilities several factors beyond academic achievement influence the ability of these youth to pass such assessments, including accurate identification of disability and provision of needed accommodations and educational supports that make learning possible regardless of disability-related factors. In particular, the provision of accommodations ensures that assessments measure a student's true academic skills, rather than elements of his or her disability. There is a strong need for evidence-based practices for transition-related activities, specifically as they relate to vocational competence, career preparation, and competitive employment. To address these important issues, we have added Chapter 4, "Accessing the General Curriculum Within a Functional Curriculum Framework."

This book focuses on key priorities in helping students with disabilities prepare for independence and employment. For example, we know that students need to attain competitive employment *before* leaving school through assistance from school personnel in conjunction with the state–federal vocational rehabilitation program and other community agencies. One of the most powerful ways to interfere with the progression of a large number of youth onto Supplemental Security Income (SSI) long-term benefits is to create a competitive employment work history. This could be done by strengthening the Individuals with Disabilities Education Act (IDEA; 1997) to provide stronger language supporting local education agencies' responsibility to provide employment and career-building services. It could also be done by establishing a grant authority in IDEA for states to earmark dollars strictly for funding local education agency competitive employment initiatives, including supported employment.

We also know that one-stop career centers supported through the Workforce Investment Act of 1998 (WIA; P.L. 105-202) need to accommodate students with disabilities. Much of the curriculum material in this book could be used to help staff in one-stop centers implement their job placement efforts. Although recent efforts have improved architectural accessibility, "invisible walls" remain that restrict access to and prevent coordination of services. Federal and state policies should be amended to require inclusion of students, beginning at age 16 (age 14 when appropriate), in the one-stop centers, while the students are still in special education. An expansion of WIA could involve (a) opening all services to a younger population (e.g., ages 16–21) and (b) opening one-stop training services under some parameter while students are still in school.

Clearly, the U.S. Congress and the president's administration should work to ensure that federal monies appropriated through the WIA, Titles XIX and XX of the Social Security Act, the Rehabilitation Act of 1973, and the IDEA are used to support competitive employment and career development alternatives for students. For example, federal and state agencies should expand the use of funding mechanisms that encourage joint funding of career development and work experience that begins early in the educational process for youth with disabilities. Illustrations include the following:

1. Local school districts and developmental disabilities agencies could jointly fund job placement and ongoing support services for students with significant disabilities who may already be receiving SSI benefits.

2. Local school districts and vocational rehabilitation offices could jointly fund the development of apprenticeship and mentor programs or corporate partnership initiatives.

Vocational rehabilitation (VR) needs to be funded in such a way that students can participate more fully and sooner in the transition process. Many, if not most, state VR agencies follow a policy of not providing rehabilitation placement services until a student is within 6 months of graduation.

In this book, we have assembled contributions from some of this nation's leading authorities in curriculum design; they have provided dozens of highly relevant tables, charts, and instructional programs for direct service providers. We hope this material can be used not only in teacher preparation but in leadership training as well. At the same time, each chapter is based on the most recent research and the most contemporary thinking to help teachers and other instructional personnel be current in their planning. The chapters in this book deal with areas of expertise that most students will need. For example, self-determination skills, functional academics, transportation, home and community living, and activities of daily living, as well as work preparation and socialization, are all critical to success in adulthood. The chapters have a heavy curriculum format that is designed to be as user-friendly as possible to teachers, instructional personnel, counselors, and occupational therapists, in addition to other people in the special education, psychology, and rehabilitation fields with interest in this area.

We are extremely grateful to the contributors in this book. People such as Pam Targett, Paul Sale, James Martin, Pam Wolfe, Richard Kubina, Kathryn Banks, Shirley Chandler, Sara Pankaskie, Marty Agran, Cheryl Hanley-Maxwell, Michael West, Colleen Thoma, Kathe Wittig, Vicki Dowdy, Kelly Ligon, Lana Collet-Klingenberg, Daniel Steere, Stacy Dymond, Fred Spooner, Wendy Wood, and Teri Burcroff all willingly gave their time to make this an outstanding curriculum book for either preservice or in-service use. We are most grateful to them as well as our many colleagues who provided insights about the best way to develop this book. It is our hope that it will have tremendous utility to students in training and professionals in the field.

REFERENCES

Individuals with Disabilities Education Act Amendments of 1997, 20 U.S.C. § 1400 *et seq.*
Rehabilitation Act of 1973, 29 U.S.C. § 701 *et seq.*
Social Security Act, 42 U.S.C. § 301 *et seq.*
Workforce Investment Act of 1998, 29 U.S.C. § 2801 *et seq.*

CHAPTER 1

Principles of Curriculum Design

Road to Transition from School to Adulthood

Paul Wehman and Pam Sherron Targett

Lucy is a 6-year-old with severe mental retardation and who is deaf and blind. She is cortically blind but responds to sounds with gazes and turns her head toward sounds on occasion. She smiles when stimulated by touch, and she seems to enjoy music. A team of professionals, using modern technology, has rigged switch devices that allow Lucy to activate toys and musical devices by eyebrow and tongue movements. She is also physically prompted to use switches to control devices in her environment such as the toaster. This technology allows her to participate partially in daily activities. Staff members also communicate what is happening with her using tactile cues and prompts during all activities. Different staff members wear different colognes to facilitate her identification of them. Opportunities for choice are constantly presented to Lucy. Many instructional activities take place in community settings such as the mall or fast-food restaurant. The family and professionals plan together to be sure that everyone exposes Lucy to multiple sensory experiences.

Ted attends a middle school and has been learning to participate in grocery shopping at a neighborhood supermarket. Because he uses a walker for support, he has been paired with a peer for the shopping activity. Typically, Ted identifies the correct item while the peer pushes the cart. For the past year, the school occupational therapist has become increasingly discouraged with the use of an isolated therapy model. She works with Ted in the occupational therapy room twice a week and is concerned that he may not use newly learned skills in natural settings. As a result, she and Ted's teacher decided to incorporate the occupational therapy objective of transferring to and from the walker with the grocery shopping activity. The therapist developed a program to teach Ted to leave his walker at the front of the store, transfer to the grocery cart, and use the cart as support while he shops. At first, this task was difficult for Ted because the cart would roll as he attempted to transfer. Also, Ted could not let go of the cart with both hands when retrieving an item or he would lose his balance. Thus, they taught him to move through an aisle of the store selecting items only on the right-hand side. At the end of the aisle, he makes a U-turn so that he can pass down the aisle again to select items on the left side. Although he still shops occasionally with a peer, Ted is especially proud that he can go through the store alone while his teacher waits at the front of the store or his mother completes her own shopping.

Miguel is a young man with severe mental retardation who is involved in a high school vocational training program. His mother expressed her concern to the instructional team during the Individualized Education Plan (IEP) conference that her son was not involved in household routines. In fact, he depended on family members for most activities of daily living such as selecting clothing, grooming, preparing meals, and maintaining his bedroom. Miguel can count to five, but has not mastered many academic skills such as color identification, reading, and typical readiness skills.

Miguel recently began training at a new work site that requires employees to wear uniforms. The instructional staff noticed immediately that Miguel was highly motivated to wear the uniform. In fact, his mother had problems with Miguel wanting to wear his uniform every day rather than only on Tuesdays and Thursdays when he reports to the training site. The instructional team worked with the family to incorporate this newfound motivation into critical home routines. The teacher adapted a calendar by placing large green dots on Tuesdays and Thursdays and attaching a red marker on a string. Now when Miguel gets up in the morning, he goes to the refrigerator with his mother to look at the calendar. He locates the current day to determine whether it is a uniform day. After making this decision, he takes the marker and places an X on the day so that he will know where to look for the next day. Then he is ready to assist in the selection of clothing. The instructional team also decided to teach Miguel to participate in washing the uniform. This has now become a Saturday chore in the home. Miguel cannot yet perform all the steps, but he does load and unload the machine and operate the controls, which are adapted with colored tape. Even though Miguel is still not independent in performing household tasks, he is certainly more involved than he was before. Not only are his parents pleased with his progress, but his younger siblings have begun to comment about their older brother going to work.

These three case studies represent individual students with disabilities who could be found in any school system throughout the country. These are students who have significant learning and behavioral challenges and who require extensive training in independent living skills before they become adults. This book has been developed because in today's complex society, there is a greater need than ever before for students with disabilities to receive a comprehensive independent living skills curriculum. In the past 20 years, thousands of such children have entered the public school system for the first time; furthermore, state institutions and other segregated programs are on the wane. As a result, the need for competence in a broad array of independent living skills has become paramount for students with all disabilities and throughout the school system.

The primary purpose of this book is to provide a solid foundation of longitudinal curriculum for teachers and other direct service providers as they design and implement independent living skills training programs. Longitudinal curriculum involves continuity of planning, instruction, and communication across student age levels by teachers and parents. The enormous amount of research literature published during the past 10 years needs to be put into practical use by teachers in classrooms and other training environments toward this goal of a longitudinal curriculum. One of the major goals of this book is to use this research information as a basis for sound educational planning that will lead to positive community outcomes for students as they leave school.

A second major focus of this book is to present curriculum across the major age levels within schools at the elementary, middle, and secondary levels. Although a number of curriculum books have been published, many of them focus exclusively on those with mild versus severe disabilities or on the elementary versus the secondary age levels. This book covers the major independent living areas in which students need to demonstrate competence and adapts them across the different age levels.

In this chapter, we briefly review the major principles of curriculum design, critical areas of independent living, and interagency planning and service delivery.

MAJOR PRINCIPLES OF CURRICULUM DESIGN

There are numerous approaches to designing curriculum, from commercially available "canned" programs to those that are "homemade." Many schools also provide a standard curriculum that all teachers must follow for students. In some cases, state departments of education have mandated the use of certain types of curricula for students, which presumably lead to the passing of competency or literacy tests. These differing approaches to curriculum design are some of the reasons that many students leave school without the necessary building blocks of independent living skills that are essential for competence in today's society. For true continuity across the age groups in school for the purpose of having a genuine longitudinal curriculum, four key instructional design tenets need to be followed. The curriculum must be

1. individualized and person centered,
2. functional or practical,
3. adaptive, and
4. ecologically oriented.

Individualized and Person Centered

Each child is an individual and requires a specialized set of instructional objectives that are particularly suited for his or her needs. In all too many U.S. classrooms, students' IEPs are virtually identical in content and scope. This type of blanket programming does a grave injustice to each student's particular needs. We should not assume, for example, that all 16-year-olds with a label of educational mental retardation should learn the capitals of all 50 states. It may be that this is an inappropriate instructional objective for all these students; on the other hand, there may be a justification for one or two to learn something like this because they hope to go on to a community college.

The concept of person-centered planning has become increasingly popular (Mount, 1994; Pearpoint, O'Brien, & Forest, 1993) and is frequently suggested as an approach to promoting individualized service planning (Reid, Everson, & Green, 1999; Whitney-Thomas, Shaw, Honey, & Butterworth, 1998). In person-centered planning, environments, services, and supports are tailored to students' dreams, wants, and needs.

First, person-centered approaches are driven by the student, family, and friends (Rogan, 1997). As an active participant in planning, the student is given tools and strategies to support him or her in taking a leadership role in the assessment and curriculum planning process (Everson & Reid, 1999; Mount, 1994, 1997). This helps ensure that goals and objectives are based on the student's desires and support needs rather than only on available program options.

Second, person-centered planning approaches are visionary and future oriented (Kregel, 1998; Pearpoint et al., 1993) because the information gathered serves as a foundation for looking toward the future and thinking about it optimistically. A student's current home and community environments are investigated with a special focus on the student's independent functioning in the future. During this process, a team is encouraged to discover the unique qualities of the student, listen to his or her dreams and desires, focus on his or her abilities first, and then support the student's wants and needs. This requires the team to dismiss any preconceived notions about the inability of people with disabilities that may stem from disability labels or formal test results.

Person-centered planning recognizes the importance of both formal and informal supports to assist a student with achieving his or her dreams and plans to maximize independence, placing emphasis on the use of natural supports (Everson & Reid, 1999; Wehman, Everson, & Reid, 2001). This does not mean that students will not need specialized services but instead encourages the team to seek new or different resources if needed to support the student's desired outcome. For example, Joan, a student with a significant physical disability, dreams of the day she will walk out of her parents' home and into her own apartment. One area of concern centers on Joan's ability to live independently. In addition to skill development, the team also focuses on what support options are available or may be required to make this possible. For example, independent living assistance could come from a variety of sources such as having a paid personal assistant, a roommate, or adaptive equipment or simply performing a task in a new way.

Person-centered planning is especially important for students and family members who need a positive vision and a road map of what the future can hold for them. The primary theme of this book is that an individualized longitudinal curriculum is the best way to provide educational programming to students with special needs. A person-centered planning approach is highly consistent with this type of long-term curriculum planning.

Person-centered planning in the context of longitudinal curriculum means that teachers must communicate across the students' different age spans and provide continuity between the curriculum objectives from year to year. The absence of this form of individualized person-centered planning has been the hallmark of many special education programs, thereby depriving students with disabilities the opportunity to reach their fullest potential. Fortunately, person-centered planning is actively combating this problem and challenging agencies to change existing schools and support services by modifying existing programs and designing new ones that focus on individualized services for the student and promote full community participation in the future.

Functional or Practical

The second design requirement for a longitudinal curriculum is that its objectives be both functional and practical in nature (Clark, 1996). Although the importance of a functional curriculum has been written about extensively, many schools continue to provide nonfunctional instructional objectives to the long-term disadvantage of the students. There is nothing especially complicated about designing and implementing functional objectives. What is involved is a careful analysis of each student's individual needs within a variety of environments, which are then prioritized according to what the student needs to learn for enhanced functioning in the community.

The functional aspects of a student's curriculum cannot be emphasized enough. No matter how good the quality of instruction, how sophisticated the equipment, or how new the school facilities, if the student is being offered inappropriate subject matter, then he or she loses the opportunity to benefit from a more useful education. For example, a teenager named John has moderate mental retardation and cerebral palsy. John has had an IEP objective to tie his shoelaces into a knot, which he has attempted to learn over the past 5 years without success. Why would any teacher continue to teach this skill when alternative styles of shoes and fasteners that John could use are available? Common sense suggests that John needs to be learning some other skills that will allow him to be competent at home and in the community rather than spending day after day with, at best, marginal success on a skill that does not build on his strengths or respond to his most pressing needs. Assessment activities and planning should address the following key question: What activities does this person need to perform to be an effective and competent human being in the weeks and months ahead? Table 1.1 shows a strategy for identifying functional activities.

Adaptive

In addition to being person centered and functional, longitudinal curriculum design must adapt to the specific goals and capabilities of a given child. It should be obvious that to provide an individualized and functional curriculum, adaptations will be necessary. Furthermore, this principle suggests that a curriculum objective identified by the IEP committee at the beginning of the school year may have to be altered 2 or 3 months later. If the team agrees that a modified objective

TABLE 1.1
Identifying Functional Activities for Instruction Across All Curriculum Domains

1. Select a broad curriculum domain (recreational, community, vocational, domestic) to be analyzed.
2. Identify a list of environments within home, school, and community settings where students may perform activities related to the identified domain.
3. Identify additional environments by surveying other professionals, the parents, and the students.
4. Observe these identified environments and list those skills that are essential for competence in each environment.
5. Verify the list of skills with other professionals and with parents.
6. Repeat this process for all domains.
7. Review and revise as needed (with a minimum of one review annually).

makes sense, then the goal should be changed. It is unethical and much more problematic to continue providing instruction to students who are not learning because the objective is inappropriate. The teacher must remember, however, that it may take some time to reach a definitive decision about adapting an objective. For example, it may very well be that functioning independently in the community is appropriate as the general area of curriculum, but riding a bus is not the right target objective at this point; instead, crossing the street might be more appropriate. Adaptation is critical for students with some sophistication in cognitive problem solving and academics. The resource teacher who is working with a student to improve reading skills must be flexible enough to change the targeted goals if the student is becoming increasingly frustrated due to failure. This is also true in learning computer skills, calculation, or arithmetic skills or in improving handwriting. The need to modify goals frequently tends to be viewed negatively by some teachers who are too rigid or who do not wish to take the time to identify new objectives.

Adapting curriculum instruction has been shown to be an effective way of providing instruction for students with significant disabilities. This book focuses on using an adaptation approach to help students learn the curriculum objectives and reach their fullest potential. The teacher must think about the need to adapt when a student is continuing to have problems in acquiring the skills that were originally targeted.

Each curriculum objective identified in this book is subject to adaptation and redesign based on students' individual needs.

Ecologically Oriented

Decades ago, Brown, Nietupski, and Hamre-Nietupski (1976) wrote eloquently about the importance of examining a student's environments when making decisions about what curriculum objectives to teach the student. Today these ideas are more viable than ever, especially when complemented with person-centered planning, functional instruction, and adaptation. An ecologically oriented program requires the student, teacher, and family to sit down and discuss the student's high-priority activities for each of the major living environments. For example, what are the student's main activities at home and in his or her immediate neighborhood? What are the major activities that the student performs or wishes to perform in the community (e.g., going to church, shopping for groceries, visiting the mall)? What are the student's major recreational activities or activities in which the student has interest? Many potential environments, or what Brown and colleagues term *subenvironments,* can be analyzed for different activities. These activities then provide the foundation for the curriculum objectives. Therefore, if a student goes with his father to church every Saturday morning to participate in a men's brunch, the student might need to place high priority on learning how to perform cleanup activities. The student could then help the father and participate with other adults in a meaningful activity. An example of a partial ecological inventory for a community grocery store is provided in Figure 1.1.

There is no end to the objectives that can be identified using an ecological approach. This design feature is viewed as being particularly useful for those with severe intellectual disabilities, but this is not necessarily true. Any student

Domain: Community living
Environment: Grocery store

Subenvironment: Parking lot
Activity: Entering the store
Sample skills: Exiting the vehicle, locating the store entrance, looking out for moving vehicles, stopping for moving vehicles, entering the store

Subenvironment: Deli
Activity: Ordering food
Sample skills: Greeting the worker, pushing a cart, waiting in line for a turn, making a choice, placing an order, thanking the worker

Subenvironment: Pharmacy
Activity: Getting a prescription filled
Sample skills: Locating the pharmacy, dropping off prescription request, waiting in line for a turn, stating name and date of birth, telling time, thanking the pharmacist

Subenvironment: Check-out register
Activity: Purchasing items
Sample skills: Locating an open lane; getting in line; loading items onto conveyor belt; answering questions related to bagging preference and type of payment; paying cashier using cash, check, or credit card; thanking cashier

FIGURE 1.1. Ecological inventory for grocery store.

with a disability is going to have some skill deficits within environments outside school, and the teacher and student, along with the family, must identify and prioritize the skills on which to focus in the coming school year.

The four principles of effective curriculum design—that it be individualized and person centered, functional or practical, adaptive, and ecologically oriented—are the glue that hold the longitudinal curriculum together. To provide continuity of instruction across the different age levels, all participants in the educational process, including administration, must adopt and adhere to these tenets. Because school systems do not always "buy in" to these ideas, parents will sometimes have to take a larger proportion of the responsibility while advocating for change and the school system to provide an appropriate education.

Many types of curriculum goals, objectives, and activities are discussed in this book; however, the four major principles related to effective curriculum design are an ongoing and major theme throughout the chapters. These principles must be understood and followed to ensure that learning takes place and behavioral competencies are developed. Table 1.2 provides a series of activities for prioritizing instructional targets for students.

CRITICAL AREAS OF INDEPENDENT LIVING

Career Education and Work

When teachers think of independent living, they do not usually think about career education or work as a curriculum area. However, the ability to get a job,

TABLE 1.2
Prioritizing Activities for Instruction

1. Identify with the student and his or her family the student's performance in each of the domain categories. Then identify desired relevant future environments in which it is projected the student will be functioning.

2. Identify activities and skills relevant to the student's current environment; identify skills necessary to function in projected future environments.

3. Review all relevant current and future activities and indicate those activities that occur in two or more domains and that are age appropriate.

4. List these activities from most to least frequent in occurrence.

5. From this list, identify those activities that are crucial for the student's safety. Next identify those activities that are critical for functioning independently in the identified future environments.

6. Select for immediate instruction:

   a. Those activities essential to the student's safety within current environments.

   b. Those activities that the student must perform frequently to function independently within current and identified future environments.

7. Select remaining objectives from the list of activities (Step 4).

hold a job, and identify a career path is an extremely important aspect of successful independent living. Most people cannot expect to have a happy and enjoyable life without some form of productive work activity.

Students need to develop an understanding of the relationships among work responsibility, pay, and getting along with others (Benz & Lindstrom, 1997). They need to understand how their involvement in the community workforce is important to the way they are perceived. Students at all levels of disability need to develop a work ethic. For example, students who work at the local grocery store not only must be able to bag groceries and carry them out to the car but also need to know how to speak politely and communicate in a positive way to all customers, even though some customers are unfriendly or rude. All too often, schools have been slow to provide ongoing career education and vocational education instruction for students, particularly those with more significant disabilities (Blackorby & Wagner, 1996; Colley & Jamison, 1998; Wagner, 1992), yet the multiple stages of career development are very important. Figure 1.2 shows how this process unfolds, as a student grows older.

If a student is going to be employed once he or she leaves school, working while still in school can be advantageous. Students will not only learn valuable work skills but can also begin to develop a work ethic. Many kinds of vocational training can be considered in the curriculum; these goals will be covered in Chapter 8. Some examples of skills that may be taught in the context of a community-based vocational training program are described in the following case study.

	Career Awareness	Career Exploration	Career Preparation	Job Placement
Elementary	███	███		
Junior High		███	███	
Senior High			███	
At graduation				███

FIGURE 1.2. Stages of career education.

NICK

Nick is a 15-year-old student with severe mental retardation. He expresses his basic needs (e.g., eat, drink, bathroom) using utterances that those who know him best can understand. He can read some sight words and can count to 20 without assistance. Nick responds best to one- to three-step verbal instructions paired with modeling and verbal praise. He does not spend much time around his disabled peers but is particularly fond of interacting with other male students. Nick lives with his parents and two older male siblings. Last semester he visited a number of community jobs representative of business in his local community and participated in three situational assessments.

A person-centered planning meeting was held to discuss future vocational goals and objectives. The team decided that Nick should continue to gain exposure to employment opportunities and begin to develop work skills by participating in the school's community-based vocational skills program. Training takes place in a number of different settings, including grocery store, department store, manufacturer, hospital, and hotel. The team agreed that Nick would participate in the hospitality training program. The decision was based on a number of factors:

- Nick's parents report that he helps at home and seems to enjoy performing basic household chores.

- During football and basketball seasons, Nick helps in the locker room by folding and handing out towels to the team.

- There are numerous hotels in the immediate area and many on the public bus line.

- Situational assessment results revealed that Nick did not like handling groceries and had extreme difficulty staying on task in an environment with a lot of environmental stimuli (i.e., noise and constant movement).

The teacher will use systematic instruction to provide training to Nick and three other students 4 hours a day. Table 1.3 shows some of the skills that Nick will learn.

TABLE 1.3
Example of Skills Nick Will Learn in the Vocational Training Program

Teaching Environment	Skills To Learn
School	Putting on uniform Brushing hair Managing time
On route to and at the bus stop	Following directions Recognizing a bus stop
Bus	Paying the fare Communicating with strangers Getting off the bus at the correct stop
Hotel (in general)	Punching in and out on time clock Riding an elevator Exiting a building during an emergency
Hotel housekeeping department	Locking and unlocking a door Making a bed Choosing an activity to perform Taking turns
Hotel laundry and linen department	Operating a washer Folding towels Asking for assistance
Hotel break room	Socializing with others Using vending machines Using a pay phone

In addition to the daily 4-hour skills training, the students will meet with a member of the hotel management team once a week for customer service training. During this time, the students will practice interviewing, greetings, and other customer service skills.

In general, the selection of training tasks can be best accomplished by exploring a student's vocational interest, aptitudes, and support needs. Another key consideration is the needs of the business community. The local labor market should be surveyed continuously to identify current hiring trends and future labor needs. Vocational education teachers and school administrators must develop partnerships with area employers who operate in or near the school district. It is these employers who will judge the success or failure of the school's efforts in vocational education. Staying abreast of current and future hiring needs ensures that realistic employment goals are set for students. The following list suggests sample goals for students.

1. Pat will sample jobs in a variety of community settings with the assistance of a job coach.

2. Marcie will explore a career as a baker's assistant and visit a minimum of three area businesses with this type of occupation.

3. Talisha will work part-time as a stocker in a building supply store that offers the opportunity to work full-time and receive medical benefits.

4. Joaquin will explore telecommuting employment options.

5. Max will use supported employment services to assist him with locating and learning how to perform a part-time, entry-level job at a retailer that is located on the bus line.

Community Participation and Living Skills

Community living skills are frequently grouped into broad clusters such as domestic skills, mobility skills, activities of daily living, personal social interactions, and communication. Actual independence, however, depends on the competence a student shows in community living, as well as the availability and quality of support services in the community. The adequacy of support is a critical factor that will determine whether a student will do well. For example, Mick, a young man with cerebral palsy and mild intellectual disability, may choose to live in a community that has strongly adhered to the Americans with Disabilities Act (ADA; 1990). The community has several different transportation options, accessible walkways and retailers, and a user-friendly telecommunications system. Mick will be able to more actively access and participate in his community than Sandy, a woman with comparable physical abilities who lives in an environment where there has been indifference or apathy in making transportation and community facilities accessible.

What this means to the teacher is that despite even Herculean efforts at instruction, it may still be difficult for a student to get around the community successfully if the community does not adhere to ADA guidelines. Fortunately, since the enactment of the ADA and the advent of universal design practices, this is becoming less of a barrier. Nevertheless, it is extremely important for teachers to develop each student's community living skills to help him or her reach full potential. Listing community living skills is almost impossible because there are so many, but some general examples of skills taught in a community skills curriculum are listed in Table 1.4.

Again, the four principles of curriculum design described earlier should be used to identify and narrow down the key target skills for instruction into a manageable number.

Independent living skills training helps persons with disabilities establish a sense of self and enhances self-esteem. It is one thing for students to go to school and to live at home, but once they "age-out" of a school, they face a major transition to the postschool world. As students become adults, they will have to develop some form of a career, find their own place to live, and learn how to get about in a complex and challenging community. Chapter 10 will further delineate the skills needed to succeed in the community. It also is necessary to recognize the roadblocks to making this successful transition and become accustomed to overcoming these real or perceived barriers with creative supports that can bolster a student's competence and participation in the community. The following are examples of community living goals:

1. Leon will attend the movies one weekend a month.

2. Jean will live in a supervised apartment setting with no more than one roommate.

3. Monty will dine out with her friends once a month at the restaurant of her choice.

TABLE 1.4
Community Participation: Examples of Curriculum Areas and Activities

Area	Activities
Shopping	Purchasing deodorant at the drugstore Purchasing food to make a meal at the grocery store Purchasing supplies in the school store
Banking	Opening a checking account Making a deposit Operating an automatic teller machine
Eating out	Placing an order at a fast-food restaurant Using good manners Paying for a meal
Recreation	Joining a gym Calling a theater for a movie schedule Riding a bicycle
Medical services	Scheduling an appointment Locating the office Checking in at the office upon arrival
Communication	Mailing a letter at the post office Using a calling card at a pay telephone at a mall Using a cell phone to call the operator for assistance
Community safety	Asking for assistance if lost Responding to strangers Walking in a parking lot

Note. Skills selected for training must be based on individual student needs and priorities.

4. Tina will deposit her allowance in her bank account and make a withdrawal.

5. Maria will move into a supervised apartment setting by age 22.

Personal Health and Safety

To successfully assimilate into their communities, students with disabilities must learn about personal health and safety. Although some basic skills may be taught, such as applying a Band-Aid or crossing a two-lane street, emphasis should be placed on training the student to attend to his or her own unique health needs and safety issues within the context of his or her current and future daily living environments. In addition, students with significant disabilities may be at much greater risk for accidents and emergency situations than other students, and thus it becomes critical to prepare them to respond appropriately.

Although health and safety are not new areas of instruction—for almost 30 years, students with mild disabilities have received basic training in crossing streets, using simple first aid, calling 911, and so on—today the teaching of health and safety issues focuses on the specific needs of the student. For example, the training of a student with diabetes may focus on teaching the student how to independently monitor his or her blood sugar and properly administer insulin.

Chapter 13 will present a more sophisticated approach to safety skill instruction in the way that Agran, Marchand-Martella, and Martella (1995) have suggested. With dangers such as AIDS, playground injuries, and drugs in schools, it is easy to see how students with disabilities could be at risk. Again, educators must go beyond teaching basic skills and focus on the student's unique health and safety needs. In creating an educational plan for each student, it is essential to include issues related to safety and health as illustrated in the following goals:

1. Garland will independently take her medication to maintain control over seizures.

2. Scott will use proper procedures when handling and grooming animals.

3. Ernestine will use proper procedures for lifting and carrying heavy items.

4. David will receive wheelchair maintenance and adjustment as needed.

5. Juwhal will reduce incidents of self-injury through stress management or other self-management techniques.

Self-Determination

Only recently have community programs begun to teach students critical self-determination skills. These skills extend well beyond learning how to make choices and self-advocate (Wehmeyer, 1994). Instead, students are prepared for adulthood by learning how to take control of their lives and establish their rightful place in the community and society at large. Far too often, people with disabilities, particularly those with more significant disabilities, become highly dependent on others to take care of them. This reliance on others often inhibits independence for many individuals with disabilities. Self-determination refers to teaching students about their rights and providing training on the skills and experience needed to take control of their lives. Some examples of personal attributes that relate to self-determination include self-awareness, goal setting, decision making, assertiveness (Wehmeyer, Kelchner, & Richards 1995; Wehmeyer & Lawrence, 1995), and transition supports (Hughes & Carter, 2000).

If students with disabilities are going to become independent, integrated, and included in the community and society at large, then self-determination skills must be taught starting at infancy and practiced throughout life. The self-determination curriculum content may range from teaching basic rights to how to be assertive in a given situation. Chapter 3 will describe this critical area in much greater detail. Table 1.5 provides a brief explanation of the types of skills that may be taught in this area.

It is extremely important to note that these should be taught to students early, and opportunities to practice these skills must take place across all environments, including home, school, and community, on an ongoing basis.

Self-determination should be introduced into all areas of the school curriculum, but it will require some thought on the part of educators and parents on how to make sure that self-determination is introduced across various community environments. Parents play a critical role in fostering self-determination and must be actively engaged in this process (Cook, Brotherson, Weigel-Garrey, & Mize, 1996). Educators must also be willing to go beyond simply teaching basic

TABLE 1.5
Sample Content for Self-Determination and Advocacy Curriculum

Curriculum Area	Possible Content
Choice and decision making	Students are given real-life opportunities to identify preferences, make choices, and identify long-term risk and consequences associated with decisions.
Problem solving	Students are given real-life opportunities to solve problems in the context of activities of daily living, interpersonal relationships, and so on.
Goal setting and attainment	Students are given opportunities to set personal short- and long-term goals, then evaluate and refine their plans.
Self-advocacy	Students are taught assertiveness, effective listening skills, negotiation skills, and so on.
Self-awareness and knowledge	Students have opportunities to discover their strengths and support needs, learn how to express personal needs and praise, and give feedback to others.

knowledge and skills in this most important area. Instead, students must be afforded with a multitude of opportunities to practice and build on these skills in real-life situations.

The idea that students will acquire self-determination and self-advocacy over the long term is extremely important if they are to become truly independent and reasonably self-sufficient adults. Again, this training is critical and must begin with very young children to prevent the cycle of dependency and feelings of personal inadequacy to evolve. Here are five examples of self-advocacy goals:

1. Margaret will attribute her success or failure to her efforts rather than to her ability or luck.

2. Krystal will actively set goals for her future education by systematically evaluating her options for postsecondary employment and selecting the school of her choice.

3. Brody will know what he needs and be able to explain this to his personal care assistant so that he or she can help him with his daily living routine.

4. Cara will actively seek information to help her develop coping skills.

5. Dorothy will decide what kind of supports she requires to live in the community.

Transportation

Getting to and from various destinations within the community is a major aspect of transitioning from childhood dependence to adulthood independence (West, Barcus, Brooke, & Rayfield, 1995). Unfortunately, due to school concerns, this goal is all too often passed over by educators and left to family members or others. Although most secondary school students can enroll in driver education programs, schools seldom consider the transportation needs of students who cannot drive because of their disability.

Transportation goals need to reflect a continuum of mobility options ranging from a student selecting an appropriate wheelchair to the design and purchase of a specially equipped vehicle. In addition to teaching students to use different modes of transportation, the curriculum should also consider teaching skills related to transportation planning. This may include topics and skills such as knowing their rights under the ADA, developing a personalized transportation plan, and identifying needed accommodations and assistive technology. Table 1.6 provides some ideas for instruction related to transportation options.

With the passage of the ADA, physical accessibility of public facilities in the community is now mandatory and seen by the U.S. Congress as a civil right. This law provides statutory support to facilitate travel for people with disabilities. However, if funds are not available to localities or individuals with disabilities to purchase necessary equipment, or if individuals do not receive appropriate training and support in certain travel skills, the impact of this law cannot be realized.

As with a number of these individual transition plan (ITP) goals, the student and family, along with the educational team, must prioritize their transportation goals. Remember, many goals in other areas will be extremely difficult to implement unless the student has adequate transportation skills. Going to college, holding a steady job, or participating on the YMCA jogging team requires the ability to get from one point to the other. Travel skill development is extremely important because it increases community access and participation for the student.

The integral relationship between community mobility and community functioning requires educators to focus on preparing individuals with disabilities to travel more independently. How much self-empowerment and control over life are possible for a person with serious travel restriction? Program initiatives in this area must focus on increasing the opportunity for community travel and

TABLE 1.6

Transportation Curriculum: Ideas for Instruction Based on Mode of Transport

Mode of Transportation	Possible Instructional Ideas
Operating a motor vehicle	Following driving rules Reading road signs Practicing driving skills Reading maps Using roadside emergency services
Using specialized transportation services	Selecting a service provider Getting documents to access services Purchasing a ticket Scheduling a ride Solving service problems
Riding public transportation (bus, subway, train, or taxi)	Reading a schedule Locating the stop Riding Problem solving
Walking	Reading street signs Following written directions Using a map Crossing streets

teaching specific mobility skills. Although the ADA addresses only accessibility, instruction and support are also needed to improve the mobility of persons with disabilities in the community. Here are five examples of transportation goals:

1. Jasper will travel independently to designated locations within a 2-mile radius of his residence.

2. Darla will learn how to access the local paratransit services.

3. Monique will learn how to cross the street.

4. Nick will use public transportation to get to work and social and recreational activities.

5. Tom will study for his driver's license and explore purchasing a modified van.

Home Living Skills

Home living skills include many different activities. Although many of these skills such as toileting or washing hands are used in other environments, home living skills are defined as those skills that are not directly related to a specific vocational skill or community task. The importance of home living skills is most evident with individuals who have significant disabilities and may continually need help. Even in this day and age, a person with a significant disability who is unable to perform key activities of daily living in the home may very well be sent to a nursing home because no one in his or her natural home is able to provide adequate care. An individual who cannot perform the necessary home living skills will be at great risk for long-term institutionalization and will be less likely to engage in other life activities such as employment or integrated community living.

Independent living skills for students with disabilities are a major component of transition (Blacher, 2001). Teachers must continually assess the home living competence of students because these skills are critical building blocks for long-term community adjustment. Table 1.7 provides some examples of what might be taught in a home living skills curriculum.

The wide range of skills required for community domestic living means that educators must systematically prioritize these skills for training. Some of the factors that need to be considered when selecting a living option include the following:

- The desires of the student and his or her family
- Current abilities and future support needs of the student
- Availability of community-based support services
- Student's finances (or those of the person paying the bill)
- Proximity to community destinations

The family and student must decide on the optimal living environment for the student and then determine what skills are essential for success in the chosen environment. Wherever possible, self-instruction and self-management methods should be developed. The ultimate goal of instruction is to teach students skills that will increase their independence as adults. Early instruction of

TABLE 1.7
Home Living: Examples of Curriculum Areas and Activities

Curriculum Area	Activities
Personal management	Organizing belongings Making a schedule of things to do Setting an alarm clock
Housekeeping	Vacuuming a carpet Operating a dishwasher Removing trash
Laundry	Sorting laundry to wash Folding towels Putting away clothes
Food preparation	Storing refrigerated foods Using a microwave oven to prepare food Making a salad
Home safety	Communicating an emergency Locking the doors and windows Avoiding electrical accidents
Home maintenance	Changing a light bulb Calling for repairs Mowing the lawn
Personal hygiene and grooming	Toileting Shaving Dressing
Leisure time	Operating a television Playing a card game Planting a garden

Note. Skills selected for training should be based on individual student needs and priorities.

this type increases the likelihood of success in future years and adulthood. Skills that include activities of daily living must be in the curriculum, particularly for those students who come to school with significant deficits in their abilities to perform them. Goals for a home living skills curriculum might include the following:

1. Richard will pack a lunch.

2. Clive will prepare a simple breakfast (e.g., bowl of cereal or cheese sandwich).

3. Brian will strip down and make up a bed.

4. Rosi will shampoo and dry her hair.

5. Ash will lock the door and windows.

Functional Academics and Postsecondary Education

Historically, special education programs for students with disabilities have emphasized academic skills training. Students who were not ready for instruction and academics were taught prerequisites such as sorting colors and shapes. Many students with disabilities, especially significant disabilities, do not learn at the rate of nondisabled children and often do not progress beyond learning these prerequisites. Protracted instruction on such basic academic skills not only becomes boring but also is a tragic waste of resources for students who have limited time before losing their school entitlement. The skill of sorting colors and shapes is low in functionality when compared with being able to order a meal at a fast-food restaurant or purchase a ticket to a local movie theater.

The solution to this problem is a move toward a functional academic curriculum that involves life skills, independent living skills, daily living skills, vocational and career education, and career development concepts.

The key way to determine whether to teach an academic skill is to ask, Will the student be able to use this information currently or in the future? The most definitive way of figuring out whether this is likely is to study the student's current and probable future environments and identify those academic or academic-like skills that are necessary in those environments. The functionality of an academic skill will be defined by the student and his or her family based on their home and community environments.

The increased involvement of students in functional academics may determine whether it is viable for students to move into postsecondary education. At a certain level of student functioning, concentrating on postsecondary education does not make much sense; getting a job is more important, particularly identifying a job that requires little in the way of academics. On the other hand, many students with traumatic brain injury, learning disabilities, sensory impairments, and severe physical disabilities are seeking some form of higher education. If possible, the student's educational team and family need to aim as high as possible in terms of goals and expectations. Postsecondary education will be appropriate for thousands of students who decide to focus less on vocational training and more on higher education while working part-time. For some students, the dual track of some employment and a limited educational load in a 2-year or 4-year college or trade school makes a great deal of sense.

Educational goals for these students are associated with selecting a course of study and career goal, taking appropriate entrance exams, choosing a school, and learning about ways to enhance personal learning and to request accommodations from the institution and professors. Students who can identify their own strengths and weaknesses and effectively communicate their accommodation needs will increase their likelihood of success in higher education. Students should be given opportunities to learn about their rights and what is required by state law, what documentation is needed to make requests for accommodations, and what their own learning processes are.

The student and family must keep in mind, however, the importance of developing the necessary building blocks for a career, as opposed to an isolated job. Increasing academics at a selective level, along with providing meaningful employment experiences, can make all the difference in the world for students as they grow into adulthood. Here are five examples of academic goals:

1. Samuel will complete a bachelor's degree in social work.

2. Mona will take a word-processing course at the local community college.

3. Madeline will complete a 2-year community college associate's degree program in culinary arts, with support services.

4. Pablo will train to be a mechanic at the local vocational technical center.

5. Lester will request accommodations for taking tests and class notes.

Financial Planning and Management

Economic self-sufficiency is a major goal for most people, and individuals with disabilities are no different. Amazingly, educators do not help students focus adequately on budgeting, financial planning, investment strategies, and comparative shopping. Not surprisingly, some individuals with disabilities are among the most vulnerable and susceptible to being taken advantage of by scams and unfair marketing practices.

If employment and postsecondary education are worthwhile transition goals, then certainly financial goals should not be overlooked. Considering that Social Security payments and medical assistance account for the overwhelming number of dollars spent on disability in the United States, individuals with disabilities need to be educated about their rights and entitlements as related to these payments. Because Social Security regulations are complex and sometimes difficult to understand, students need to learn how to get help in resolving special questions.

Educational goals in this area may range from simple money management and opening a bank account to more complex topics such as investment strategies and estate planning. Money management has always been part of the special education curriculum, but most schools have not advanced to a more contemporary and functional approach for many areas of financial planning and economic self-sufficiency. Many school programs still do not teach money skills in community settings; there is a false assumption that students will automatically know how to perform a skill in the community that was taught in the classroom. The world is much more complicated for today's students than it was for previous generations. Personal competence is heavily dependent on the ability to manage financial affairs, to know what questions to ask, to know how to obtain help, and to know what pitfalls to avoid. Educational goals should not ignore these needs. Examples of goals in this area follow:

1. Tiffany will receive a weekly allowance for performing chores at home.

2. Sid will withdraw money from his trust fund with support.

3. Chris will develop and maintain a budget with support.

4. Isahia will open a checking account and learn how to use checks to make purchases at community stores.

5. Tashell currently receives Supplemental Security Income (SSI) and will learn how her earned income will affect this benefit.

Socialization, Recreation, and Leisure

Appropriate social and interpersonal skills are important in all aspects of life. Those students with disabilities who possess good social and interpersonal skills will have an easier time assimilating to normal community activities, whereas those who do not will be more likely to be ignored and avoided by others.

Many wonderful materials and curricula have been developed for age-appropriate social and leisure activities. It is important to perform ongoing assessment of students' abilities and needs across community settings to determine what skills and supports are necessary for them to succeed. Students who are taught to behave according to social norms increase their chances of successfully functioning in community life (Moon & Inge, 2000).

Within the context of interpersonal skills are recreational and leisure skills. These are activities that the student chooses for his or her free time instead of a narrow range of stereotypical activities (Dattilo & Schleien, 1994). Some activities may take place in isolation such as watching television or playing a video game, whereas others take place with people such as attending the school's basketball game or skating at the community ice rink. Selecting appropriate recreation goals hinges on the following criteria:

- What recreational interests does the student express or demonstrate?

- Are these interests age appropriate, and is exposure to other options needed?

- Are these interests consistent with his or her intellectual and physical capabilities? If not, what supports does the student need to participate in the activity?

- What opportunities are available in the student's community and home to enjoy this leisure activity?

There are so many leisure activities that this curriculum area can be overwhelming. Generally, it will be most advantageous to encourage the student to select an activity that has a high probability of being enjoyed repeatedly. Common sense must also enter into goal development. For instance, wanting to be on the swimming team may be great, but if the pool is 40 miles away and there is no transportation, this might be a futile plan. The following are some examples of goals in this area:

1. Terri will develop a daily exercise and therapy routine with the YWCA and the physical therapist to strengthen healthy muscles.

2. Tito will apologize when at fault.

3. Wendy will join the Girl Scouts.

4. Charles will learn how to fish from the pier using adaptive equipment.

5. Karen will smile and express positive feelings to peers.

TRANSITION PLANNING

A curriculum that follows good design principles is not enough. For students to succeed, comprehensive transition planning that follows these principles must be put into place. In this section, we present important information about how this transition planning process can go forward.

Transition from school to work is a process that focuses on the movement of students with disabilities from school into the world of work (Bullis, Bull, Johnson, & Peters, 1995). Facilitating a student's transition from a school program to the workplace requires movement through school instruction, transition process planning, and placement into meaningful community-integrated employment. Currently, special education and vocational rehabilitation programs are required to cooperatively plan for the transition of students with disabilities into the work environment. Effective transition planning and implementation requires the participation, cooperation, and coordination of all local school and adult agencies that provide services and supports to individuals with disabilities (Blackorby & Wagner, 1996). A systematic team effort increases the chances that all the necessary services and supports are made available to a student to ensure a smooth transition into the community labor force after graduation (Hasazi, Furney, & Destefano, 1999). The rehabilitation counselor is a key player in the transition of students from school into the labor force and must be an active participant in the transition team planning and implementation (Wittenburg, Golden, & Fishman, 2002).

A rehabilitation counselor's role in transition programs varies according to local needs and resources. In a few instances, rehabilitation counselors are school based and employed by a school district or cooperative of districts; however, most counselors are employed by state vocational rehabilitation agencies and often have limited time and resources to devote to coordination of transition services. Whether a counselor is school based or state agency based, his or her activities may include career and psychosocial counseling, consultation with special education and vocational education teachers, and coordination with school, family, and community efforts in career planning and implementation. Additionally, job search assistance, identification of job support service, referral to and coordination with other adult services, and planning and coordination with postsecondary programs may be provided (Wehman, 1995). Later in this chapter, we provide an example of a transition plan for a student named Eric.

The key components of the transition planning process include the following:

- Functional, community-referenced secondary educational curriculum (Alberto, Taber, Brozovic, & Elliot, 1997)
- Community-based instruction and service delivery (Inge, Wehman, Clees, & Dymond, 1996)
- Interagency planning and service delivery efforts
- Availability of an array of postsecondary options, including vocational training or employment during high school (Benz, Yovanoff, & Doren, 1997)
- Availability of ongoing community-based support services
- Student, parent, and family involvement throughout the transition process

INTERAGENCY PLANNING AND SERVICE DELIVERY EFFORTS

An interagency transition planning team should be composed of professionals from various disciplines who provide direct educational services or who are targeted to provide adult services to transition-age students, the student, and the student's family. The team's major responsibility is to use a systematic approach to develop, implement, and monitor the ITP for the student (Blackorby & Wagner, 1996; Hasazi et al., 1999). The team should develop a plan that identifies the target adult outcomes in the areas of employment, community living, and recreation that the student and his or her family desire at the time of the student's graduation (Wehman, 1995). The plan should identify the supports necessary to achieve and maintain these outcomes, the steps that are needed, and the person who is responsible for each step.

The ITP addresses goals in a number of postsecondary areas, such as career and community integration. These are future goals and are not achieved while the student is in his or her secondary program. However, the ITP can serve to focus educational services on the development and practice of skills that will enhance the opportunity for the student to achieve these goals upon completion of his or her secondary-level program (Alberto et al., 1997). Issues that a transition team needs to consider for each student include the following:

- Has formal transition planning begun for a student at age 16?

- Are the appropriate school and adult service personnel involved?

- Has a transition planning meeting been held? Has an ITP been developed?

- Does the transition plan cover the appropriate target areas such as employment, postsecondary education, independent living services, financial and income needs, recreation and social needs, medical and therapeutic needs, transportation needs, and advocacy and legal needs?

- Does the plan reflect a true vision of the potential of the student, or is it merely a plan that offers only what the service delivery system currently provides?

- Is the plan updated as needed?

- Are exit meetings held to finalize plans for the transition from school to employment?

- Are appropriate elements of the transition plan included in the IEP?

Broad Array of Employment Options

Employment is a major element in the lives of people with or without disabilities. The type of work people do, the amount of money they earn, and the career advancement opportunities they have directly affect how individuals look at themselves (Unger, 1995; Wehman & Moon, 1988). What is most important is to develop multiple employment choices for individuals with disabilities that reflect the array of job opportunities available to nondisabled individuals in the same community. Conducting a labor market screening of employment opportunities can help ensure that individuals with disabilities receive choices. Consider some of the following issues when conducting a screening:

- What jobs are available in the community? Who hires entry-level employees, and is there opportunity for advancement?
- What wages and benefits are offered for various positions?
- Are individuals with disabilities working in their community alongside nondisabled individuals?
- What employers are new to the area?
- What businesses have growing or declining hiring needs?

Career Counseling

Career and job choices are difficult for all individuals. Frequently, students with disabilities have had little or no exposure to the vocational options available within the community, thus making it difficult for them to choose a certain job or career at graduation. The educational team, especially the vocational rehabilitation counselor, should begin career counseling with students by the time they reach age 16. The vocational rehabilitation counselor should arrange to meet with the student, his or her family, and school personnel to discuss the array of employment opportunities available in the community. The counselor should act as a consultant to the teachers and other school personnel involved in the development of IEPs to ensure that students are exposed to the variety of vocational opportunities available in the community. Concerted efforts on the part of all involved parties can provide the student with experiences that will assist him or her in making career choices prior to graduation.

At times, such as in a heavily populated urban area, the size of a special education program makes it unrealistic for the vocational rehabilitation counselor to meet with all students age 16 and older. In this instance, the counselor might work with schools to prioritize those students who are most in need of services, such as students with the most significant disabilities who face additional challenges (Blackorby & Wagner, 1996).

Case Management

Traditionally, rehabilitation counselors working with a public agency have assumed primary responsibility for case management (Neal & Bader, 1991). As a member of a transition planning team, the counselor may also ensure dissemination of accurate information to parents and educators. The following are some typical responsibilities of a case manager:

- Develop agreements with community service providers.
- Establish local agreements with key agencies.
- Participate in local interagency transition planning.
- Provide in-service training to school personnel and parents about the federal–state vocational rehabilitation criteria for eligibility and provision of services.
- Attend individual transition planning meetings.
- Serve as a member of the transition team throughout the secondary years.

- Gather and interpret vocational assessment information.

- Coordinate and monitor supported employment placement of postsecondary students.

- Identify referral needs and ensure referrals are made to the appropriate agencies or services.

Transition planning involves various members of the educational team and community service providers; it should also include persons chosen by the student and family. Transition planning is key to planning for life after exiting school.

WHAT EDUCATORS NEED TO KNOW ABOUT THE ADULT SERVICES SYSTEM

We now move to a discussion of what special educators at the secondary level need to know about working with the adult service community. Educators at the high school level must be informed about postschool services because they will be the major source of information to concerned parents (Miner & Bates, 1997) and their teenage students about what awaits them after school. These educators must become informed about the world of adult services and resources that exist outside the school. The following questions and responses from parents in a large suburb of Virginia illustrate some of the issues facing families in the school-to-work transition process. These questions were asked of parents by a local parent resource center that serves families of children in special education. These questions and answers were provided by Gail Epps (personal communication, 1993).

▶ Question to parents

For a student with a disability going from high school to the adult service system, what information do you, the family, want to know from professionals about working, living, and recreation in the adult community?

▶ Parents' answers

"We want to know what is available in the job market, what we can expect when our child is no longer in school. Will there be someone to take over where the school left off or will our child be forced to stay at home being nonproductive? Suppose she is placed in a situation where she is not happy. Will she go to the bottom of the list again? Are there enough personnel in the adult service system to take over this task or is the person with a disability put on the back burner until something or someone becomes available to assist?"

"I believe the family needs to know what services are available, exactly what they can or cannot offer the young adult, and who is to be contacted to obtain services."

"The special education staff should be updated about the services available to each student. There should be close communication between the local community services board and the school."

"Information on issues such as recreation programs that include persons without disabilities, vocational training, behavior management, independent living skills, Social Security, supported employment, and so forth, should be given to families as early as possible."

⮕ Question to parents

What is your hope for your family member? What are your fears or concerns about his or her entering the adult world? One response that seemed to communicate most clearly both the hope and uncertainty of all the persons assembled as they looked toward the rapidly approaching time when they would be actively involved with the adult community was the following.

⮕ Parents' answers

"We want them to live as independently as possible in the least restrictive setting and to work in the community, live in a group home or apartment, and to have opportunities for recreational activities and social outings for continual social growth. We have fears and concerns: not enough resources available, not enough finances to fund programs for our family members, family members being ridiculed or not accepted for who they are by persons *without* disabilities, and opportunities not being offered to them because of lack of understanding and fear on the part of employers and coworkers."

These above responses speak volumes to the need for information and resources about existing services and possible opportunities. There are references to work, living arrangements, community, recreation, financial supports, and, most important, where to find this information. The responses also reveal parent hopes that promises be fulfilled, guarded optimism about opportunities for students to obtain meaningful work and grow as adults, and concerns about isolation, misunderstanding, and fear of rejection. For typical teenage youth, thoughts about preparing for and entering the adult community can be puzzling. For teenage youth with disabilities and their families—who must not only deal with the normal difficulties of entering adult life but also the additional complexities of an unfamiliar service and support system—preparation for the transition process can be a challenge.

The informational and support needs identified by these parents point to two primary issues facing the secondary-level educator. First, to be meaningful and long lasting, education programs must help students with disabilities prepare to live and work in the community. Therefore, educational programs must provide these students with regular opportunities to go to school with nondisabled peers. Also, the curriculum must be value ladened, functional (Clark, 1994), and community referenced and involve the necessary community representatives such as case managers (Wehman, 1992). Second, because the special educator is frequently the primary person to whom students with disabilities turn with questions about future education, work, and community living options, today's educators must be able to respond to such requests accurately and confidently. This requires educators to become familiar with this information and to develop linkages with adult community service providers (Whitney-Thomas & Hanley-Maxwell, 1996). The following section discusses the school's role in fostering transition.

SCHOOL'S ROLE IN IMPLEMENTING TRANSITION PLANNING

The services available through the assistance of a vocational rehabilitation counselor and other resources are most effective if the school program aggressively incorporates transition planning into middle school and secondary-level activities. For example, the family of a young adolescent with a disability should sign up for service coordination assistance from local mental health and mental retardation (MHMR) services programs early in the student's school career. The service coordinator is then invited to attend selective IEP meetings to assist with issues such as living arrangements, respite services, and recreation.

As early as middle school, the process of situational or formal vocational assessment can be initiated as a starting point in vocational planning. Student résumés with vocational information are started at this level (Parent, 1991; Wehman, 1992). In the first years of high school, the student can secure a picture ID and begin vocational exploration activities. During the last years of high school, the state vocational rehabilitation counselor can help the student and family make plans for work after exiting school. By spreading these activities over a number of years, the school system gradually assists students and their families in planning for life after secondary education. When schools use a systematic approach that follows set time lines, they prevent students and families from failing to make long-range plans, potentially delaying services, or dropping through the cracks. Ongoing planning procedures also make students and faculty members aware of the different agencies that offer services to assist students with the transition to adult life (Marchant, 1993).

A number of administrative procedures within the school are necessary to implement effective transition planning. It is helpful to designate the teacher who is responsible for a student's IEP as his or her transition service coordinator. This teacher then develops an ITP in cooperation with the MHMR case manager, vocational rehabilitation counselor, and any other persons whom the student or family wishes to invite to transition-oriented IEP meetings. The written transition plan can be filed with the active IEP and updated each time the IEP is reviewed. These procedures assist in establishing clear communication among all persons involved in long-range planning for a student. In instances when transition services are not being delivered or objectives are not being met in a timely manner, the IDEA legislation indicates that the school system is responsible for reconvening the transition committee. The transition committee should assign a person to be responsible for each objective and should set a time line for carrying out specific strategies (Marchant, 1993). See Figure 1.3 for a sample ITP, created for a student named Eric. Goals were established for Eric across major program areas of economic self-sufficiency, community integration, and personal competence.

(*text continues on p. 29*)

INDIVIDUALIZED TRANSITION PLAN

I. Career and Economic Self-Sufficiency

1. Employment Goal

Eric will work full-time on a mobile work crew on apartment complex cleaning.

Level of Present Performance

Eric must be closely supervised while in the community. He tolerates working for approximately 45 minutes at a time without a break. He requires prompts for three-step tasks.

Steps Needed To Accomplish Goal

1. Make referrals for vocational rehabilitation and Hermitage Enterprises.
2. Develop a PASS (Plan for Achieving Self-Support) via Medicaid waiver.
3. Decrease aggressive, destructive acts through continued behavioral intervention.

Date of Completion

3/1/04

Person(s) Responsible for Implementation

Case manager, parents, teacher, psychiatrist, Department of Rehabilitation Services, Medicaid waiver vendor, and Hermitage Enterprises.

2. Vocational Education/ Training Goal

Eric will learn six key cleaning skills, such as picking up trash, which is necessary for apartment complex cleaning.

Level of Present Performance

Eric shows little interest in work and tires easily. He completes tasks for specific immediate reinforcement but close supervision is essential.

Steps Needed To Accomplish Goal

1. Complete vocational situational assessments at varied sites.
2. Design and implement vocational instruction program at community job site.

Date of Completion

3/1/04

Person(s) Responsible for Implementation

Teacher, vocational assessment center senior evaluator

3. Postsecondary Education Goal

N/A

Level of Present Performance

Steps Needed To Accomplish Goal

Date of Completion

Person(s) Responsible for Implementation

4. Financial/Income Needs Goal

Eric will independently keep wallet with change and small bills on his person to make small purchases during daily routine.

Level of Present Performance

Eric currently receives SSI benefits and is dependent on others for all uses of money.

Steps Needed To Accomplish Goal

1. Teach simple purchasing skills.
2. Teach use of wallet.
3. Make frequent shopping trips available for use.

Date of Completion

5/1/04

Person(s) Responsible for Implementation

Teacher, parents

(continues)

FIGURE 1.3. Individualized transition plan, created for Eric.

II. Community Integration and Participation

5. Independent Living Goal

Eric will live in two- to three-occupant group home with 24-hour supervision/assistance and near parents.

Level of Present Performance

Eric lives in parents' home and receives assistance with self-care activities 5 hours a day, 6 days a week via Medicaid waiver. He is destructive at home.

Steps Needed To Accomplish Goal

Schedule meetings that include parents, student, case manager, representative from Center for Independent Living, Medicaid waiver vendor, and teacher (as advocate) to explore options for appropriate residential service.

Date of Completion

8/1/04

Person(s) Responsible for Implementation

Case manager, parents, teacher, vendor, and Center for Independent Living staff

6. Transportation/Mobility Goal

Eric will travel safely and without incident to and from work and in the community.

Level of Present Performance

Eric grabs people and throws items in all settings. He has grabbed drivers of vehicles. Requires close supervision even in restrooms.

Steps Needed To Accomplish Goal

1. Increase community-based instruction.
2. Develop consistent behavioral intervention plan across his day.
3. Increase alternative means of communication to express needs.

Date of Completion

6/1/04

Person(s) Responsible for Implementation

Teacher, parents, student, speech therapist, Medicaid waiver vendor, principal, university behavioral intervention staff, and MHMR psychiatrist

7. Social Relationship Goal

Eric will engage in cooperative activities with peers without one-to-one supervision.

Level of Present Performance

Eric needs and greatly enjoys social interactions with parents and staff. He has difficulty interacting with peers. He has no peer interactions outside of school.

Steps Needed To Accomplish Goal

Structure cooperative recreational activities in which Eric can interact with peers with less staff or parental intervention, such as participating in bicycling club.

Date of Completion

1/1/04

Person(s) Responsible for Implementation

Teacher, parents, Medicaid waiver vendor

8. Recreation/Leisure Goal

Eric will participate in a variety of community-supported recreational activities.

Level of Present Performance

Eric's behavior has excluded him from a variety of available programs offered by Henrico Parks and Recreation, YMCA, and so on.

Steps Needed To Accomplish Goal

1. Schedule meetings with program coordinators to plan for Eric's integration into available programs.
2. Identify appropriate support staff.
3. Contact and arrange for local volunteers.

(continues)

FIGURE 1.3. *Continued.*

Date of Completion	3/1/04
Person(s) Responsible for Implementation	Case manager, Henrico Parks and Recreation, Medicaid waiver vendor, and Parent Resource Center

III. Personal Competence

9. Health/Safety Goal — Eric will function in all community settings without running away and will cease aggressive, destructive incidents.

Level of Present Performance — Eric runs from designated areas, showing no concern for his safety. He has injured others and himself during acts of aggression.

Steps Needed To Accomplish Goal
1. Teach safety awareness in community (e.g., streets, parking lots).
2. Fade close supervision in all settings as much as possible.
3. Pair Steps 1 and 2 with appropriate behavior management strategies.

Date of Completion — 1/1/04

Person(s) Responsible for Implementation — Teacher, parents, university behavioral intervention staff, and MHMR psychiatrist

10. Self-Advocacy/Future Planning Goal — Eric will improve communication to make needs known and as alternative to acting out. He will also develop an appropriate trust fund and documented future plan.

Level of Present Performance — Eric's difficulty in communicating affects his self-control. Eric will always need services. He receives SSI benefits and stands to receive inheritance from mother, stepfather, and natural father.

Steps Needed To Accomplish Goal
1. Continue to teach communication skills.
2. Seek legal advice with family regarding trust and wills on Eric's behalf.

Date of Completion — 6/1/04

Person(s) Responsible for Implementation — Teacher, speech therapist, parents, and Parent Resource Center

Student Career Preference — Cleaning in an outdoor environment

Student Major Transition Needs
1. Social relationships
2. Community residential services
3. Safety in all settings
4. Employment
5. Participation in community activities

FIGURE 1.3. *Continued.*

Community-Based Instruction with Students

Many students with disabilities and their families feel isolated from the community (O'Brien & O'Brien, 1992; O'Connell, 1992; Whitney-Thomas & Hanley-Maxwell, 1996) and have discomfort due to the uncertainty that may face them during the postschool years (Ferguson, Ferguson, & Jones, 1998). A primary example of this isolation is the limited participation of students with disabilities in work and work-related activities. By encouraging and supporting middle and secondary age students with disabilities to obtain ID cards, develop and maintain résumés, and seek work opportunities, the school program can expand students' involvement in the community, knowledge of work requirements, and awareness of individual interests. These activities provide a firm base of information for the transition committee to use in assisting the student in planning for postsecondary interests and services needs.

A formalized approach to expanding the community awareness and participation of a secondary age student with a disability is the incorporation of community-based instruction and supported employment into school activities (Moon & Inge, 1993). Community-based instruction was defined by Wehman (1992) as involving "teachers and other education personnel teaching educational objectives in natural environments, such as work sites, shopping malls, and restaurants" (p. 170). Training experiences in the community help students with disabilities determine job preferences and develop a work history (Inge, Simon, Halloran, & Moon, 1993). The focus of community experiences can also move from training to actual employment as students near completion of secondary education.

Community-based training experiences in local businesses where wages are not paid to students must follow specific criteria to be in accordance with the Fair Labor Standards Act of 1938 and its subsequent amendments. For a "non-employment relationship," as defined by the U.S. Department of Labor (U.S. Department of Education, 1992), to be established, the following seven criteria must be met:

1. Participants will be youth with physical and/or mental disabilities for whom competitive employment at or above the minimum wage level is not immediately obtainable and for whom, because of their disability, intensive ongoing support will be needed to perform in a work setting.

2. Participation will be for vocational exploration, assessment, or training in a community-based placement work site under the general supervision of public school personnel.

3. Community-based placement will be clearly defined components of IEPs developed and designed for the benefit of each student. The statement of needed transition services established for the exploration, assessment, training, or cooperative vocational education components will be included in students' IEPs.

4. Information contained in a student's IEP will not have to be made available; however, documentation as to the student's enrollment in the community-based placement program will be made available to the U.S. Departments of Labor and Education. The student and his or her parent or guardian must be fully informed about the IEP and the community-based placement component and must participate voluntarily with the understanding that such participation does not entitle the student to wages.

5. The activities of students at a community-based placement site will not result in an immediate advantage to the business.

6. Although the existence of an employment relationship will not be determined exclusively on the basis of the number of hours of student

participation, as a general rule, each work experience will not exceed the following limitations during any one school year:

Vocational exploration: 5 hours per job experienced

Vocational assessment: 90 hours per job experienced

Vocational training: 120 hours per job experienced

7. Students will not be entitled to employment at the business at the conclusion of their placement program. However, once a student has become an employee, he or she cannot be considered a trainee at that particular community-based placement unless in a clearly distinguishable occupation. (Inge et al., 1993)

For a nonemployment relationship between the business and the student to exist, all seven of the U.S. Department of Labor criteria must be met. Furthermore, the departments of labor for individual states also have their own guidelines. Finally, the liability insurance issues and protections involved in transporting and training the students must be understood by teachers, employers, students, and their families.

Role of the School Principal

For a teacher to use community-based instruction effectively, assistance and support from the school principal are critical. The school principal or other administrator can use a number of strategies to encourage teachers to implement community-based instruction. It is imperative that an administrator develop a philosophy and put in writing a mission statement that promotes functional and community-based programming for students with disabilities. The administrator should share the mission statement with all staff and patrons and provide an opportunity to discuss concerns regarding the program. Such a mission statement gives clear direction to everyone involved. In addition to developing a mission statement, the administrator should provide formal staff development activities to teach techniques for implementing and assessing community-based activities. It is also helpful if teachers can be sent to conferences or to other school divisions to learn needed skills. If possible, each site administrator who supervises the program should also attend such training activities.

The foundation of effective vocational training is the training a student receives during his or her school years. A number of studies have shown that successful employment after exiting school is related to whether a student participated in community-based training during his or her educational years (Doren & Benz, 1998; Rylance, 1998). Many teachers, however, feel uncomfortable leaving their "safe" classroom environments for the world of work. This may be caused by teachers simply not knowing how to go about setting up training sites for students.

Vocational training programs should be designed with the local community in mind. The program designer should analyze the community and identify jobs that are appropriate for students with severe disabilities. Training experiences should provide students with the opportunity to become a part of the work culture and train alongside regular employees. Finally, training programs should be designed so that they increase the number of hours a student spends in the community as he or she nears graduation. Ideally, a student will obtain employment

**DESIGNING AND IMPLEMENTING
A COMMUNITY-BASED INSTRUCTIONAL PROGRAM**

Steps	Activities
I. Conduct a job market analysis to identify potential jobs in the community that would be appropriate for students with severe disabilities.	1. Survey the yellow pages of a telephone directory. 2. Read the classifieds section of the newspaper. 3. Contact local business organizations, such as the Chamber of Commerce. 4. Survey school graduates to determine what jobs are held by individuals with disabilities in the community.
II. Identify businesses with the targeted jobs.	1. Establish a school policy for contacting businesses. 2. Identify school personnel responsible for making business contacts. 3. Determine school insurance coverage and liability issues. 4. Develop a list of employers to approach. 5. Schedule a time to write letters, make telephone calls, and visit employers. 6. Create a file for each business contacted.

III. Contact the personnel director or employer.	1. By letter and/or telephone:
	  a. Briefly describe the school's community-based program.
	  b. Identify jobs that may be appropriate for training.
	  c. Schedule a time to visit and explain the program further.
	2. In person:
	  a. Describe the purpose of community-based instruction.
	  b. Discuss the employer, teacher, and student responsibilities on the job site.
	  c. Discuss the school's insurance and liability policies.
	  d. Target tasks and time periods for training.
	  e. Schedule a work site visit to observe the identified tasks to develop job duty and task analyses.
	  f. Send thank you note.

IV. Select and analyze appropriate jobs for community-based training.	1. Visit the job site location. 2. Discuss the identified jobs with the site supervisor. 3. Discuss the job site rules and regulations. 4. Observe coworkers performing the job. 5. Select the tasks best suited for students with severe disabilities. 6. Develop a job duty schedule and task analyses for the activities selected. 7. Identify available times with the employer or supervisor for training. 8. Request at least 1- to 2-hour blocks of time for each site identified. 9. Agree on a program start date.

(continues)

FIGURE 1.4. A guide for teachers in setting up community-based training sites.

Steps	Activities

V. Schedule community-based training.	1. Identify students to receive vocational training.
	2. Hold IEP/ITP meetings for students.
	   a. Identify student training needs.
	   b. Discuss purpose of community-based vocational training with transition team members.
	   c. Write vocational goals and objectives.
	3. Match students to available sites.
	4. Sign community-based training agreements (student, parents, employer, school representative).
	5. Develop a daily schedule.
	6. Develop a transportation schedule.
	7. Send a copy of the schedules to the school principal, special education supervisor, parents, employers, and so on.
	8. Provide parents with information about individual insurance coverage for liability.

VI. Design individual systematic instruction programs.	1. Modify job duty schedules and task analyses based on student characteristics. 2. Select a data collection procedure. 3. Take a baseline of student performance on all tasks to be taught. 4. Select an instructional procedure. 5. Select a reinforcer. 6. Implement the training program. 7. Take probe data on student performance. 8. Routinely review student data and modify program format as needed. 9. Review student goals and objectives for training and update as needed.

FIGURE 1.4. *Continued.*

by the end of the school years. The result of an effective community-based placement program is a student résumé that demonstrates inclusion in a variety of jobs in a number of different work settings. The information in Figure 1.4 is offered as a guide to teachers for setting up community-based training sites.

REFERENCES

Agran, M., Marchand-Martella, N., & Martella, R. (1995). *Safety for persons with developmental disabilities*. Baltimore: Brookes.

Alberto, P. A., Taber, T. A., Brozovic, S. A., & Elliot, N. E. (1997). Continuing issues of collaborative transition planning in the secondary schools. *Journal of Vocational Rehabilitation, 8,* 197–204.

Americans with Disabilities Act of 1990, 42 U.S.C. § 12101 *et seq.*

Benz, M., & Lindstrom L. (1997). *Building school-to-work programs: Strategies for youth with special needs.* Austin, TX: PRO-ED.

Benz, M. R., Yovanoff, P., & Doren, B. (1997). School-to-work components that predict post-school success for students with and without disabilities. *Exceptional Children, 3,* 151–165.

Blacher, J. (2001). The transition to adulthood: Mental retardation, families, and culture. *American Journal of Mental Retardation, 106,* 173–188.

Blackorby, J., & Wagner, M. (1996). Longitudinal postschool outcomes of youth with disabilities: Findings from the National Longitudinal Transition Study. *Exceptional Children, 62*(5), 399–413.

Brown, L., Nietupski, J., & Hamre-Nietupski, S. (1976). Criterion of ultimate functioning. In M. Thomas (Ed.), *Hey don't forget about me!* (pp. 212–242). Reston, VA: Council for Exceptional Children.

Bullis, M., Bull, B., Johnson, B., & Peters, D. (1995). The school-to-community transition experiences of hearing young adults and young adults who are deaf. *Journal of Special Education, 28*(4), 405–423.

Clark, G. (1994). Is a functional curriculum approach compatible with an inclusive educational model? *Teaching Exceptional Children, 26*(2), 36–39.

Clark, G. (1996). Transition planning for secondary-level students with learning disabilities. *Journal of Learning Disabilities, 29*(1), 79–92.

Colley, D. A., & Jamison, D. (1998). Post school results for youth with disabilities: Key indicators and policy implications. *Career Development for Exceptional Individuals, 21,* 145–160.

Cook, C. C., Brotherson, M. J., Weigel-Garrey, C., & Mize, I. (1996). Homes to support the self-determination of children. *Self-Determination Across the Life Span,* 91–110.

Dattilo, J., & Schleien, S. J. (1994). Understanding leisure services for individuals with mental retardation. *Mental Retardation, 32,* 43–52.

Doren, B., & Benz, M. R. (1998). Employment inequality revisited: Predictors of better employment outcomes for young women with disabilities in transition. *Journal of Special Education, 31,* 425–442.

Everson, J. M., & Reid, D. H. (1999). *Person-centered planning and outcome management: Maximizing organizational effectiveness in supporting quality lifestyles among people with disabilities.* Morganton, NC: Habilitative Management Consultants.

Fair Labor Standards Act of 1938, 29 U.S.C. § 201 *et seq.*

Ferguson, P. M., Ferguson, D. L., & Jones, D. (1988). Generations of hope: Parental perspectives on the transitions of their children with severe retardation from school to adult life. *Journal of the Association for Persons with Severe Handicaps, 13,* 177–187.

Hasazi, S. B., Furney, K. S., & Destefano, L. (1999). Implementing the IDEA transition mandates. *Exceptional Children, 65,* 555–566.

Hughes, C., & Carter, E. W. (2000). *The transition handbook: Strategies high school teachers use that work!* Baltimore: Brookes.

Inge, K., Wehman, P., Clees, T. J., & Dymond, S. (1996). Transition from school to adulthood. In P. J. McLaughlin & P. Wehman (Eds.), *Mental retardation and developmental disabilities* (2nd ed., pp. 69–84). Austin, TX: PRO-ED.

Inge, K. J., Simon, M., Halloran, W., & Moon, M. S. (1993). Community-based vocational instruction and the labor laws: A 1993 update. In K. J. Inge & P. Wehman (Eds.), *Designing community-based vocational programs for students with severe disabilities.* Richmond: Virginia Commonwealth University.

Kregel, J. (1998). Developing a career path: Application of person centered planning. In P. Wehman & J. Kregel (Eds.), *More than a job: Securing satisfying careers for people with disabilities.* Baltimore: Brookes.

Marchant, J. (1993). *Responses of a school administrator to questions on transition.* Unpublished manuscript, Virginia Commonwealth University, Richmond.

Miner, C. A., & Bates, P. E. (1997). The effect of person centered planning activities on the IEP/transition planning process. *Education and Training in Mental Retardation and Developmental Disabilities, 32,* 105–112.

Moon, M. S., & Inge, K. (1993). Vocational preparation and transition. In M. E. Snell (Ed.), *Instruction of students with severe disabilities* (4th ed., pp. 556–587). New York: Merrill.

Moon, M. S., & Inge, K. (2000). Vocational preparation and transition. In M. Snell & F. Brown (Eds.), *Instruction of students with severe disabilities* (pp. 591–628). Upper Saddle River, NJ: Merrill.

Mount, B. (1994). Benefits and limitations of personal futures planning. In V. J. Bradley, J. W. Ashbaugh, & B. C. Blaney (Eds.), *Creating individual supports for people with developmental disabilities: A mandate for change at many levels* (pp. 97–108). Baltimore: Brookes.

Mount, B. (1997). *Person-centered planning: Finding direction for change using personal futures planning* (2nd ed.). New York: Graphic Futures.

Neal, S., & Bader, B. (1991). Case management. In P. McLaughlin & P. Wehman (Eds.), *Mental retardation and developmental disabilities* (pp. 172–183). Austin, TX: PRO-ED.

O'Brien, J., & O'Brien, C. (1992). Members of each other: Perspectives on social support for people with severe disabilities. In J. Nisbet (Ed.), *Natural supports in school, at work, and in the community for people with severe disabilities* (pp. 217–231). Baltimore: Brookes.

O'Connell, M. (1992). *Community building in Logan Square: How a community grew stronger with contributions of people with disabilities.* Evanston, IL: Northwestern University Center for Urban Affairs and Policy Research.

Parent, W. (1991). Situational assessment and vocational evaluation. In S. Griffin & G. Revell (Eds.), *Rehabilitation counselor desktop guide to supported employment* (pp. 117–131). Richmond: Virginia Commonwealth University.

Pearpoint, J., O'Brien, J., & Forest, M. (1993). *PATH: A workbook for planning positive possible futures.* Toronto, Canada: Inclusion Press.

Reid, D. H., Everson, J. M., & Green, C. W. (1999). A systematic evaluation of preferences identified through person-centered planning for people with multiple disabilities. *Journal of Applied Behavior Analysis, 32*(4), 467–477.

Rogan, P. (1997). *Review and analysis of post-school follow-up results: 1996–1997 Indiana post-school follow-up study.* Indianapolis: Indiana Department of Education, Division of Special Education.

Rylance, B. J. (1998). Predictors of post-high school employment for youth identified as severely emotionally disturbed. *Journal of Special Education, 32,* 184–192.

Unger, K. V. (1995). Unfinished business: Providing vocational services to transition-aged youth with serious emotional disturbance. *Journal of Vocational Rehabilitation, 5*(2), 159–165.

U.S. Department of Education. (1992). *Guidelines for implementing community based educational programs for students with disabilities.* Washington, DC: Author.

Wagner, M. (1992). *What happens next? Trends in post school outcomes of youth with disabilities.* Menlo Park, CA: SRI International.

Wehman, P. (1992). *Life beyond the classroom: Transition strategies for young people with disabilities.* Baltimore: Brookes.

Wehman, P. (1995). *Individual transition plans: The teacher's guide for helping youth with special needs.* Austin, TX: PRO-ED.

Wehman, P., Everson, J., & Reid, D. H. (2001). Beyond programs and placements: Using person centered practices to individualize the transition process and outcomes. In P. Wehman (Ed.), *Life beyond the classroom: Transition strategies for young people with disabilities* (3rd ed., pp. 91–124). Baltimore: Brookes.

Wehman, P., & Moon, M. S. (Eds.). (1988). *Vocational rehabilitation and supported employment.* Baltimore: Brookes.

Wehmeyer, M. L. (1994). Interpersonal cognitive problem solving skills of individuals with mental retardation. *Education and Training in Mental Retardation, 29,* 265–278.

Wehmeyer, M. L., Kelchner, K., & Richards, S. (1995). Individual and environmental factors related to the self-determination of adults with mental retardation. *Journal of Vocational Rehabilitation, 5,* 291–305.

Wehmeyer M. L., & Lawrence, M. (1995). Whose future is it anyway? Promoting student involvement in transition planning. *Career Development for Exceptional Individuals, 18*(2), 68–84.

West, M., Barcus, M., Brooke, V., & Rayfield, R. G. (1995). An exploratory analysis of self-determination of persons with disabilities. *Journal of Vocational Rehabilitation, 5*(4), 357–369.

Whitney-Thomas, J., & Hanley-Maxwell, C. (1996). Packing the parachute: Parents' experiences as their children prepare to leave high school. *Exceptional Children, 63,* 75–87.

Whitney-Thomas, J., Shaw, D., Honey, K., & Butterworth, J. (1998). Building a future: A study of student participation in person-centered planning. *Journal of the Association for Persons with Severe Handicaps, 23*(2), 119–133.

Wittenburg, D., Golden, T., & Fishman, M. (2002). Transition options for youth with disabilities: An overview of programs that affect the transition from school. *Journal of Vocational Rehabilitation, 17*(3), 195–206.

CHAPTER 2

Designing Instructional Programs

John Kregel

Developing and implementing a functional curriculum for students with moderate and severe disabilities requires a thorough understanding of student abilities, interests, and support needs, as well as knowledge about the competencies required to successfully function in home, school, employment, and community environments. Instruction must be individualized to meet the needs and preferences of individual students. Working with the student and his or her family to select the goals and objectives that are most relevant to the student, that enable him or her to function independently in the local community, and that enhance the student's ability to control and direct his or her own life is a crucial component of educational programming for students with moderate and severe disabilities. However, knowing *what* to teach a student is only part of the process. Equally important is knowing *how* to each a student. Effective instructional strategies enable students to acquire, maintain, and generalize essential skills.

Instructional technology changes constantly. Teaching strategies now viewed as "state of the art" will someday be questioned and rejected. Research and technological advances in the recent past have led to the following series of current best practices in instructional approaches for students with disabilities:

- Instructional goals should be determined by analyzing the employment, educational, residential, community, and recreational environments the student will encounter both in and out of school.

- Whenever possible, tasks should be grouped and taught together as integrated activities, as opposed to merely teaching isolated skills.

- Instruction should not just prepare students to perform skills in one setting, but rather enable students to generalize their new abilities to new environments in their own communities.

- Instruction, to the extent possible, should occur in the community-based settings where students will actually use the skills.

This chapter does not provide a comprehensive discussion of all aspects of instructional technology and program development. Many fine resource texts do this quite well and should be consulted (e.g., Orelove & Sobsey, 1987; Snell & Brown, 1999). Rather, the purpose of this chapter is to familiarize the reader with the terminology used in the remaining chapters, provide an outline of the key decisions a practitioner should make in using the programs and curriculum suggestions presented below, and provide general guidelines for instructional programming with students with significant disabilities.

DECIDING WHETHER TO TEACH A SPECIFIC SKILL

Chapter 1 described the process of using information from a variety of sources to assess a student's strengths and weaknesses; involve the student, his or her family, and community members in the assessment process; and develop individualized goals and objectives that address the student's primary educational needs. The first decision to be made after an interdisciplinary assessment reveals a skill deficit is to determine whether the skill deficit is significant enough to warrant instruction. Although there are many reasons for teaching or not teaching a specific skill to an individual student, at least three criteria should be applied to the decision-making process—functionality, feasibility, and student preferences.

Functionality

The first decision to be made is whether the skill or behavior being considered for instruction is functional for the student. Will the skill enable the student to be more independent in the future? If the student will have the opportunity to use the skill in his or her home, community, or job, it is far more likely that the skill will be retained over time. Therefore, the specific environments in which the student spends the greatest amount of time (e.g., home, classroom, neighborhood, church, community settings) will determine the skills to be included in the student's Individualized Education Program (IEP). A skill that is functional for one student may be irrelevant for another. As a result, there is no universal curriculum that is equally applicable for all students.

It is also important to consider how well the student's environment will support a skill once it is acquired. Will the student be able to practice what he or she has been taught? If the skill is performed successfully, will the student receive naturally occurring consequences that will reinforce the behavior? The test of whether a skill has been acquired is whether the student performs it in the environment where he or she will need it to be independent. If opportunities for practice and reinforcement do not exist, it may be appropriate to delay instruction on a particular skill. Some specific examples of environmental issues include the following:

- If a student is taught to make purchases in retail stores or order food in restaurants, will he or she be able to use this skill outside the instructional setting?

- If a student learns to operate a VCR or DVD player at school, will he or she be able to use this recreational skill at home or in community settings?

- If the student is taught to cross streets with stoplights and crosswalks, will he or she have the opportunity to use this skill when traveling independently in the community?

Another consideration is whether the student will be able to use the skill in both current and future environments. For example, learning to fill out a job application may be useful for some students at some point in time, but teaching this skill may be questionable if the student is several years away from actually applying for a job. Ideally, skills should be taught that have both immediate relevance and opportunity for long-term usage.

Feasibility

A second important decision is whether instruction on a skill is feasible. Although thousands of potentially functional skills might be taught to a given student, the decision to teach a specific skill should be based on efficiency, in addition to functionality. It could be argued that one can teach almost any skill to a learner if the proper techniques are used and a sufficient amount of instructional time is alotted. However, the anticipated length of time to teach a particular skill may be so great that it is practical to teach only a portion of a skill at one time. Furthermore, an alternative way to perform the skill should be identified to reduce instructional time.

The feasibility criterion is routinely applied in educational decision making.

- For students at the elementary level, the decision to focus on verbal speech as opposed to alternative communication modalities is often made in part based on the feasibility of instruction.

- At a certain point in many students' educational experiences, a decision is made about the feasibility of continuing instruction in a basal reading series, as opposed to concentrating on functional reading skills.

- For adolescents, the feasibility of teaching driving versus using public transportation, using ATM cards and paying cash for purchases as opposed to writing checks, or preparing processed foods as opposed to preparing complex recipes is often considered when identifying the skills and behaviors most relevant to a particular student.

Student Preferences

The criteria of functionality and feasibility in no way outweigh the importance of student and family preferences in the identification of potential skills for instruction. Of crucial significance is whether the student is interested in the skill and has had a role in selecting the instructional objectives. If the student has been involved in selecting instructional objectives, he or she likely will be more motivated to learn the skill. Self-selected skills will be far more likely to be used outside the school setting. Also, acquiring a skill that a student feels is important can often add his or her positive self-concept and sense of accomplishment.

In some instructional areas, the importance of student preferences is readily apparent. Few would discount the significance of student preference in identifying a job or selecting potential recreational activities. However, student likes and preferences should be considered in all areas of instruction. For example, a student's hairstyle, the menu items selected for cooking instruction, and the community settings frequented by the student should all be based on the preferences and desires of the student and his or her family.

After a specific skill has been determined to be (a) functional for the student, (b) able to be acquired in a reasonable amount of time, and (c) consistent with the preferences and desires of the student and his or her family, an instructional program can be developed to assist the student in acquiring the skill. In the sections that follow, specific procedures will be described that can be used to teach new skills to students of various ages who require unique supports and accommodations.

DEVELOPING INSTRUCTIONAL PROGRAMS

Developing an instructional program to teach a specific skill requires several important choices. How should the student complete the task? How should it be broken down for instruction? What type of feedback should be provided to the student if he or she makes an error during instruction? When making these decisions, the teacher should focus on the unique needs of the specific student and his or her specific learning deficits. The particular disabilities of a student will determine the most effective way to perform a task, organize task content, and provide instruction. Instead of using instructional programs that theoretically work for all students with disabilities, a teacher will be far more effective if he or she designs a program for a unique student, with specific skill sets and support needs. For example, the student's abilities (e.g., speaking using extremities, understanding and profiting from feedback) will dramatically affect the strategies used to deliver instruction. Some of the major steps involved in developing instructional programs are identified in Table 2.1.

TABLE 2.1
Steps in the Design of Instructional Programs

Step	Description
1. Develop instructional objectives	Define the scope, conditions, and performance criteria
2. Identify the method of task performance	Determine the way in which the student can most effectively and efficiently perform the task
3. Complete the task analysis	Identify the steps involved in task completion
4. Determine program format	Select among forward chaining, backward chaining, and total task presentations
5. Collect baseline information	Validate the task analysis and assess the length of time required for instruction
6. Develop instructional prompts	Identify the structured system of supports and prompts that will minimize student errors: a. System of least prompts b. Time delay
7. Schedule the training session	Determine the frequency and location of training sessions: a. Massed versus distributed training trials b. Community-based instruction
8. Develop reinforcement strategies	Motivate student to learn the skill
9. Plan for generalization	Generalize across settings, trainers, and behaviors

The effort to individualize instructional programming should be reflected in all aspects of program format. For example, some programs may be designed to make use of specific sensory modalities in the learning process and therefore would be appropriate for a student who is deaf, blind, or deaf and blind. The way in which the task will be performed should also be considered. Many of the instructional programs described in upcoming chapters reflect alternate methods for performing conventional skills in ways that capitalize on a student's strengths and abilities. For example, a teacher may be teaching three students how to purchase items in a grocery store, but he or she will be training each student to use a different method to perform the task. As a result of this need for individualization, almost all instructional programs will be specific in nature and may need frequent modification for use with other students.

Developing Instructional Objectives

After a teacher has decided to teach a particular skill to a specific student, he or she should write a behavioral objective. Numerous resources are available that do an excellent job of teaching the process of writing instructional objectives (e.g., Rusch, Rose, & Greenwood, 1988). Behavioral objectives are statements that describe what is to be taught (the behavior), where and when the behavior is to occur (conditions), and a standard of performance (criterion) that is used to determine successful acquisition of the objective.

Behavioral Statement

The behavioral statement within an instructional objective specifies the target response desired from the student. What will the student be able to do after instruction has been completed? Behavioral objectives serve a practical function in that they define the scope of the task to be taught. If the task is washing clothes, for example, an appropriate behavioral objective might be, "The student will sort, load, wash using bleach and fabric softener, dry on line, fold, and put away three loads of clothes." Another acceptable objective might be, "The student will load, wash, dry in automatic dryer, and fold one load of laundry." These two statements represent two distinct tasks that will be analyzed differently, taught differently, and evaluated differently.

The behavioral component of the instructional objective may focus on teaching the student the entirety of a specific task or provide instruction on only a portion of the skill to allow the partial participation of students unable to acquire the whole skill. The principle of partial participation (Baumgart et al., 1982) holds that even if a student is unable to learn to perform all aspects of a task due to the severity of his or her disability, the student should be taught to perform those parts of the skill that he or she has the ability to acquire. In other words, a student's inability to perform all aspects of a task in the way most people do should not prohibit instruction on any part of the task. For example, a student could be taught to prepare a portion of a meal, as opposed to an entire meal, or a student can learn to dial preprogrammed, color-coded numbers on a telephone instead of dialing an entire number. Teachers have the responsibility to work toward student participation on components of tasks identified by the student or his or her family as meaningful and relevant.

The principle of partial participation is highly related to the notion of entry behaviors or prerequisite skills. A prerequisite skill is one that is necessary before benefit from instruction on a program as it is written can be realized. However, a student's inability to perform a prerequisite skill does not necessarily mean that he or she should not be taught the targeted task. First, the student may be taught the prerequisite skill within the context of the program. For example, if a student is learning to operate a pay telephone, it may seem reasonable to identify the functional use of a pincer grasp as a prerequisite skill. A pincer grasp enables the student to pick up the coins and place them in the slot. If the student being taught does not have a functional pincer grasp, it would be possible to develop the grasp by teaching it during the highly motivating task of telephone use.

A second reason for not excluding a student from instruction on a skill because he or she lacks a prerequisite skill relates to the fact that a prerequisite skill is one necessary to complete a program *as it is written.* If a student cannot perform a specific prerequisite skill, the instructor can devise a method for performing the task that does not require the particular prerequisite skill. One of the most important skills of teachers who work with students with multiple disabilities is the ability to devise alternative methods of performing a given task.

Conditions Under Which the Behavior Will Occur

The conditions component of an instructional objective stipulates where the behavior should occur, when it should occur, and the environmental stimuli and factors that should be present in the immediate environment. Consider, for example, an instructional objective designed to teach a student to cross a four-lane street. When and where the student should perform this task would dramatically affect the instructional strategies used and the criterion that would be established for successful mastery. Potential conditions for the objective of street crossing are described in Table 2.2.

As indicated in Table 2.2, there is significant variability in the conditions under which a student may be required to cross a four-lane street. If a student only learns to cross one type of four-lane street, he or she may not automatically be able to cross all other types of streets. The specific conditions under which the

TABLE 2.2
Conditions Under Which a Street-Crossing Objective Might Occur

When	Rush hour traffic
	Non–rush hour traffic
Where	Familiar street
	Unfamiliar street
	Near school
	Near home
Environmental factors	Traffic light
	Two-way or four-way stop sign
	Crosswalk or no crosswalk
	Presence of parent or adult
	Presence of crossing guard
	Sidewalk or no sidewalk

student will acquire the behavior must be specified to ensure that he or she will acquire the skill and will be able to use it safely throughout the community.

Criterion for the Behavior

The criterion component of the instructional objective delineates the anticipated standard of success. Criteria are usually stated in quantifiable terms, such as frequency, rate, duration, or percentage correct. The criteria specified for a particular objective should reflect the unique characteristics of both the student and the skill to be taught. For example, in the street-crossing example described above, the criterion would necessarily be quite rigid (e.g., 20 consecutive times with no errors), due to the dangers inherent in just one situation where the student fails to perform the skills successfully. The criterion could be much less demanding for a recreational task, such as shooting a basketball through a hoop (e.g., 30% accuracy across 10 trials on 2 consecutive days), because 100% accuracy on this skill is neither necessary nor anticipated. Similarly, the criterion level established for a student whose performance is stable from day to day may be significantly different from that established for a student whose disability results in wide variation in performance from day to day. For example, a student with significant memory deficits resulting from a traumatic brain injury, a condition that often varies widely from day to day, would require an extremely stringent criterion on tasks that rely heavily on memory skills (e.g., distinguishing between poisonous and nonpoisonous materials in a work setting).

Any criterion level identified for a particular student is little more than an arbitrary designation of a level of proficiency at which the student can be said to have learned the task. There is nothing magical about the criteria delineated in an IEP or for an instructional objective. Even if a student can perform a skill with 80% accuracy for 3 consecutive days, he or she may not have learned the skill to the point at which it can be used at all times in all places. Answering the question of proficiency is a complex task, and a number of variables should be considered. Does the student perform the skill well enough and fast enough? Will the student be able to perform the skill after a vacation or illness? How well will the skill generalize to other environments? It may be useful for teachers to distinguish between achievement of artificial criteria for education measurement purposes and the actual performance of the skill in the environment in which it will be used.

Acquisition, Fluency, Generalization, and Maintenance

To ensure instruction results in functional skills that can assist the student in a number of different settings, the instructor must develop a systematic plan to move the student from initial acquisition to complete mastery of the skill. Mastery may be viewed as having four components: acquisition, fluency, generalization, and maintenance.

The *acquisition* phase refers to the student's ability to learn the skill under the conditions and criteria established in the original objective. At this point, the student is able to successfully perform the skill independently and to the satisfaction of the instructor. However, the student's initial ability to perform a task such as using a copying machine, entering data into a computer, or preparing a meal may not reflect the ultimate standards that would be expected of an

TABLE 2.3
Steps for Michael in Mastering the Use of a Pay Telephone

Acquisition	Michael will deposit the appropriate amount of money and dial the correct telephone number 70% of the time across 10 consecutive opportunities.
Fluency	Michael will deposit the correct amount of money and accurately dial an appropriate telephone number 90% of the time across 20 consecutive opportunities.
Generalization	Michael will use various coin combinations to dial different telephone numbers, using a number of different pay telephones, 90% of the time across 20 consecutive opportunities.
Maintenance	Michael will use various coin combinations to dial different telephone numbers, using a number of different pay telephones, at random monthly intervals over a period of 2 years.

experienced performer. *Fluency* refers to the increased accuracy and speed of performance that reflect a student's improved competence as he or she benefits from further practice. For example, as the student masters the skill of using a copying machine, he or she will able to process jobs more quickly and efficiently, anticipating when paper might need to be replaced and removing copies from the machine with greater dexterity. *Generalization* reflects a further expansion of the student's abilities. Generalization is usually defined as exhibiting a behavior or performing a skill under different conditions (e.g., stimuli, settings, time of the day) than were present in the initial acquisition phase. Can the student use various types of copying machines with little difficulty after learning the skill on an initial machine? Specific procedures for promoting generalization are described later in this chapter. Finally, *maintenance* refers to the student retaining the ability to perform a skill over time. If the student can perform copying tasks, then no longer performes them for a short time, can he or she return to the copying tasks and perform than successfully months or even years after the skill was initially acquired?

Table 2.3 provides an example of the acquisition, fluency, generalization, and maintenance stages for the skill of using a pay telephone for a student named Michael. Initially, Michael learns to use a single pay phone with 70% accuracy. However, to stop instruction at this point would leave Michael in a situation where he might be considered a novice telephone user, prone to frustration and more than occasionally dialing a wrong number. During the fluency stage, efforts are undertaken to improve his accuracy. In the generalization phase, Michael expands his abilities so that his proficiency in using the phone is not limited by the change in his pocket, the number he is dialing, or the type of telephone that might be available. Finally, because Michael has spent a considerable amount of effort learning this skill, it is important that he be able to perform it for the foreseeable future. Maintenance procedures are used to ensure that once skills are acquired, students can use them indefinitely.

METHOD OF PERFORMING THE TASK

The method of the task is the manner in which it is performed, or the process or strategy that the student will use to complete a complex activity such as cleaning a bedroom, playing a video game, or self-administering medication. It is an area of instructional program development that requires a great deal of innovation and creativity on the part of the teacher. The method selected for instruction will determine (a) whether the student will acquire the task, (b) the amount of time required for instruction, and (c) the potential for the acquired skill to generalize across a large number of settings.

Several factors influence the method that will work best with a given student. When possible, the student should be taught to perform the task in the same manner that most other individuals complete it. A student who dresses very differently from his or her peers, orders meals differently in a restaurant, or uses a different procedure to swim the length of a swimming pool may unnecessarily feel that his or her accomplishments are somehow inferior to those of others. For this reason, the instructor should determine the typical manner in which various skills are performed and attempt to teach students the method used by most people in society. To do this, the instructor can observe people performing the task, interview individuals in employment settings, or consult developmental literature or curriculum guides in areas such as motor or communication skills.

When the most common method cannot be used, two factors should be considered and balanced in developing alternative methods. The first factor is the speed and convenience of the method for the learner. If the task can be performed more quickly and with less effort by using an alternative method, then such a method should be considered. Examples of alternative methods that will improve the speed and efficiency of a student's performance include threading a belt through belt loops while the student's pants are held on his or her lap rather than while the student is wearing them, using a language board to order a meal in a fast-food restaurant, or using Velcro fasteners as opposed to zippers or snaps.

The second factor to consider about an alternative method of performing a task is whether the method will enable the student to perform the task in a variety of environments. For example, an alternative method may enable a person who cannot count money to operate a vending machine, but the number of different vending machines the student can operate may be limited. In this case, the alternative method identified may make the task easier for the student to perform but limit the environments in which the student can use the skill. Consider the following methods for teaching a student with limited money-counting skills (i.e., unable to combine coins into various amounts of money) to use drink or snack food vending machines in which the items cost between $0.25 and $1.50.

Method 1. The student is provided a small number of $1 bills. The student uses the bills to purchase items from vending machines. When approaching the machine, the student locates the dollar bill slot, inserts the bill, and selects the desired item. If the item is not dispensed, the student inserts a second bill, in case the item costs more than $1.00. The student never inserts more than two bills.

This method is effective when used with vending machines that accept currency in addition to coins, and it does not require any counting skills. However, if the vending machine approached by the student is not equipped to accept currency, the student will be frustrated in his or her efforts to obtain an item. In addition, in situations when the machine is malfunctioning (i.e., bills are inserted but not returned and nothing is dispensed), the student will lose $2.00.

Method 2. The student is provided several quarters. The student approaches the vending machine, locates the slot where coins are inserted, and inserts a single quarter. The student then pushes the button (pulls the selection lever, etc.) that dispenses the desired item. If the item is not dispensed, the student repeats the process of inserting another quarter and again pushing the button. The process is repeated until the item is dispensed.

Method 2 has the advantage of working on a wider range of vending machines than Method 1, including those machines that do not accept currency. However, it fails to keep the student from losing money if a machine is malfunctioning. In addition, inserting coins and pressing selection buttons before the correct amount of change has been inserted may increase the likelihood of malfunction.

Method 3. The student is provided a large number of dimes and one or more nickels. The student approaches the machine, then locates the writing on the machine that identifies the amount a specific item costs. The student points to the number in the amount that is on the right (either 0 or 5). If the number is a 5, the student inserts the nickel. The student then covers that number with his or her finger and looks at the remaining number(s). The student then inserts that many dimes into the machine and presses the button to select the desired item.

Method 3 has several advantages. It will work on all vending machines with items costing up to $1.50. It enables the student to enter all the needed coins before selecting the item, thereby reducing the chance of causing a malfunction. It ensures that the student will not insert up to $2.00 in coins or currency into machines that are not working. However, this approach is significantly more complicated than the other two methods. It requires the student to (a) discriminate between dimes and nickels, (b) discriminate left from right in a series of numerals, and (c) count accurately up to 15.

All of the three methods may be appropriate for an individual student. In addition, there are many other effective methods for teaching generalized use of vending machines to students with significant disabilities. The precise method for teaching a skill that will be best for a specific student depends on the skill, the student's ability to perform various components of the skill, and the range of settings in which the skill must be used after instruction. The instructor must remember not to use the student's lack of prerequisite skills to limit his or her ability to learn skills that are functional and meaningful.

TASK ANALYSIS

After a method for task performance has been selected, the next step is a formal task analysis. Task analysis is the process of breaking down a skill or set of skills into its component parts to help a student learn the skill. The number and specificity of the steps identified in the task analysis should relate to the student's ability level. For example, one student may benefit from instruction on washing a sink full of dishes when the task is divided into a series of 10 distinct steps. Another student may need even more, smaller steps and require a 30-step or 40-step task analysis.

Numerous strategies can be used to generate task analyses. Published resources can be consulted (Wehman & Targett, 1999; Wolery, Bailey, & Sugai, 1988); they may provide a basic guide that a teacher could modify or adapt to be appropriate for his or her students. In employment settings, businesses may have developed detailed procedures that are used to train all employees and that can form the basis of individualized task analyses that are designed for a specific student. In most instances, a teacher will have to construct a task analysis without any additional resources.

In such cases, the teacher can take several approaches. The teacher may decide to perform the task himself or herself and note the steps employed along the way. Alternatively, the teacher can list the steps based on a logical analysis of the task to be performed. The teacher could also observe an individual performing the task. Finally, in situations when the teacher is analyzing complex vocational or recreational skills, he or she may interview an experienced individual to learn the "tricks of the trade" developed by individuals who have practiced the skill for extended periods of time.

The following are guidelines for developing a task analysis:

1. Each step of the task analysis should be clearly stated to allow the instructor (or other individual) to accurately and objectively determine whether the student has completed the step.

2. Each step of the task analysis should be written so that it can also be used as a verbal prompt to the student during instruction. For example, a step could be written, "Put the quarter in the machine," as opposed to "Use a pincer grasp to grasp a quarter and insert into appropriate slot."

3. If important to the completion of the task, specify the hand the individual will use to perform a specific action.

4. If a step has the word *and* in it, carefully review the step to determine whether it should be broken into multiple steps. For example, in the step "Remove the tray and place it on the counter," the student may successfully complete part of the step but have difficulty completing the entire step. Separating this step into two will allow the teacher to better identify the specific component of the task on which the student is experiencing difficulty.

5. After developing the task analysis, the teacher should test the task analysis with the student and make modifications if necessary before initiating instruction.

An example of a task analysis for using an ATM card to obtain cash from a checking account is provided in Table 2.4. Although this basic task analysis contains most of the steps involved in using an ATM, the analysis may need to be modified to accommodate the needs of a specific student. For example, because many different types of ATM exist, steps may need to be performed in a different order. The student may be required to swipe his or her card through a slot instead of inserting it into the machine. Specific security procedures may need to be identified to make certain that the student does not leave money or the card behind. Individuals with orthopedic or sensory impairments may need to perform the steps in a completely different manner. As such, the analysis presented

TABLE 2.4
Task Analysis of Using an Automated Teller Machine (ATM)
To Make a Cash Withdrawal from a Checking Account

Steps
1. Approach ATM.
2. Remove ATM card from purse, wallet, or pocket.
3. Insert card into machine, orienting the card as necessary.
4. Select language to be used to display directions.
5. Enter Personal Identification Number (PIN).
6. Accept or decline additional transaction fees as necessary.
7. Select type of transaction.
8. Select specific account (i.e., checking) to be used for transaction.
9. Select "receipt requested" when prompted by ATM.
10. Enter amount of transaction.
11. Remain at ATM while processing occurs.
12. Collect money when dispensed.
13. Place money in purse, wallet, or pocket.
14. Select "transaction complete" when prompted by ATM.
15. Collect receipt when dispensed.
16. Collect ATM card when dispensed.
17. Place receipt and ATM card in purse, wallet, or pocket.

in Table 2.4 illustrates how an initial task analysis should be viewed as only an initial guide that must be modified to meet the needs of specific learners.

Several different types of task analyses are included in the remaining chapters. Most task analyses are a sequential listing of the steps to be performed in completing complex behavioral chains. Other task analyses are distance based; that is, the steps listed are used to teach the student to perform the skills across increasing distances, such as catching a ball at 5-foot, 10-foot, and 20-foot distances. These types of task analyses are particularly useful in teaching vocational skills or recreational skills in situations when the student needs to orient throughout a large area. In other types of skills, the action the student performs remains the same throughout the course of the task; what is analyzed may be the complexity of the conditions under which the skill will be performed, the amount of assistance given to the student while he or she is performing the skill, or the duration or rate at which the skill is performed.

INSTRUCTIONAL PROCEDURES

All of the steps involved in developing instructional programs discussed to this point have dealt with designing the task in the way in which it will be presented to the student. The remaining steps will deal with designing the teaching strategies and methods for evaluation. The following procedures will be discussed: program format, collecting baseline information, instructional prompts, scheduling the training session, reinforcement, and generalization.

Program Format

Program format relates to how much and what part of a task will be presented to a student for instruction during one training trial. The three most common program formats are forward chaining, backward chaining, and total task presentation. The primary difference between the chaining procedures and the total task procedure is the number of steps that the student will be asked to perform independently during each trial. In both the forward and backward chaining procedures, the student receives instruction on just one step of the task on any given trial. In the total task presentation format, the student receives instruction on all steps of the task analysis during each training trial.

In forward chaining, the student learns the first step of the task first. Instruction is provided on the first unlearned step of the task analysis. The teacher allows the student to attempt to perform the designated step. If successful, reinforcement is delivered. If unsuccessful, assistance is provided. After the student has mastered that step, instruction proceeds to the next step.

In practice, few skills are taught using forward chaining because this approach prevents the student from successfully completing the last step of the task and experiencing the natural consequences of successful performance until all steps in the task analysis have been completely learned. Forward chaining may have its greatest application on tasks such as tying shoes, in which the last steps of the task analysis are generally the most difficult to acquire. In this instance, the student can benefit from the assistance received on the latter steps of the analysis while he or she practices and learns initial steps.

In backward chaining, the last step of the task is taught first. This approach has the advantage of linking the naturally occurring reinforcement that inherently results from the completion of the task with the performance of the activity. Backward chaining may be beneficial for tasks in which the student is able to complete a large number of the steps at the end of the task analysis. In backward chaining the ATM task in Table 2.4, the student would first be taught to secure the ATM card and receipt in his or her purse, wallet, or pocket. Then the student would be taught to complete the last two steps of the task, which are to grasp the receipt and card when dispensed from the machine and to secure the ATM card and receipt in his or her purse, wallet, or pocket, and so on.

In the total task presentation format, the student receives training on every step of the task analysis in one session. In the ATM example, the student would be allowed to attempt Step 1, approaching the ATM. If successful, reinforcement would be provided; if unsuccessful, assistance would be delivered. In either case, instruction moves to the next step, and the student would be allowed to attempt Step 2, eventually moving through all remaining steps.

Total task presentation has several advantages. Some research indicates that total task presentation is more effective than chaining strategies for some students with disabilities (Kayser, Billingsley, & Neel, 1986). Total task presentation is generally viewed as more natural than other procedures because instruction is generally provided in the context of daily routines. In addition, it should be noted that in some instances, strategies can be used in combination. For example, a particularly difficult step of a task could be further broken down and isolated for instruction using a chaining strategy, but the main task can be taught through total task presentation.

The following example may serve to illustrate the differences between the three types of formats. Suppose the task one wishes to teach is hand washing. If a forward chaining procedure is used, the student will first learn the first step of the task, "Turn on the cold water." Several trials may be provided during the course of a training session on the same step. After the student learns that step, another step is added and the student attempts to perform the first and second steps of the task, "Turn on the cold water; turn on the hot water." Additional steps are added to the chain until the student performs the whole task. In a backward chaining program, however, the student would first learn the last step, then the last two steps, and so on. In all chaining programs, a criterion is set (called a phase-change criterion) and used to determine when to add an additional step. For example, when the student performs the first step correctly for three consecutive times, the second step will be added, and so on.

In a total task presentation, the student attempts to independently perform each step of the task on each trial. In the hand-washing example, the student first attempts to independently perform the first step, "Turn on the cold water." If the student performs the step correctly, reinforcement is given. If the student does not perform the step correctly, a correction procedure is initiated and the student is given assistance until he or she is able to perform the step. Then, on the same trial, the student continues the task, attempting to perform the second step. This process continues, with the student attempting to perform each step of the task independently and then receiving reinforcement or assistance, until the task has been completed. Total task presentation is generally used when the teacher feels that the student can benefit from instruction on more than one step of a task training program within a single training session.

Collecting Baseline Information

After the teacher has identified a method of task performance and developed a task analysis, he or she can begin instruction. The first step in instruction is the collection of baseline assessment information. The purposes of the baseline assessment are (a) to determine whether instruction on the task is required, (b) to verify that the task analysis developed for the skill is appropriate for the student, and (c) to identify any particular steps of an analysis that may cause particular problems for the student.

The format of the baseline assessment will vary depending on the nature of the task. If the task being assessed contains a lengthy list of complex steps, it may be appropriate to observe the student's performance across all steps of the task. On shorter tasks, assessment may stop at the student's first mistakes. Some skills, such as the introduction of a new vocational skill that the student has never seen or attempted before, may only need to be assessed once or twice. Other skills, such as telling time or counting money, may require lengthier baseline periods because the student's first response may not indicate his or her overall level of mastery of the skill. Whatever assessment strategy is used, the teacher should ensure that assessment occurs under the same conditions that the student will face when using the skill in daily life. Community-based skills must be assessed *in the community,* at the time of day during which they typically would be used.

Instructional Prompts

The teaching procedures identified to this point assume a situation in which the student learns the skill with no difficulty whatsoever. If all a teacher was required to do was to reinforce students for tasks performed correctly, teaching would be a much easier job. In reality, students may make numerous errors and require a significant amount of assistance on many steps of a task until they acquire the desired skill. When a student performs a step incorrectly or fails to perform a step after a specified period of time, assistance, in the form of a *prompt,* should be delivered to allow the student to successfully perform the task.

Many types of prompts can be used to assist students with disabilities in acquiring complex skills. The type of prompt that will be most effective in a specific situation depends on the characteristics of the learner, the type of task being taught, and the specific step within the task on which the student is experiencing difficulty. Table 2.5 describes several prompts that have proven effective in many different instructional settings. Each of these types of prompts is described in detail below.

Ambiguous Verbal Prompts. In some situations, a student needs only a minimal amount of assistance to complete the next step of a task analysis. For example, he or she may be uncertain or lack confidence that the step can be performed correctly. In these situations, an ambiguous verbal statement such as, "What's next?" can help the student initiate the next step. Ambiguous verbal cues have their greatest applicability in situations in which the teacher feels that the

TABLE 2.5
Types of Instructional Prompts

Prompt	Description
1. Ambiguous verbal prompts	Comments such as, "Keep going," or "What's next?" that encourage a student to go on without specifying what needs to be done.
2. Specific verbal prompts	Specific information that tells the student what to do next, such as, "Pick up the plate."
3. Modeling	Teacher performs the correct action and then allows the student to attempt to perform the step.
4. Gestures	These are methods of nonverbal communication, such as pointing to the place where an object belongs or gesturing to the student to turn an object over.
5. Priming	The student is given just enough physical assistance to initiate performance of the step. When the student begins to move on his or her own, the teacher's assistance is removed.
6. Physical assistance	The student is given hand-over-hand assistance to enable him or her to complete the task. This assistance is then faded from the hand, to the wrist, to the forearm, to the elbow, to the shoulder; the fading process is called *graduated guidance.*

student knows how to perform the next step, or has completed the step properly in the past, but is reluctant for whatever reason to initiate it.

Specific Verbal Prompts. Direct verbal instruction is an effective way to guide a student into performing the correct action. Verbal prompts must be stated in a manner that the student will understand. A consistent verbal prompt should be developed for each step of a task analysis, which is why the steps in a task analysis should be written in a manner that allows them to be directly stated as specific verbal cues, as mentioned previously in this chapter. Specific verbal cues are most applicable in the initial stages of teaching a task with students who can benefit from verbal instructions. In addition, verbal prompts are best used for steps of the task analysis that involve discrimination among actions, objects, or other stimuli and will be less effective with behaviors that require complex motor movements.

Modeling. The use of modeling as an instructional prompt refers to demonstrations of the appropriate action completed by a teacher, who then allows the student to copy the teacher's action. Modeling is effective when (a) the student can benefit from demonstrations performed by the instructor, and (b) the step of the task analysis to be completed does not lend itself to the use of verbal cues.

The use of modeling assumes that the student will attend to the model and copy the actions seen to complete the task. Because the student must turn his or her attention away from the instructional task to attend to the teacher's demonstration, modeling should only be used when other strategies are ineffective. In addition, when models are used, they should be combined with verbal cues so that over time the verbal cue becomes an effective prompt and modeling is no longer required.

In most instances, modeling refers to actions performed by the teacher. However, a classmate or coworker in the actual setting may also model an action for the student. In recreational settings, such as a fitness center, other individuals may be used to model actions.

Gestures. Gestures are simply teacher motions or actions that indicate to the student what action should be performed next. Gestures are most appropriate when used in situations in which the student (a) does not understand a specific verbal prompt provided by the teacher, or (b) the action required at a specific step of a task analysis is difficult to state verbally. For example, if a student does not know what a Phillips-head screwdriver is, it will difficult for him or her to respond to a specific verbal prompt such as, "Pick up the Phillips-head screwdriver." In this case, pointing to the screwdriver may be an effective prompt. As with modeling, it is important that gestures be paired with a specific verbal prompt, so that over time the verbal direction itself becomes an effective prompt. Gestures are also effective in situations where the step of the task analysis requires the student to place an object in a specific location or orientation. Prompts such as, "Turn it over" or "Rotate it 90 degrees," may be very difficult to understand for many students if not accompanied by a gesture.

Priming. Priming is a type of physical prompt in which a student is given gentle physical contact that directs him or her to initiate action on a step of the task analysis. Priming is sometimes referred to as partial physical assistance.

Priming is often effective in situations where the step involved requires physical manipulation and the student seems to know what to do next, yet is hesitant about initiating the action. In these situations, a gentle touch on the student's elbow or shoulder may be sufficient to assist the student in completing the next step of the task analysis, such as clicking the left mouse button, inserting a token into a machine, pressing a doorbell, or other similar actions.

Physical Assistance. Physical assistance involves the delivery of hand-over-hand assistance to help a student complete a specific step of the task. Physical assistance is the most intrusive of all prompts and, therefore, should only be used when absolutely necessary. The assistance should be delivered in a gentle manner that provides the student only the amount of assistance that is needed. Physical assistance is most effective on steps that require complex physical manipulations. In these situations, the teacher can assist the student in developing the appropriate motor movements and control the pace of the action, such as using a computer mouse to scroll down a screen, turning a key in a lock, or shifting the manual transmission of an automobile.

When a student begins to make an error on a step of a task analysis, the teacher should move quickly to stop the student's behavior. Research indicates that "errorless" learning is the most effective approach to instruction (Schriebman, 1975; Sidman, 1990). In other words, learning occurs most efficiently when few errors are made. When a student starts to perform a step incorrectly, such as turning on the cold water instead of the hot water, he or she is "practicing" the mistake. Stopping the student when he or she begins to make an error and immediately providing the amount of assistance necessary to enable the student to perform the step independently helps him or her learn the task in the shortest amount of time.

System of Least Prompts

Prompts are most frequently used in combination. In most instances, various types of prompts will be ordered into a hierarchy that can be delivered in a most-to-least or least-to-most sequence. A prompt hierarchy is typically divided into three levels of assistance and delineates what the teacher will do when the student makes a mistake. In such cases, the teacher first stops the student's ongoing behavior. Then the teacher delivers the assistance identified on the first level of the prompt hierarchy. If the student still does not complete the step, the teacher should implement assistance according to the second level of the prompt hierarchy, and then the third level, if necessary.

Different prompt hierarchies can be employed depending on the type of error made by the student. Student errors are either *discrimination* errors or *manipulation* errors. A discrimination error occurs when a student's behavior is not under the control of the appropriate discrimination stimulus (S^D). Examples of frequently occurring discrimination errors include selecting an inappropriate object, placing an object in an inappropriate place, orienting an object incorrectly, failing to initiate a step, completing a step out of order, and so on. Generally, ambiguous verbal prompts, specific verbal prompts, and gestures are considered the most effective prompts for discrimination errors.

A manipulation error occurs when a student is unable to perform the physical manipulation necessary to complete a step. Consider, for example, an 8-year-old student named Emily, who is attempting to learn to insert a compact disc into a CD player but is unable to easily grasp the outside edges of the CD and insert it into the narrow slot on the player. In this situation, the following prompt hierarchy could be used to correct Emily's manipulation errors. Initially, Emily will be allowed to attempt the physical manipulation (i.e., inserting the compact disc) for 15 seconds. If she has not completed the step after the time period, the teacher will do the following:

1. Provide a physical prompt in the form of hand-over-hand physical manipulation, beginning with Emily's fingers and hand.

2. Fade the manipulation from the fingers, to the back of the hand, to the wrist as Emily becomes more proficient at the task.

Different types of prompts should be used to correct discrimination errors and manipulation errors. For example, if Emily is attempting to insert the compact disc into the player upside down (a discrimination error), a specific verbal cue or gesture indicating that she should turn it over might be very effective. However, if she is having difficulty grasping the disc and inserting it properly into the narrow slot (a manipulation error), verbal or gestural prompts will have limited value. Discrimination errors and manipulation errors frequently require different prompt hierarchies.

If a student is making the same error on the same step over successive trials, it might prove effective to provide assistance *prior* to the performance of the step. This assistance will preclude the possibility of the student independently performing the step correctly, but it does have several advantages. First, prior assistance enables the student to practice performing the appropriate action, and that action only, in the presence of the particular S^D for that step. Second, it maintains the continuity and rhythm of the task because the student will be more likely to perform the step correctly. Third, it prevents the student from practicing incorrect responses, which lessens the risk of ineffective habits being developed. Again, the type of error will determine the type of prior assistance given.

As the student progresses through training, the amount of assistance provided should decrease until no assistance is being provided. If at any time during the fading process a student makes an error, even after having been given prior assistance, more assistance should be provided until the student is performing the step accurately.

Time Delay

Time delay is a type of prompting procedure that is especially useful for promoting errorless learning. In time delay, prompts are provided immediately after the instructional cue, thereby greatly reducing the number of errors that the student will make. As the student begins to master the task, the time period between the cue and the prompt is gradually and systematically increased. In the *progressive delay approach,* the length of time between cue and prompt increases through a series of small increments. In a *constant delay approach,* the length of time between cue and prompt varies from an immediate to a constant (e.g., 5 seconds) level.

Time delay has been used effectively to teach skills such as using a vending machine (Browder, Snell, & Wildonger, 1988) and reading sight words (Ault,

Gast, & Wolery, 1988). Although in some instances time delay has been used to teach lengthy behavioral chains, such as bed making (Snell, 1982), time delay is most suited for teaching skills such as communication and functional academics.

In the following example, a teacher named Mr. Young uses progressive time delay to teach Lance, a 12-year-old boy with significant memory deficits, to state his home telephone number. Mr. Young first gives the cue, "Lance, what is your telephone number?" and immediately prompts (0-second time delay) Lance by verbally stating the first digit of his telephone number, then the second digit, and so on until the number is complete. After a series of practice trials in this manner, Mr. Young initiates a 1-second delay between the cue and each of the prompts. As practice sessions continue, Lance begins to occasionally say a digit of his phone number in the interval between Mr. Young's cue and his verbal prompt. Over time, as Lance's performance improves, Mr. Young increases the period of time from 1 second to 3 seconds and then 5 seconds. As Lance begins to master the skill, he is then ready to generalize the use of this skill to a wide range of community-based settings.

Scheduling the Training Session

Scheduling where and when instruction will occur is often one of the most challenging aspects of instructional planning. Current trends emphasize instruction of entire tasks and sequencing common activities that usually occur at the same time (in areas such as work tasks, grooming, home maintenance), as opposed to instruction on isolated skills. Activity sequencing results in the need for lengthy instructional periods that may not easily fit into the structure of the school day. In addition, instruction should be provided in the natural environments where the skill will be performed, such as a grocery store or post office. This emphasis often runs counter to other trends such as inclusion, which stresses the importance of students spending a maximum amount of time with their same-aged peers, and educational reform, which stresses instruction on academic skills necessary for basic adult literacy. As a result, finding the time and resources necessary to teach the type of skills identified in the remaining chapters often becomes difficult.

Massed Versus Distributed Trials

In the 1970s, best practices for teaching students with significant disabilities suggested that instruction for students be "massed" in certain periods of the day. For example, if a student was learning to turn on a radio, he or she would practice turning it on, the teacher or student would turn it off, the student would practice the task again, and this sequence would be repeated three, five, or nine times until an instructional session was completed.

In the 1980s, a number of professionals began to question the concept of massed trials (Guess & Helmstetter, 1986; Mulligan, Guess, Hoelvet, & Brown, 1980), and they were rejected as an artificial, overly rigid technique that reduced the likelihood that skills taught in the training setting would transfer to natural community settings. As an alternative, the concept of "distributed" trials was developed. Under this concept, training occurs in community-based settings and focuses on activities as opposed to isolated skills. Considerable evidence suggests that distributed trials result in improved performance and more positive student response than massed trials (Dunlap & Koegel, 1980; Mulligan, Macy, & Guess, 1982). Although the intensive practice afforded by the massed trial approach may be beneficial in a limited number of situations, the advantages of community-based training have proven significant.

Community-Based Instruction

Community-based instruction offers the student the opportunity to learn new skills in the environment in which he or she will use them. The student is able to experience the environmental factors that form the context for the skills the student is learning. For example, the presence of coworkers, the relationship to an employment supervisor, and the duration of a work day are all factors that influence a student's ability to learn new job skills. Similarly, adjusting to the pace and noise of downtown sidewalks is crucial to learning bus-riding skills. Distributed trial instruction is more likely to take place at various times and across settings, thereby promoting generalization.

Although the student, the task being taught, and the structure of the school may affect scheduling, there are a number of guidelines in this area. First, whenever possible, instruction should focus on activities rather than isolated skills. Meal preparation could focus on preparing the meal, eating, and performing kitchen cleanup chores. Second, instruction should take place at the time of day when the task is usually performed. Third, when possible, the student should spend the maximum amount of time possible with his or her same-aged peers. The concept of community-based instruction is not inconsistent with the concept of inclusion. Students without disabilities, family members, employers, and community members can all be involved in instructional settings. Fourth, the length of time between instructional sessions should be determined by the needs of an individual student and the nature of the task being taught. For some students, instruction that occurs one time per week may enable them to acquire community skills. Other students may benefit from community-based instruction more frequently. Some activities, such as doing laundry, may occur once or twice per week. Other activities, such as banking, may occur less than one time per week.

Reinforcement

Little has been said in this chapter about the role of reinforcement in the design of instructional programs. Although reinforcement is often overemphasized in simplistic explanations of the learning process, few would argue that a motivated learner will be more likely to quickly learn a task than one who is not motivated. Besides motivation, reinforcement also has the effect of providing the learner with feedback as to whether his or her behavior was correct.

In many instances, no specialized reinforcement program is needed because completing a set of tasks may lead to results that are inherently reinforcing (e.g., cooking a meal, making a purchase). However, some students will require additional reinforcement in the form of activities or verbal praise, and a few students may need more tangible forms of reinforcement. Some individuals may feel that the use of tangible reinforcement is not a natural approach and that it bribes students to perform skills they should want to learn on their own. Remember, however, that tangible reinforcement during the initial stages of instruction on a task does not mean that the student will always require tangible reinforcement to perform the task. Reinforcement can be faded, just as physical assistance can be faded. If a student is not learning a skill and appears to be unmotivated and unfocused on the task, then tangible reinforcement techniques may be highly appropriate.

Generalization

The final component of instructional program design is generalization. Generalization refers to situations in which a student (a) demonstrates a skill learned in one setting in related but not previously experienced environments, (b) continues to display a behavior after the training conditions have been removed (also known as maintenance), or (c) develops new, untrained responses as a result of initial training. Generalization is an extremely important, often neglected area of educational programming. After all, teachers do want students to be able to cross all streets of a specific type, not only the single street or streets on which instruction occurred, or to be able to purchase foods in all grocery stores, not just in a single location.

Generalization can be said to have occurred if the behavior endures over time, occurs in a variety of settings, or occurs across a set of related behaviors. Generalization can occur along a number of different dimensions, usually identified as stimulus generalization, maintenance, and response generalization. Examples of each of the three generalization dimensions are provided in Table 2.6.

A wide variety of strategies can be used to promote the generalization of newly learned skills across employment, residential, community living, and recreational situations.

TABLE 2.6
Dimensions of Generalization

Type of Generalization	Description
1. Stimulus generalization	The student should be able to perform a skill in a variety of community settings or with a variety of materials. For example, a student who has learned to purchase a meal in a fast-food restaurant should be able to do so in a variety of fast-food settings. A student who has learned to use a screwdriver should be able to use screwdrivers of various shapes and sizes.
2. Maintenance	The student should be able to independently perform a skill learned several weeks or months earlier without any of the prompting or reinforcement provided in the initial training stages. For example, if the student has learned to prepare a specific meal, the student should be able to prepare the meal in the absence of any instruction 6 to 12 weeks after the initial training has occurred.
3. Response generalization	A student who learned to perform a skill in the presence of a specific stimulus should be able to perform related skills in the presence of the same stimulus. For example, a student who has learned to use a written checklist to assist in the completion of a part of his or her job (e.g., watering plants in a greenhouse) will begin to develop and use written checklists to assist with other tasks, such as housecleaning or car maintenance activities.

Rely on Natural Reinforcers

In some instances, providing reinforcement through verbal praise or activity reinforcers is an effective way of motivating students with disabilities to learn new skills. However, an overemphasis on artificial reinforcement during initial training may actually reduce the likelihood that skills taught in one setting will generalize to an array of settings throughout the community. Whenever possible, instructional programs should be designed so that the student experiences the natural reinforcement that comes from completing an activity. For example, the natural consequence of completing an employment task may be praise from a supervisor or a paycheck. The natural consequence of successfully operating a CD player is to listen to music. Exposing students to the consequences of task completion, as opposed to adding artificial types of reinforcement that must ultimately be faded, is an effective strategy for encouraging stimulus generalization.

Train with Sufficient Examples

If the intent of instruction is to enable a student to perform a skill in a variety of settings and situations, then special care should be taken to ensure that training sites reflect the range of settings the student will experience after learning the skill. One process for generalizing skill usage across various community settings is *general case instruction*. In general case instruction, careful selection of teaching examples enables students to learn to perform skills across a variety of settings (e.g., Horner & McDonald, 1982; Sprague & Horner, 1984). This type of approach has proven effective with skills ranging from using telephones and vending machines to learning vocational skills and appropriate social behaviors.

When using general case instruction, the teacher should first identify the universe of possible settings in which a skill might be used. The teacher then carefully selects teaching examples and testing examples that reflect the natural variation across all the settings that comprise the universe. For example, if the task being taught is purchasing food in a fast-food restaurant, the selected teaching examples should include fast-food restaurants that have salad bars and those that do not, restaurants with condiments in various locations, restaurants where customers are responsible for getting their own drinks from a drink machine, and so on. Instruction then begins at several (2–4) teaching example sites. After the student is able to order food at these teaching example sites, testing occurs at a similar number of sites to see if the student is able to generalize his or her newly learned skill to untrained settings. If generalization has not yet occurred, instruction continues in additional teaching sites until the student is able to easily perform the task in a variety of untrained settings.

Train Loosely

For many years, best practices in the instruction of individuals with significant disabilities emphasized standardized instructional strategies and rigid adherence to proven learning principles. Baer (1981) argued that instruction that is too rigid (i.e., repeated the same way each time without variation) may actually inhibit generalization. Baer suggested randomly varying the number of instructors, the settings in which instruction occurs, and the time of day at which instruction takes place. The teacher is also encouraged to vary his or her tone of voice, position in relation to the student, and the words he or she uses during instruction. The instructional setting should also vary in terms of lighting, sound, decorations, and presence of other individuals. Baer urged teachers to "do all this as often and unpredictably as possible" (Baer, 1981, p. 25).

Program Common Stimuli

Another effective strategy for promoting both stimulus and response generalization is to identify stimuli (e.g., items or objects) that can be present in both the initial training environment and the generalization environments. The extent to which common stimuli are available in all settings to prompt the student's appropriate behavior will greatly determine the amount of generalization the student will display. Personal data assistants (PDAs), pocket calculators, written checklists of daily activities at school, work, or home, and even portable computers can serve as stimuli to assist the student in performing a newly learned behavior across settings.

For example, the use of pocket calculators in a wide variety of settings may promote stimulus generalization in students learning basic financial management skills. A student who uses a calculator to make purchases in a grocery store, for example, may generalize its use to restaurants, banks, and other retail settings. The common stimulus (i.e., the pocket calculator) enhances the student's confidence in each of these settings. Similarly, response generalization can be enhanced when a common stimulus, such as a written checklist, is used to manage a student's morning routine at home, to manage his or her time effectively at work, and to organize errands that must be completed during the weekend.

Teach Self-Management Strategies

Self-management strategies involve students directly in their own instruction and promote generalization. All children and adults use a variety of self-management strategies on a daily basis. We make lists to prompt us about what to buy at the grocery store. We reinforce ourselves with a short break and a cool drink after completing a tiring task such as mowing grass or playing basketball. We record data about ourselves when we keep track of how much we weigh or the number of laps we swim. When used as an instructional technique for students with disabilities, self-management may refer to activities such as self-instruction, self-monitoring and evaluation, and self-reinforcement.

Self-instruction occurs when a student prompts himself or herself to perform one of the steps involved in the task analysis of a particular skill. Recipe cards, picture booklets (Wacker & Berg, 1984), pocket-sized calendars, and tape-recorded instructions (Alberto, Sharpton, Briggs, & Stright, 1986) have all been used to assist students in acquiring and maintaining new skills. Self-instruction strategies have been particularly effective in assisting individuals in learning and performing job-related duties in employment situations. Kreutzer and Wehman (1991) described an array of compensatory strategies and other self-instructional strategies that have been used by individuals to overcome memory and other learning problems and to successfully maintain employment.

Self-monitoring and evaluation occur when an individual observes and records his or her own behavior. A child who checks off the various tasks involved in cleaning his or her own room (e.g., making bed, emptying trash, dusting) as they are completed, an adolescent who keeps track of his or her high score on a video game, or an adult who checks off job duties as they are completed are all using self-monitoring strategies. Self-monitoring is effective for several reasons. Some evidence suggests that the very act of recording one's own behavior may change it for the better (e.g., Koegel & Koegel, 1990; Koegel, Koegel, Hurley, & Frea, 1992). Self-monitoring can also involve the subjective evaluation of the quality of one's own efforts, such as when an individual samples a dish that he or she has prepared or evaluates the cleanliness of a kitchen after it has been cleaned.

Self-reinforcement occurs when a student selects a reinforcer that will be administered when a behavior has occurred or makes the decision to implement the reinforcement contingency. Determining when to take breaks and identifying what to do during break time has effectively enhanced employee performance in a variety of work settings. Rewarding oneself by watching a favorite television program after completing a series of housekeeping activities such as doing laundry and ironing can enhance the maintenance of these skills over a long period of time.

In summary, the need to plan and program for generalization places a difficult burden on the instructional staff. Programming for generalization is a complex task. But what is certain is that generalization will occur if systematically planned for; it may not spontaneously occur without specific interventions designed to promote it. The teacher should work both during and after initial training to see that generalization will occur.

DESIGNING INSTRUCTIONAL UNITS

For students with significant disabilities, a great deal of instructional time will be spent acquiring skills while working one-to-one with a teacher or instructional aide. Most of the functional skills included in a student's IEP will require the student to perform complex actions that cannot be effectively mastered, or even practiced, in large-group situations. For example, crossing the street with a group of students is a much different task than crossing the street alone. Cooking a meal with a group of students does not ensure that a student can independently cook a complete meal when he or she is alone. Most students with significant support needs require extensive, individualized instruction, using the strategies described above, to practice and master the skills they will need to lead productive, independent lives after graduation.

Despite the need for individualized instruction, many students spend a great deal of time working in small- or large-group settings in resource rooms or self-contained special education classrooms. A teacher or aide may be working with a small group of students while an additional instructor is providing other one-to-one instruction in another area of the classroom, school, or community. Or a teacher may be providing instruction to students with disabilities and other students in a mainstream or inclusion setting. In these types of situations, it is important that the group instructional activities be designed and delivered so that each student is able to benefit from instruction that takes into consideration his or her unique strengths and support needs.

The development of an instructional unit may be an effective method of providing instruction to students with significant disabilities in small groups. The purpose of an instructional unit is to teach functional skills to a number of students with significant disabilities simultaneously while ensuring that the activities provided are relevant to each member of the group. There are many similarities between an instructional unit and the individual instructional programs identified above. First, both units and programs have clear, student-based performance objectives that have been selected to meet the functional goals identified in the student's IEP. Second, each requires the student to complete some type of performance activity each day. In an instructional program, the student will complete one or more *trials* each day. In an instructional unit, each group member will complete some type of *performance activity* each day. A performance activity is something each student does to indicate mastery of a specific objective. Performance activities may include such things as answering questions, making a poster, drawing a picture, or taking a test. Third, both units and instructional programs can and should be individualized to assist students with specific support needs, such as students with limited expressive language, significant cognitive disabilities, or orthopedic impairments that may limit movement or mobility. Finally, both units and individual programs result in a student mastering a specific functional skill that can subsequently be applied in school, home, or community settings.

An effective instructional unit contains a number of specific components, including a targeted student group, statement of instructional goal, instructional objectives, instructional activities, and a method of evaluating instruction. Each of these components is described below.

Targeted Student Group. Instructional units should be designed for a specific group of students. Content must be functional, relevant, and feasible for all students. The characteristics and support needs of the students will directly affect the objectives and activities selected for instruction. The service delivery setting (e.g., general education classroom, resource room, self-contained class) will shape the scope and pace of instruction. Accommodations will be required to ensure that individuals with orthopedic or sensory impairments can participate in, and benefit from, all aspects of instruction. The need to customize the unit to the individual students targeted for instruction means that commercially available curricula should rarely be used without extensive modifications. Commercial materials should be viewed as guides that can assist teachers and instructional personnel in developing instructional units of immediate relevance to targeted students.

Statement of Instructional Goal. The instructional unit should have a clearly stated behavioral goal. Similar to an instructional objective in an individualized instructional program, the goal should define the scope of the behavior the student will learn, the conditions under which he or she will display the behavior, and the appropriate evaluation criteria. Unlike an instructional program, however, a goal statement in an instructional unit will be the summative activity in a series of small instructional objectives that lead to the final goal.

Instructional Objectives. In an instructional unit, a specific performance objective is established for each day during which the unit is taught. For example, if the unit will be taught during six 90-minute periods, six instructional objectives will be established. This approach has two advantages. First, it guarantees that the daily instructional activities all lead to the acquisition of the overall

TABLE 2.7
Possible Instructional Activities

Class discussion	Guest speaker
Internet search	Role-playing
Drawing a picture	Making a poster
Classroom demonstration	Field trip or site visit
Storytelling	Simulation
Problem-solving activities	Instructional games

instructional goal. Second, it ensures that the student will perform an activity during each instructional period that will reflect his or her mastery of a short-term objective and verify that the instructional content is relevant to the individual student.

Instructional Activities. The unit plan should identify specific activities that will effectively teach each of the instructional objectives. Instructional activities can vary widely depending on the ages, abilities, and interests of the students. Activities should include an introduction that links the daily lesson to the overall instructional goal, elicits the students' attention, and motivates the students to exhibit their best performance. The activities should allow each student to demonstrate competence on the daily instructional objective. A list of potential instructional activities is provided in Table 2.7.

Method of Evaluation. At the end of an instructional unit, all students should complete a summative evaluation activity that assesses their mastery of the overall instructional goal for the unit. As opposed to assessing the class as a whole, each student should be independently assessed to make certain that the critical content has been acquired. If a student has difficulty with the summative evaluation activity, adaptations, accommodations, additional practices, and other techniques can be employed to assist the student in achieving the specific goal.

An example of a unit plan is provided below. The sample unit illustrates the type of instructional content that might be taught in small- or large-group settings, the way in which multiple instructional objectives can combine to achieve a larger instructional goal, and the array of instructional activities that can be used to deliver content to students with significant disabilities.

SAMPLE UNIT PLAN: WHY WORK PAYS

Grade Level: This unit is designed for students in Grades 10 to 12. It is appropriate for students between the ages of 14 and 21.

Targeted Students: The unit is designed for students with significant cognitive disabilities served in a resource room or self-contained class. It may also be appropriate for some students with significant learning disabilities or emotional disturbance.

Time Required: The unit will be taught daily, for 50 minutes each day, for a period of 6 days.

Statement of Instructional Goal: The student will be able to identify a job he or she is interested in, determine the rate of pay for the job, and describe how the earnings will affect his or her purchasing ability.

Statement of Instructional Objectives:

1. Each student will be able to describe reasons why people are paid to work.

2. Each student will be able to identify reasons why some jobs pay more than others.

3. Each student will be able to discuss the salary they expect to earn upon graduation.

4. Each student will be able to discuss the personal needs that are met through employment earnings.

5. Each student will be able to describe the relationship between earnings and purchasing ability.

6. (Culminating Objective) Each student will be able to identify a job he or she is interested in, determine the rate of pay for the job, and describe how the earnings will affect his or her purchasing ability.

List of Instructional Activities:

Objective 1: Each student will be able to describe reasons why people are paid to work.

- Have a panel of workers from different jobs discuss their job responsibilities and types of remuneration.

- Students will discuss the jobs and list the reasons why someone would be paid for performing each job (e.g., community needs the service, long hours spent, education and/or training to perform the job).

Objective 2: Each student will be able to identify reasons why some jobs pay more than others.

- Students interview their parents to determine the amount of training and/or education required for their jobs.

(continues)

Objective 2 Continued.

- Students categorize jobs based on education/training required, hours worked per week, salary versus hourly wage, amount of wages, and so on.

Objective 3: Each student will be able to discuss the salary he or she expects to earn upon graduation.

- Students will research a job that they are interested in, identifying wages paid, experience required, and so on.
- Students will identify and communicate to class members the salary they wish and expect to earn upon graduation.

Objective 4: Each student will be able to discuss the personal needs that are met through employment earnings.

- Students will discuss personal needs they hope to meet with their salaries.
- Students will prepare a list of necessary payments that must be made from one's salary (e.g., rent, food, car, recreation).

Objective 5: Each student will be able to describe the relationship between earnings and purchasing ability.

- A panel of recent graduates will describe their present jobs and how their earnings relate to their purchasing power.
- Students will compute the salaries of workers based on hourly wages and number of hours worked per week. They will then discuss the purchasing ability of various workers based on the wages calculated.

Culminating Objective: Each student will be able to identify a job he or she is interested in, determine the rate of pay for the job, and describe how the earnings will affect his or her purchasing ability.

Method for Evaluating Instruction. Each student will develop a poster that contains information on a specific job, including wages and paycheck deductions, number of hours worked per week, education and training required, and other relevant information. Each student will present his or her poster to the class and describe the extent to which the job will meet the student's personal needs.

SUMMARY

Effective instruction for students with disabilities involves many decisions and an ability to adapt basic strategies to the unique characteristics and needs of individual students. This chapter described some of the important decisions and steps involved in developing instructional programs in the curricular areas described in the remainder of the book. Determining whether to teach a particular skill, developing an instructional objective, developing a creative method for performing the task, and completing task analyses require commitment and cooperation by a number of individuals, including the student, his or her family, and members of the community. Developing prompting procedures, providing reinforcement, and promoting generalization are essential components of instructional programs that build on a student's current skills to enable the student to achieve self-selected instructional goals.

Current best practices in instructional programming include using task analyses for instruction, training in actual community settings, using coordinated prompting procedures, and planning instruction to maximize generalization. Through careful planning and the cooperation of all individuals involved, effective instructional strategies can be used to promote the independence and inclusion of students with disabilities in employment, educational, and recreational settings in their local communities.

REFERENCES

Alberto, P., Sharpton, W., Briggs, A., & Stright, M. (1986). Facilitating task acquisition through the use of a self-operated auditory prompting system. *Journal of the Association of Persons with Severe Handicaps, 11,* 85–91.

Ault, M., Gast, D., & Wolery, M. (1988). Comparison of progressive and constant time-delay procedures in teaching community sign–word reading. *American Journal on Mental Retardation, 93,* 44–56.

Baer, D. (1981). *How to plan for generalization.* Austin, TX: PRO-ED.

Baumgart, D., Brown, L., Pumpian, I., Nisbet, J., Ford, A., Sweet, M., et al. (1982). Principle of partial participation and individualized adaptations in educational programs for severely handicapped students. *Journal of the Association of Persons with Severe Handicaps, 7,* 17–27.

Browder, D., Snell, M., & Wildonger, B. (1988). Simulation and community-based instruction of vending machines with time delay. *Education and Training in Mental Retardation, 23,* 175–185.

Dunlap, G., & Koegel, R. (1980). Motivating autistic children through stimulus variation. *Journal of Applied Behavior Analysis, 13,* 619–627.

Guess, D., & Helmstetter, E. (1986). Skill cluster instruction and the individualized curriculum sequencing model. In R. Horner, L. Meyer, & H. D. Fredericks (Eds.), *Education of learners with severe handicaps* (pp. 221–248). Baltimore: Brookes.

Horner, R., & McDonald, R. (1982). A comparison of single instance and general case instruction in teaching a generalized vocational skill. *Journal of the Association for the Severely Handicapped, 7,* 7–20.

Kayser, J., Billingsley, F., & Neel, R. (1986). A comparison of in-context and traditional instructional approaches: Total task, single trial versus backward chaining, multiple trials. *Journal of the Association for Persons with Severe Handicaps, 11,* 28–38.

Koegel, R., & Koegel, L. (1990). Extended reductions in stereotypic behavior of students with autism through a self-management treatment package. *Journal of Applied Behavior Analysis, 23,* 119–127.

Koegel, R., Koegel, L., Hurley, C., & Frea, W. (1992). Improving social skills and disruptive behavior in children with autism through self-management. *Journal of Applied Behavior Analysis, 25,* 341–353.

Kreutzer, J., & Wehman, P. (Eds.). (1991). *Cognitive rehabilitation for persons with traumatic brain injury.* Baltimore: Brookes.

Mulligan, M., Guess, D., Hoelvet, J., & Brown, F. (1980). The individualized sequencing model (I): Implications from research on massed, distributed, or spaced trial training. *Journal of the Association for the Severely Handicapped, 5,* 325–336.

Mulligan, M., Macy, L., & Guess, D. (1982). Effects of massed, distributed, and spaced trial training on severely handicapped students' performance. *Journal of the Association for the Severely Handicapped, 7,* 48–61.

Orelove, F., & Sobsey, R. (1987). *Educating children with multiple disabilities: A transdisciplinary approach.* Baltimore: Brookes.

Rusch, F., Rose, T., & Greenwood, C. (1988). *Introduction to behavior analysis in special education.* Englewood Cliffs, NJ: Prentice Hall.

Schriebman, L. (1975). Effects of within-stimulus and extra-stimulus prompting on discrimination learning in autistic children. *Journal of Applied Behavior Analysis, 8,* 91–112.

Sidman, M. (1990). Equivalence relations: Where do they come from? In D. Blackman & H. Lejeune (Eds.), *Behavior analysis in theory and practice: Contributions and controversies* (pp. 93–114). Hillsdale, NJ: Erlbaum.

Snell, M. (1982). Analysis of time delay procedures in teaching daily living skills to retarded adults. *Analysis and Intervention in Developmental Disabilities, 2,* 139–156.

Snell, M., & Brown, F. (Eds.). (1999). *Instruction of students with severe disabilities* (5th ed.). Mahwah, NJ: Prentice Hall.

Sprague, J., & Horner, R. (1984). The effects of single instance, multiple instance, and general case training on generalized vending machine use by moderately and severely handicapped students. *Journal of Applied Behavior Analysis, 17,* 273–278.

Wacker, D., & Berg, W. (1984). Use of peer instruction to train a complex photocopying task to severely retarded adolescents. *Analysis and Intervention in Developmental Disabilities, 4,* 219–234.

Wehman, P., & Targett, P. S. (Eds.). (1999). *Vocational curriculum for individuals with special needs: Transition from school to adulthood.* Austin, TX: PRO-ED.

Wolery, M., Bailey, D. B., & Sugai, G. (1988). *Effective teaching: Principles and procedures of applied behavior analysis with exceptional children.* Needham Heights, MA: Allyn & Bacon.

CHAPTER 3

Self-Determination

Paul Sale and James E. Martin

 ZEKE

Zeke is a 15-year-old young man living with his aging adoptive parents in a midsize suburban western city. Zeke has received special education support services since the third grade. At that time, he had significant problems reading and experienced many poor social interactions with peers and educators. During grade school and the first few years of middle school, Zeke was placed into a self-contained program where he spent all day with other children who had social interaction and academic problems. Toward the end of Zeke's middle school years, the district changed philosophies and began placing most students from self-contained classrooms into general education programs. Zeke now receives special education services through an inclusion facilitator who works with general education teachers to provide needed supports, accommodations, and strategies within his high school classes.

Zeke's academic performance plateaued during the last 2 years of middle school and has not increased since. Even though he received instruction in basic academic skills during elementary and middle school, his performance improved only marginally. He now reads at the 4.1 grade level. His math skills are at the 5.5 grade level, and his written language performance is about that of a typical fourth grader. The more teachers insisted that he spend time learning to read, write, and calculate better, the more he acted out. This avoidance response resulted in Zeke being suspended three times last year. His recent arrest and conviction for burglary and possession of a controlled substance are closely tied to his desire to join a street gang. He told his counselor and probation officer that he may drop out of school. The vice principal and some of the faculty secretly wish Zeke would leave. His parents are frustrated and do not know what to do.

Throughout Zeke's school years, educators and parents have told Zeke what to do, when to do it, and how he did. Zeke is not engaged in the education process. The more his academic and social performance decline, the more direction the adults in his life provide. In short, Zeke does not know what to do, where to go, or how to get there. Peers and situations seem to direct Zeke's life.

A school-based self-determination curriculum may help Zeke learn to decide for himself what to do, where to go, and how to get there. This chapter provides an overview of self-determination, reviews sample self-determination assessment and curricula, and discusses curriculum design for building self-determination skills.

DESCRIPTION OF CURRICULUM

During the past few years, educators have made increasing efforts to teach students with special needs the generalizable skills they need to be successful during the school years and beyond. Educators have realized that simply teaching the three Rs and social skills does not adequately prepare students for life after school. Many policymakers and educators are starting to suggest that self-determination may be one of the keys to student success during the school years and afterward. But why focus on self-determination? What is it? The purpose of this section is to examine the foundation of a self-determination-based curriculum and to provide a general overview and specific examples of a self-determination curriculum.

Curriculum Foundation

Self-determination curricula attempt to teach a set of skills that successful people use. The roots of these materials come from the self-determination psychological literature, research in business and sports psychology, self-efficacy writings, and the self-management literature, to mention a few. Wehmeyer (1999) presented behavioral autonomy, self-regulation, psychological empowerment, and self-realization as essential characteristics of self-determined behavior. Diaz-Greenberg, Thousand, Cardelle-Elawar, and Nevin (2000) suggested that an analysis of educational psychology's concept of self-regulation, critical pedagogy's concept of conscientization, and the current discussion of special education's concept of self-determination intersect. Self-determination materials bring together in one package the best of these different approaches. Alternatively, an understanding of self-determination can be found in an analysis of what successful people do.

Successful people know what they want and persistently go after it (Hill, 1960; Hill & Stone, 1987). They decide on major goals, set a time line, develop specific plans to attain their goals, determine the benefits that reaching the goals will bring, close off discouraging influences and thought, and build coalitions with others who share similar goals and who will encourage each other in reaching them—things that Zeke has never done. Most students with special needs are never taught how to be successful.

Garfield (1986) interviewed more than 1,500 successful people from business, science, sports, and the arts. He found that successful people excel at making decisions, self-managing their behavior, and adapting to changing situations. When successful people make decisions, they (a) choose a goal, (b) envision and communicate that goal, and (c) develop an action plan of specific objectives and means to evaluate performance. Successful people do the following:

- They learn as they go, taking educated risks and building confidence in their skills along the way. "It is not fear of failure that drives them along, but a strong desire for achievement" (Garfield, 1986, p. 138).

- They see themselves "as the originator of actions in one's life . . . [viewing] events in life as opportunities for taking action and [seeing] themselves as the agents who must precipitate action" (Garfield, 1986, p. 141).

- They adapt by making course corrections and managing change through lifelong learning, expecting to succeed, mapping alternative futures, and updating their mission.

Garfield reached two conclusions in his study of successful people: First, regardless of age, education, or profession, the most successful people share the same basic set of skills. Second, individuals can learn these skills (Garfield, 1986). In education, these are called self-determination skills.

Individuals with Disabilities and Success

Self-determined individuals know how to choose—they know what they want and how to get it. From an awareness of personal needs, self-determined individuals choose goals, then doggedly pursue them. This involves asserting their presence, making their needs known, evaluating progress toward meeting their goals, adjusting their performance, and creating unique approaches to problem solving (Field & Hoffman, 1994; Martin, Huber Marshall, & Maxson, 1993; Mithaug, 1991, 1993; Schloss, Alper, & Jayne, 1993; Ward, 1988; Wehmeyer, 1992a, 1992b, 1998). People who are self-determined choose and enact their choices in persistent pursuit of their best interests. Self-determined people are their own best advocate (Martin et al., 1993). The Council for Exceptional Children's Division on Career Development supports and affirms self-determination approaches in its 1998 position statement (Field, Martin, Miller, Ward, & Wehmeyer, 1998). The authors note that

> self-determination is highly important to the career development and transition process and it needs to be encouraged throughout the lifespan. It is important for all students, with and without disabilities, including those students with the most severe disabilities. Self-determination instruction can be provided within an inclusive framework and is important for educators as well as students. Family participation is important to the development of self-determination. (p. 113)

Do these same success and self-determination behaviors apply to people with disabilities? Yes, they do. In a unique study, Gerber, Ginsberg, and Reiff (1992) interviewed a group of adults with learning disabilities to determine why some succeeded and others failed. They found that successful individuals with learning disabilities had the following:

- a desire to succeed
- well–thought-out goals
- persistence
- adapted to their environment
- built a social support network that facilitated their success

Gerber et al. (1992) realized that successful individuals decided, long before they became successful, that they would be successful. The authors concluded that successful adults with severe learning disabilities wanted to succeed, set achievable goals, and confronted their learning disability so that they could take appropriate measures to increase the likelihood of success. One highly successful young man explained it like this: "Successful people have a plan. You have to have a plan, goals, strategy, otherwise you are flying through the clouds and then you hit the mountain" (Gerber et al., 1992, p. 480).

Wehmeyer and Schwartz (1999) conducted a content analysis of all transition goals presented in the Individualized Education Plans (IEPs) of 136 students with mental retardation or other developmental disabilities. Results were very disappointing. "Out of nearly 900 transition-related goals, there were none that indicated students were being taught the skills they need to make choices, solve problems, make decisions, set and achieve goals, or understand themselves" (p. 82). Although these findings were related to individuals with mental retardation and other disabilities only and are therefore not generalizable to individuals with other disabling conditions, there is a dearth of literature to suggest that the situation is much better with other populations.

The findings of the Wehmeyer and Schwartz (1999) study are supported in another study in which 44 teachers of students with mild mental retardation were asked about participation of their students in transition planning (Zhang & Stecker, 2000). The authors found that students participated relatively little. The authors concluded that students need to be taught self-determination skills.

Finally, Wehmeyer, Agran, and Hughes (2000) surveyed 1,219 teachers about their beliefs and practices regarding self-determination. Although the vast majority of teachers noted that self-determination was an important area of instruction, only 22% of the teachers indicated that all of their students had IEP goals in the area of self-determination. Furthermore, 31% of the teachers indicated that none of their students had goals in this area.

In summary, though improving some over the past decade or so, the special education programs continue to do little to empower youth with learning and behavior problems. As a result, these youth do not learn the skills they need to manage their lives. They remain dependent on other people to make decisions, provide support, and make changes (Mithaug, Martin, & Agran, 1987). Little effort is expended to teach students how to gain control of their lives and how to adapt to changes in their environments (Martin & Huber Marshall, 1995). When considering the employment success of adults with disabilities, Wehman, West, and Kregel (1999) noted that self-determination is the number-one need for program development, research, and policy analysis.

But there is hope: Agran, Blanchard, and Wehmeyer (2000) used the Self-Determined Learning Model of Instruction to teach 19 adolescent students to set goals, take action, and adjust goals based on the results of their actions. The study found that 17 of the 19 students changed dramatically in their independence skills, exceeding teacher expectations. Of the goals the students set, 89% were attained at or above the expected level. The model "was found effective across students with a variety of disabling conditions" (p. 361). We believe that the use of techniques such as those described below will facilitate similar results in a wide array of students.

Self-Determination Curricula Exemplars

During the past several years, the U.S. Department of Education, Office of Special Education Programs, has funded numerous self-determination curriculum development projects across the country. In addition, several other curricula have been developed through other efforts. The curricula use a variety of approaches and strategies to facilitate the development of self-determination skills for students with special needs.

The curriculum examples below come from two sources: a 1995 and 1996 review of self-determination curricula by a team of University of Colorado faculty and public school educators (Martin, Huber Marshall, Miller, Kregar, & Hughes, 1996) and an updated review of the literature. This section provides an overview of several of these curricula.

***Become Your Own Expert!* (Carpenter, 1995).** This is a well-written curriculum that may be used to teach high school students with learning disabilities self-advocacy skills during a one-semester course. The self-advocacy skills that are directly taught in this curriculum include identifying individual academic strengths and weaknesses, determining learning styles, and setting goals for completing high school and continuing postsecondary education and training. In addition, students learn about classroom and workplace accommodations that can help them be successful and about federal and transition laws that support them in their efforts. The skill development activities use a variety of instructional techniques and strategies such as structured group problem solving, videotaped self-evaluations, site visits to postsecondary programs, and activities involving postsecondary students and adults with learning disabilities. A corresponding parent program accompanies this curriculum that teaches parents how to support students while they acquire new skills. Available from Winnelle D. Carpenter, Minnesota Educational Services, Capitol View Center, 70 West Colorado Road, B2, Little Canada, MN 55117-1402 (800/848-4912, ext. 2401).

***100 Activities for Transition* (Lyle, 2000).** This activity-based manual describes goals in five basic transition areas: communication and problem solving, daily living, securing and keeping a job, career awareness, and self-determination. The program shows sample goals and objectives for each of the areas and provides a compendium of activities, worksheets, and direct teaching ideas that teachers can use immediately. The program is appropriate for students in elementary through secondary school. Available from Hawthorne Educational Services, 800 Gray Oak Drive, Columbia, MO 65201 (573/874-1710 or 800/542-1673).

***Learning with PURPOSE: An Instructor's Manual for Teaching Self-Determination Skills to Students Who Are At Risk for Failure* (Serna & Lau-Smith, 1995).** This is a comprehensive self-determination curriculum designed for students with mild and moderate disabilities and students who are at risk for failure in home, school, and community environments. The program is appropriate for students between the ages of 12 and 25 years, and its systematically teaches the self-determination skills of self-evaluation, self-direction, networking, collaboration, persistence and risk taking, and dealing with stress. Students define the skill, learn how the skill will be useful to them, rehearse the skill, evaluate their own performance, reach skill mastery, and participate in activities that will help them use their skills in other environments. A corresponding parent program accompanies this curriculum that teaches parents how to support students while they acquire new skills. Available from Loretta A. Serna, University of New Mexico, College of Education, Albuquerque, NM 87131 (505/277-5119).

I Want My Dream, New Hat, and Profile Decks—It's My Life: Preference-Based Planning, Facilitator's Guide, and Goal Planner's Workbook **(Curtis, 1995).** A facilitator uses numerous It's My Life awareness-building materials to show how students can take an active role in making decisions, self-advocating, and creating their own lifestyle plans and goals. Preference-based planning supports a process whereby students learn how to string together thoughts to get an idea, make a plan, evaluate the progress, and adjust. Materials include the New Hat Card Deck, I Want My Dream Deck, *It's My Life* workbook, and other materials. The contents of the workbook include "Organizing My Planner," "Hopes, Dreams, and Preferences," "Possibilities, Priorities, and Goals," and "My Meeting." Supplemental materials, which are available from the author, are used in different workbook chapters. Available from New Hats, P.O. Box 57567, Salt Lake City, UT 84157 (801/268-9811).

Steps to Self-Determination **(Field & Hoffman, 1995).** This curriculum supports students in developing skills, knowledge, and experience to help them be more self-determined. The activities engage students in experiences designed to increase their self-awareness and self-esteem and provide instruction in skills to assist students in reaching their goals. The curriculum follows a five-step model: (a) know yourself, (b) value yourself, (c) plan, (d) act, and (e) learn. Each curriculum activity relates back to one of these steps. The lessons begin with a 6-hour workshop session, followed by 16 weekly sessions that take place in a scheduled class or extracurricular activity. The 16 sessions include topics such as, "What Is Important to Me?" "Setting Long-Term Goals," "Creative Barrier Breaking," "Assertive Communication," "Negotiation," and "Conflict Resolution." Available from PRO-ED, 8700 Shoal Creek Boulevard, Austin, TX 78757-6897 (512/451-3246).

Whose Future Is It Anyway? A Student-Directed Transition Planning Process **(Wehmeyer, 1995).** This instructional package provides students the opportunity to acquire the knowledge and confidence necessary to take part in the transition process as an equal partner. The package emphasizes disability as a part of the human condition and stresses that students need to be aware of their own learning abilities and needs. Each session teaches students something they can use in their transition or other educational meeting. Students learn how to write and track goals, how to identify community resources, how informed consent affects them, how to communicate in small groups, and how to participate in a meeting. Students select a coach to help them through the process. The six major parts of the program are (a) getting to know you; (b) making decisions; (c) how to get what you need; (d) goals, objectives, and the future; (e) communication; and (f) thank you. Students use the materials on their own—they read and complete the 40 lessons in about 5 days. The materials are designed for students to read and complete most of the activities independently, and also includes a detailed facilitator's guide. Available from The Arc, 500 East Border Street, Suite 300, Arlington, TX 76010 (817/261-6003).

ChoiceMaker Self-Determination Transition Curriculum. This curriculum includes three instructional packages that teach seven self-determination constructs: self-awareness, self-advocacy, self-efficacy, decision making, independent performance, self-evaluation, and adjustment through leadership and management of the IEP process. The *Self-Directed IEP* (Martin, Huber Marshall,

Maxson, & Jerman, 1996) is designed for use by students receiving special education services; the others are for use by all secondary students. The *Self-Directed IEP* teaches students the leadership skills needed to manage their IEP meeting; disclose their interests, skills, and limits; and build necessary support to reach their goals. *Choosing Employment Goals* (Huber Marshall, Martin, Maxson, & Jerman, 1996) teaches students a process for learning and articulating their employment interests, skills, limits, and goals. *Taking Action* (Huber Marshall, Martin, McGill, Maxson, & Jerman, 1996) teaches students how to break their long-term goals into tasks that can be accomplished in a week and shows students a process they can use to attain goals. Each package comes with at least one student video, teacher guide, and student materials. Somewhat unique to the ChoiceMaker curriculum is the inclusion of a detailed self-evaluation process whereby students reflect about their choices and then compare them with reality. For example, in *Choosing Employment Goals,* students identify job characteristics they like, then compare those characteristics with those that exist at different job sites. Similarly in *Choosing Employment Goals,* students self-evaluate their work, social, and personal behaviors; then this rating is compared with an evaluation done by a job-site supervisor. Students decide if their evaluation matches that of the supervisor. Available from Sopris West, 1140 Boston Avenue, Longmont, CO 80501 (303/651-2829).

General Approaches to Assessment

Assessment of a student's self-determination knowledge and skills is essential before and after instruction. The assessment of self-determination skills is complementary to, but distinct from, the assessment of task-related or academic skills. For example, when a student is assessed at a community-based training site, information such as rate, endurance, and quality of task performance is measured. These narrow data need to be complemented by an assessment of the process that the student uses to self-evaluate, formulate plans, and implement changes in task-related, social, and other behaviors.

Measurement of a student's self-determination, knowledge, and skills is primarily accomplished through the use of third-party assessment checklists or self-report tools. Each self-determination assessment tool is rooted in its authors' unique understanding of self-determination. This section will present four examples of different assessment approaches and their associated tools.

The Arc Approach. Wehmeyer and Kelchner (1995) described self-determination as "acting as the primary causal agent in one's life and making choices and decisions regarding one's quality of life free from undue external influence or interference" (p. 1). *The Arc's Self-Determination Scale* uses this definition for students with disabilities to assess their own beliefs about themselves and their self-determination. The scale also provides a means for students with disabilities and educators to work together to identify strengths and limitations relative to self-determination goals and objectives (Wehmeyer & Kelchner, 1995). The scale is a self-report measure designed for use by adolescents with disabilities, particularly students with mild mental retardation and learning disabilities.

The scale has 72 items divided into four sections: (a) autonomy, (b) self-regulation, (c) psychological empowerment, and (d) self-realization. Behavioral autonomy consists of self- and family care, self-management, recreation, and social and vocational categories. Self-regulated behavior includes self-management strategies, goal setting and attainment behaviors, problem-solving behaviors, and observational learning strategies. Psychological empowerment refers to perceived control, including its cognitive, personality, and motivational domains. Self-realization is self-knowledge and self-understanding through experience and interpretation of one's environment and is influenced by evaluations of significant others, reinforcements, and opinions of one's own behavior.

The Arc's Self-Determination Scale requires a different type of response for each of the four sections. The autonomy section asks the student to respond to a Likert-type scale for 32 questions. The self-regulation section requests respondents to fill in the middle of the story, given the beginning and ending of the story, for six situations. The self-regulation section asks 3 open-ended questions related to living, working, and transportation plans in the future. The psychological empowerment section asks 15 two-item forced-choice questions. Last, the self-realization section provides 15 forced-choice (agree/disagree) items. *The Arc's Self-Determination Scale* is scored in a five-step process that converts the raw section scores into percentile scores from a nationwide norming sample of 500 special education students primarily with learning disabilities (44%) and mental retardation (35%).

The Arc's Self-Determination Scale is available from The Arc, 500 East Border Street, Suite 300, Arlington, TX 76010 (817/261-6003).

The AIR Approach. Wolman, Campeau, DuBois, Mithaug, and Stolarski (1994) believe that self-determined people know and express their needs, interests, and abilities. They set goals, make plans, and follow through with actions to achieve their goals. Wolman et al. believe that "self-determination depends on students' capacities and opportunities" (p. 5). *Capacity* is defined as the student's knowledge and skills, whereas *opportunity* refers to the student's chances to use his or her self-determination skills. Capacity, opportunity, and conditions form the foundation of Wolman et al.'s *AIR Self-Determination Scale*. Thinking, doing, and adjusting are all components of the AIR assessment process. The purpose of the scale is to provide an easy tool for assessing and teaching self-determination. The scale is designed for all school-age students—with and without disabilities.

Four versions of the scale are available. The parent, educator, and research versions are all third-party report scales that rely on previously obtained information. The student version can be completed independently by students with sufficient reading skills or with assistance for those who cannot read the scale.

The educator version of the scale is the most comprehensive. It contains three capacity sections (knowledge, ability, and perception) and two opportunity sections (school and home). Knowledge is the understanding a student has about self-determination. Ability includes those skills needed to identify and satisfy one's interests and needs. Perception includes motivation, confidence, self-esteem, and the "sense of freedom to meet interests and needs" (Wolman et al., 1994, p. 15). Opportunities at school and at home are those supporting environmental events that can enable the student to become more self-determined. Each section has 6 items for a total of 30 items on the scale. The educator uses previous observations of the student to complete a 5-point Likert-type scale for each item. The raw scores for each of the five sections are tabulated, graphed, and compared with the total points available to find the percentage level of self-determination.

"The student and parent forms are shorter and the headings on them are slightly different. For example, the ability section is called 'What Do I Do' in the student form and 'Things My Child Does' in the parent form. The student and parent forms include six items each for ability, opportunity at school, and opportunity at home. The student form also includes six items for perception" (Wolman et al., 1994, p. 22).

This tool is a criterion-referenced assessment used in a nonnormative manner. The tool was validated on 450 students with and without disabilities in San Jose, California, and New York City.

The *AIR Self-Determination Scale* is available from Dennis Mithaug, Special Education Program, Teachers College, Columbia University, New York, NY 10027 (212/678-3859).

University of Colorado Approach. Martin et al. (1993) believe that self-determined people know how to choose—they know what they want and how to get it. From an awareness of personal needs, self-determined individuals choose goals and then persistently pursue them. This involves individuals asserting their presence, making their needs known, evaluating progress toward meeting goals, adjusting performance, and creating a plan to solve problems. The *ChoiceMaker Self-Determination Transition Assessment* (Martin & Huber Marshall, 1996) is based on the ChoiceMaker curriculum (see Table 3.1). The assessment results are used to determine teaching goals and objectives. The assessment is unique in that it can be tied directly to the ChoiceMaker curriculum and thus can be used as a curriculum-based assessment. The assessment is designed for middle and high school students who have mild to moderate learning and behavior problems.

The *ChoiceMaker Self-Determination Transition Assessment* is a third-person scale that contains 62 items for evaluating student self-determination skills; it also evaluates the opportunities students have at school to exercise these skills. Each domain (student skills and opportunities at school) is divided into three major sections: Choosing Goals, Expressing Goals, and Taking Action. The Choosing Goals section assesses skills and opportunities related to students' understanding of their rights and goal-setting roles; expression of transition interest across school, employment, post–high school education, and other areas; expression of skills and limits of the foregoing transition areas; and options and goals for those transition areas. The Expressing Goals section assesses student leadership and expression of interests, skills, limits, and goals at their IEP and transition meetings. The Taking Action section measures planning, action, self-evaluation, and adjustment.

The *ChoiceMaker Self-Determination Transition Assessment* requires completion of a 5-point Likert-type scale for each of the 62 items across the two domains. The raw scores for each of the three sections are tabulated, graphed, and compared with the total points available to find the percentage level of self-determination in each domain. The scale is a criterion-referenced assessment used in a nonnormative manner, and it has been validated using more than 300 students with learning disabilities, mental retardation, and behavior problems from four states.

(*text continues on p. 78*)

TABLE 3.1
ChoiceMaker Self-Determination Transition Curriculum Matrix

Teaching Objectives

Sections	Teaching Goals							
1: *Choosing Goals*	A. *Student Interests*	A1. Express school interests	A2. Express employment interests	A3. Express post–high school education interests	A4. Express personal interests	A5. Express housing and daily living interests	A6. Express community participation interests	
(through school and community experience)	B. *Student Skills and Limits*	B1. Express school skills and limits	B2. Express employment skills and limits	B3. Express post–high school education skills and limits	B4. Express personal skills and limits	B5. Express housing and daily living skills and limits	B6. Express community participation skills and limits	
	C. *Student Goals*	C1. Indicate options and choose school goals	C2. Indicate options and choose employment goals	C3. Indicate options and choose post–high school education goals	C4. Indicate options and choose personal goals	C5. Indicate options and choose housing and daily living goals	C6. Indicate options and choose community participation goals	
2: *Expressing Goals*	D. *Student Leading Meeting*	D1. Begin meeting by stating purpose	D2. Introduce participants	D3. Review past goals and performance	D4. Ask for feedback	D5. Ask questions if don't understand	D6. Deal with differences in opinion	D7. State needed support	D8. Close meeting by summarizing decisions
	E. *Student Reporting*	E1. Express interests (from A1–6)	E2. Express skills and limits (from B1–6)	E3. Express options and goals (from C1–6)				

(continues)

76

TABLE 3.1 Continued.

Sections	Teaching Goals	Teaching Objectives							
3: *Taking Action*	F. *Student Plan*	F1. Break general goals into specific goals that can be completed now	F2. Establish *standard* for specific goals	F3. Determine how to get *feedback* from environment	F4. Determine *motivation* to complete specific goals	F5. Determine *strategies* for completing specific goals	F6. Determine *support* needed to complete specific goals	F7. Prioritize and *schedule* to complete specific goals	F8. Express *belief* that goals can be obtained
	G. *Student Action*	G1. Record or report performance	G2. Perform specific goals to *standard*	G3. Obtain *feedback* on performance	G4. *Motivate* self to complete specific goals	G5. Use *strategies* to perform specific goals	G6. Obtain *support* needed	G7. Follow *schedule*	
	H. *Student Evaluation*	H1. Determine if goals are achieved	H2. Compare performance to *standards*	H3. Evaluate *feedback*	H4. Evaluate *motivation*	H5. Evaluate effectiveness of *strategies*	H6. Evaluate *support* used	H7. Evaluate *schedule*	H8. Evaluate *belief*
	I. *Student Adjustment*	I1. Adjust goals if necessary	I2. Adjust or repeat goal *standards*	I3. Adjust or repeat method for *feedback*	I4. Adjust or repeat *motivations*	I5. Adjust or repeat *strategies*	I6. Adjust or repeat *support*	I7. Adjust or repeat *schedule*	I8. Adjust or repeat *belief* that goals can be obtained

Note: From *ChoiceMaker Self-Determination Transition Assessment*, by J. Martin and L. Huber Marshall, 1996, Longmont, CO: Sopris West. Copyright 1996 by Sopris West. Reprinted with permission.

The *ChoiceMaker Self-Determination Transition Assessment* is available from Sopris West, 1140 Boston Avenue, Longmont, CO 80501 (303-651-2829).

CURRICULUM DESIGN

We have discussed the general parameters of self-determination, reviewed several curricula, and described several assessment tools. Based on this review, we find that the essential components of a self-determination curriculum are goal setting, choice, self-evaluation, and adjustment. These self-determination concepts must be infused into the daily instructional cycle; they cannot be taught in a vacuum. Learning self-determination is a function of opportunities to practice and to learn the skills. Students must have real choice, too, once they and their IEP team have chosen goals across curriculum domains and various environments. Students, in conjunction with other IEP team members, need also to choose their strategies and supports for meeting their goals and the criteria by which they want to be evaluated. This can only occur if teachers, schools, and districts provide flexible, individualized, student-driven curricula, as opposed to only set, group-oriented, and teacher-directed activities.

For full implementation of a self-determination philosophy, goal setting, choice, and self-evaluation must occur across common curricular domains, such as reading, math, science, and social studies. Or, in the case of some students, goal setting, choice, and self-evaluation may occur within the common domains of functional academics, such as domestic, recreational, community, and vocational activities. Students must also engage in choice and goal setting in relation to how their needs can best be met. Examples of student choice and goal setting include selecting a career, engaging in recreational activities, and spending time with friends.

Wehmeyer, Palmer, Agran, Mithaug, and Martin (2000) have most recently proposed an extension of their Adaptability Model: The Self-Determined Learning Model of Instruction. In this model, three instructional phases lead students to solve three broad problems: What is the goal? What is my plan? and What have I learned? The model takes the student through 12 specific questions (e.g., "What do I want to learn?"). Based on this cycle of questions and objectives, the students choose a variety of learning goals, objectives, and actions. The model has been field tested, and students have attained educationally relevant goals.

This section provides examples of how self-determination instruction can be implemented for individuals, schoolwide, and districtwide at the elementary, middle, and high school levels.

Elementary School Curriculum Considerations

Self-determination activities during the early elementary years focus on teaching students helpful strategies for setting goals, planning to achieve goals, and self-evaluating performance. During the elementary years, students have repeated opportunities to practice goal setting, planning, and self-evaluation.

Student Assessment

Currently, one of the few elementary self-determination assessment tools available is the *AIR Self-Determination Scale* (Wolman et al., 1994). As mentioned earlier, the *AIR Self-Determination Scale* measures student opportunity and capacity at school, which is critical for students in elementary schools.

Zeke, the student described at the beginning of this chapter, can be used as an example of elementary assessment. Figure 3.1 is a hypothetical profile of Zeke's level of self-determination as measured with the educator version of the *AIR Self-Determination Scale* when Zeke was a fourth grader. The profile shows that Zeke had an overall self-determination level of 61 of the possible 150 points, for a score of 40%. His capacity and opportunity scores were similar at 28 and 33, respectively. Interestingly, he had many more opportunities at home to practice self-determination than at school. Please note that the *AIR Self-Determination Scale* provides no normative data from which to compare Zeke's score with that of other students his age. Zeke's overall scores can be used to compare his fourth-grade profile with that scored later in life.

Zeke had not received any self-determination instruction at this point in his life. These assessment results can be used to determine an instructional beginning point for Zeke. The IEP team looked at the responses to each of the assessment items. Figure 3.2 shows how Zeke's teacher scored his knowledge of self-determination behaviors on four items. The results of these items and the others provide insight into Zeke's self-determination behavior strengths and deficits. For example, as shown in Figures 3.1 and 3.2, Zeke almost never identifies his personal strengths and talents and therefore never sets expectations and goals to satisfy his own interests and needs. Likewise, the school almost never provides opportunities for that behavior and never asks Zeke to identify his goals and expectations.

Sample IEP Goals

The IEP team, with Zeke's input and agreement, next sets goals based on the findings from the assessment. Likewise, Zeke's educational team decides to provide increased opportunity for Zeke to practice self-determination skills. The team used the *AIR Self-Determination User Guide* (Wolman et al., 1994) to arrive at the following two annual goals.

Annual Goals

1. To increase Zeke's knowledge of own interests, abilities, and limitations.

   Sample Activities:

   a. Racing against the clock, five students (including Zeke) in a cooperative group list 15 school and out-of-school interests in 5 minutes.

   b. The five students will discuss with the teacher their skills and limitations associated with each interest.

2. To increase Zeke's knowledge of how to set goals that satisfy interests.

   Sample Activities:

   a. Zeke will interview three adults to determine the adults' goals.

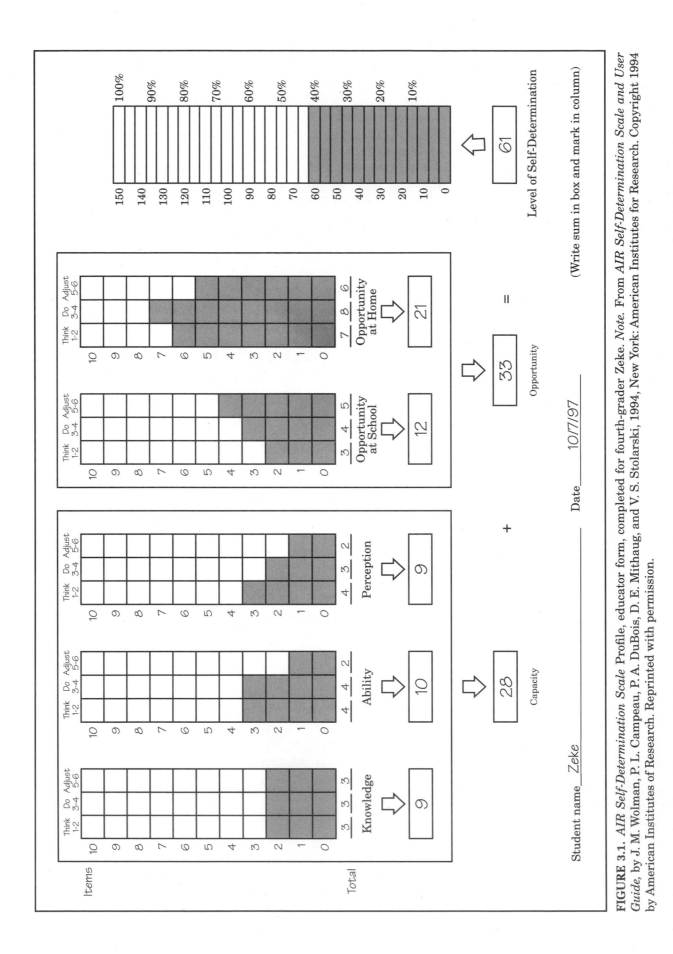

FIGURE 3.1. *AIR Self-Determination Scale* Profile, educator form, completed for fourth-grader Zeke. *Note.* From *AIR Self-Determination Scale and User Guide,* by J. M. Wolman, P. L. Campeau, P. A. DuBois, D. E. Mithaug, and V. S. Stolarski, 1994, New York: American Institutes for Research. Copyright 1994 by American Institutes of Research. Reprinted with permission.

Perception of Knowledge and Ability to Perform Self-Determination Behaviors	1 Never	2 Almost Never	3 Sometimes	4 Almost Always	5 Always
1. Student feels free to express own needs, interests, and abilities, even when facing opposition from others—*Example:* Fran defends her needs and interests to anyone who questions them.	1	2	③	4	5
2. Student feels free to set own goals and expectations, even if they are different from the expectations others have for the student—*Example:* Trevor does not feel constrained by others' opinions in setting goals and expectations for himself.	①	2	3	4	5
Perception Total: Items 1–2				[4]	
3. Student feels free to make own choices, decisions, and plans, to meet own goals and expectations—*Example:* Corine often considers her parents' suggestions when making choices and plans, but the final plans taken to meet her goals are her own.	①	2	3	4	5
4. Student feels confident about being able to successfully complete own plans—*Example:* When Nicholas schedules his own activities, he is confident he can complete them accurately and on time.	1	②	3	4	5
Perception Total: Items 3–4				[3]	

FIGURE 3.2. Zeke's knowledge of self-determination behaviors, as reported by his teacher in the *AIR Self-Determination Scale.*

Sample Activities continued

b. Zeke will examine the commonalties of the goals identified during his interviews (e.g., long-range nature of goals, type of goals).

c. Zeke will write two goals for his academic work to be achieved in the next week (e.g., 90% correct on spelling test, 24 math facts completed in 1 minute).

Elementary Self-Determination Curricula. Few elementary-level self-determination curricula exist. Much of what teachers will need to do is to take the basic assessed skills and develop activities. The preceding list of sample activities are illustrative of how this can be done. One of the few available elementary packages that we know of is *Connections: A Transition Curriculum for Grades 3 Through 6* (Aspinall, Roberts, & Robinson, 1992). This curriculum provides an equal balance between several concepts, including career awareness; attitudes, values, and habits; human relationships; occupational information; and acquisition of job and daily living skills. Its purpose is to make an impact on work personalities in the early school years through teaching crucial career education and self-determination concepts. Although not directly addressed, many self-determination concepts are discussed through units on career development, career orientation, and career exploration. Unit 1, "Me and My Shadow," introduces the self-determination skills of self-awareness and goal setting through sections on "getting to know me," "positive self-esteem," and "goal setting."

Middle School Curriculum Considerations

Self-determination activities for middle school students should focus on refining strategies for setting goals, planning ways to achieve goals, and self-evaluating performance. It is during the middle school years that students begin to focus increasingly on goals and plans beyond middle and high school. Career exploration (Brolin, 1989) is common during these years, with students assessing career interests and abilities and setting some trial plans for meeting career goals.

Student Assessment

The Arc's Self-Determination Scale (Wehmeyer & Kelchner 1995) is a good assessment for use with middle school students because it examines autonomy, self-regulation, psychological empowerment, and self-realization, which are skills consistent with the emergence of this level of emotional development. Figure 3.3 is a hypothetical profile of Zeke's level of self-determination as measured with *The Arc's Self-Determination Scale* when he was in the seventh grade. Unlike the *AIR Self-Determination Scale* (Wolman et al., 1994), the Arc's scale provides normative data from which to compare Zeke's score with the scores of other adolescents. Zeke's self-determination level overall is better than only 11 out of 100 students (as noted in the graph under Step 4 and based on the normative sample of 500 adolescent students). Compared with the normative sample, Zeke's skills related to self-regulation are relatively strong. Autonomy and self-realization are Zeke's two weakest assessed areas at the 11th and 3rd percentile, respectively.

The IEP team looked at the responses to each assessment item. Figure 3.4 shows how Zeke's teacher scored the Independence: Personal Care section. For example, Zeke never cares for his own clothes, but he always keeps together his own personal items. He will sometimes make his meals, do home chores, do simple first aid, and groom himself. Figure 3.5 depicts the results of Zeke's psychological empowerment subscale. Of the 16 possible items, Zeke felt empowered on 10 responses. Although this gave Zeke a high positive score (see Figure 3.3), when compared with the norm group, Zeke's results were low. For example, Zeke said, "Trying hard at school doesn't do me much good," "I need good luck to get what I want," and "My choices will not be honored." These responses provide an excellent beginning point for the IEP team to start determining Zeke's goals for the next school year.

Scoring Step 1:
Record the raw scores from each section:

Autonomy
1A = 7
1B = 6
1C = 9
1D = 8
1E = 7
1F = 7
Domain Total: 44

Self-Regulation
2A = 7
2B = 6
Domain Total: 13

Psychological Empowerment
3 = 10
Domain Total: 10

Self-Realization
4 = 5
Domain Total: 5

Scoring Step 2:
Sum each Domain Total for a Total Score:

Self-Determination
Total = 72

Scoring Step 3:
Using the conversion tables in Appendix A, covert raw scores into percentile scores for comparison with the sample norms (Norm Sample) and the percentage of positive responses (Positive Scores):

	Norm Sample	Positive Scores
Autonomy		
1A =	9	39
1B =	49	50
1C =	18	50
1D =	44	53
1E =	29	39
1F =	13	47
Domain Total:	11	46
Self-Regulation		
2A =	79	58
2B =	79	67
Domain Total:	80	
Psychological Empowerment		
3 =	17	62
Domain Total:	17	62
Self-Realization		
4 =	3	33
Domain Total:	3	33
Self-Determination Total Score =	11	43

Scoring Step 4:
Fill in the graph for the percentile scores from the norming sample. From the appropriate percentile down, darken the complete bar graph (See example in Scoring Manual).

Scoring Step 5:
Fill in the graph for the percentile scores indicating the percent positive responses.

FIGURE 3.3. Zeke's level of self-determination, as recorded on *The Arc's Self-Determination Scale. Note.* From *The Arc's Self-Determination Scale–Adolescent Version,* by M. Wehmeyer and K. Kelchner, 1995, Arlington, TX: The Arc National Headquarters. Copyright 1995 by The Arc. Reprinted with permission.

Sample IEP Goals

Like his elementary IEP team, Zeke's middle school IEP team, with Zeke's input and agreement, sets goals based on the assessment results. In this instance, the first goal is for Zeke to use the assessment tool himself to develop a plan of action prior to his IEP meeting.

Annual Goals

1. To increase Zeke's knowledge of his own self-determined behaviors and attitudes.

   Sample Activities:

   a. Quarterly, Zeke will complete *The Arc's Self-Determination Scale* (e.g., the current assessment demonstrates that Zeke needs to improve his performance in the areas of personal autonomy and psychological empowerment).

   b. Zeke will discuss the assessment results with peers, parents, and school personnel.

   c. Zeke will develop a plan of action to improve at least one subdomain per quarter and discuss his progress weekly with peers, parents, and educators. For example, Zeke has asked his father for instruction in how to do his laundry. Zeke has asked his peers and school staff to point out to him how each lesson relates to his adult life.

   d. Zeke will present his assessment, plan of action, and results at his next IEP meeting.

2. To increase Zeke's participation in school activities.

   Sample Activities:

   a. Zeke will identify with a counselor all extracurricular activities options available at his school.

   b. Zeke will select three extracurricular activities to explore.

   c. Zeke will regularly participate in at least one extracurricular activity throughout the school year.

High School Curriculum Considerations

Activities during the high school years should focus on teaching self-determination through student leadership of the IEP process. While in the elementary and middle school grades, Zeke actively participated in his IEP meetings and collaborated with his educators to develop goals, interventions, and self-evaluation strategies. Now in high school, Zeke needs to develop these skills further to learn the self-determination skills he will need after leaving school. The IEP process provides the perfect opportunity to learn these crucial skills.

(text continues on p. 87)

SECTION ONE
Autonomy

Directions:

Check the answer on each question that BEST tells how you act in that situation. There are no right or wrong answers. Check only one answer for each question. (If your disability limits you from actually performing the activity, but you have control over the activity (such as a personal care attendant), answer like you performed the activity).

1A. Independence: Routine personal care and family oriented functions

	I do not even if I have the chance	I do sometimes when I have the chance	I do most of the time I have a chance	I do every time I have the chance
1. I make my own meals or snacks.	[ ]	[X]	[ ]	[ ]
2. I care for my own clothes.	[X]	[ ]	[ ]	[ ]
3. I do chores in my home.	[ ]	[X]	[ ]	[ ]
4. I keep my own personal items together.	[ ]	[ ]	[ ]	[X]
5. I do simple first aid or medical care for myself.	[ ]	[X]	[ ]	[ ]
6. I keep good personal care and grooming.	[ ]	[X]	[ ]	[ ]

*1A. Subtotal 7

FIGURE 3.4. Zeke's scores on the Independence section of *The Arc's Self-Determination Scale. Note. From *The Arc's Self Determination Scale–Adolescent Version,* by M. Wehmeyer and K. Kelchner, 1995, Arlington, TX: The Arc National Headquarters. Copyright 1995 by The Arc. Reprinted with permission.

SECTION THREE
Psychological Empowerment

Directions:

- Check the answer that BEST describes you.
- Choose only one answer for each question.
- There are no right or wrong answers.

42. [X] I usually do what my friends want . . . or
    [ ] I tell my friends if they are doing something I don't want to do.

43. [X] I tell others when I have new or different ideas or opinions . . . or
    [ ] I usually agree with other people's opinions or ideas.

44. [X] I usually agree with people when they tell me I can't do something . . . or
    [ ] I tell people when I think I can do something they tell me I can't.

45. [ ] I tell people when they have hurt my feelings . . . or
    [X] I am afraid to tell people when they have hurt my feelings.

46. [X] I can make my own decisions . . . or
    [ ] Other people make decisions for me.

47. [X] Trying hard at school doesn't do me much good . . . or
    [ ] Trying hard at school will help me get a good job.

48. [ ] I can get what I want by working hard . . . or
    [X] I need good luck to get what I want.

49. [ ] It is no use to keep trying because that won't change things . . . or
    [X] I keep trying even after I get something wrong.

50. [X] I have the ability to do the job I want . . . or
    [ ] I cannot do what it takes to do the job I want.

51. [ ] I don't know how to make friends . . . or
    [X] I know how to make friends.

52. [X] I am able to work with others . . . or
    [ ] I cannot work well with others.

53. [ ] I do not make good choices . . . or
    [X] I can make good choices.

54. [X] If I have the ability, I will be able to get the job I want . . . or
    [ ] I probably will not get the job I want even if I have the ability.

55. [ ] I will have a hard time making new friends . . . or
    [X] I will be able to make friends in new situations.

56. [X] I will be able to work with others if I need to . . . or
    [ ] I will not be able to work with others if I need to.

57. [X] My choices will not be honored . . . or
    [ ] I will be able to make choices that are important to me.

Section 3 Subtotal 10

FIGURE 3.5. Zeke's scores on the Psychological Empowerment subscale of *The Arc's Self-Determination Scale. Note.* From *The Arc's Self Determination Scale–Adolescent Version*, by M. Wehmeyer and K. Kelchner, 1995, Arlington, TX: The Arc National Headquarters. Copyright 1995 by The Arc. Reprinted with permission.

Student Assessment

The *ChoiceMaker Self-Determination Transition Assessment* (Martin & Huber Marshall, 1996) evaluates the self-determination skills students will need to be successful in their adult life and the opportunities available to engage in these skills. This scale is designed for use by middle and high school students with learning and behavior problems. The ChoiceMaker assessment measures students' self-determination skills and opportunities across three areas: Choosing Goals, Expressing Goals, and Taking Action. Figure 3.6 is a hypothetical profile of Zeke's level of self-determination and the opportunities his school provides as measured with *ChoiceMaker Self-Determination Transition Assessment* from his freshman year. Unlike the other assessments, the ChoiceMaker tool is a curriculum-based assessment keyed directly to the ChoiceMaker self-determination transition curriculum, which teaches self-determination skills through active participation and leadership of the IEP process. This criterion-referenced scale profiles Zeke's skills in relation to the ChoiceMaker curriculum. Zeke performs only about 44% of the Choosing Goals skills, 15% of the Expressing Goals skills, and 25% of the Taking Action skills. It should be noted, however, Zeke's skill performance is only slightly below the opportunities available at his school. Therefore, although Zeke's skill development still needs to improve, systematic reform must also occur at Zeke's school to provide greater opportunities for self-determined behaviors.

Zeke's IEP team looked at the assessment results section by section to develop goals and activities. Figure 3.7 shows how Zeke's teacher scored the Student Interests section of Choosing Goals. Zeke's teachers have never seen him express any employment, post–high school education, or housing and daily interests. Not surprisingly, Zeke's school program provided little to no opportunity for him to express interests in these areas, except for asking him about his school interests, which carried over from his middle school educational plan. Expressing Goals results are depicted in Figure 3.8. Zeke attended his IEP meetings but did little once there. He talked briefly about his past goals and his performance and responded to questions when asked about his school interests and goals.

Sample IEP Goals

Once Zeke's IEP team reviewed the Opportunity at School section, they realized they needed to improve their curriculum to allow for more self-determined behaviors to occur at school. Concurrently, Zeke and his IEP team set goals and discussed activities to achieve those goals based on the ChoiceMaker assessment results. The IEP team used the goals and objectives from the ChoiceMaker transition curriculum guide to assist them in this process.

Annual Goals

1. Zeke will express his employment and post–high school education interests, skills, limits, and goals at his next IEP meeting.

(*text continues on p. 91*)

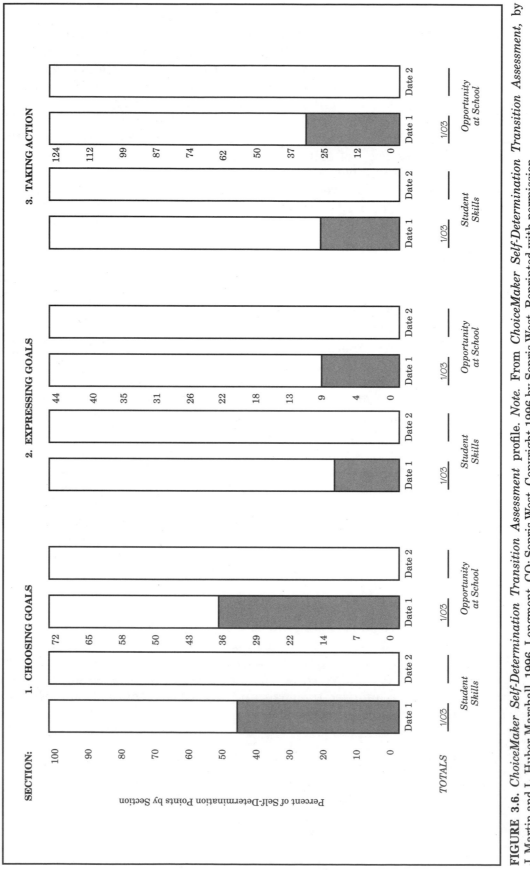

FIGURE 3.6. *ChoiceMaker Self-Determination Transition Assessment* profile. *Note.* From *ChoiceMaker Self-Determination Transition Assessment,* by J. Martin and L. Huber Marshall, 1996, Longmont, CO: Sopris West. Copyright 1996 by Sopris West. Reprinted with permission.

SECTION 1: CHOOSING GOALS

A. Student Interests—Does the student:	Student Skills (Does the student do this?)					Opportunity at School (Does school provide structured time?)				
	(not at all) 0	1	2	3	100% 4	(not at all) 0	1	2	3	100% 4
A1. Express school interests (e.g. classes, sports, clubs)?	0	1	2	3	④	0	1	2	3	④
A2. Express employment interests (e.g., jobs, careers)?	⓪	1	2	3	4	⓪	1	2	3	4
A3. Express post–high school education interests (e.g., colleges, trade school)?	⓪	1	2	3	4	⓪	1	2	3	4
A4. Express personal interests (e.g., relationships, leisure, health, legal)?	0	①	2	3	4	0	1	2	③	4
A5. Express housing & daily living interests?	⓪	1	2	3	4	0	①	2	3	4
A6. Express community participation interests (e.g., transportation, adult services)?	0	①	2	3	4	0	1	②	3	4
	Subtotal: 6					**Subtotal: 10**				

FIGURE 3.7. *ChoiceMaker Self-Determination Transition Assessment*, Section 1. *Note.* From *ChoiceMaker Self-Determination Transition Assessment*, by J. Martin and L. Huber Marshall, 1996, Longmont, CO: Sopris West. Copyright 1996 by Sopris West. Reprinted with permission.

SECTION 2: EXPRESSING GOALS	Student Skills (Does the student do this?)					Opportunity at School (Does school provide structured time?)				
	(not at all)				100%	(not at all)				100%
D. Student Leading Meeting— Does the student:										
D1. Begin meeting by stating purpose?	⓪	1	2	3	4	⓪	1	2	3	4
D2. Introduce participants?	⓪	1	2	3	4	⓪	1	2	3	4
D3. Review past goals and performance?	0	1	②	3	4	0	1	2	③	4
D4. Ask for feedback from group members?	⓪	1	2	3	4	⓪	1	2	3	4
D5. Ask questions if student doesn't understand something?	⓪	1	2	3	4	⓪	1	2	3	4
D6. Deal with differences in opinion?	⓪	1	2	3	4	⓪	1	2	3	4
D7. State needed support?	⓪	1	2	3	4	⓪	1	2	3	4
D8. Close meeting by summarizing decisions?	⓪	1	2	3	4	⓪	1	2	3	4
	Subtotal: 2					**Subtotal: 3**				
E. Student Reporting—Does the student:										
E1. Express interests (from SECTION 1: CHOOSING GOALS)?	0	1	2	③	4	0	1	2	③	4
E2. Express skills & limits (from SECTION 1: CHOOSING GOALS)?	⓪	1	2	3	4	0	1	2	③	4
E3. Express options and goals (from SECTION 1: CHOOSING GOALS)?	0	1	②	3	4	0	1	②	3	4
	TOTAL (D+E): 7					**TOTAL (D+E): 11**				

FIGURE 3.8. *ChoiceMaker Self-Determination Transition Assessment*, Section 2. *Note.* From *ChoiceMaker Self-Determination Transition Assessment*, by J. Martin and L. Huber Marshall, 1996, Longmont, CO: Sopris West. Copyright 1996 by Sopris West. Reprinted with permission.

Sample Activities:

a. In his transition class and community work experiences, Zeke completes the Choosing Employment Goals lessons. These lessons provide Zeke the opportunity to learn the job characteristics he likes and determine whether they match different community job sites.

b. In his learning strategies class, Zeke will complete the Choosing Education Goals lessons. Among other skills, Zeke will learn to identify the classroom characteristics he likes best (e.g., lecture or hands-on, small-group activities) and compare them with classes available next semester.

2. To increase Zeke's leadership of his IEP process.

Sample Activities:

a. Zeke will complete the Self-Directed IEP lessons. For example, Zeke will learn the 11 steps needed for him to lead his own IEP meeting.

b. Prior to his IEP meeting, Zeke will videotape a role-play using the 11 steps needed to lead his own IEP meeting. Zeke and his teacher will each assume varying roles. After the role-play, Zeke will review his performance with assistance from his peers and teacher.

CONCLUSION

Self-determination skills development should be an integral part of every student's educational program. Various self-determination assessment and curricula are now available to facilitate the teaching of these skills within the overall curriculum. Opportunities must be created across elementary, middle school, and high school programs for students to exercise self-determination, and self-determination-oriented goals need to be a part of each student's IEP. Successful adults use self-determination skills. Does it not make sense to teach students the skills needed to be successful while they are still in school?

REFERENCES

Agran, M., Blanchard, C., & Wehmeyer, M. L. (2000). Promoting transition goals and self-determination through student self-directed learning: The Self-Determined Learning Model of Instruction. *Education and Training in Mental Retardation and Developmental Disabilities, 35*(4), 351–364.

Aspinall, R. S., Roberts, L., & Robinson, R. (1992). *Connections: A transition curriculum for Grades 3 through 6.* Denver: Colorado Department of Education.

Brolin, D. E. (1989). *Life centered career education: A competency-based approach* (3rd ed.). Reston, VA: Council for Exceptional Children.

Carpenter, W. D. (1995). *Become your own expert! Self-advocacy curriculum for individuals with learning disabilities.* Minneapolis: Minnesota Educational Services.

Curtis, E. (1995). *I want my dream, new hat, and profile decks—It's my life: Preference-based planning, facilitator's guide, and goal planner's workbook.* Salt Lake City, UT: New Hats.

Diaz-Greenberg, R., Thousand, J., Cardelle-Elawar, M., & Nevin, A. (2000). What teachers need to know about the struggle for self-determination (conscientization) and self-regulation: Adults with disabilities speak about their education experiences. *Teaching and Teacher Education, 16,* 873–887.

Field, S., & Hoffman, A. (1994). Development of a model for self-determination. *Career Development for Exceptional Individuals, 17*(2), 159–169.

Field, S., & Hoffman, A. (1995). *Steps to self-determination.* Austin, TX: PRO-ED.

Field, S., Martin, J., Miller, R., Ward, M., & Wehmeyer, M. (1998). Self-determination for persons with disabilities: A position statement of the Division on Career Development and Transition. *Career Development for Exceptional Individuals, 2*(2), 113–128.

Garfield, G. (1986). *Peak performers: The new heroes of American business.* New York: Avon.

Gerber, P. J., Ginsberg, R., & Reiff, H. B. (1992). Identifying alterable patterns in employment success for highly successful adults with learning disabilities. *Journal of Learning Disabilities, 25,* 475–487.

Hill, N. H. (1960). *Think and grow rich.* New York: Ballantine.

Hill, N. H., & Stone, W. C. (1987). *Success through a positive mental attitude.* New York: Prentice Hall.

Huber Marshall, L., Martin, J. E., Maxson, L. L., & Jerman, P. (1996). *Choosing employment goals.* Longmont, CO: Sopris West.

Huber Marshall, L., Martin, J. E., McGill, T., Maxson, L. L., & Jerman, P. (1996). *Taking action.* Longmont, CO: Sopris West.

Lyle, M. E. (2000). *100 activities for transition.* Columbia, MO: Hawthorne Educational Services. (ERIC Document Reproduction Service No. ED444285)

Martin, J. E., & Huber Marshall, L. H. (1995). ChoiceMaker: A comprehensive self-determination transition program. *Intervention in School and Clinic, 30*(3), 147–156.

Martin, J. E., & Huber Marshall, L. H. (1996). *ChoiceMaker self-determination transition assessment.* Longmont, CO: Sopris West.

Martin, J. E., Huber Marshall, L., & Maxson, L. L. (1993). Transition policy: Infusing self-determination and self-advocacy into transition programs. *Career Development for Exceptional Individuals, 16*(1), 53–61.

Martin, J. E., Huber Marshall, L., Maxson, L. L., & Jerman, P. (1996). *Self-directed IEP.* Longmont, CO: Sopris West.

Martin, J. E., Huber Marshall, L., Miller, T. L., Kregar, G., & Hughes, W. (1996). Self-determination curricula: A detailed review. In S. Field, J. E. Martin, R. J. Miller, M. Ward, & M. L. Wehmeyer (Eds.), *Student self-determination guide.* Reston, VA: Council for Exceptional Children, Division on Career Development and Transition.

Mithaug, D. E. (1991). *Self-determined kids: Raising satisfied and successful children.* Lexington, MA: Heath.

Mithaug, D. E. (1993). *Self-regulation theory: How optimal adjustment maximizes gain.* Westport, CT: Praeger.

Mithaug, D. E., Martin, J. E., & Agran, M. (1987). Adaptability instruction: The goal of transitional programs. *Exceptional Children, 53,* 500–505.

Schloss, P. J., Alper, S., & Jayne, D. (1993). Self-determination for people with disabilities: Choice, risk, and dignity. *Exceptional Children, 60*(3), 215–225.

Serna, L. A., & Lau-Smith, J. (1995). *Learning with PURPOSE: An instructor's manual for teaching self-determination skills to students who are at risk for failure.* Albuquerque: University of New Mexico.

Ward, M. J. (1988). The many facets of self-determination. *National Information Center for Children and Youth with Handicaps: Transition Summary, 5,* 2–3.

Wehman, P., West, M., & Kregel, J. (1999). Supported employment program development and research needs: Looking ahead to the year 2000. *Education and Training in Mental Retardation and Development Disabilities, 34*(1), 3–19.

Wehmeyer, M. L. (1992a). Promoting self-determination using the Life-Centered Career Education Curriculum. In D. E. Brolin (Ed.), *Life-Centered Career Education Curriculum.* Reston, VA: Council for Exceptional Children.

Wehmeyer, M. L. (1992b). Self-determination: Critical skills for outcome-oriented transition services. *Journal for Vocational Special Needs Education, 15,* 3–9.

Wehmeyer, M. L. (1995). *Whose future is it anyway? A student-directed transition planning process.* Arlington, TX: Arc National Headquarters.

Wehmeyer, M. L. (1998). Self-determination and individuals with significant disabilities: Examining meanings and misinterpretations. *Journal of the Association for Persons with Severe Handicaps, 23*(1), 5–16.

Wehmeyer, M. L. (1999). A functional model of self-determination: Describing development and implementing instruction. *Focus on Autism and Other Developmental Disabilities, 14*(1), 53–61.

Wehmeyer, M. L., Agran, M., & Hughes, C. (2000). A national survey of teachers' promotion of self-determination and student-directed learning. *Journal of Special Education, 34*(2), 58–68.

Wehmeyer, M. L., & Kelchner, K. (1995). *The Arc's Self-Determination Scale–Adolescent version.* Arlington, TX: Arc National Headquarters.

Wehmeyer, M. L., Palmer, S. B., Agran, M., Mithaug, D. E., & Martin, J. E. (2000). *Exceptional Children, 66*(4), 439–453.

Wehmeyer, M. L., & Schwartz, M. (1999). The self-determination focus of transition goals for students with mental retardation. *Career Development for Exceptional Individuals, 21*(1), 75–86.

Wolman, J. M., Campeau, P. L., DuBois, P. A., Mithaug, D. E., & Stolarski, V. S. (1994). *AIR Self-Determination Scale and user guide.* Palo Alto, CA: American Institutes for Research.

Zhang, D., & Stecker, P. M. (2000, May). *Infusing self-determination into transition planning: Current practice and recommendations.* Paper presented at the annual meeting of the American Association of Mental Retardation, Washington, DC. (ERIC Reproduction Service No. ED449588)

CHAPTER 4

Accessing the General Curriculum Within a Functional Curriculum Framework

Colleen A. Thoma, Kelly Ligon, and Katherine Wittig

With the passage of the Individuals with Disabilities Act (IDEA) Amendments of 1997, a new element was added to the process of developing an Individualized Education Program (IEP) for students with disabilities. This element has been called "access to the general education curriculum," and it ensures that what is taught to students with disabilities during the school day is directly related or tied to what their peers without disabilities are learning. This change mandated that not only were students with disabilities to learn what all other students learn, but they were also required to participate in the same districtwide or statewide assessments as students without disabilities.

More specifically, the IDEA Amendments of 1997 require that the following be included as part of a student's IEP:

- A statement of how the student's disability affects his or her involvement with and progress in the general curriculum
- A statement of measurable goals to enable the student to be involved with and progress in the general curriculum while meeting each of the student's other unique educational needs
- A statement of the services, program modifications, and supports necessary for the student to be involved and progress in the general curriculum
- A statement of the extent, if any, to which the student will not participate with the students without disabilities in general education classes and activities
- A statement of any individual modifications in the administration of state or district assessments of student achievement that are needed for the student to participate in the assessments

These requirements differ significantly from what was included previously in IDEA and necessitate a change in the strategies used both to teach the general curriculum and to develop IEPs.

Prior to 1997, students with disabilities were ensured an opportunity for a free and appropriate education, with *appropriate* being defined by a team. Annual goals for a student were determined based on information obtained from a series of assessments of student strengths and needs and frequently focused on remediating or eliminating those "needs." Typically, there was little, if any, focus on relating those individualized educational goals and objectives to the general education curriculum. Including students with these individualized goals in general education classrooms was difficult at best, and students who had IEPs that primarily included functional goals were the most difficult to accommodate in general education classrooms (e.g., Gersten, Walker, & Darch, 1988).

IDEA now requires that teams develop IEPs from a new starting point: the general education curriculum. Access to the general education curriculum does not necessarily mean that the team cannot make many of the same decisions for a student's education program that it made before 1997. IEPs can still contain functional goals, and students can still receive their education in the most appropriate environment and receive any necessary therapy they require to benefit from their education. But decisions are based now on helping students with disabilities participate in the same educational experiences as students without disabilities.

This chapter explains what access to the general education curriculum means and how such access is achieved. This chapter also demonstrates how standards-based learning can be linked to functional and age-appropriate activities for students with cognitive disabilities, particularly mental retardation. The chapter concludes with case studies that show how this can be accomplished at both the elementary and secondary grade levels.

WHAT DOES ACCESS TO THE GENERAL CURRICULUM MEAN?

IDEA regulations state that general curriculum refers to "the same curriculum as for nondisabled children" (*Federal Register,* March 12, 1999, p. 12592). Although the law is not specific about whether this includes both informal and formal aspects of the curriculum, Wehmeyer, Sands, Knowlton, and Kozleski (2002) assert that access to both the formal and the informal aspects of the general curriculum is implied. Formal curriculum is defined as the clearly defined learning objectives that are developed for students, whereas the informal curriculum includes all of the social and unplanned learning that takes place in the school and classroom. Wehmeyer et al. point to IDEA's emphasis on educating students with disabilities in the least restrictive environment, preferably in the general education classroom, as an indication that students with disabilities should also benefit from access to the informal aspects of the general education curriculum.

State and local performance and content standards must be a key part of any discussion about general education curriculum. State and local standards have gained new importance in today's era of standards-based reform. Nolet and McLaughlin (2000) describe standards-based reform as a "policy response to the dissatisfaction with the performance of American schools that has been growing in both the public and private sectors for a number of years. Major elements of standards-based reform are (a) higher content standards, (b) use of assessments aimed at measuring how schools are helping students meet the standards, and (c) an emphasis on holding educators and students accountable for student achievement" (p. 2). Such reform efforts affect the general education curriculum and therefore need to be considered when ensuring that students with disabilities have access to that curriculum and describing the degree to which the access will occur. These three elements of standards-based reform are discussed in this section.

Standards. Standards are general statements of what students should know or be able to do as a result of their education. Most states have passed legislation to incorporate standards into their state's public education, and states have the freedom to decide what these standards will include. As Nolet and McLaughlin (2000) point out, "No standard exists for these new state standards" (p. 3).

Assessments. As states adopt new standards, they implement new assessments to measure student progress in meeting the standards. Many of these statewide assessments include an exit or graduation test that students must pass before they receive standard high school diploma (e.g., Nevada). Other states require subject area assessments (e.g., New York). Students with disabilities must participate in their districtwide or statewide assessments unless their team decides that an alternative assessment is necessary. It is easy to see that students with disabilities who have not had access to the general education curriculum would not perform well on these standardized tests.

Accountability. Schools and districts are being held accountable for the performance of their students on statewide assessments. Tests designed to measure student achievement in curriculum areas are now being used to make decisions about a school's performance, a use for which the test was not developed or evaluated. Decisions about which students with disabilities are included in these assessment procedures are affected by this additional use for standardized tests.

HOW IS ACCESS TO THE GENERAL EDUCATION CURRICULUM ACHIEVED?

Research studies that document the experiences of students with disabilities in general education classrooms prove that providing access to the general education curriculum means more than a student simply being present in a general education classroom (Klinger & Vaughn, 1999). "Access requires that students with disabilities be provided with the supports necessary to allow them to benefit from instruction" (Nolet & McLaughlin, 2000, p. 9). It also requires that instruction be provided in ways that meet the needs of the majority of students with and without disabilities.

Universal Design

Universal design, a term that once referred to architecture and other construction design, is now being applied to the design of curriculum and instruction. The concept refers to curriculum and instruction being "constructed" so that the majority of students with and without disabilities can access the instruction and learn (Rose & Meyer, 2002). For example, consider the development of an electronic file for a lesson. Such an electronic file could be printed for most students (both those with and without disabilities), accessed on a computer that had voice output for group of students who had visual or learning disabilities, and printed in Braille for a student who has a visual and hearing impairment. The Center for

Applied Special Technology has outlined three essential features of universal design for learning:

1. multiple means of representation of content/material

2. multiple means of expression to allow students to respond with their preferred method

3. multiple means of engagement to spark interest and increase motivation (Rose & Meyer, 2002)

Although these features of universal design for learning are typically considered within the context of the academic curriculum, they also provide a rationale for functional activities. Many students find their educational experiences unfulfilling because they do not understand why they have to learn certain subjects. When instruction is tied to real life (i.e., functional), students are often more motivated to learn. In particular, when instruction is tied to job skills, all students report increased motivation and are less likely to drop out (e.g., Saddler, Thoma, & Whiston, 2002). For many students with disabilities, the changes to curriculum, instruction, and assessment that follow universal design principles may be all that is required to ensure access to the general education curriculum.

Assistive Technology

For students who need additional supports or accommodations to access the curriculum, assistive technology is the first step to consider. Assistive technology is a very specific type of accommodation and modification that can increase access to the curriculum. It is different from universal design in that its use typically benefits students with disabilities only and, at times, may benefit only one particular student. Like universal design for learning, the use of assistive technology does not necessarily involve changing the content of the curriculum being taught in a general education classroom.

Assistive technology includes devices and services. IDEA (1997) defined assistive technology devices and assistive technology services as follows:

> Assistive technology device means any item, piece of equipment or product system, whether acquired commercially off the shelf, modified or customized, that is used to increase, maintain, or improve the functional capabilities of a child with a disability. (§1401, ¶1)
>
> Assistive technology service means any service that directly assists a child with a disability in the selection, acquisition, or use of an assistive technology device. (§1401, ¶2)

Assistive technology can have a variety of applications in the classroom and can meet a variety of needs. To benefit from their education, some students with disabilities may require assistive technology for mobility (e.g., moving from classroom to classroom), and others may require assistive technology for communication so that they can "tell" others what they have learned. There are many ways to describe assistive technology, but most describe it by its degree of complexity and its primary use. *Low tech* refers to devices that are passive or simple, with few moving parts (Mann & Lane, 1991), such as picture communication boards, pointers, and switches. *High tech* refers to devices that are complex and typically contain electronic components (Inge & Shepherd, 1995), such as voice output communication aides, electric wheelchairs, universal remote controls, and computers. Typically, the complexity of assistive technology devices can be conceptualized as a continuum from low or no tech to high tech.

The IDEA amendments (1997) require that assistive technology be considered for each student with a disability as part of the process of developing an IEP, which requires that team members know what technology is available that could possibly meet a student's educational needs. Assistive technology devices are typically categorized by their major uses, although some can have multiple uses for an individual student. Bryant and Bryant (2002) grouped assistive technology devices into seven categories: "positioning, mobility, augmentative and alternative communication, computer access, adaptive toys and games, adaptive environments, and instructional aides" (p. 4). Because the devices change often and quickly, the best source of information about available technology is the Internet. Table 4.1 lists some of the most comprehensive Web sites devoted to assistive technology.

Once assistive technology has been considered by the team, a more comprehensive assessment process should begin. There are many approaches to technology assessment, but the one that provides the most comprehensive information and follows a person-centered approach is the Matching Person and Technology (MPT) format (Scherer, 1998). Scherer's assessment strategy involves not only examining the uses of the technology but also looking at individual preferences and comfort with technology in making assistive technology recommendations.

TABLE 4.1
Internet Resources for Assistive Technology

Internet Address	Name	Category	Comments
www.aacproducts.org	Communication Aid Manufacturers Association	Communication	Has search engine for devices; provides information about conferences
www.enablemart.com	Enable Mart	All	Allows user to purchase devices and download software programs
www.rjcooper.com	R. J. Cooper	Computer Access/ Instructional Aides	User can request CD-ROM with product information
www.abledata.com	Abledata	All	Very comprehensive Web site contains search engine
www.accessiblesolutions.net	Accessible	Computer Access Solutions	Has computer access and software for work, home, school
www.cast.org	Center for Applied Special Technology	Instructional Aides	Contains information about universal design, computer access

Accommodations and Modifications

A smaller number of students with disabilities will require still more supports to access the general curriculum than universal design and assistive technology can provide. It is for these students that adaptations, augmentation, and alterations are necessary. Figure 4.1 provides a step-by-step sequence that teams can follow to determine a student's IEP or individualized curriculum (Wehmeyer et al., 2002).

The starting point for this sequence is the universally designed curriculum that meets the needs of students without disabilities and a large number of students with disabilities. For students who cannot access the universally designed curriculum, their teams would consider what assistive technology could help provide access to the curriculum and meet the students' needs. Again, a percentage of these students with disabilities would now have access to the general curriculum, but a small percentage would not. This is the point at which adaptations,

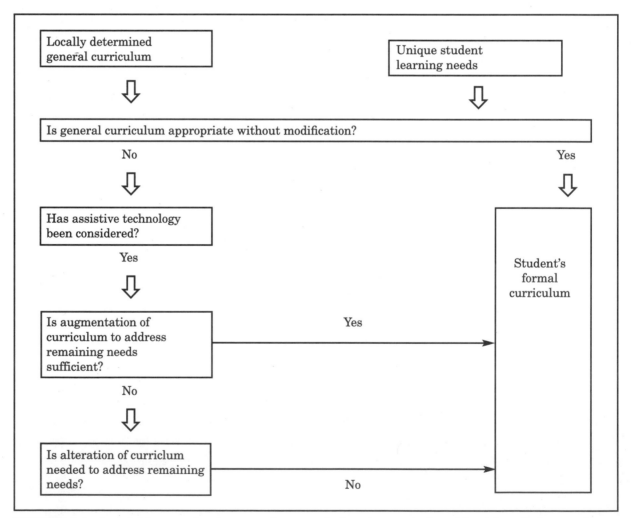

FIGURE 4.1. A model for ensuring access to the general education curriculum. *Note.* From "Achieving Access to the General Curriculum," by M. L. Wehmeyer, D. J. Sands, H. E. Knowlton, and E. B. Kozleski, in *Teaching Students with Mental Retardation: Providing Access to the General Curriculum* (p. 55), edited by M. L. Wehmeyer, D. J. Sands, H. E. Knowlton, and E. B. Kozleski, 2002, Baltimore: Brookes. Copyright 2002 by Brookes. Reprinted with permission.

augmentation, and alterations would be considered. A team would not consider a more intrusive or restrictive approach when a less intrusive or restrictive one is sufficient. When a student is able to access the general curriculum, the student's formal, individualized curriculum would be complete.

Curriculum Adaptation

Wehmeyer et al. (2002) define *curriculum adaptation* as "any effort to modify the representation or presentation of the curriculum or to modify the student's engagement with the curriculum to enhance access and progress" (p. 52). Many of the same strategies or techniques that could be used in a universally designed curriculum could also be used to adapt the general education curriculum. The difference between the two is that the techniques for adaptation are used to meet the needs of a small number of students and are not available to all students.

Like universal design, curriculum adaptations can include modifications to instructional materials, the delivery of instruction, the manner in which a student engages in instruction, or the process of assessing what a student has learned. Because instructional materials are typically print based (e.g., textbooks, worksheets, notebooks), adaptations to these materials can include books on tape, Braille, computer-based work, audiocassette tapes, videotapes, and CD-ROMs.

Teachers generally deliver instruction verbally through lectures or in written format on chalkboards, overheads, and worksheets. Changes in instructional delivery can make learning more functional through the use of community-based instruction, hands-on or discovery learning, guest speakers, and authentic learning.

Engaging the student in learning is a key factor in ensuring access to the general curriculum. Students must learn how to take advantage of opportunities for learning to occur. Adaptations to student engagement in learning can also be adaptations to how one would measure student progress in the curriculum. Students typically engage in learning through oral and written methods. That is, they write what they know and occasionally have opportunities to tell others what they know. For students who have difficulty in verbal expression (oral or written), engagement can be difficult and student performance may not demonstrate a student's knowledge about a subject. Alternative assessment processes to verbal expression include demonstrations of mastery, projects, portfolios, and recitals (Thoma & Held, 2002).

Curriculum Augmentation

For some students with disabilities, access to the general curriculum involves more than changing its format, methods in delivery, and engagement. Students may also need instruction and supports in learning how to learn. "These augmentations do not change the curriculum but, rather, add to or augment the curriculum to provide students with strategies for success" (Wehmeyer et al., 2002, p. 53). Skills that make up the core component skills of self-determination such as goal setting, problem solving, self-monitoring, and self-management are more successful in an inclusive environment, which leads to the assumption that such students are better able to access the general curriculum (e.g., Agran, Fodor-Davis, & Moore, 1986; Hughes & Petersen, 1989). Mithaug, Wehmeyer, Agran, Martin, and Palmer (1998) developed a model for teaching self-determination skills to students and assisting them in using the skills to learn. This model teaches students to follow a three-phase sequence to enhance their learning: set a goal, take action, and adjust the goal or plan. This model has been the only one used with students with mental retardation and more significant disabilities. Other strategies such as learning strategy instruction (Knowlton, 1998) have been primarily used with students with learning disabilities. Although many researchers and educators believe that other strategies may be useful for students with mental retardation, they recommend that systematic research be conducted (e.g., Borkowski, Weyhing, & Turner, 1986; Bulgren & Lenz, 1996).

Curriculum Alteration

Altering the curriculum should occur only when all other attempts at providing access to the general education curriculum have been ineffective at meeting the needs of an individual student. Too often, special education begins here, with the individualized curriculum designed to meet student needs without sufficient grounding in the general curriculum. The overarching premise for any alteration of the general curriculum must be in its functionality for the individual student. That is, what does the student need to learn to achieve his or her goals for a quality life at any age? Strategies that typically have been used in special education can be used in individualizing an altered curriculum, including community-based instruction, vocational training, and functional curriculum. None of these strategies need to be discarded for students to access the general education curriculum. The examples in the following section will demonstrate how the two approaches can be successfully integrated.

CASE STUDY: PAIGE

Paige is a 9-year-old girl who has a medical condition with an unknown etiology. She can walk independently, although she has a lack of flexibility and easily loses her balance. Her lack of flexibility in her joints also affects her fine motor skills. Paige communicates verbally, and her language is understandable to a familiar listener. She uses profane language at times. Paige is the oldest of three girls and lives with her parents in a small, rural eastern town. Her father is self-employed and her mother is a homemaker. Paige has a large, supportive extended family, and her mother is very involved in her education. Paige has a history of grand mal seizures and has been hospitalized for them in the past. She is on medication that causes her to become extremely drowsy at times during the day.

Paige is enrolled in a rural elementary school where she is in a self-contained classroom with five other students with various disabilities. Paige enjoys coming to school and interacts with adults and classmates. Her IEP includes goals for improving appropriate oral communication, increasing the amount of time on task, planning and preparing simple meals or snacks, following safety rules in the school and community, improving money skills, and completing assigned classroom jobs, chores, and errands. Paige's family hopes that she will hold a competitive job with supports when she gets older. Paige would like to live independently in a personally selected supported living arrangement.

Paige is well liked by her typical peers. She attends resource classes (e.g., art, music) with these peers daily. The challenge for Paige's educational team will be to provide access to the general curriculum in typical settings and to explore options for Paige to become more involved and engaged in learning with her typical peers.

An example of her typical daily schedule is shown in Figure 4.2, including subjects and teachers. Ms. Williams is Paige's case manager and Ms. Burke is the third-grade teacher. The schedule represents a segregated educational setting that follows the standard pullout model for therapy service delivery. Paige clearly has limited access to typical peers during academic activities. Her special education teacher provides Paige's daily instructional activities. Although Paige has access to general education teachers within the context of art and music, the settings include special education students only. This model provides limited opportunities for the general and special education teachers on Paige's grade level to collaborate about Paige's IEP goals.

Figure 4.3, on the other hand, shows how Paige's schedule might look following an integrated teaching model. Ms. Williams and Ms. Burke are using a cooperative teaching model. Paige is involved in all aspects of the third-grade classroom. She participates with her typical peers to reach her IEP goals and to access the general curriculum. Paige's activities are adapted to meet her needs. Ms. Williams provides Ms. Burke the support and resources necessary to assist with Paige's education, as well as the education of other students in the class. The teachers in Paige's school apply universal design for learning (Rose & Meyer, 2002) theories in their everyday practices. "The basic premise for universal design for learning should include alternatives to make it accessible and applicable to students, teachers, and parents with different background, learning styles, abilities and disabilities in widely varied learning contexts" (Rose & Meyer, 2002, p. 4). Here are several examples of IEP goals for Paige.

Student Name: Paige Turner   Grade: 3

Subject	Teacher	Time
Morning meeting	Williams	9:15
Functional academics: math and language arts	Williams	9:30
Lunch	Williams	11:00
Recess	Williams	11:30
Functional academics: science or history	Williams	12:00
Adaptive PE: Ms. Williams's class only	Adaptive PE teacher	1:00
Resource classes (art, music, etc.)	General education teachers	1:45
Individual work time	Williams	2:45
Speech therapy; physical therapy; occupational therapy	Related services personnel in therapy room	3:00

FIGURE 4.2. Daily schedule for Paige in a segregated setting.

Student Name: <u>Paige Turner</u>		Grade: <u>3</u>
Subject	**Teacher**	**Time**
Journal writing	Burke/Williams	9:15
Math	Burke/Williams	9:30
Self-selected reading time	Burke/Williams	10:30
Character education	School counselor	10:45
Lunch	Burke/Williams	11:15
Recess	Burke/Williams	11:45
Language arts	Burke/Williams	12:15
Resource classes (art, music, etc.)	General ed. teachers	1:15
Science or history	Burke/Williams	2:00
Individual work time	Burke/Williams	3:00

FIGURE 4.3. Daily schedule for Paige in an integrated setting.

⮞ IEP Goal for History/Social Sciences

Paige will improve her communication skills by using appropriate language 100% of the time when communicating with peers and adults in three of four planned interactions daily, to be reported each 9-week grading period.

Access Skill:

The student will explain the responsibilities of being a good citizen, with emphasis on the following:

- Respecting and protecting the rights and property of others
- Taking part in the voting process when making classroom decisions
- Demonstrating self-discipline and self-reliance

(Source: Virginia Department of Education, Standards of Learning, 2001, History/Social Science 2.10)

Activity:

Paige will use an augmentative communication device such as a voice output device with picture cue, then fading to picture cue only, to communicate with peers and adults.

For communication skills to generalize, research has shown that students with disabilities need to practice these skills across a variety of settings with a variety of listeners (Browder & Ware, 2001). In Virginia, the Alternate Assessment Program requires each participant to perform IEP goals across a variety of settings and social interactions (Virginia Department of Education, 2001). Teachers must provide evidence of that access with photographs, videos, handwritten or typed letters from general education teachers and typical peers, and other types of evidence.

➔ IEP Goal for Science

Paige will plan and prepare a simple snack, following visual picture directions, in four of five opportunities with 90% accuracy, to be reported each 9-week grading period.

Access Skill:
The student will plan and conduct simple investigations in which

- predictions and observations are made,
- volume is determined,
- temperature is measured,
- time is measured.

(Source: Virginia Department of Education, Standards of Learning, 1995, Science 3.1)

Activity:
Paige will participate with peers in making Kool-Aid. They will make predictions about the change in color or the difference in taste before and after the sugar is added, measure the volume of water needed, measure the temperature, and measure the amount of time taken to complete the task.

Students with disabilities should participate in activities that are age-appropriate with reasonable expectations in terms of performance (Steere & Burcroff, 1997). It is important that students actively participate in their daily routines, including planning and preparing snacks and meals, as independently as possible (Browder, 2001).

➔ IEP Goal for Math

Paige will increase her amount of time on task by 8 minutes by the end of the first semester.

Access Skill:
The student will tell time to the nearest 5-minute interval and to the nearest minute.

(Source: Virginia Department of Education, Standards of Learning, 2001, Math 3.15)

Activity:
Paige will use a Time-Timer to keep track of her time on task and the amount of time for breaks. She will increase the amount of time between break periods, thereby increasing her amount of time on task.

Managing oneself is critical for success, and it also encourages independence and opportunities to learn many other skills (Kleinert, Denham, et al., 2001). Older students on job sites may learn to self-monitor their time during work and break periods, assisting them in maintaining current skills and acquiring new ones (Wehman, 1997).

➔ IEP Goal for Math

Paige will improve her money skills by accurately counting her lunch money daily, with 100% accuracy by the end of the first 9-week grading period.

Access Skill:

The student will determine value by counting a collection of bills or coins up to $5.00, compare the value of the coins or bills, and make change.

(Source: Virginia Department of Education, Standards of Learning, 2001, Math 3.13)

Activity:

Paige will use a money jig to count her lunch money daily and place the money in her wallet.

The ability to perform functional mathematical skills is essential for the success of individuals in their communities. Students need opportunities to generalize money skills in a variety of settings, including the community, for personal competence (Wehman, 1997).

➜ IEP Goal for English

Paige will improve her written communication skills by completing a four-sentence paragraph, with adaptations, in four of five attempts during the first 9-week grading period.

Access Skill:

Students will write stories, letters, simple explanations, and short reports across all content areas.

(Source: Virginia Department of Education, Standards of Learning, 1995, English 3.8)

Activity:

Using IntelliKeys and IntelliPics, the teacher will create a template for Paige to use to write about a current topic studied in class. Paige will make choices between written words to complete the paragraph. See Figure 4.4 as an example of how Paige's English goal might be recorded.

As parents/caregivers spend time with their children reading, children learn the basic mechanics of reading (e.g., holding the book right side up, starting at the front) and become aware of print and the alphabet (Erickson & Koppenhaver, 1999). With this exposure at an early age, children are more prepared as they

---

Student's Name: ___Paige___　　　　Academic Year: ___2004–2005___

Grade Level: ___3___　　　Teacher Name: ___Ms. Williams___

IEP Goal	Access Skill	Activity
Paige will improve her written communication skills by completing a four-sentence paragraph, with adaptations, in four of five attempts during the first 9-week grading period.	*English:* Students will write stories, letters, simple explanations, and short reports across all content areas (Virginia Department of Education Standards of Learning English 3.8).	Using IntelliKeys and IntelliPics, the teacher will create a template for Paige to use to write about a current topic studied in class. Paige will make choices between written words to complete the paragraph.

FIGURE 4.4.　Paige's goal in English.

enter school to move through the reading and writing process (Musselwhite, 2001). Literacy and communication are intertwined. To learn literacy skills, one needs communication skills, and vice versa (Musselwhite, 2001). Figure 4.4 shows how Paige will access the general education curriculum in English.

CASE STUDY: JAMES

James is a 17-year-old adolescent with a severe neuromuscular disorder. He uses a power wheelchair in his urban high school and in the community. James has severe hand tremors on his left side and paralysis in his lower left leg and foot. His speech is understandable to a familiar listener. James is enrolled in a transition/career development program. His IEP goals stress a successful transition to adult life. James will graduate with a special education diploma emphasizing his successes in the supported employment services program. Now in 11th grade, he works part-time in a large bookstore located at a shopping mall near his high school placing bar codes on books. James also participates in on-campus activities, such as managing the track team and serving as an office assistant in the media center. James is a gregarious well-liked student at Wakefield High School.

James is one of many students whose IEP involves access to the general curriculum. Let us first compare two schedules for James, one for James in a self-contained environment, the other his actual schedule. Figure 4.5 shows what James's schedule might look like in a self-contained environment. Note the block schedule, with Block 5 meeting every day.

It is clear in the schedule in Figure 4.5 that James's contact with peers without disabilities would be severely limited. One may surmise that his access to the general curriculum is restricted by receiving instruction from one teacher in one classroom all day, every day. Most high school students change classes every block, travel throughout the school campus all day, and have numerous opportunities to interact with various teachers and peers. Compare James's hypothetical schedule in Figure 4.5 with his actual schedule in Figure 4.6. This schedule reflects a typical high school student who changes classes throughout the day and has access to many peers and teachers.

Student Name: _James Washington_		Grade: _11_	
Block	**Subject**	**Teacher/Room**	**Time**
1	Functional English	Mrs. Tyler: A13	8:00
2	Functional Government	Mrs. Tyler: A13	8:00
3	Functional Math	Mrs. Tyler: A13	9:40
4	Functional Science	Mrs. Tyler: A13	9:40
5	Adaptive PE/Lunch/Activity	Mr. Jones: Gym	11:10
6	Functional Employment	Mrs. Tyler: A13	1:00
7	Functional Employment	Mrs. Tyler: A13	1:00

FIGURE 4.5. Hypothetical schedule for James, based on self-contained environment.

Block	Subject	Teacher/Room	Time
	Student Name: _____ James Washington _____ Grade: ___ 11 ___		
1	Education for Employment	Weaver: 218	8:00
2	Computer Technology	Bonner: C2	8:00
3	Ecology and Technology	Smith: C16	9:40
4	Consumer Math	Izzi: B31	9:40
5	Activity/Lunch	Tyler: 101	11:10
6	Career Connections	Tyler: 101	1:00
7	Career Connections	Weaver/Tyler: 218	1:00

FIGURE 4.6. James's actual schedule, with access to the general curriculum.

➔ IEP Goal for English

James will develop and communicate his career goals through the use of written and verbal language by June 2004.

Access Skill:

The student will write, revise, and edit personal and business correspondence to a standard acceptable in the workplace and higher education.

(Source: Virginia Department of Education, Standards of Learning, 1995, English 11.8)

Activity:

James will participate in the Education for Employment class to develop a personal career résumé. He will use assistive technology and a template to organize his ideas in a logical sequence. He will, with assistance, revise his writing for clarity. Inclusive opportunities are available for James so that he can learn targeted skills throughout the school day with typical peers.

Kleinert, Hurte, et al. (2001) emphasized the value of instruction in multiple settings in the context of learning activities for other students. Clearly, James will have many opportunities to share his work experiences and career goals with typical peers in the context of a general education classroom and in the various settings of his school campus. He enjoys daily access to the general curriculum.

➔ IEP Goal for Math

James will develop a personal monthly budget based on his Social Security Income (SSI), paycheck, and allowance with 95% accuracy, to be reported to his SSI program manager quarterly (i.e., September, December, March, June).

Access Skill:

The student will compare and order whole numbers, fractions, and decimals, using concrete materials, drawings or pictures, and mathematical symbols.

(Source: Virginia Department of Education, Standards of Learning, 2001, Math 6.4)

Activities:

James has many skills in math. He makes purchases to an exact amount, discriminates money equivalence, and has mastered math standards to at least a fourth-grade level. Browder (2001) emphasized banking skill acquisition through the use of actual check registers and in community settings.

James works with his mother and his IEP case manager to maintain an accurate log of financial activities. He deposits paychecks and SSI checks into a local credit union savings account on a biweekly basis. James's teacher has enlarged credit union deposit and withdrawal slips on the school copier. James then fills out the enlarged credit union deposit slip, stating each number aloud as he writes it. He maintains his account information with the use of a budget template on a computer, using assistive technology for input.

James has access to nondisabled peers and age-appropriate activities as he performs his budget activities in the community. Many of his school-aged friends use the same credit union as James for their financial activities.

⊵ IEP Goal for Science

James will use assistive technology to communicate written assignments at least 50% of day as measured by personally developed daily checklists.

Access Skill:

The student will communicate through application software.

(Source: Virginia Department of Education, Standards of Learning, 2001, Computer/Technology 8.1)

Activities:

James will use a custom computer overlay to access keyboard keys in classroom, work, and community settings with typical peers and coworkers and use the computer to communicate within those settings. James began using assistive technology devices in fifth grade. His occupational, speech–language, and physical therapists collaborated with a local college's technology students and professors to devise a personalized communication system. These early efforts contributed to the success James enjoys today.

⊵ IEP Goal for History/Social Sciences

James will monitor his progress in his employment setting 100% time using a template and supporting software.

Access Skill:

The student will analyze career opportunities in terms of individual abilities, skills, and education and the changing supply and demand for those skills in the economy.

(Source: Virginia Department of Education, Standards of Learning, 2001, Civics/Economics 12)

Activities:

James will use an adapted template to measure his work output as he places bar codes on books in the employment site (bookstore). His supervisor or employment specialist will compare James's records with actual output at least once per employment shift. James has access to nondisabled peers at work because most employees are within 4 years of his age.

SUMMARY

Clearly, students with disabilities can and should have access to the general education curriculum. The law (IDEA, 1997) mandates that it occur, and the challenge for teams is to develop IEPs that meet a student's needs for functional skills while providing opportunities to learn academic content with peers without disabilities. This chapter provided examples of how to make this process work at both the elementary and secondary levels, but additional examples and demonstrations will be necessary to ensure that access to the general education curriculum occurs in individualized ways. The concept of universal design for instruction will open doors currently closed to students with disabilities, and the increase in our knowledge about student strategies for learning (particularly goal setting, problem solving, self-management, and self-assessment) will further the efforts of teachers to offer quality, individualized education based on the general curriculum. We look forward to seeing how much this field will progress in the next few years.

REFERENCES

Agran, M., Fodor-Davis, J., & Moore, S. (1986). The effects of self-instructional training on job-task sequencing: Suggesting a problem-solving strategy. *Education and Training in Mental Retardation, 21,* 273–281.

Borkowski, J. G., Weyhing, R., & Turner, L. (1986). Attributional retraining and the teaching of strategies. *Exceptional Children, 53,* 130–137.

Browder, D. (2001). Functional math. In D. M. Browder (Ed.), *Curriculum and assessment for students with moderate to severe disabilities* (pp. 225–226). New York: Guilford.

Browder, D. M., & Ware, K. (2001). Communication and social skills. In D. M Browder (Ed.), *Curriculum and assessment for students with moderate to severe disabilities* (pp. 320–321). New York: Guilford.

Bryant, D. P., & Bryant, B. R. (2002). *Assistive technology for people with disabilities.* Boston: Allyn & Bacon.

Bulgren, J. A., & Lenz, K. (1996). Strategic instruction in the content areas. In D. D. Deshler, E. S. Ellis, & B. K. Lenz (Eds.), *Teaching adolescents with learning disabilities: Strategies and methods* (2nd ed., pp. 409–473). Denver, CO: Love.

Erickson, K., & Koppenhaver, D. (1999, October). *Technology supports for balanced word level instruction in beginning reading.* Paper presented at the Closing the Gap Preconference, Minneapolis, MN.

Federal Register. (1999, March). Washington, DC: Government Printing Office.

Gersten, R., Walker, H., & Darch, C. (1988). Relationship between teachers' effectiveness and their tolerance for handicapped students. *Exceptional Children, 54,* 433–438.

Hughes, C. A., & Petersen, D. L. (1989). Utilizing a self-instructional training package to increase on-task behavior and work performance. *Education and Training in Mental Retardation, 24,* 114–120.

Individuals with Disabilities Education Act Amendments of 1997, 20 U.S.C. § 1400 *et seq.*

Inge, K. J., & Shepherd, J. (1995). Assistive technology applications and strategies for school system personnel. In K. F. Flippo, K. J. Inge, & J. M. Barcus (Eds.), *Assistive technology: A resource for school, work, and community* (pp. 133–166). Baltimore: Brookes.

Kleinert, H., Denham, A., Groneck, V., Clayton, J., Burdge, M., Kearns, J., et al. (2001). Systematically teaching the components of self-determination. In H. Kleinert & J. Kearns (Eds.), *Alternate assessment* (pp. 114–115). Baltimore: Brookes.

Kleinert, H., Haigh, J., Kearns, J., & Kennedy, S. (2000). Alternate assessments: Lessons learned and roads to be taken. *Exceptional Children, 67*(1), 51–53.

Kleinert, H., Hurte, M., Groneck, V., Fay, J., Roszmann-Millican, M., Hall, M., et al. (2001). Demonstrating performance across multiple environments. In H. Kleinert & J. Kearns (Eds.), *Alternate assessment* (pp. 186–187). Baltimore: Brookes.

Klinger, J. K., & Vaughn, S. (1999). Students' perceptions of instruction in inclusion classrooms: Implications for students with learning disabilities. *Exceptional Children, 66*(1), 23–37.

Knowlton, H. E. (1998). Considerations in the design of personalized curricular supports for students with developmental disabilities. *Education and Training in Mental Retardation and Developmental Disabilities, 33,* 95–107.

Mann, W. C., & Lane, J. P. (1991). *Assistive technology for persons with disabilities: The role of occupational therapy.* Rockville, MD: American Occupational Therapy Association.

Mithaug, D. E., Wehmeyer, M. L., Agran, M., Martin, J. E., & Palmer, S. (1998). The self-determined learning model of instruction: Engaging students to solve their learning problems. In M. L. Wehmeyer & D. J. Sands (Eds.), *Making it happen: Student involvement in educational planning, decision-making, and instruction* (pp. 299–329). Baltimore: Brookes.

Musselwhite, C. (2001, November). *Balanced literacy! Literacy for students with disabilities: It's a balancing act!* Paper presented at Techknowledgy, Virginia Commonwealth University Training and Technical Assistance Center, Richmond, VA.

Nolet, V., & McLaughlin, M. J. (2000). *Accessing the general curriculum: Including students with disabilities in standards-based reform.* Thousand Oaks, CA: Corwin Press.

Rose, D. H., & Meyer, A. (2002). *Teaching every student in the digital age: Universal design for learning.* Alexandria, VA: Association for Supervision and Curriculum Development.

Saddler, S., Thoma, C. A., & Whiston, S. (2002). School-to-career services and experiences: Are they linked with lower dropout rates for high school students in Nevada? *Workforce Education Forum, 29*(1), 41–50.

Scherer, M. J. (1998). *Matching person and technology (MPT) model manual* (3rd ed.). Webster, NY: Institute for Matching Person and Technology.

Steere, D. E., & Burcroff, T. L. (1997). Living at home. In P. Wehman & J. Kregel (Eds.), *Functional curriculum* (pp. 22–249). Austin, TX: PRO-ED.

Thoma, C. A., & Held, M. (2002). Measuring what's important: Using alternative assessments. In C. L. Sax & C. A. Thoma (Eds.), *Transition assessment: Wise practices for quality lives* (pp. 71–85). Baltimore: Brookes.

Virginia Department of Education. (n.d.). *Standards of learning.* Retrieved January 4, 2003, from http://www.pen.k12.va.us/VDOE/Superindendent/Sols/home.shtml

Virginia Department of Education. (2001). *Virginia alternate assessment implementation manual.* Richmond, VA: Author.

Wehman, P. (1997). Curriculum design. In P. Wehman & J. Kregel (Eds.), *Functional curriculum* (pp. 13–14). Austin, TX: PRO-ED.

Wehmeyer, M. L., Sands, D. J., Knowlton, H. E., & Kozleski, E. B. (2002). Achieving access to the general curriculum. In M. L. Wehmeyer, D. J. Sands, H. E. Knowlton, & E. B. Kozleski (Eds.), *Teaching students with mental retardation: Providing access to the general curriculum.* Baltimore: Brookes.

CHAPTER 5

Functional Academics

Pamela S. Wolfe and Richard M. Kubina Jr.

In this chapter you will be introduced to three students with disabilities: Jennifer, who has moderate to severe cognitive and physical disabilities; Casey, who has been labeled as behaviorally disordered; and Robert, who has a specific learning disability. Throughout the chapter we will define and discuss the importance of functional academic skills for students with disabilities. Further, we will examine practical activities in the goal area of functional academics for Jennifer, Casey, and Robert.

JENNIFER

Jennifer is 10 years old and has been diagnosed as having moderate to severe mental retardation and cerebral palsy. She began receiving early intervention services when she was 1 year old. Jennifer is currently enrolled in an inclusion classroom in her neighborhood school.

Jennifer lives at home with her mother and father, both of whom are employed full-time. Her mother works in the school district as a secretary and her father is an accountant. Fortunately, both of her parents are actively involved in Jennifer's educational planning and participate in a number of advocacy groups. Jennifer is an only child, but she is rarely alone because she has many friends from the community and her school.

Due to cognitive disabilities, Jennifer has low receptive and expressive language skills. She communicates using a DynaVox, which is an assistive device used to augment communication. Jennifer points to a picture board menu with icons that represent words. Communication aids such as the DynaVox permit Jennifer to "say" words to her nondisabled peers. Currently, a personal aide assists Jennifer with hygiene, toileting, eating, and mobility needs. She uses a manual wheelchair to travel throughout her environment. She is also able to use a computer in her classroom with a single switch. Jennifer's Individualized Education Program (IEP) team has identified a number of functional goals for her, including working toward greater independence in her environment. Specific goal areas include increased hygiene skills, greater mobility throughout the school, and more opportunity to access the community. Even though Jennifer has a severe cognitive disability, the team has also identified a number of functional academic goals in her IEP, including reading functional signs and using functional math such as number identification and time management.

CASEY

In the third grade, Casey was labeled as behaviorally disordered. Casey recently changed schools because his mother did not like him spending all of his time in a self-contained classroom. At his new school, Casey divides his time between a general education classroom and an emotional support room.

The school psychologist who diagnosed Casey, now age 14, believes many of his problems stem from his parents' painful divorce years ago. Casey sees his father, who moved to another state, during holidays and in the summer for 8 weeks. An only child, Casey does not have siblings in which to confide, nor does he have many friends at school. The last friendship Casey had fell apart when he aggressively bit his acquaintance over an innocuous argument.

Casey takes medication to help control his aggressive outbursts. To the chagrin of his mother and teacher, however, the medication does not seem to help at all. Casey often becomes angry when confronted with situations that cause even minimal discomfort. For example, in math class one day, Casey's teacher asked him to explain how he got an answer to an addition problem; Casey responded with profanities. He behaves similarly in English. He frequently misspells words and becomes very angry when his teacher provides corrective feedback. Although he has many redeeming qualities, such as a sense of fair play, good manners, and frequent displays of affection, Casey's inappropriate behaviors have interfered with his academic development and threaten to seriously disrupt his tenuous relationship with his teachers. Academically, Casey has a number of strengths and weaknesses. In the area of math, he has difficulty with money management. However, he has expressed a desire to "get out of school and get a job" and seems committed to that goal. Casey's IEP team has worked hard to permit him to explore a number of jobs in the community. Job exploration placements generally have been successful, but Casey's behavior has sometimes been an issue.

ROBERT

Robert, a 17-year-old of average intelligence, has a specific learning disability. In the fourth grade, Robert's teacher and a multidisciplinary team referred him for special education services. Robert had longstanding problems learning to read and had an extremely difficult time keeping pace with the class. His mother strongly supported Robert's placement in a learning support classroom for part-time instruction. Since the fourth grade, Robert has continued to receive special education services.

Robert lives at home with his mother, father, and two younger sisters. Both his father and mother work full-time, his father as an electrician and his mother as a postal clerk. Robert often watches his two younger sisters after school until one of his parents arrives home. Robert's sisters especially like when he makes peanut butter toast as a snack for them.

Robert has many strengths. His interpersonal qualities include a great sense of humor, a generous nature, and a commitment to his family and friends. Academically,

(continues)

Robert has good verbal skills and understands mathematical concepts well.

According to his teacher, however, Robert needs help with problem solving, planning and completing activities, and decoding and comprehending written text. Still, Robert does reasonably well in many of his classes, and he and his parents have considered his future graduation and postsecondary plans. IEP and transition team members believe Robert could attend community college or a university. His parents agree and believe that Robert could succeed in a higher education setting.

FUNCTIONAL CURRICULA

Perhaps one of most difficult yet fundamental questions teachers face is, "What is the goal of education?" What should teachers be doing with the valuable but limited time they have to educate students, particularly students with special needs who may require more time and practice to master skills? Traditional models of education have suggested that students be taught academic and enrichment content with the expectation that they will acquire the skills needed for living and working incidentally and on their own (Brolin, 1995). However, when this model was applied to students in special education, some students were found to lack necessary survival skills needed to function beyond the classroom. Further, the bottom-up or developmental approach in which students proceeded through stages of development before they could master other skills often resulted in nonfunctional, artificial, and inappropriate skill development (Brown et al., 1979). That is, students with a discrepancy between their mental age and chronological age would not get the opportunity to learn age-appropriate skills.

The need for functional curricula is evidenced by data illustrating poor school and postschool outcomes for special education students. Blackorby and Wagner (1996) found that students with disabilities lagged behind their nondisabled peers in graduation rates and other achievement indicators. The number of students with disabilities graduating with a high school diploma remains low at 30% (U.S. Department of Education, 1998). A national poll by Louis Harris and Associates (2000) reported that two thirds of Americans with disabilities between the ages of 16 and 64 are not working; the unemployment rate for people with disabilities currently ranges from 50% to 75% (Louis Harris and Associates, 2000). Given such data and a legislative mandate for transition planning, educators are realizing that students such as Jennifer, Casey, and Robert will need to be exposed to functional curriculum that enables them to succeed beyond the school's doors.

The ideology behind providing students with meaningful or functional skills was in evidence in the early 1900s when Dewey spoke of the need to learn by doing (Weaver, Landers, & Adams, 1991). Terms associated with functional curriculum have included criterion of *ultimate functioning, life skills, independent living skills, adaptive skills, daily living skills, work experience, vocational education, career education,* and *career development* (Brolin, 1995; Brown, Nietupski, & Hamre-Nietupski, 1976). The construct of functionality can be conceptualized as a thinking process used by teachers to answer questions such as, "How, when, and where will my students use this knowledge in their lives now and in the future?" (Weaver et al., 1991). Functional skills are useful in current as well as future environments and are determined by looking to the future (Browder & Snell, 2000; Morse & Schuster, 2000). Further, functional activities can be used in natural environments and focus on skills needed in areas such as employment and education, home and family, leisure pursuits, community involvement, physical and emotional health, and personal responsibility and relationships (Clark, 1994; Cronin & Patton, 1993). The functionality of a skill is contextually defined by each student and his or her own family. What is functional for one student may not necessarily be functional for another student in the same class. To determine whether a skill is functional for a particular student, educators should ask themselves several questions:

- Is the instructional content of the student's current educational placement appropriate for meeting the student's personal and social, daily living, and occupational adjustment needs?

- Does the content focus on necessary knowledge and skills to function as independently as possible in the home, school, or community?

- Does the content provide a scope and sequence for meeting future needs?

- Do the student's parents think the content is important for both current and future needs?

- Does the student think the content is important for both current and future needs?

- Is the content appropriate for the student's chronological age and current intellectual, academic, or behavioral performance level?

- What are the consequences of not learning the content or skills inherent in the current educational placement? (Clark, 1994, p. 37)

Cronin and Patton (1993) have identified a four-stage model of functional curriculum development, as outlined in Figure 5.1. The model suggests that functional curriculum can be developed by (a) identifying the major adult domains and subdomains that students need to function in as adults, such as employment and education, home and family, leisure pursuits, community involvement, physical and emotional health, and personal responsibility and relationships; (b) identifying major life demands or situations that most adults will encounter; (c) identifying specific life skills needed to meet each of the life demands that will be used as the basis for instructional objectives in the student's IEPs or transition plans; and (d) organizing instruction to teach functional skills by deciding what content to cover and how to do so.

Functional curricula traditionally have been associated with students who have severe cognitive disabilities. It was assumed that traditional academic content would not be useful for persons with severe disabilities but that training in adaptive skills would be necessary. Although adaptive skills often were viewed as dichotomous with traditional academic content, greater numbers of educators are now arguing that functional curricula should be a priority for all students (Algozzine & Audette, 1992; Brolin, 1995). That is, any skill that is taught in school should be examined to determine how it is of use to the student and when the skill will be used in everyday life.

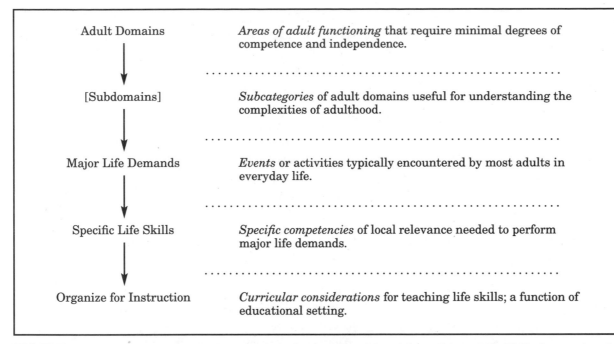

Adult Domains	*Areas of adult functioning* that require minimal degrees of competence and independence.
[Subdomains]	*Subcategories* of adult domains useful for understanding the complexities of adulthood.
Major Life Demands	*Events* or activities typically encountered by most adults in everyday life.
Specific Life Skills	*Specific competencies* of local relevance needed to perform major life demands.
Organize for Instruction	*Curricular considerations* for teaching life skills; a function of educational setting.

FIGURE 5.1. Top-down approach to curriculum development. *Note.* Adapted from *Life Skills Instruction for All Students with Special Needs* by M. E. Cronin and J. R. Patton, 1993, Austin, TX: PRO-ED, Inc. Copyright 1993 by PRO-ED, Inc. Adapted with permission.

FUNCTIONAL ACADEMIC CURRICULUM

Functional curricula can encompass a number of domain areas, including academic subjects. Functional academic domains include the three Rs of reading, writing, and arithmetic (Browder & Snell, 2000), as well as other related content areas of instruction, such as social studies, history, and science. Functional academic content areas are appropriate for all students with disabilities. A functional academic curriculum can cover any curricular skill. Table 5.1 lists traditional academic content areas and examples of functional activities that may be used to convey academic subject matter. Even when students are not able to master all the academic skills that are needed to participate in an activity, students can be taught to use adaptations (Browder & Snell, 2000).

Because functional academics can encompass a variety of life skills, it is important to identify what activities students may undertake when they leave the school system. Several authors have identified major activities or life demands that most adults must be able to perform and have developed curricula to aid educators in teaching those functional skills (e.g., Cronin & Patton, 1993; Dever, 1988). These curricula provide teachers with an idea of what skills may be needed and enable them to identify objectives, goals, and daily instructional activities. Tables 5.2 and 5.3 present matrices for elementary and secondary students, were developed by Cronin and Patton (1993), and illustrate the relationship between scholastic and social skills, as well as adult domains. The matrices illustrate how functional academic skills can be taught across a variety of curricular domains. Whether a student has a cognitive disability like Jennifer, a behavioral disorder

TABLE 5.1
Traditional Academic Content Areas and Examples of Functional Activities

Academic Content Area	Examples of Functional Activities
Reading	Read a newspaper article Read a recipe Read the signs on restroom doors Read instructions for video game Read a job application Read a course schedule of classes for college
Math	Add sales tax to purchase order Use calculator to add grocery item totals Compare prices at a local video store Calculate income tax return Compute square footage for a carpentry task
Science	Calculate boiling point for candy recipe Use medication chart Plant and harvest vegetable garden Identify weather to select appropriate clothing
Social Studies	Register to vote Identify cultural holidays and customs Identify headlines in newspapers Determine bus route in the community
Health	Brush teeth and practice proper oral hygiene Plan balanced meals Identify and purchase items for class first aid kit Identify health services in the community Label sexual feelings and attitudes
Expressive writing	Write a thank-you note Dictate a personal story Write a biography for college entrance application

such as Casey, or a learning disability like Robert, teachers can readily incorporate functional academic curricula into the student's daily lessons.

Jennifer, for example, the 10-year-old with mental retardation and cerebral palsy, is working on a functional academic curriculum in reading. Her teacher has devised a number of effective strategies that help Jennifer not only read better but target her reading materials and activities so they will have immediate use in her environment. Jennifer receives instruction and guided practice with "see-and-say" sight words. In the see-and-say sight word intervention, the teacher preselects a number of functional words and then teaches a small number of those words daily.

The teacher makes a deck of cards by printing each word on one side of an index card. She shows Jennifer one card and says the word (modeling). The teacher then asks Jennifer to say the word with her (guided practice). Then, the teacher asks Jennifer to say the word by herself (testing). This process is repeated with all of the cards. The procedure allows the teacher to immediately identify what words give Jennifer problems and allows Jennifer to receive immediate corrective feedback. After Jennifer can say the words correctly 2 days in a row, they go into a

(text continues on p. 121)

TABLE 5.2
Elementary School Matrix Showing Relationship of Scholastic and Social Skills to Adult Life Domains

	Employment/ Education	Home and Family	Leisure Pursuits	Community Involvement	Emotional/ Physical Health	Personal Responsibility/ Relationships
Reading	Read library books on various occupations	Read directions to prepare brownies from a mix	Look for ads in the newspaper for toys	Read road signs and understand what they mean	Locate poison control numbers in the phone-book	Read a story to a younger child
Writing	Write to the school board about a pothole in the school driveway	Make a list of items needed from the grocery store	Fill out a magazine order form completely	Complete an application to play Little League	Keep a daily diary of food you eat in each food group	Write a thank-you note to a relative for a gift
Listening	Listen to a lecture by a bank official on savings accounts	Listen to a lecture on babysitting tips	Listen to radio/TV to see if a ball game is rained out	Listen to a lecture on how children can recycle	Listen to the school nurse explain the annual eye exam for your class	Listen to a friend describe his or her family vacation
Speaking	Discuss reasons we work	Ask parents for permission to stay at a friend's house	Invite friends over to play Monopoly	Discuss park and play-ground improvements with the mayor	Ask the school nurse how to care for mosquito bites	Discuss honesty, trust, and promise. Define them.
Math Applications	Calculate how much you would make baby-sitting at $1.25 an hour for 3 hours	Compute the cost of a box of cereal using a coupon	Compute the cost of going to the movies	Compute tax on a video game	Calculate and compare the cost of different types of Band-Aids. Include tax.	Ask a friend to share a candy bar. Calculate your part of the cost.
Problem Solving	Decide which environment you work best in: out or in, quiet or noisy, active or at a desk, etc.	Decide how to share TV time with a sibling	Given $15 for the afternoon, which would you do: go to the movies, go bowling, or play videos?	Role-play the times you would use the 911 emergency number	Decide how many hours of sleep you need per night	Decide if you have enough coins to purchase a vending machine soda for you and your friend
Survival Skills	Keep homework assignments in a special notebook	Develop a checklist of what to do before and after school	Use a map to find the best way to the mall	Draw a map of the way you go to/from school	Mark the calendar for your next dental appointment	Identify important table manners
Personal/Social	Ask a classmate to assist you with a job	Settle a dispute with a sibling	Call a video store to see if they have a specific movie	Role-play asking a police officer for help if you're lost	Ask a friend to go bicycling with you	Role-play appropriate behavior for various places (movies, church, restaurant, ballpark)

Note. From *Life Skills Instruction for All Students with Special Needs* (pp. 32–33), by M. E. Cronin and J. R. Patton, 1993, Austin, TX: PRO-ED, Inc. Copyright 1993 by PRO-ED, Inc. Reprinted with permission.

TABLE 5.3

Secondary School Matrix Showing Relationship of Scholastic and Social Skills to Adult Life Domains

	Employment/ Education	Home and Family	Leisure Pursuits	Community Involvement	Emotional/ Physical Health	Personal Responsibility/ Relationships
Reading	Reading classified ads for jobs	Interpreting bills	Locating and understanding movie information in a newspaper	Following directions on tax forms	Comprehending directions on medication	Reading letters from friends
Writing	Writing a letter of application for a job	Writing checks	Writing for information on a city to visit	Filling in a voter registration form	Filling in your medical history on forms	Sending thank-you notes
Listening	Understanding oral directions of a procedure change	Comprehending oral directions about making dinner	Listening for forecast to plan outdoor activity	Understanding campaign ads	Attending lectures on stress	Taking turns in a conversation
Speaking	Asking your boss for a raise	Discussing morning routines with family	Inquiring about tickets for a concert	Stating your opinion at the school board meeting	Describing symptoms to a doctor	Giving feedback to a friend about the purchase of a compact disc
Math Applications	Understanding difference between net and gross pay	Computing the cost of doing laundry in a Laundromat versus at home	Calculating the cost of a dinner out versus eating at home	Obtaining information for a building permit	Using a thermometer	Planning the costs of a date
Problem Solving	Settling a dispute with a co-worker	Deciding how much to budget for rent	Role-playing appropriate behaviors for various places	Knowing what to do if you are the victim of fraud	Selecting a doctor	Deciding how to ask someone for a date
Survival Skills	Using a prepared career planning packet	Listing emergency phone numbers	Using a shopping center directory	Marking a calendar for important dates (e.g., recycling, garbage collection)	Using a system to remember to take vitamins	Developing a system to remember birthdays
Personal/Social	Applying appropriate interview skills	Helping a child with homework	Knowing the rules of a neighborhood pool	Locating self-improvement classes	Getting a yearly physical exam	Discussing how to negotiate a price at a flea market

Note. From *Life Skills Instruction for All Students with Special Needs* (pp. 32–33), by M. E. Cronin and J. R. Patton, 1993, Austin, TX: PRO-ED, Inc. Copyright 1993 by PRO-ED, Inc. Reprinted with permission.

"know" pile. The "practice" pile contains the words Jennifer has not mastered and a small number of new words. Jennifer's teacher made the see-and-say sight word method functional by selecting "survival words" based on interviews with Jennifer's parents and observations of Jennifer in community environments. Some of the words indicate potential hazards, such as *poison, danger,* and *stop.* Other words come from the community, such as *restroom* and *enter.* Jennifer is given many opportunities to use the functional sight words in actual community settings.

In the case of Casey, the 14-year-old with a behavior disorder, his teacher has found a functional curriculum very practical. Casey did not have a firm grasp on addition, and his teacher found that Casey understood better when actual coins were used in teaching. The teacher used nickels and dimes to help Casey learn "skip counting" or "count byes." Skip counting refers to a student learning to count by a number of a specific multiple (Stein, Silbert, & Carnine, 1997). By lining up 20 nickels, Casey quickly learned to skip-count or count by 5s (i.e., 5, 10, 15, 20, 25, 30, 35, 40, and so on, up to 100). He then learned to skip-count by 10s with the dimes.

The teacher made the task functional by having Casey count by multiples of 5 and 10, thereby teaching Casey the value of money. Casey found it took more nickels than dimes to make a dollar, a functional aspect of money usage. Additionally, the skip counting serves as an important foundation for learning other money skills. For example, making equivalent change involves grouping smaller value coins for larger ones such as giving two dimes and a nickel for a quarter (Stein et al., 1997).

The last student, Robert, the 17-year-old with a learning disability, also has benefited from a functional curriculum. As Robert prepares to make the transition from high school to a community college, his teacher has focused on several skills to prepare him for the demands of a postsecondary environment. Expressive writing is one of the many important skills Robert will need for entrance into college and throughout his educational experience. Thus, his teacher decided to use a strategy known as *mediated scaffolding* to help Robert become a better writer. Mediated scaffolding refers to different types of assistance teachers provide to help students better understand instruction (Dixon, Isaacson, & Stein, 1998). Robert has learned to use "think sheets," which guide writers in using effective planning or organizational strategies (Dixon et al., 1998). Robert's teacher has made the skill functional by using the think sheets with writing tasks that Robert will face in college, such as expressing himself on the college entrance exam.

ASSESSMENT OF FUNCTIONAL ACADEMIC SKILLS

Assessment is an essential feature of meaningful educational programming; teachers assess students to gain information for the purposes of screening, placement, curriculum development, and student evaluation (Salvia & Ysseldyke, 2000). Traditional assessment measures primarily have consisted of standardized tests that compare a student's academic and behavioral performance with that of other students. When using functional curricula, however, educators need assessment techniques that yield meaningful information about how well an individual will perform in natural environments (Brolin, 1995). Although some functional academic skills can be assessed using standardized tests, other functional assessment strategies can include rating scales and inventories, as well as performance-based measures such as portfolios, curriculum-based assessment, precision teaching, and ecological inventories.

Rating Scales and Inventories

Rating scales and inventories can be developed commercially or by teachers to assess functional academic skills. Information for assessment is collected in a variety of ways, including review of the student's file, staffing notes, interview results, observations, test and work sample administrations, situational assessments, and curriculum-based assessments (Brolin, 1995; Brown & Snell, 2000). Scales and inventories typically list a number of functional competencies that teachers, parents, and other persons involved in the student's life can use as a benchmark to assess whether the student has the specified competency.

Performance Assessment

Performance assessment is concerned with how a student applies knowledge, rather than how he or she simply acquires knowledge or facts. The central difference between traditional and performance assessment is the type of response that is required by the student. Standardized tests require that a student select and mark the correct response; performance assessment requires the student to produce or perform a response (Poteet, Choate, & Stewart, 1993). Closely related to performance assessment is authentic assessment. Performance assessment becomes authentic when it requires the tasks to be performed in natural contexts and under natural conditions and demands (Meyer, 1992). Authentic performance assessments frequently have been used in vocational domains through the use of situational assessments, work samples, and simulations (Poteet et al., 1993) and are easily applied to assessment of functional academic skills. An example of an authentic performance assessment for Robert occurred when his teacher videotaped his actual college entrance interviews and then provided him with constructive feedback. Types of authentic performance assessment include portfolio and curriculum-based assessment, precision teaching, and ecological inventories.

Portfolio Assessment

Portfolio assessment continues to gain favor among educators as a means for collecting observable evidence or products of performance assessment (Poteet et al., 1993). Portfolio assessment uses records of a student's work over time that illustrate the depth, breadth, and development of the student's academic abilities. It should involve a purposeful and systematic collection of the student's work (Pierce & O'Malley, 1992). Portfolios have helped evaluate the performance of writers with disabilities in both general and special education settings (Jochum, Curran, & Reetz, 1998). Portfolios also have supported secondary students with mental retardation in advancing self-determination skills (Ezell, Klein, & Ezell-

Powell, 1999). Additionally, early childhood teachers have used portfolios to increase the acceptance of children with disabilities with their peers (Morrison, 1999).

The purpose of a portfolio will determine its content, but teachers generally use two common types of portfolios: working portfolios that represent the student's academic work in progress and permanent portfolios that present the best and most comprehensive assessment of the student's work (Grady, 1992). If needed, a portfolio can provide a method for generating support strategies (Shure, Morocco, & DiGisi, 1999) and assessment of instructional programs in inclusion settings (Salend, 2000). Robert's teacher took advantage of portfolio assessment by maintaining a working portfolio of Robert's expressive writing from the last marking period. The portfolio showed noticeable improvement in Robert's writing. For example, his paragraph length increased to four to five sentences, and he demonstrated more syntactic maturity. Table 5.4 illustrates some examples of the kinds of materials used in an assessment portfolio for several functional academic domains.

Curriculum-Based Assessment

Curriculum-based assessment, another type of performance assessment, is conducted in the curriculum of the school and is tied to the actual classroom material being taught so that teachers are able to directly determine the extent to which students are learning (Fuchs & Deno, 1994). Although there are a number of curriculum-based assessment methods available, all share three features: (a) student proficiency is sampled from materials found in the school's curriculum, (b) assessments recur over time, and (c) information from the assessment is used to formulate instructional decisions (Tucker, 1987). Figure 5.2 presents an example of a curriculum-based assessment conducted for Jennifer. A graph of the correct and incorrect sight words Jennifer learned is displayed. The graph shows a lack of progress for the first week. However, when her teacher applied a goal-setting intervention, Jennifer showed steady progress toward her goal of 10 correct functional words with no errors. Both Jennifer and her teacher liked seeing Jennifer's progress visually, and the progress provided an opportunity to celebrate success.

Precision Teaching

Originally founded by Ogden Lindsley, Precision Teaching refers to methods and practice procedures that promote the systematic and precise evaluation of instruction or curricula (Lindsley, 1972, 1990, 1997; West & Young, 1992). A group of tenets best exemplifies the Precision Teaching method: (a) basing curricular decisions on the student's performance (i.e., "The student knows best"), (b) using frequency for measurements, (c) using the standard celeration chart to display frequency data, and (d) focusing instruction and practice on directly observable behavior (Lindsley, 1972; White, 1986). Precision Teaching also has an extensive database of research examining fluency, that is, the highly accurate and automatic responses typical of a competent performer (Binder, 1996).

Casey's teacher used Precision Teaching to help him become more fluent in money computation. His teacher used the Standard Celeration Chart that showed a low line of progress (see Figure 5.3). By projecting the line of progress into the future, Casey's teacher realized it would take 3 months for Casey to reach his fluency aim of adding basic coins if he proceeded at his current rate of progress. To

TABLE 5.4
Examples of Assessment Portfolios

Type of Portfolio	Contents
Reading portfolio	Audiotape of oral reading of selected passages Original story grammar map Transcript of story retelling Log of books read with personal reactions, summaries, vocabulary Representative assignments: responses to pre- and postreading questions Favorite performance Journal entries including self-evaluation
Science portfolio	Representative work samples Student-selected best performance Report from hands-on investigation Notes on science fair project Journal entries including self-evaluation Learning progress record Report cards Personal journal
Writing portfolio	Scrapbook of representative writing samples Selected prewriting activities Illustrations or diagrams for one piece Log or journal of writing ideas, vocabulary, semantic maps, compositions, evaluations Conference notes, observation narratives Student-selected best performance Self-evaluation checklists and teacher checklists
Social studies portfolio	Representative work samples Student-selected best performance Design of travel brochure, packet or itinerary of trip Notes on history fair project Journal entries including self-evaluation
Generic portfolio	Tests Significant daily assignments Anecdotal observations
Mathematics portfolio	Reports of mathematical investigations Representative assignments Teacher conference notes Descriptions and diagrams of problem-solving processes Video, audio, or computer-generated examples of work Best performance Journal entries including self-evaluation
Arts portfolio	Best performance Favorite performance First, middle, and final renderings of projects Tape of performance Journal entries including self-evaluation Photographs Awards Personal goals

Note. From "Performance Assessment and Special Education: Practices and Prospects," by J. A. Poteet, J. S. Choate, and S. C. Stewart, 1993. *Focus on Exceptional Children, 26,* 9. Copyright 1993 by Love. Reprinted with permission.

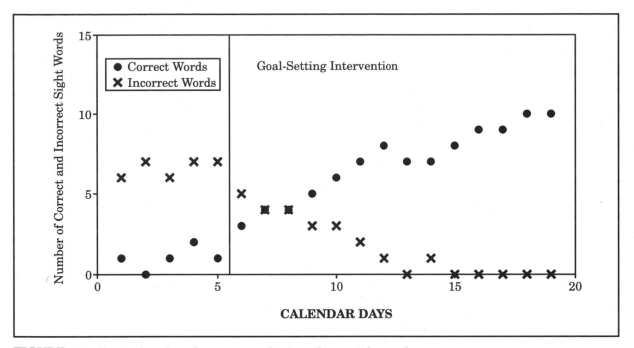

FIGURE 5.2. Curriculum-based assessment for Jennifer on sight words.

find a more effective method of instruction, Casey's teacher first tried using a ticket system, whereby Casey earned tickets for a raffle at the end of the week. The data showed that the ticket system did not produce rapid growth in Casey's learning. Casey's teacher tried another intervention called sprinting (i.e., taking small chunks of the behavior and practicing it), which did result in a dramatic improvement. Casey spent greater time-on-task, exhibited fewer behavioral issues during the intervention, and liked seeing his performance charted daily.

Ecological Inventories

Ecological inventories are another way to conduct a functional assessment and are typically associated with students who have more severe disabilities. An ecological inventory is based on the top-down approach to skill development and focuses on skills needed in the natural environment as the source of curriculum content (Brown et al., 1979). Ecological inventories assess a student's strengths and weaknesses within natural environments; information from the inventories can help determine how well a student performs activities within frequently accessed environments. Environments selected to be inventoried typically are identified through primary caregiver interviews and represent activities of present and future importance to the student (Browder, 1987). Results of ecological inventories are of particular use in functional assessment because instructional objectives can be directly identified from functional performance of the skill. The results of the inventory can be used to help decide whether to teach an adaptive skill or adapt the situation to facilitate student performance (Downing & Perino, 1992). Steps in conducting an ecological inventory include (a) identifying the appropriate

(text continues on p. 128)

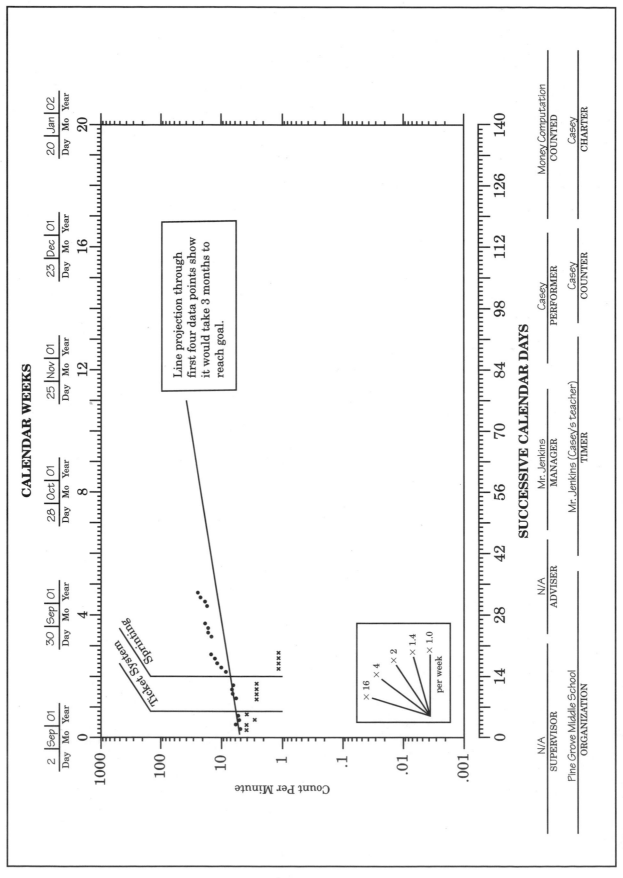

FIGURE 5.3. Chart showing how precision teaching improved Casey's money computation.

Domain: Domestic

Environment: Elementary Classroom

Subenvironment: Kitchen

Activity: Lunch preparation

Activity 1: Planning lunch menu
  Skill 1: Determine meal (sandwich, milk, dessert).
  Skill 2: Determine if ingredients are available in cupboards and refrigerator.
  Skill 3: If item is unavailable, place on shopping list.
  Skill 4: Determine amount of food necessary to make meal.

Activity 2: Food preparation—sandwich
  Skill 1: Read recipe.
  Skill 2: Locate ingredients and utensils.
  Skill 3: Take bread out of wrapper.
  Skill 4: Using butter knife, spread peanut butter on one slice of bread.
  Skill 5: Spread jelly on the other slice of bread.
  Skill 6: Assemble sandwich.
  Skill 7: Cut sandwich in half.

Activity 3: Food preparation—beverage
  Skill 1: Take milk out of refrigerator.
  Skill 2: Get glass out of cupboard.
  Skill 3: Pour milk into glass.

Activity 4: Food preparation—dessert
  Skill 1: Choose fruit from cupboard or refrigerator.
  Skill 2: Open can of fruit.
  Skill 3: Obtain bowl from cupboard.
  Skill 4: Pour fruit into bowl.

Student: Jennifer Godshall	Domain: Domestic
Date: November 1, 2003	Environment: Elementary Classroom
Teacher: Sue Smith	Subenvironment: Kitchen

Nonhandicapped Person Inventory	Student Inventory	Discrepancy Analysis	What-To-Do Options
Activity: Planning lunch menu			
Skills: Determine meal (sandwich, milk, dessert)	+		
Determine if ingredients are available in cupboards and refrigerator	−	No strategy to determine	Add picture cues to cupboards and refrigerator
Place on shopping list if unavailable	−	Unable to write	Develop a menu of pictures to use to construct shopping list
Determine amount of food needed to make meal	+		

(continues)

FIGURE 5.4. Ecological inventory for Jennifer. *Note.* Adapted from *Community-Based Curriculum* (2nd ed.), by M. Falvey, 1989, Baltimore: Brookes.

Nonhandicapped Person Inventory	Student Inventory	Discrepancy Analysis	What-To-Do Options
Activity: Food preparation—sandwich			
Skills: Read recipe	−	Not able to read	Develop picture recipes and teach
Locate ingredients and utensils	−	Unable to find	Add picture cues for ingredients and utensils and teach
Take bread out of wrapper	−	Lacking pincer grasp	Use bread without twist ties and improve pincer grasp skills
Spread peanut butter on one slice of bread	−	Bread tears	Use toast
Spread jelly on the other slice of bread	−	Bread tears	Use toast
Assemble sandwich	+		
Cut sandwich in half	+		
Activity: Food preparation—beverage			
Skills: Take milk out of refrigerator	−	Not enough muscle strength to open refrigerator	Teach her to use two hands or provide hand-over-hand assistance
Get glass out of cupboard	−	Drop glass	Use unbreakable cup
Pour milk into glass	−	Often tips glass over	Use holder to steady glass
Activity: Food preparation—dessert			
Skills: Choose fruit from cupboard or refrigerator	−	Unable to find	Provide picture cues on cupboard and refrigerator
Open can of fruit	−	Lack of muscle strength and pincer grasp	Teach to use electric can opener
Obtain bowl from cupboard	+		
Pour fruit into bowl	+		

FIGURE 5.4. *Continued.*

curriculum domain; (b) identifying the environment; (c) identifying subenvironments within the environment; (d) identifying activities that occur in the subenvironment; (e) determining whether the student has the skills to perform the activities required in the subenvironment; and (f) if the student does not have the skills, deciding how to teach the skills, teach an adaptation, or modify the environment (Falvey, 1989). Figure 5.4 presents an ecological inventory that has been conducted for Jennifer. Notice that even in the domestic domain the inventory revealed a number of academic skills for Jennifer to work on in areas of functional reading and math.

INSTRUCTIONAL METHODS FOR TEACHING FUNCTIONAL ACADEMICS

A number of methods may be used to teach functional academic skills to students with disabilities. Critical to any successful teaching strategy, however, is empirical research. Instructional methods such as direct instruction, learning strategies, and applied behavior analysis all have a common empirical basis that indicates their effectiveness for teaching functional academic content.

Direct Instruction

Direct instruction (Engelmann, 1997; Engelmann & Carnine, 1991) is a teaching approach that offers a variety of research-based practices aimed at helping learners achieve academic content at high rates. Direct instruction emphasizes sequenced tasks verified and modified by field tests, instructional sequences that teach the learner skills directly and efficiently, and procedures that take into account research on learning (Engelmann, 1997). Direct instruction tenets can improve functional academic content areas such as reading, expressive writing, mathematics, science, and social studies (Kame'enui & Carnine, 1998).

One useful strategy of direct instruction is a correction procedure that helps students quickly grasp content. In the correction procedure, the teacher models the correct answer, leads the student response, and then tests the student for a correct response (Carnine, Silbert, & Kame'enui, 1997). By immediately receiving feedback in a systematic manner, students quickly learn from their mistakes and acquire the instructional content.

Casey's teacher used direct instruction to teach functional spelling words. The words selected were deemed functional because Casey will use them when he obtains employment. Casey learns *morphographs,* which include prefixes, (e.g., *un-, re-*) suffixes (e.g., *-ed, -ing*), and word bases (*late, do*). By learning morphographics, Casey can spell many words by making combinations. For instance, he could spell *relate, unrelated, undoing, redo,* and *doing.* When Casey makes a mistake, his teacher uses a model–lead–test correction procedure. Casey's teacher immediately stops the group lesson and models the correct response, leads the group saying the correct response, and then tests to see if the group can perform the correct word. Casey experiences success with this method because he does not practice errors and quickly applies his new skills to the task at hand.

Learning Strategies

Due to their disability, some students may experience difficulty acquiring information in traditional formats. Learning strategies help compensate for limitations brought about by a disability by enabling students to acquire academic content. The University of Kansas Center for Research on Learning (n.d.) has developed and researched a variety of learning strategies in content areas such as reading and math and other areas such as demonstrating competence, improving social interactions, and storing, remembering, and expressing information.

Robert has benefited from learning strategy instruction. Robert's teacher knew that Robert's reading disability would make reading and comprehending text difficult. Strategy instruction was critical for Robert because he will soon enter college where he will encounter a variety of tasks that call for reading comprehension. To prepare Robert for upcoming college life, his teacher taught Robert a learning strategy called RAP (Schumaker, Denton, & Deshler, 1984). RAP helps students comprehend written text by using the following mnemonic:

Read a paragraph.

Ask, "What were the main idea and details of the paragraph?"

Put the main idea and details in your own words.

Robert's teacher gave Robert a variety of materials with which to test the RAP strategy. One reading task called for Robert to identify a major he would like to pursue in college and then read his college's undergraduate degree program booklet to determine what he needed to graduate with a degree in the major. Using the RAP strategy, Robert identified the main ideas presented in the program booklet and listed in his own words what courses he needed to graduate.

Applied Behavior Analysis

Applied behavior analysis is rooted in the influential work of B. F. Skinner and the theory of operant conditioning. Central to the theory is the notion that consequences can be arranged to modify human behavior (Alberto & Troutman, 1999). Elements of applied behavior analysis can be used to teach functional academic skills. Useful principles include prompts and consequences arranged to affect student performance.

Prompts are used to aid student responses and can vary depending on the task and the student. Prompts can be verbal, pictorial or written, gestural, model, or partial or full physical (Snell & Brown, 2000). Jennifer's teacher has used a variety of prompts when working on Jennifer's functional academic skills. For example, when instructing Jennifer on functional reading and math activities, such as following a recipe, her teacher uses verbal prompts and modeling at some steps of a task analysis. In addition, her teacher color-coded some utensils to aid Jennifer in the activity.

Consequence strategies also can be used to enhance student performance. One consequence strategy is the use of positive reinforcement. Positive reinforcement increases the rate and probability of a correct student response. Reinforcement can include primary and secondary reinforcers. Primary reinforcers are unlearned and include edibles (i.e., food or liquids) and sensory reinforcers (i.e., visual, auditory, tactile, olfactory, or kinesthetic experiences). Secondary reinforcers are those whose meaning has been learned and can include tangible reinforcers (e.g., privileges or activities), generalized reinforcers (e.g., tokens, points, credits), and social reinforcers (e.g., verbal expressions, physical proximity; Alberto & Troutman, 1999). Reinforcers should be as natural as possible; objects and activities that are typically part of an environment should be used rather than introducing new items to the environment. Reinforcers are individually determined and can vary for each student and over time. Jennifer's teacher used positive reinforcement when working on functional academic skills. For example, Jennifer received verbal reinforcement at each step of a task when "reading" a recipe. Once Jennifer completed the recipe, she was naturally reinforced by getting to consume her efforts.

IMPLEMENTING FUNCTIONAL ACADEMIC CURRICULA

Because the functionality of curricula is contextually bound, each individual student will need different skills to function in future environments. In all cases, however, educators must attend to *where* and *how* functional academic skills are taught. Where skills are taught may include instruction in integrated and community settings. How skills are taught should include attention to issues of social validity.

Implementing Functional Academic Curricula in Integrated Settings

Functional academic skills can be taught to students with special needs in any educational environment, including integrated settings (Browder & Snell, 2000). Table 5.5 depicts a method for integrating functional curricula into a student's educational program based on models developed by Bradley, King-Sears, and Tessier-Switlick (1997); Giangreco, Cloninger, and Iverson (1998); and Janney and Snell (2000). Also given in the table is a practical example of each level of integration. The model illustrates how functional academic content can be taught to students of any disability level in integrated settings. Because of the range of possible adaptations and accommodations, educators can ensure that functional

TABLE 5.5
Functional Academic Instruction in Integrated Settings and Examples for Jennifer

Level of Integration	Description	Example
1. Unadapted participation in the regular curriculum	Same activities, same objectives, same setting	Jennifer participates with the rest of the class in visiting the library to locate a book or magazine.
2. Adaptations to the regular curriculum	Same activities, different (related) objectives, same setting	Jennifer participates in a game of Nerf dodgeball and uses her wheelchair to ambulate.
3. Embedded skills within the regular curriculum	Similar activity, different (related) objectives, same setting	While the class is working on writing a short story about community workers, Jennifer uses the newspaper to identify pictures of community workers.
4. Functional curriculum in the regular education classroom	Different activities, different (related) objectives, same setting	While the class is working on fractions, Jennifer identifies necessary measuring cups for a recipe.
5. Functional curriculum outside the regular education classroom	Different activities, different (unrelated) objectives, different setting	While the class works on a science project, Jennifer is briefly removed from the classroom to practice hygiene skills.

academic skills outlined in the student's IEP are being addressed in inclusive settings.

Implementing Functional Academic Curricula in Community Settings

Functional academic skills can be taught outside the classroom in the community itself. Community-based instruction, also referred to as community-referenced instruction or in situ instruction (Browder & Snell, 2000; Kluth, 2000), entails taking students into the community for skill acquisition and practice in the setting where the skills will be used. Community-based instruction has been used with students who have a variety of disabilities in both self-contained and inclusive settings (Kluth, 2000). Further, community-based instruction has been used to teach functional academic skills such as reading (e.g., signs, menus, schedules) and math (e.g., calculating a tip, paying for a purchase; Beakley & Yoder, 1998; Morse & Schuster, 2000). Jennifer and Casey currently are involved in community-based training. Jennifer is working on functional math skills in the community. As written in her IEP, she spends part of each week visiting restaurants and stores where she is learning to handle money using a next-dollar strategy (i.e., counting "one-more-than" when making a purchase; McDonnell & Ferguson, 1988). Casey also is participating in community-based instruction. Because of his goal to attend a vocational trade school, Casey spends a few hours each week in an employment setting where he is able to explore vocational interests and practice his math skills.

Social Validation of Methods, Materials, and Outcomes

The concept of social validity is a critical component in the development of functional curriculum. Social validity can be used to evaluate the social acceptability of what and how skills are taught. A large body of research on social validity focuses on treatment acceptability or the appropriateness of the treatment procedures (Gresham & Lopez, 1996). For a curriculum to be deemed functional, it must be judged to be socially valid. Social validity can be determined by asking whether the goals, procedures, and effects of an intervention or instructional goal are acceptable as judged by the person with a disability, educators, and the community at large (Bernstein, 1989).

Closely related to the concept of social validity is the concept of age appropriateness. Functional curriculum focuses on the development of skills that are representative of a student's chronological rather than developmental age. For example, even though Jennifer may be functioning on a lower cognitive level, she is working on age-appropriate goals. As indicted on her IEP, Jennifer is working on reading functional signs in present and future environments. Further, instead of learning a nonfunctional and age-inappropriate skill such as counting blocks, Jennifer is working on functional math skills such as using money and measuring. Jennifer's teacher also is making certain that the manner in which she instructs Jennifer is socially valid. For example, because Jennifer is in an included classroom, her teacher uses the same reinforcers and consequences that are available to all students in the class. Robert's teachers also are cognizant of the need to help Robert attain socially valid outcomes in his coursework. For Robert to succeed in a college setting, he will need to read and comprehend materials as accurately as his peers without disabilities. As a result, Robert is using learning strategies to help him achieve his academic goals. Attention to the social validity of goals, instructional procedures, and outcomes cannot be underscored; research has shown that individuals with disabilities who are depicted engaging in non-functional and age-inappropriate activities are perceived less favorably by others in the community (Bates, Morrow, Panscofar, & Sedlak, 1984; Calhoun & Calhoun, 1993). Obviously, educators who are teaching functional skills are more likely to be teaching socially valid skills.

FUNCTIONAL ACADEMICS IN IEPs AND TRANSITION PLANNING

IEPs typically consist of annual goals and short-term objectives; they are used by many educators as a basis for daily instructional programming and curricular development (Sands, Adams, & Stout, 1995). Functional academic objectives should be part of every IEP. Each IEP team should question whether the goals and objectives are functional for the student and whether they will have real-life use. Tables 5.6, 5.7, and 5.8 list functional academic objectives and related activities for Jennifer, Casey, and Robert, respectively. For example, Jennifer is working on skills such as reading a picture schedule and identifying her first and last name. Casey is developing skills in math by creating a budget and working with money. Casey's teachers have developed activities that build on each other. In one instance, his social studies teacher is involving him in planning a trip. Casey's activities will include planning the route, figuring the cost of the trip, and determining what sights to see. Robert also is involved in functional academic activities. His IEP objectives are centered on skills he will need while in college. For example, he is working on test-taking strategies and time management. The IEP objectives in Tables 5.6, 5.7, and 5.8 illustrate that, although they may differ based on the age and disability of the student, the academic goals are functional and have real-life applications.

The Individuals with Disabilities Education Act of 1990 mandates that transition planning occur for every student with a disability by the age of 16 to better ensure a smooth transition from school to postschool environments. A transition plan provides a plan for services rather than a plan for skill or knowledge acquisition. Typically, a transition plan is organized around content areas similar to those in functional curricula and may include areas such as employment, living arrangements, getting around in the community, financial independence, making friends, sexuality and self-esteem, and having fun (Wehman, 2001). Casey and Robert both have transition plans in place. Casey's plan details, among other things, how he will continue to be involved in vocational exploration and paid job experiences. Robert is working on transition into a college setting. His transition plan details specific steps to make admission into the college of his choice a reality. For example, his transition team has listed activities such as filling out applications, visiting colleges, and speaking with college disability personnel. In addition, the transition team is making sure that Robert is taking necessary classes

TABLE 5.6
Selected IEP Functional Academic Objectives and Related Activities for Jennifer

Objective	Related Activity
Mathematics	
Use next-dollar strategy to purchase items in school and community.	Use appropriate predetermined bills in vending machines (e.g., soda, candy, gum, laundry detergent).
	Use public telephones.
	Use public transportation.
	Shop and buy needed personal hygiene materials.
Demonstrate knowledge of concept of one-to-one correspondence.	Set table placing one plate, napkin, fork, knife, spoon, cup, and saucer at each place setting for class snack.
	Conduct class lunch count.
Use picture schedule for daily scheduled activities.	Select items needed for class activities according to picture schedule.
	Independently move to activity when given a verbal cue.
Measure liquid and powdered substances using measuring cups.	Measure detergent to wash laundry for gym clothes. Measure to prepare simple meals.
Reading	
Identify first and last name.	Find school locker, gym locker, personal basket, and work materials by using printed name as a cue (picture cues provided as needed).
Read functional signs and demonstrate the meaning of each sign.	Use functional signs to distinguish between women's and men's restrooms in school and in the community.
	Recognize basic safety signs and follow them (e.g., stop, green light, poison).
	Place poison stickers on unsafe containers in school and home (with parent assistance).
	Read picture thermometer and select clothing appropriate for the weather.

while in high school that will prepare him for college. He also is working with team members on self-advocacy skills so that he is able to communicate with college personnel about his needs while at college.

SUMMARY

The need for functional curricula has been highlighted by current postschool outcomes for students with disabilities. Functional academic curricula include reading, math, and related content areas such as science, social studies, and language arts. Functional academic curricula should be included in the IEPs of all students

TABLE 5.7
Selected IEP Functional Academic Objectives and Related Activities for Casey

Objective	Related Activity
Mathematics	
Prepare a shopping list using newspaper circulars to compare prices and identify items to purchase within budget guidelines.	Construct a shopping list of grocery items needed to make a simple meal.
	Use circulars from local grocery stores to make price comparisons to determine the better buy.
	Choose and cut out appropriate coupons for items on grocery list.
	Compute total for purchases, including special prices and coupons.
	Shop for items for home economics class at the local grocery store.
	Use catalogs and local circulars to choose items to purchase within a set budget.
	Fill out order form for those catalog items and calculate price, including sales tax and shipping costs.
	Calculate the total for the same catalog order using a credit card (including finance charges).
Social Studies	
Identify and participate in discussions about local, national, and world current event topics from newspapers, television, and current periodicals.	Use newspapers to identify current event topics.
	Discuss current event issues with regular education peers.
	Watch news and discuss events with parent, peers, and teacher.
	Read and recall current event articles from periodicals (e.g., *Newsweek*).
	Participate in current event games.
Use a map to plan a trip, calculating number of miles for the trip, identifying restaurants and hotels, and estimating the total cost for the trip.	Choose a rental car from a local dealership. Call or visit dealerships and compare prices, miles per gallon, safety features, and available options.
	Determine items needed for trip such as location, planned activities, and season of the year and write a detailed packing list.
	Plan route using map, including miles, cities, routes to follow, time required for trip, and when to stop for gas.
	Call travel agencies (e.g., AAA) for literature on hotels, restaurants, leisure activities, and local tourist attractions.
	Estimate costs of trip.

TABLE 5.8
Selected IEP Functional Academic Objectives and Related Activities for Robert

Objective	Related Activity
Note Taking	
Use effective note-taking strategies for both visual and auditory media.	Take notes from oral lectures.
	Use effective note-taking techniques such as abbreviation.
	Make notes when reading textbooks.
	Make notes from different textbooks (science, history).
	Outline chapters in textbooks.
Time Management	
Organize and schedule daily events that occur in school.	Schedule activities for a Saturday in a day planner.
	Prepare a schedule for studying, working, and leisure time.
	Self-check a planned schedule and determine if all the objectives were met.
Test Taking	
Use various forms of study to prepare for an exam.	Use different strategies for taking tests in general (e.g., listen to tape-recorded lectures).
	Respond to different kinds of test items, including true–false, multiple choice, completion, and essay.

with special needs. Educators should be challenged to reflect on whether what is being taught includes activities and skills with real-life application. The precise functional academic skills to be taught should be individualized and can be determined by using meaningful assessment strategies. Assessment techniques can include the use of rating scales and inventories, as well as performance-based measures such as curriculum-based assessment, precision teaching, portfolios, and ecological assessments. Empirically based teaching strategies can be used to teach functional academic skills, including direct instruction, learning strategies, and applied behavior analysis. Further, functional academic skills can be taught in a variety of settings such as inclusive settings and in the community. Whatever and wherever skills are taught, educators should ensure that the goals, procedures, and outcomes are socially valid. By including functional academic skills into IEPs and daily programming, educators can be sure that students such as Jennifer, Casey, and Robert can participate and succeed in integrated settings, whatever the students' goals.

REFERENCES

Alberto, P. A., & Troutman, A. C. (1999). *Applied behavior analysis for teachers* (5th ed.). Upper Saddle River, NJ: Merrill.

Algozzine, B., & Audette, B. (1992). Free and appropriate education for all students: Total quality and the transformation of American public education. *Remedial and Special Education, 13*(6), 8–18.

Bates, P., Morrow, S. A., Panscofar, E., & Sedlak, R. (1984). The effect of functional vs. nonfunctional activities on attitudes/expectations of nonhandicapped college students: What they see is what we get. *Journal of the Association for Persons with Severe Handicaps, 9*(2), 73–78.

Beakley, B., & Yoder, S. L. (1998). Middle schoolers learn community skills. *Teaching Exceptional Children, 30,* 16–21.

Bernstein, G. S. (1989). In response: Social validity and the report of the ABA task force on right to effective treatment. *Behavior Analyst, 12*(1), 97.

Binder, C. (1996). Behavioral fluency: Evolution of a new paradigm. *Behavior Analyst, 19,* 163–197.

Blackorby, J., & Wagner, M. (1996). Longitudinal postschool outcomes of youth with disabilities: Findings from the National Longitudinal Transition Study. *Exceptional Children, 62,* 399–413.

Bradley, D. F., King-Sears, M. E., & Tessier-Switlick, D. M. (1997). *Teaching students in inclusive settings.* Boston: Allyn & Bacon.

Brolin, D. E. (1995). *Career education: A functional life skills approach* (3rd ed.). Englewood Cliffs, NJ: Prentice Hall.

Browder, D. (1987). *Assessment of individuals with severe handicaps: An applied behavior approach to life skills assessment.* Baltimore: Brookes.

Browder, D. M., & Snell, M. E. (2000). Teaching functional academics. In M. S. Snell & F. Brown (Eds.), *Instruction of students with severe disabilities* (5th ed., pp. 493–542). Upper Saddle River, NJ: Merrill.

Brown, F., & Snell, M. E. (2000). Measurement, analysis, and evaluation. In M. E. Snell & F. Brown (Eds.), *Instruction of students with severe disabilities* (5th ed., pp. 173–206). Upper Saddle River, NJ: Merrill.

Brown, L., Branston, M. B., Hamre-Nietupski, S., Pumpian, I., Certo, N., & Gruenewald, L. (1979). A strategy for developing chronological-age-appropriate and functional curricular content for severely handicapped adolescents and young adults. *Journal of Special Education, 13*(1), 81–90.

Brown, L., Nietupski, J., & Hamre-Nietupski, S. (1976). Criterion of ultimate functioning. In M. A. Thomas (Ed.), *Hey, don't forget about me!* (pp. 2–13). Reston, VA: Council for Exceptional Children.

Calhoun, M. L., & Calhoun, L. G. (1993). Age-appropriate activities: Effects on the social perception of adults with mental retardation. *Education and Training in Mental Retardation, 28,* 143–148.

Carnine, C. W., Silbert, J., & Kame'enui, E. J. (1997). *Direct instruction reading* (3rd ed.). Upper Saddle River, NJ: Prentice Hall/Merrill.

Clark, G. M. (1994). Is a functional curriculum approach compatible with an inclusive education model? *Teaching Exceptional Children, 26*(2), 36–39.

Cronin, M. E., & Patton, J. R. (1993). *Life skills instruction for all students with special needs.* Austin, TX: PRO-ED.

Dever, R. B. (1988). Community living skills: A taxonomy. In D. E. Brolin (Ed.), *Career education: A functional life skills approach* (pp. 4–5). Englewood Cliffs, NJ: Prentice Hall.

Dixon, R. C., Isaacson, S., & Stein, M. (1998). Effective strategies for teaching writing. In E. J. Kame'enui, D. W. Carnine, R. C. Dixon, D. C. Simmons, & M. D. Coyne (Eds.), *Effective teaching strategies that accommodate diverse learners* (2nd ed., pp. 93–119). Upper Saddle River, NJ: Merrill.

Downing, J., & Perino, D. M. (1992). Functional versus standardized assessment procedures: Implications for educational programming. *Mental Retardation, 30*(5), 289–295.

Engelmann, S. (1997). Direction instruction. In C. R. Dills & A. J. Romiszowski (Eds.), *Instructional development paradigms* (pp. 537–554). Englewood Cliffs, NJ: Educational Technology.

Engelmann, S., & Carnine, D. (1991). *Theory of instruction: Principles and applications* (Rev. ed.). Eugene, OR: ADI Press.

Ezell, D., Klein, C. E., & Ezell-Powell, S. (1999). Empowering students with mental retardation through portfolio assessment: A tool for fostering self-determination skills. *Education and Training in Mental Retardation and Developmental Disabilities, 34*(4), 453–463.

Falvey, M. (1989). *Community-based curriculum: Instructional strategies for students with severe handicaps* (2nd ed.). Baltimore: Brookes.

Fuchs, L. S., & Deno, S. L. (1994). Must instructionally useful performance assessment be based in the curriculum? *Exceptional Children, 61*(1), 15–24.

Giangreco, M. F., Cloninger, C. J., & Iverson, V. S. (1998). *Choosing outcomes and accommodations for children* (2nd ed.). Baltimore: Brookes.

Grady, E. (1992). *The portfolio approach to assessment.* Bloomington, IN: Phi Beta Kappa Educational Foundation.

Gresham, F. M., & Lopez, M. F. (1996). Social validation: A unifying concept for school-based consultation research and practice. *School Psychology Quarterly, 11,* 204–227.

Individuals with Disabilities Education Act of 1990, 20 U.S.C. § 1400 *et seq.*

Janney, R., & Snell, M. E. (2000). *Teachers' guide to inclusive practices: Modifying schoolwork.* Baltimore: Brookes.

Jochum, J., Curran, C., & Reetz, L. (1998). Creating individual educational portfolios in written language. *Reading and Writing Quarterly: Overcoming Learning Disabilities, 14*(3), 283–306.

Kame'enui, E. J., & Carnine, D. W. (1998). *Effective teaching strategies that accommodate diverse learners.* Upper Saddle River, NJ: Prentice Hall.

Kluth, P. (2000). Community-referenced learning and the inclusive classroom. *Remedial and Special Education, 21,* 19–26.

Lindsley, O. R. (1972). From Skinner to precision teaching: Teaching the child knows best. In J. B. Jordan & L. S. Robbins (Eds.), *Let's try doing something else kind of thing* (pp. 1–11). Arlington, VA: Council for Exceptional Children.

Lindsley, O. R. (1990). Precision teaching: By teachers for children. *Teaching Exceptional Children, 22*(3), 10–15.

Lindsley, O. R. (1997). Precise instructional design: Guidelines from precision teaching. In C. R. Dills & A. J. Romiszowski (Eds.), *Instructional development paradigms* (pp. 537–554). Englewood Cliffs, NJ: Educational Technology.

Louis Harris and Associates. (2000). *The N.O.D./Harris survey program on participation and attitudes: Survey of Americans with disabilities.* New York: Author.

McDonnell, J., & Ferguson, B. (1988). A comparison of general case in vivo and general case simulation plus in vivo training. *Journal of the Association for Persons with Severe Handicaps, 13,* 116–124.

Meyer, C. A. (1992). What's the difference between authentic and performance assessment? *Educational Leadership, 49*(8), 39–40.

Morrison, R. (1999). Picture this! Using portfolios to facilitate the inclusion of children in preschool settings. *Early Childhood Education Journal, 27,* 45–48.

Morse, T. E., & Schuster, J. W. (2000). Teaching elementary students with moderate intellectual disabilities how to shop for groceries. *Exceptional Children, 66,* 273–288.

Pierce, L. V., & O'Malley, J. M. (1992). *Performance and portfolio assessment for language minority students.* Washington, DC: National Clearinghouse for Bilingual Education.

Poteet, J. A., Choate, J. S., & Stewart, S. C. (1993). Performance assessment and special education: Practices and prospects. *Focus on Exceptional Children, 26,* 1–20.

Salend, S. (2000). Strategies and resources to evaluate the impact of inclusion programs on students. *Intervention in School and Clinic, 35*(5), 264–270.

Salvia, J., & Ysseldyke, J. E. (2000). *Assessment* (6th ed.). Boston: Houghton Mifflin.

Sands, D. J., Adams, L., & Stout, D. M. (1995). A statewide exploration of the nature and use of curriculum in special education. *Exceptional Children, 62,* 68–83.

Schumaker, J. B., Denton, P. H., & Deshler, D. D. (1984). *The paraphrasing strategy.* Lawrence: University of Kansas Press.

Shure, A., Morocco, C. C., & DiGisi, L. L. (1999). Pathways to planning. *Teaching Exceptional Children, 32,* 48–54.

Snell, M. E., & Brown, F. (2000). Development and implementation of educational programs. In M. E. Snell & F. Brown (Eds.), *Instruction of students with severe disabilities* (5th ed., pp. 115–172). Upper Saddle River, NJ: Merrill.

Stein, M., Silbert, J., & Carnine, D. (1997). *Designing effective mathematics instruction: A direct instruction approach* (3rd ed.). Upper Saddle River, NJ: Prentice Hall/Merrill.

Tucker, J. (1987). Curriculum-based assessment is no fad. *Collaborative Educator, 1*(4), 4, 10.

University of Kansas Center for Research on Learning (n.d.). *Strategic instruction model learning strategies.* Retrieved October 14, 2002, from http://www.ku-crl.org/htmlfiles/lscurriculum/lsdescription.html

U.S. Department of Education. (1998). *Implementation of the Individuals with Disabilities Act: Twentieth annual report to Congress.* Washington, DC: Author. (ERIC Document Reproduction Service No. ED424722)

Weaver, R., Landers, M. F., & Adams, S. (1991). Making curriculum functional: Special education and beyond. *Intervention in School and Clinic, 25,* 284–287.

Wehman, P. (2001). *Life beyond the classroom* (3rd ed.). Baltimore: Brookes.

West, R. P., & Young, K. R. (1992). Precision teaching. In R. P. West & L. A. Hamerlynck (Eds.), *Designs for excellence in education: The legacy of B. F. Skinner* (pp. 113–146). Longmont, CO: Sopris West.

White, O. R. (1986). Precision teaching–Precision learning. *Exceptional Children, 52*(6), 522–534.

CHAPTER 6

Financial Planning and Money Management

Kathryn Banks

The primary goal of a longitudinal curriculum designed to teach financial planning and money management skills is for the learner to be able to manage personal finances independently upon his or her transition to adult life. Elementary, middle, and high school teachers; administrators; special education directors; parents; and adult service agencies must believe that this goal is both realistic and attainable and must coordinate their efforts for it to become a reality for students with cognitive disabilities.

The 1997 reauthorization of the Individuals with Disabilities Education Act sharply criticized special education programs for ineffectiveness. Congress charged that the expensive programs in place were not based on proven research and expected too little of students with disabilities (Wright & Wright, 1999). Special educators must become more adept in providing instruction that enables all students with disabilities to lead successful and independent lives to the fullest extent possible. Productive adults in our society are financially responsible and are able to manage their money independently. If disabled individuals are to be regarded as productive adults, they must learn the same financial planning and money management skills that are required of their nondisabled peers.

THOMAS

Thomas is 21 years old. He completed high school with a special education diploma. He has a mild intellectual disability and a measured full-scale IQ of 58. He participated in the vocational evaluation and work adjustment programs at Goodwill Industries through funding provided by the Georgia Division of Rehabilitation while he was still enrolled in high school. After 6 months of training, he had a productivity rate of between 85% and 90% of the industry standard required to hold a competitive job. Therefore, he was deemed ready for entry-level employment 2 years before his graduation and was placed at a local restaurant as a custodial worker.

Over a 3-year period, Thomas held three jobs. His first placement was successful insofar as Thomas learned the duties of the job, how to travel independently, and the social skills necessary to maintain employment. Neither his teacher nor vocational counselor identified his lack of money management and financial planning skills as a potential problem.

Early in his first placement, he developed the habit of cashing his paychecks and stopping by the mall to make unnecessary purchases. He would come home

(continues)

without the funds he needed for bus fare and lunch the following week. Thomas's teachers talked to him about being more responsible with his money, but they did not intervene with this behavior. They assumed that personal finances were private issues for Thomas and his mother to address. He was taught basic money management skills using general worksheets and lessons that were unrelated to his real-life situation. His limited cognitive ability made it difficult for him to generalize the skills he learned in the classroom to his current predicament. His lack of maturity was also a factor in his behavior.

Thomas's family members experienced a loss of income directly related to his job placement because their public assistance check was reduced to reflect Thomas's earnings. As a result of this development, as well as Thomas's inability to manage money and plan for expenses, his mother encouraged him to quit his job and insisted that he return to school. She complained to his vocational counselor that Thomas did not understand how to manage his money, and she asked that his teachers help him build these skills so that he could return to work without spending his earnings inappropriately.

For the next year, Thomas remained in school where he worked to develop money management and financial planning skills. His teachers were able to increase his counting skills from sums of up to $5.00 to sums of up to $20.00. He demonstrated an understanding of job-related expenses using individualized lessons and drill activities. During Individualized Education Program (IEP) meetings, he stated that he understood the importance of spending his money wisely and promised to do so when he returned to work. The team decided that it was time to try a job placement again.

Thomas's next job lasted only 3 weeks. He was unable to gain the speed necessary to maintain employment at a local dry cleaner. He ironed all of his own clothes extremely well and was proud of this skill. Thomas was very disappointed in the company's decision to let him go and had a difficult time overcoming the rejection.

He was soon placed at a neighborhood grocery store as a courtesy clerk earning minimum wage plus tips. Thomas was provided a job coach to assist him with locating merchandise in the store because his reading deficit made it difficult for him to do this essential job function fast enough without additional training. He was able to transfer to this job the mobility skills he had developed from his placement at the restaurant. Thomas maintained this job, although his mother reported that he continued to cash his checks at work and come home with little or no money. He made inappropriate purchases, and she feared that he was being cheated out of some of the money. He often needed her assistance with transportation and lunch money to continue to maintain his employment.

DESCRIPTION OF CURRICULUM

Financial responsibility and money management skills that allow individuals with disabilities to function independently in the community are appropriate and realistic educational outcomes that must be taught early. Financial responsibility as an outcome of the educational experience for students with disabilities requires mastery of the same money management and financial planning skills that are required of all learners. However, the curriculum and methods of instruction for these students will differ significantly from those of their nondisabled peers (Langone, 1992).

Special Needs

Students with mild to moderate cognitive deficits fall significantly behind general education students academically. By the time they reach high school, students with intellectual disabilities will have attained functional grade-level scores that are 6 or more years behind those of their nondisabled peers (Dreshler & Schumaker, 1986). In addition, the ability to generalize or transfer skills from one setting to another is poor for students with mild cognitive disabilities, and the difficulty students have with generalization increases with the severity of impairment (Langone, 1992). These factors make it difficult for instructors to teach money management and financial planning skills in the context of the traditional classroom setting. Yet, students with mild to moderate intellectual disabilities are most often served in traditional classroom settings that afford limited opportunity for community-based instruction (Roessler, 1991). The curriculum accepted by many teachers of students with mild to moderate cognitive impairment will focus primarily on money management and financial planning skills taught in isolation using repetition of facts and lists (Langone, 1992).

It is well documented through research that students with mild to moderate cognitive impairment retain to the greatest degree those skills learned in the situation where the skills will be used. Although students with mild disabilities express the same need and desire for independence as their nondisabled peers, their slower ability to learn, retain, and transfer skills requires a more concrete approach to instruction. Instructional methods that use functional materials in the most realistic setting possible will promote the retention and transfer of money management and financial planning skills more adequately than other curriculum designs (Brolin, 1993).

Curriculum for this population is most effective when it is longitudinal in design, that is, when money management and financial planning skills are systematically presented beginning in the elementary grades. The curriculum should build on a network of prerequisite skills that are continued throughout secondary school until the student transitions into adult life as a financially responsible individual. Materials used in instruction must mimic those most often used in adult environments. For example, money used to teach counting skills should be a copy of real money. Teachers may photocopy currency at either 75% or 150% of its actual size for bills and at the exact size of coins using black ink. Teachers should make sure that any copies of U.S. currency could not be mistaken for the real thing. All materials used to facilitate the mastery of money management and financial planning skills from elementary through secondary school should mimic, as close as possible, the same items used in the adult world.

Sequence of Instruction

A longitudinal curriculum for money management and financial planning must reflect the sequence of events that will take place when the skill is to be used in real life. For example, a houshold's once-a-week grocery shopping trip requires that food purchases be planned ahead using lists and coupons; this process involves the development of sound financial planning skills. To develop these skills, teachers should plan lessons using a classroom shopping center and focus on classroom activities that build skills for the buying process. Community-based shopping trips will then be used to reinforce the skills introduced and practiced in the classroom. In Table 6.1, the sequence of activities for students to practice grocery shopping skills in a real-life environment is described.

Teachers should use a variety of similar activities to encourage skill mastery and promote the transfer of money management and financial planning skills to the adult environment. Community-based sites should also vary as much as possible to further encourage the transfer of skills once they have been learned. Skill maintenance activities are continued after the teacher has recorded and analyzed data on worksheets that document mastery of objectives. More complex shopping trips that involve major purchases such as appliances, electronics, furniture, or real estate could be added as student skill levels increase. As students prepare to transition into the adult world, teachers need to communicate the level of support that a student will need with adult agencies, so making the transition is seamless. Often, individuals with cognitive impairment do not continue to demonstrate mastery of these skills after graduation without some assistance from adult service providers, parents, friends, or advocates. The transition planning process should be used to pass on this information to the next individual responsible for assisting the individual.

The sequence of activities described in Table 6.1 is at an advanced level and appropriate for students in the upper grades. Students who have achieved advanced mastery of these skills should also be taught to compare layaway purchases with credit card and rent-to-own purchases. High-priced items at a rent-to-own store can often tempt adults with mild to moderate disabilities into mistakenly signing a contract for immediate gratification rather than using a layaway plan. The difference in cost between the two options is extreme and difficult for individuals with cognitive disabilities to distinguish without prior training. Using credit and checking accounts, as well as understanding interest

TABLE 6.1
Learning Grocery Purchasing Skills

Sequence	Activity
Monday	Students plan individual weekly menus to include food items needed for breakfast, lunch, supper, and snacks.
Tuesday	Students compile a list of individual items and food amounts needed to complete the menu. Menus are based on student preference.
Wednesday	Students check weekly advertisements and coupons against items needed. Substitutions may be made for specials and coupon items that save money.
Thursday	Students compute the approximate cost of the menu using pricing information obtained from store advertisements and coupons. Students will compare the cost of the items with their personal weekly budget. Weekly budgets are based on realistic income potential.
Friday	Students visit the supermarket and practice selecting the items on the list. Students will calculate the difference between estimated and actual cost. Calculators with tapes can be used to total items for purchase as these items are selected. Students will record the information in a weekly budget ledger.

rates and billing procedures, are important skills that can only be addressed successfully at the secondary level if the required prerequisite skills have been mastered in the earlier grades.

Some budgeting skills mentioned in Table 6.1 are examples of the prerequisite skills required of students learning how to use credit and banking services appropriately. Students must first learn how to budget money effectively. They must then understand how their budget translates into shopping for necessities before they can master appropriate use of credit cards and checking accounts.

Elementary and middle school teachers must foster student mastery of these skills by presenting longitudinal lessons in the context of where the skill will be used in adult life. Successful mastery of basic financial planning and money management skills in early grades has a direct impact on the mastery of more advanced financial concepts in later grades. In turn, students who are expected from elementary school to master independent skills will have a better chance to become adults who are able to live independently.

Table 6.2 shows how an elementary or middle school teacher would plan a group lesson around a shopping trip. Group activities for elementary and middle school students assist students with developing prerequisite skills such as measurement, vocabulary, and creative writing in the context that the students will be expected to use later. Teachers could creatively promote a contest where classes compete for prizes for the best cookie or the best advertisement. The income produced by the sale will provide a tangible and realistic avenue for teaching prerequisite skills such as budgeting and projecting food costs. Students with well-developed skills should serve as peer tutors for those students who need more extensive remediation and drill to master the objective. Activities such as these also promote inclusion in the regular education classroom. Students with disabilities who are taught using a challenging curriculum will more easily fit in with their nondisabled peers (Jones & Carlier, 1995).

TABLE 6.2
Planning a Shopping Trip

Sequence	Activity
Monday	As a group, students will discuss and make plans for a cookie sale. They decide on the cookie of choice. Students will plan the sale and begin to advertise the sale to peers, adults, and family.
Tuesday	Students will make a list of the required ingredients to make the cookie of choice. Amounts needed for each ingredient are calculated. Students will continue to advertise the sale to peers, adults, and family.
Wednesday	Students will compute the estimated cost of ingredients needed. They will look at store advertisements and coupons available to reduce costs. Students will estimate the cost of the ingredients and determine the price of the cookie. Students will add the price per cookie to their sale advertisements. Students will take orders and collect money.
Thursday	Students will go to the supermarket to select and purchase ingredients. They will compare estimated costs to actual costs. Students will return to school and make a schedule for baking and distributing the cookies the next day. They will continue to collect money.
Friday	Students will bake, package, and deliver cookies to customers. Students will compute the cost and profit of the sale. The students will evaluate their sale, discuss possible changes, and decide how to continue the program.

Lessons using a similar plan-of-action format are useful in teaching money management and financial planning skills because they focus on the development of skills in the context of their use. Students also find such lessons more interesting than the paper-and-pencil rote learning activities currently taught in many special needs classrooms. The prerequisite skills that students develop in the learning process will serve as a foundation for the higher order thinking skills required for learning to budget money and prepare for both expected and unexpected expenses as an adult. If these concepts are introduced in the elementary grades, students will become accustomed to planning for expenses, comparing prices, calculating food amounts, estimating costs, and adjusting menus to save money, making it easier for the high school teacher to use the community as a classroom for more advanced lessons.

Students taught using this type of instructional format would also learn how to write number words using a check and how to sign their name using the method that they will most often employ as adults. They will be exposed to and master the real-life skills necessary for true financial responsibility as they prepare for transition into the community as productive citizens. Teachers employing this type of curriculum will become agents of positive change in the lives of their students and their families.

Self-Determination

Students with mild to moderate cognitive impairments need training and support that will empower them to take control of their finances. Anyone who assumes that a student cannot achieve mastery of these skills, especially a young student, is delaying the instruction and support that fosters independence. Such delay may also perpetuate the assumption in the general public that students with disabilities are unable educationally to attain this goal.

A person who takes control of a cognitively impaired individual's personal finances may feel as though he or she is providing appropriate assistance, but in reality, such assistance only fosters dependence. When adults with disabilities depend on others to perform their adult tasks for them, they are unlikely to feel empowered by their income, and some may not see the need to remain employed. This perception of dependence will diminish their ability to function in the community independently in their own minds as well in the minds of others (Wehmeyer & Kelchner, 1995). Students with disabilities have a right to expect that their planned educational program will focus on the acquisition of skills that will foster their ability to live independently as adults.

The 1997 reauthorization of IDEA blatantly accuses special education classrooms of being expensive havens of lowered expectations and few educational results. Far too many adults who were classified as cognitively impaired as children and who received many years of costly special education services have left school unable to hold jobs or live independently in the community, thus requiring expensive intervention by government-funded programs. The law demands that special education programs be revised to support classrooms where students with disabilities master the skills they need to become self-actualized adults. IDEA also demands that students with disabilities receive these services in a regular education setting with their nondisabled peers to the greatest extent possible. In many classrooms across the United States, this is not the case (Wright & Wright, 1999).

IDEA clearly makes it necessary that all special education programs reevaluate current curriculum and hold teachers accountable for meeting the individual educational needs of students with disabilities using curricula and teaching methods that are research based and focused on increased expectations for learning. Although school systems can rightfully argue that implementation of IDEA has been seriously underfunded in past years, it will be difficult to convince Congress to allocate even more money for programs that have shown little success in meeting even the most basic learning needs of students with disabilities (Wright & Wright, 1999). Dedicated educational professionals have a responsibility to provide quality instruction that will support our students as they make a successful transition into the adult world.

Community-Based Instruction

Community-based instruction is an essential tool in a longitudinal curriculum for money management and financial planning for the learner with special needs. Teachers must develop relationships with local bankers and retail managers that allow frequent access to community sites for instructional purposes. These positive relationships with community sites should begin in the elementary grades and continue throughout the secondary level as a regular component of any curriculum that is designed to teach financial planning and money management skills.

Educators should find a wealth of support in the community because educational programs that strive to develop independent skills in potential customers are extremely useful to local businesses and industry leaders. Well-trained consumers make good customers. Usually banks and retail stores have slower periods that will facilitate student visitation, and most have customer service representatives who will be eager to assist teachers with training. Many communities have established school–business partnerships in an organized effort to link the school and community. These business partners often provide staff time and resources that encourage employee participation in school-related activities.

Classroom Learning Centers

Teachers who photograph or videotape community-based excursions will find the tapes and pictures useful in the development of authentic classroom learning centers. Teachers must get written permission to photograph and videotape both students and business locations ahead of time (Salend, 1995). Learning centers link the classroom setting to community sites and can be used to reinforce a variety of skills. These centers should be developed at every grade level to replicate the essential functions of the community sites.

For example, a classroom banking center that is equipped with the appropriate forms can be developed by a team of teachers and shared between classrooms. A well-stocked classroom banking center allows students to concentrate on the repetition of banking skills while in a simulated banking environment. Local banks can provide samples of the forms needed to build these skills. Teachers will need to adapt the forms based on the instructional level of the student. The center must be constructed as close as possible to the physical structure of a bank. Teachers will find that constructing realistic community learning centers in the classroom is a creative and fun activity. A supermarket or drugstore center could also be built using the same format. Teachers who undertake such a project with a team of their peers in surrounding schools will decrease the labor and expense involved, as well as foster communication with teachers across grade levels. Teachers who work in teams to create community centers will improve the quality of their instruction and increase the availability of useful instructional tools. Realistic banking and marketing centers will enhance students' ability to generalize financial planning and money management skills from the classroom to the community. A classroom that resembles the community is more functional than a traditional classroom because it helps students blend the two locations and assists teachers with facilitating successful adult transitions by promoting student generalization of these skills.

To construct a classroom banking center, creative teachers could enlist the help of volunteers to design and build a center that is appropriate for the classroom situation. The design must be as portable as possible so that the teachers sharing the center could easily transport and store the components when it is not in use. For instance, art students could draw and paint cardboard sections to mimic the teller window at a local bank. Folding tables could be covered in paper and arranged in the room to display the forms students need to complete their transactions. Cardboard tubes could be dressed up using contact paper, and inexpensive rope could be strung between the tubes to simulate the materials that direct customers to form one line like those at local banks.

Creative teachers should approach center design in much the same way that a drama teacher would create a set for a school play. Involving general education teachers and students in the process can promote an inclusive environment in a fun setting. Some school systems and colleges require that their students participate in volunteer projects, and savvy special education teachers can benefit from students' time. Parents also make great volunteers.

Teachers should always involve their students in the design and building process to create even greater learning opportunities. Teachers should document the entire process with photographs or video, both to record the events and to make a visual reminder that can be used later by others interested in creating their own classroom centers. Again, teachers must get signed consent forms in advance for persons who will appear in photographs or videos. With a little elbow grease and a vivid imagination, special educators can turn their classrooms into community learning environments and reap many rewards by watching their lessons come alive for students.

Parental Support and Participation

Perhaps the single most often overlooked factor in the process of developing skills related to financial planning and money management for students with disabilities is that of parental participation and support. Too often, teachers initiate only limited connections with parents, usually centered on IEP meetings or school behavioral problems. Parental participation and support for the development of the skills that lead to independence is critical. Without this support, teachers often find that even the most creative and coordinated instructional lessons do not translate into a student's success in the real world.

There are many possible barriers to parental participation and support. Parents may feel out of place or intimidated by the school setting or the advanced educational level of the professionals involved with their child. Educational jargon may be difficult for parents to translate into the action steps they must take to be true participants in the skill-building process. They may be reluctant to accept their child's disability and unable to provide assistance at that particular time.

The amount of time needed for a parent to participate may be difficult to arrange around work or the care of small children and elderly or ill family members. The parent's level of competence in the skills related to money management may be below that which is necessary to assist in the skill-building process, and the parent may be reluctant to tell the teacher that he or she lacks the required skills.

There may be a cultural or a language barrier between parent and teacher. Parents may have a different financial agenda for their child than one that leads to independence. They may place reading skills at a higher priority than money management and financial planning skills. Or parents may not see the need to start early, especially if the student is in the elementary grades. The parents themselves may have a physical or emotional disability. Teachers may feel that it is easier to plan for and carry out lessons without parental assistance. Some teachers will make little effort to involve parents beyond what is required by law because such a relationship is time-consuming and difficult to maintain.

The problem with a teacher using an isolated approach is that very little personally appropriate and realistic financial skills training can occur within a vacuum. Students with mild to moderate intellectual disabilities need the support of everyone involved in their educational program to successfully develop the skills they need to become independent adults. Smart teachers realize the significant contributions that parents can make and will be relentless in their efforts to involve their parents in the quest to teach financial planning and money management skills.

Every family has a unique method for managing household finances. Issues surrounding personal finances are extremely private in many cultures and are often considered off-limits to everyone but the individuals immediately involved. At best, the subject is tricky to discuss in the school setting.

The teacher who shows true concern for the student's need and desire for an independent future can overcome many of the barriers involved to parental participation. A teacher who is tactful and nonjudgmental in approaching parents will more easily gain true support. Teachers who build a bridge of support between home, school, and community will see their students become successful money managers with at least an active role in planning their financial future.

When a teacher focuses questions on the student's access to money, parents should become more willing to share personal information. In addition, the parents' responses will give the teacher an idea of how money is managed in the student's home. Teachers also can determine parents' attitudes about their child's ability to gain independence through this type of dialogue. It goes without saying that parents must believe that the personal information they share with teachers will be kept strictly confidential. Privacy is of particular importance in issues related to money management and financial planning.

When a teacher has built a bridge of support with parents, he or she should ask the parents the following question: What goals do you have for your child related to money management and financial planning in the coming year?

When the parents respond, the wise teacher will work diligently to develop the particular skill that is requested, even if it is not the skill the teacher would have chosen. The teacher will contact the parent often to report progress and to solicit help in reaching the goal. The best approach when communicating with parents is to treat them as equal partners in their child's education. Partners always work together better when everyone involved feels that their assistance is equally vital to the successful outcome of the collaboration. Teachers may find this difficult when a parent is uneducated or demanding, but parents will usually become more reasonable when they feel that the teacher is a partner and not the one with all the answers. Parents with limited skills know their limitations and will appreciate teachers who can remain nonjudgmental and focus on their child's success despite the obstacles.

If a parent wants a teacher to develop skills for his or her child that are not related to money management and financial planning, the teacher should target beginning instruction objectives to the skills that were requested by the parent. Because the teacher demonstrates a sincere respect for the parent's initial request, a climate of mutual respect begins to develop, paving the way for the teacher to initiate instruction in other subject areas.

Parents of students with special needs often complain that teachers seldom give homework. Teachers who assign homework related to parents' initial skill development request often uncover the perfect opportunity to initiate ongoing parental support. Parents rarely refuse a teacher's request when that teacher has demonstrated a personal commitment to their child's success. Cooperation is contagious on every level. Wise teachers often find that when they use this same approach in dealing with administrators and inclusion teachers, the special needs child becomes welcome in the general education environment.

Parents know the needs of their children better than anyone else, and teachers who work with parents in this way will achieve positive results. Even if a parent requests something totally outside of what can be reasonably accomplished, the teacher should break the task down into manageable objectives and work toward the requested goal. Once the student has made tangible progress, the teacher can request parental assistance for meeting additional objectives.

Teachers must document this information in the minutes of IEP reviews so that the next teacher will be able to continue to build the bridge of support with the family. If possible, teachers should contact each other to share information such as, "Tom's mother is really sensitive about his inability to count money. She will welcome and assist with any home assignments you send to reinforce this skill." Further, teachers will save each other time by sharing this type of information. This knowledge will also assist the new teacher in making a positive initial contact with the parent.

Nothing fosters support more than when a teacher calls a student's home at the beginning of the school year with information that lets the parent know that the teacher is knowledgeable about the needs of the child and is ready to begin at the point where the former teacher left off. This process also builds esteem in parents because it helps them feel that the teacher appreciates that they are crucial to their child's educational progress. Parents who feel like active participants in the IEP process will be more available to support the teacher (Roessler, 1991). These parents may also help the teacher build support from other parents.

As parents begin to see their child gain the skills required for independence, it should become easier for them to relinquish the control that fosters dependence. A true partnership between school and home will help build the confidence and self-determination skills that are necessary for students to learn the skills they need to become independent adults. When the process begins in the early grades and is fostered throughout high school and into adult life, independent living will become more of a reality than it is presently. The special education classroom will be transformed from a room of lowered expectations to a center of true educational achievement.

GENERAL APPROACHES TO ASSESSMENT

The purpose of assessment is to determine a student's present level of performance of an individual skill or group of skills related to money management and financial planning. An accurate assessment of student performance will enable the IEP team to develop goals and objectives that will target the skills that need to be developed or increased. An ongoing evaluation of performance will assist teachers with the task of moving as rapidly as possible from one skill level to the next and provide information for planning skill maintenance activities. The assessment process is key to the success of a longitudinal curriculum for money management and financial planning because by targeting specific skill areas that need work, teachers can make the best use of their limited instructional time.

The main components of an accurate assessment include observation, task analysis, situational assessment, and measurement of general knowledge. The evaluator combines the results of these evaluations for an accurate picture of the student's money management and financial planning skills. Consistently accurate data collected over a designated period of time is a key factor to reporting accurate results. Simply measuring student skills once or twice per year to obtain a general grade-level score will do little to document the true present level of a student's performance.

Data collection is painstaking and time-consuming and usually not the favorite activity of most teaching professionals. Yet this aspect of the assessment process is extremely important for accurate evaluation. Teachers who are disciplined in the collection of data will find that the process enables them to make real progress with students and use their time wisely.

General Knowledge Assessment

Many reliable instruments are available that determine the general performance level of money management and financial planning skills for students with cognitive impairment. The *Brigance Inventory of Essential Skills* (Brigance, 1981) can be used to determine functional skill levels for students with mild disabilities, particularly the section of the test related to money and finance skills. The *Brigance Life Skills Inventory* (Brigance, 1995) also has a comprehensive assessment for money and finance skills and ranges in difficulty from second- to eighth-grade levels. A "quick-screen" battery contains a small sample of items to provide teachers with a short diagnostic placement level, but this quick screening tool should be used only to assess skills, not to make placement decisions. Teachers may also use the quick-screen battery to verify results obtained from other assessments and to identify those skills that need more extensive evaluation. A number of the skills assessed in the full money and finance section of the *Brigance Life Skills Inventory* are listed in Table 6.3. Both inventories are comprehensive criterion-referenced assessments that identify the skills that have been previously mastered by the student, assisting the teacher in determining the next step in instruction.

The *Scales of Independent Behavior–Revised* (Brunininks, Woodcock, Weatherman, & Hill, 1996) includes a section on money and value that can be used with students who function below second-grade level. This battery would be useful for students who have not yet reached the skill level assessed by the *Brigance Life Skills Inventory* (Brigance, 1995). Both instruments include norms to obtain standard scores when they are needed. These assessment batteries serve as useful tools for evaluating a student's present level of performance and general knowledge related to money and finance skills.

Situational Assessment

Situational assessment refers to the process of observing a student when he or she is performing a skill or group of skills, then recording the level of independence demonstrated by the student performing the task over time to determine the mastery level of the skill being measured. The situation where the skill is observed and recorded can be in a classroom or the community, depending on the skill being assessed and the instructional level of the student (Clees, 1992). For example, a teacher may use a grocery store learning center to assess a student's readiness for instruction at a community site. Observation data on how the student negotiates the grocery center's checkout, how quickly the purchase is made, and how accurately the transaction is handled will help determine when the student is ready to move into the community classroom.

Situational assessments are extremely valuable components of a total assessment battery because teachers can observe and rate the skill as the student is performing it in the situation where it is to be used. The student's general knowledge of the skill in isolation does not indicate the extent to which the skill will transfer to a real-life situation.

A situational assessment for check-writing skills of a secondary-level student would involve teacher observation of the student writing a check. The assessment would be even more accurate if the student used his or her own checkbook to purchase a significant personal item, such as a class ring or automobile insurance. The closer the assessment situation is to the real-life event, the more accurately the teacher will be able to determine the student's true performance level.

An elementary teacher performing a similar situational assessment of check-writing skills would observe a student writing a check using an enlarged check format. If, over a designated period of time, the student has correctly written the required vocabulary and placed the appropriate information on the correct lines and in the correct boxes, then the teacher can validate that the student

TABLE 6.3
Brigance Life Skills Inventory: Money and Finance Sections

Assessment for Basic Skills

Equivalent Values of Coins and the Dollar Bills
Totals Values of Groups of Coins
Convert Coins
Price Signs
Makes Change
Computes Totals for Purchases
Comprehends and Computes Savings on Purchases
Uses Charts and Tables To Compute Expenses
Completes Application for Credit Card
Completes Deposit Slips, Writes Checks, and Computes Balance

Supplemental and Related Lists/Skill Sequences

Equivalent Values of Collections of Bill
Totals Values of Groups of Bills
Convert Bills
Price Signs
Price Signs
Makes Change
Computes Totals, Including Tax, for Purchases
Determines How Many Items of a Given Price Can Be Purchased with a Given Amount of Money
Addition of Whole Numbers
Totals for Purchases
Comprehends and Computes Savings on Purchases
Subtraction of Whole Numbers
Spends Money Wisely (Thrifty Buying)
Uses Locally Available Charts and Tables To Compute Savings/Differences
Interprets Information from Graphs
Credit Skills and Knowledge
Computes Interest on Loans
Bank Statement and Checkbook
Checking Account Skills and Knowledge
Savings Account Skills and Knowledge
Miscellaneous Money Management and Consumer Skills

Note. From *Brigance Life Skills Inventory,* by A. H. Brigance, 1995, N. Billerica, MA: Curriculum Associates. Copyright 1995 by Curriculum Associates. Reprinted with permission.

has mastered the prerequisite skills for writing personal checks. The teacher can then teach more complicated skills while providing the student with activities that will help maintain his or her newly mastered check-writing skills.

When teachers use a vocabulary, spelling, and cursive writing test to evaluate check-writing skills in isolation of the real-life format used for writing a check, they will find that their students do not easily transfer these skills to realistic situations. When students are instructed and then evaluated in isolation, teachers usually find that they need to devote additional instructional time to the development of check-writing skills related to everyday situations.

Data sheets, such as the one depicted in Figure 6.1, document skill acquisition and help the teacher decide which skills need to be assessed. Wise teachers combine grading responsibilities with data collection duties to document student progress. Data sheets enable parents and students alike to understand exactly

Student Name _____ Date _____

Day	Things To Do	Entry	Intermediate	Advanced	Exit
Monday	Breakfast Menu				
	Lunch Menu				
	Supper Menu				
	Snack Menu				
	Generic Menu				
Tuesday	Breakfast List				
	Lunch List				
	Supper List				
	Snack List				
	Generic List				
Wednesday	Breakfast: Coupons/Specials				
	Lunch: Coupons/Specials				
	Supper: Coupons/Specials				
	Snack: Coupons/Specials				
	Generic: Coupons/Specials				
Thursday	Breakfast: Cost Estimates				
	Lunch: Cost Estimates				
	Supper: Cost Estimates				
	Snack: Cost Estimates				
	Generic: Cost Estimates				
Friday	Items Found				
	Items Totaled				
	Items Compared with Budget				
	Items Recorded in Ledger				
	Generic: Butter/Sugar/Salt, etc.				

Key: **Entry: Needs Total Assistance**
  Intermediate: Needs Prompts
  Advanced: Needs Minimal Assistance
  Exit: Independent Skill

FIGURE 6.1. Data sheet for documenting skill acquisition.

how a grade is calculated. Students who see their progress visually and know their next step recognize that they are moving steadily toward a shared goal and are less likely to become disinterested in class. There are also many excellent software programs (e.g., word-processing and spreadsheet programs) available today to make data collection easier.

CURRICULUM DESIGN

The design of a longitudinal curriculum for money management and financial planning consists of a systematic series of goals and objectives formulated to build skills from elementary to middle to high school until the student with cognitive impairment has developed the highest skill mastery level possible. The design begins with the identification of the prerequisite skills needed to develop money management and financial planning skills at the elementary level. Once the prerequisite skills have been identified, they should be taught in the context that best allows the student to transfer the skill to the next level.

An example of the elementary school component of a longitudinal curriculum design for writing a personal check is described in Table 6.4. The format used

TABLE 6.4
Curriculum Design for Money Management

DOMAIN: *Daily Living Skills, Elementary Level*
COMPETENCY: *Managing Personal Finances*
SUBCOMPETENCY: *Prerequisite Skills for Writing a Personal Check*

Objective	Activities/Strategies	Adult/Peer Roles
Master prerequisite skills for writing a personal check.	• Students will demonstrate mastery of basic manuscript and cursive alphabet and number symbols. • Students will use an enlarged check format to develop the following skills: a. Write number words on appropriate lines. b. Write corresponding number symbols in appropriate boxes. c. Write proper nouns related to purchase. d. Sign name on appropriate line. • Students will demonstrate an understanding of the basic vocabulary involved in writing a check. • Students will practice skills in a classroom banking center. • Students will visit local banks to obtain information related to check writing.	• Parents will assist student with homework related to writing a check using an enlarged check format. • Parent will allow student to observe the parent writing personal checks for household expenses. • Bank personnel will discuss the types of checks and account services offered by the bank in basic terms. • Student will work in groups where students with advanced skills can tutor those needing additional instruction.

Note. Adapted from *Life Centered Career Education: A Competency-Based Approach* (4th edition), by D. E. Brolin, 1993, p. 27, Reston, VA: Council for Exceptional Children. Copyright 1993 by the Council for Exceptional Children. Adapted with permission.

is related to the *Life Centered Career Education* curriculum, developed by Donn Brolin in 1978. Elementary teachers should begin to develop students' check-writing skills as soon they have mastered the basic prerequisite skills of manuscript and cursive writing of letters and number words. The basic vocabulary and arithmetic skills needed for financial planning and money management skills are introduced using an enlarged check format designed for students to practice writing the words and symbols correctly.

Students build check-writing vocabulary and cursive writing skills throughout the elementary grades until they demonstrate a level of mastery that allows them to move to a standard-size check format. Teachers increase student check-writing skills by creating more complicated scenarios, for which their students write personal checks. To reinforce these skills, the students could work in groups where advanced students serve as peer tutors for students who need additional reinforcement for skill mastery. The peer tutor role serves to provide skill maintenance activities for the students who have mastered the objectives but continue to need to practice the skill to maintain it.

Middle school teachers continue the skill-building process by introducing more complex situations that involve check writing and using a variety of personal check formats that are available at local banks. Middle school banking centers should include many types of the materials used by adults to write personal checks. Teachers must ensure that the practice checks are not confused with real checking accounts and cashed inappropriately by local banks or business establishments.

Parents should include their child in check-writing duties at home (Brolin, 1993), such as allowing the child to be present when the parent pays bills or balances the account. The use of a variety of check formats (e.g., duplicate checks and standard checks) in every situation helps students transfer their skills to more complicated environments and make informed choices regarding the particular format they want use when opening a personal bank account.

High school teachers reinforce check-writing skills using banking centers, personal budget lessons, and community-based field trips to local banks and credit unions. If high school teachers do not have to spend time teaching students how to write a personal check because students learned the skill in earlier grades, they can devote more of their instructional day to visiting community banking institutions. Students will be able to determine which local bank has the best services for their individual needs. Students will develop a distinct frame of reference from which to choose a bank and will also have significant experience using the check format most appropriate for them.

High school teachers can assist employed students with opening and maintaining personal checking accounts. Parents who are actively involved in the skill-building process can also assist their child with developing the skills necessary to open and maintain a personal checking account. As students with disabilities receive the same type of instruction as their nondisabled peers, they will become more accepted in the inclusion setting by the general education teachers and peers. For this acceptance to occur, special education teachers must raise their expectations for what their students can accomplish. Success breeds success, and self-determination is born when students feel empowered to succeed. This empowerment will not come unless all individuals involved believe in the goal and are committed to a successful outcome, even if the goal is difficult to accomplish.

A variety of resources are available for teachers to use in developing a longitudinal curriculum for money management and financial planning. The *Life Centered Career Education* (LCCE; Brolin, 1993), a comprehensive, competency-based curriculum, can be readily used for this purpose. With a little creativity, elementary special education teachers can scale down the objectives of the LCCE curriculum into the prerequisite skills required for mastery of money management and financial planning skills. One such breakdown for the prerequisite skills needed for writing a personal check is described in Table 6.4. Additional goals and objectives for teaching money management and financial planning skills could be developed using the LCCE format such as the ones described in Table 6.5.

In 1995, Robert J. Loyd and Donn Brolin completed a modified LCCE curriculum for the moderately cognitively impaired population, taking into account that these students learn best when objectives are broken down into smaller components with increased repetition (Loyd & Brolin, 1995). This additional resource would be most beneficial to teachers developing appropriate learning objectives for students with moderate cognitive impairment.

Life Skills Instruction for All Students with Special Needs: A Practical Guide for Integrating Real-Life Content into the Curriculum, by Cronin and Patton (1993), is also an outstanding resource that will assist teachers with the

TABLE 6.5
Additional Goals for Teaching Money Management

DOMAIN: *Daily Living Skills, Secondary Level*
COMPETENCY: *Managing Personal Finances*
SUBCOMPETENCY: *Use Banking Services*

Objective	Activities/Strategies	Adult/Peer Roles
Write checks, make deposits, and record checking transactions.	• Students take a field trip to a bank to discuss procedures to follow when writing checks, making deposits, and recording checking account transactions. • Students list on a poster the process of writing checks, making deposits, and recording transactions. • Class practices with mock checks, deposit slips, check registers, and monthly bank statements. • Class discusses the importance of accurate checking account record keeping. • Class devises mock checking system and students use checks to purchase classroom items.	• Parents inform the student of the procedures for writing checks, making deposits, and recording transactions. • Parents discuss with the student the family's checking account transactions and recording. • Bank personnel discuss the procedures for writing checks, making deposits, and recording transactions. • Parents assist student in making an actual transaction and in record keeping. • Parents involve the student in balancing the family's checking account.

Note. From *Life Centered Career Education: A Competency-Based Approach* (4th edition, p. 27), by D. E. Brolin, 1993, Reston, VA: Council for Exceptional Children. Copyright 1993 by the Council for Exceptional Children. Reprinted with permission.

development of a longitudinal money management and financial planning curriculum. Information related to age level, reading level, and instructional format is given for commercially available resources in the extensive appendix. Although not as detailed as LCCE, the book is well written and easy to use by professionals for lesson planning and curriculum development.

ASSISTIVE TECHNOLOGY

Special education teachers must evaluate the different types of technology available today and adequately assess what kind of assistive technology will be needed to enable students with special needs to succeed in classroom and community environments. "Generally, assistive technology refers to those accommodations or adaptations provided for individuals with disabilities that may be mechanical, electrical, or computerized, and that enhance the routine functioning of these people" (Swith, 2001, p. 1).

The Technology-Related Assistance for Individuals with Disabilities Act of 1988 states that assistive technology includes "any item, piece of equipment, or product system, whether acquired commercially off the shelf, modified or customized, that is used to increase, maintain, or improve functional capabilities of individuals with disabilities" (§ 3002). IDEA requires that IEP teams address, at least yearly, any assistive technology devices and related services that will increase opportunities for students with disabties to access the regular education curriculum in the least restrictive setting possible. Teachers must be knowledgeable about the types and purposes of a variety of assistive technology devices that will address the IDEA requirements (Wright & Wright, 1999).

One low-tech and inexpensive assistive technology tool essential for teaching financial planning and money management skills is the pocket calculator. In fact, this device has proven to be indispensable to virtually everyone calculating personal finances, disabled or not. When teachers use a calculator with paper tape, they have a tool that assists students by producing a paper record that can be double-checked for accuracy.

When calculators are used in the learning process, students are less likely to get bogged down by basic arithmetic operations, and they can easily learn how to calculate more complex problems, such as the savings reflected by a percent-off sale item. There are also pocket calculators available at a relatively low cost that allow the user to enter the price of the item to be purchased, then the device keeps a running total of the price of the selected items to let the buyer know when he or she has gone over budget. Items can then be subtracted from the total without the buyer having to reenter all of the item prices again.

There are many excellent software packages, too numerous to list and too easily outdated to put into print, that teachers can use to help students gain financial planning and money management skills. A variety of these software packages should be standard issue for special education classrooms. Teachers can use laptop computers and software programs at both classroom and community sites to enter and download data, making accurate data collection and assessment of individual skill levels easier to maintain. Technology is fast becoming an essential tool for promoting student success and can easily make the difference in a student's ability to keep up in the fast pace of a general education classroom. School systems that have embraced technology usually have personnel that are specially trained to assist teachers with identifying and procuring assistive technology devices for classroom use. Teachers without these resources can search the Internet for information related to assistive technology use in the classroom.

 ## THOMAS

Thomas's mother told Thomas that he should let her cash his checks and handle his finances so that she can make sure the bills are paid on time and that he has enough money to pay his expenses for the upcoming workweek. She also told him that he should contribute to the household expenses. Thomas refused her requests, and said he resented her opinion that he cannot be trusted with his own money, even though he admitted that his current behavior was irresponsible. He said he felt that his mother wanted to control his life as well as his money. He acknowledged his responsibility for family expenses but expressed the desire to move into his own place. He said he could live independently if he could master the required money management and financial planning skills.

Instead of assuming responsibility for Thomas's finances, his mother could assist him in developing the skills he needs to manage his money effectively. The help of an advocate would be useful to Thomas and his mother to put the plan in motion and encourage successful completion of the objectives. For a 6-month period, Thomas and his mother commit to the following contingencies. They will acknowledge to each other that a positive change in Thomas's behavior regarding financial responsibility is important to both of them. His mother agrees to be supportive and to refrain from making negative comments if Thomas resumes his old habits as long as he gets back on task quickly.

Each payday, Thomas will go to the bank with his advocate to cash his paycheck in the form of one-dollar bills. Thomas will count the money before he leaves the bank. With permission from Thomas, the advocate could prearrange this activity for a time that would allow Thomas to complete the task without too many other customers around to ask questions. Thomas's mother may or may not go to the bank; this is a personal choice that will be made by Thomas. The advocate will decrease his or her visits to the bank when Thomas's skill level allows Thomas to complete the task independently.

Thomas earns about $150 net per week in his job as a courtesy clerk for a grocery store. He works 5 or 6 days each week on a full-time basis. His transportation expense is $20, and his weekly snack and lunch expense is $20. He needs a new supply of personal care items, which will cost approximately $20. He also will soon need two new work shirts, two pairs of work pants, a new tie, and a new pair of steel-toe shoes. If he puts aside $20 per week for 3 months, he will have saved $240 toward these purchases. The items listed will cost approximately $180.

At home, Thomas and his mother will list each expense on a single sheet of paper and arrange the sheets in order of importance. Thomas will keep a ledger of income, expenses, and savings each week. He will need assistance in doing this at

(continues)

first but should be able to develop the skills to do this task independently with support and practice.

Thomas will count out the amount of each identified expense from the stack of one-dollar bills. He will then, with his mother's assistance, decide where to keep the money safe for the next week's expenses. He will open a savings account at the bank with the assistance of his advocate. After these activities, Thomas should have about $15 to $20 left over each week for discretionary income. Although this amount may seem excessive for someone who makes $150 per week, Thomas is accustomed to having his entire paycheck as discretionary income. The transition to budgeting money and saving for purchases must be a realistic one, or it will fail.

It will be hard for Thomas and his mother to follow through with this plan. They will need to acknowledge the difficulties of the plan from the beginning and discuss their feelings. This is particularly important when the plan seems too difficult or if Thomas falls back into his former habits. Both Thomas and his mother need encouragement, support, and a high level of commitment to make the plan successful.

If Thomas returns to his previous irresponsible behavior, his mother will be faced with the decision either to continue fostering his dependence by giving in and paying his expenses or to let him walk to work and miss lunch until he receives his next paycheck. The advocate could be included as a mediator during this process. Throughout the plan period, the advocate will need to pay close attention for any signs of a return to past behavior. As the plan is implemented, the advocate will gradually reduce his or her involvement with the family and encourage them to take more and more responsibility for the plan's success.

Tables 6.6 and 6.7 show a sample IEP for the development of money management and financial planning skills for Thomas. If Thomas were a student, his special education teacher would assume the responsibilities of the advocate. When teachers use methods similar to those described in this chapter, students will learn appropriate money management and financial planning skills prior to job placement and should not need to conduct these types of activities when they enter the adult environment.

Initially, Thomas will use photocopies of one-dollar bills to practice the steps prior to cashing his checks. The guided practice will move to real currency as soon as Thomas and his advocate feel he is able to complete the task using real money. As his budgeting skills grow, Thomas will be able to replace the single dollars with larger bills, making trips to the bank less time-consuming. A checking account will replace the cash as soon as Thomas is trained and independent in his banking skills.

The advocate will assist Thomas's mother in taking a secondary role and helping her stick to her decision to encourage Thomas's financial independence. As Thomas develops skills in financial planning and money management, he and his mother will determine together, with the help of the advocate if they request it, how Thomas will meet his financial obligations to his family. As Thomas begins to see the reality of financial planning and money management as they relate to his income, expenses, and personal desires, it is hoped that he will become more responsible in his spending patterns. He will then be able to consider living on his own.

TABLE 6.6
Individual Education Program Semiannual Goal and Short-Term Instructional
Objectives for Thomas, for Skills in Budgeting

Student: <u>Thomas</u>   Person To Provide Service: <u>Advocate/Parent</u>   DOB: <u>1/1/82</u>

Dates: <u>9/1/03–3/1/04</u>

Semiannual Goal: <u>To increase skills related to cashing a payroll check, making a budget, and keeping a journal of expenses over</u>
<u>a 6-month period.</u>

Short-Term Instructional Objective	Criteria for Mastery	Method of Evaluation	Projected Date of Review	Mastery (Dates) Yes No
Thomas will do the following:				
1. Practice cashing a copy of his payroll check using photocopies of one-dollar bills.	Build mastery levels until he can maintain 100% or 10 of 10 attempts.	Observation data sheets	11/1	___ ___
2. Count the one-dollar bills to equal the amount of his check. Begin with photocopies and convert to real currency.	Build mastery levels until he can maintain 100% or 10 of 10 attempts.	Observation data sheets	11/1 3/1	___ ___ ___ ___
3. Count the one-dollar bills related to his travel and lunch expenses. Begin with photocopies and convert to real currency.	Build mastery levels until he can maintain 100% or 10 of 10 attempts.	Observation data sheets	11/1 3/1	___ ___ ___ ___
4. List expected expenses and estimate the cost of the items.	8 of 10 attempts to list and estimate actual cost of future expenses.	Lists/discussion Observation/data sheets	1/1 3/1	___ ___ ___ ___
5. Make a weekly budget of expenses related to personal needs and desires.	8 to 10 attempts to list and estimate actual cost of desired items.	Lists/discussion Observation/data sheets	1/1 3/1	___ ___ ___ ___
6. Make weekly budget of expenses related to personal needs and desires.	8 of 10 attempts to make a realistic budget of needs and desires.	Budget forms Discussion Observation/data sheets	3/1	___ ___
7. Record amounts of each expense in a journal. Document weekly and monthly amounts accurately. Review each prior week's expenses.	Build a mastery of recording skills until he can maintain 100% accuracy or 10 of 10 attempts.	Journal sheets Discussion Observation/data sheets	3/1	___ ___

TABLE 6.7
Individual Education Program Semiannual Goal and Short-Term Instructional Objectives for Thomas, for Skills in Cashing Payroll Check

Student: Thomas   Person To Provide Service: Advocate/Parent   DOB: 1/1/82
Dates: 9/1/03–3/1/04

Semiannual Goal: To increase banking skills related to cashing a payroll check using local banking facility over a 6-month period.

Short-Term Instructional Objective	Criteria for Mastery	Method of Evaluation	Projected Date of Review	Mastery (Dates) Yes	No
Thomas will do the following:					
1. Obtain a picture ID using his original birth certificate and Social Security card	100% of one attempt.	Copy of ID card	9/15	___	___
2. Travel to a local bank of choice and cash his payroll check with the assistance of the advocate	100% of one attempt per week for 8 weeks.	Self-report by Thomas/observation/data sheets/cash from check	11/1	___	___
3. Without assistance, request that the teller cash the check with one-dollar bills	100% of one attempt per week for 8 weeks.	Observation/data sheets/self-report by Thomas/correct amount of cash	11/1 3/1	___	___
4. Before leaving the bank, count the cash with the assistance of the advocate or teller for the first 8 weeks and independently for the next 4 weeks	100% of one attempt per week for 8 weeks.	Observation/data sheet/count cash with advocate/count cash with teller/self-report by Thomas	11/1 3/1	___	___
5. Secure the money on his person in a safe place and return home immediately with all cash with assistance	100% of one attempt per week for 8 weeks with assistance. 100% of one attempt per week for 4 weeks independently.	Safe return home with appropriate amount of cash/observation/data sheet/self-report by Thomas	12/1 3/1	___	___
6. Correctly complete Steps 1–5 independently	100% of one attempt per week for 4 weeks.	Observation/data sheet/self-report by Thomas/observation by mother/safe return home with all cash	3/1	___	___

SUMMARY

This chapter gave examples of appropriate money management and financial planning skills training for students with mild to moderate intellectual disabilities. The figures and tables presented provide samples of some of the different methods that can be used for instruction and examples of data collection formats for keeping track of student progress. These skills should be developed beginning in elementary grades and continuing through secondary school as a coordinated set of objectives that represent a longitudinal curriculum designed to foster financial planning and money management as independent living goals. Special education teachers should plan and present lessons in both simulated and real-life environments that promote goal achievement. If teaching professionals embrace and support the concept that students with cognitive disabilities can indeed achieve independence in the adult world and promote the high expectations necessary for their students to achieve success, then these students will transition from high school to the community as independent and productive citizens.

REFERENCES

Brigance, A. H. (1981). *Brigance Inventory of Essential Skills.* North Billerica, MA: Curriculum Associates.

Brigance, A. H. (1995). *Brigance Life Skills Inventory.* North Billerica, MA: Curriculum Associates.

Brolin, D. E. (1978). *Life centered career education: A competency-based approach.* Reston, VA: Council for Exceptional Children.

Brolin, D. E. (1993). *Life centered career education: A competency-based approach.* (4th ed.). Reston, VA: Council for Exceptional Children.

Brunininks, R. H., Woodcock, R. W., Weatherman, R. F., & Hill, B. K. (1996). *Scales of Independent Behavior–Revised.* Chicago: Riverside.

Clees, T. (1992). Community living. In P. J. McLaughlin & P. Wehman (Eds.), *Developmental disabilities: A handbook of best practices* (pp. 228–267). Boston: Andover/Butterworth/Heinemann.

Cronin, M., & Patton, J. (1993). *Life skills instruction for all students with special needs: A practical guide for integrating real-life content into the curriculum.* Austin, TX: PRO-ED.

Dreshler, D., & Schumaker, J. B. (1986). Leaving strategies: An instructional alternative for low-achieving adolescents. *Exceptional Child, 52,* 583–590.

Individuals with Disabilities Education Act Amendments of 1997, 20 U.S.C. § 1400 *et seq.*

Jones, M. M., & Carlier, L. L. (1995). Creating inclusionary opportunities for learners with multiple disabilities: A team teaching approach. *Teaching Exceptional Children, 27*(3), 23–27.

Langone, J. (1992). Mild to moderate mental retardation. In P. J. McLaughlin & P. Wehman (Eds.), *Developmental disabilities: A handbook of best practices* (pp. 1–15). Boston: Andover/Butterworth/Heinemann.

Loyd, R., & Brolin, D. E. (1995). *Life centered career education: Modified curriculum for individuals with moderate disabilities.* Reston, VA: Council for Exceptional Children.

Roessler, R. (1991). A problem-solving approach to implementing career education. *Career Development for Exceptional Individuals, 14*(1), 59–66.

Salend, S. J. (1995). Using videocassette recorder technology in special education classrooms. *Teaching Exceptional Children, 27*(3), 4–9.

Swith, Y. (2001, May). *Determining evidence-based practice in assistive technology service delivery through qualitative research.* Paper presented at the Qualitative Evidence-based Practice Conference, Taking a Critical Stance, Coventry University, Coventry, England.

Technology-Related Assistance for Individuals with Disabilities Act of 1988, 29 U.S.C. § 2201 *et seq.*

Wehmeyer, M. L., & Kelchner, K. (1995). Measuring the autonomy of adolescents and adults with mental retardation: A self-report form of the Autonomous Functional Checklist. *Career Development for Exceptional Individuals, 18*(1), 3–21.

Wright, P. W. D., & Wright, P. D. (1999). *Wrightslaw: Special education law.* Hartfield, VA: Harbor House Law Press.

CHAPTER 7

Socialization, Peer Relationships, and Self-Esteem

Shirley K. Chandler and Sara C. Pankaskie

Accurately or not, much of society continues to view students with disabilities as socially incompetent because of their behaviors. These behaviors may include disrupting the classroom environment, fighting, name-calling, withdrawal, isolation, or avoidance of peers. These students may have trouble making or sustaining relationships and interacting with others, and they may have problems with diminished self-esteem. The following case study is typical of many of the students who receive special education services.

MICHAEL

Michael is a 15-year-old middle school student. He has one sibling, a 10-year-old brother. Michael, his brother, and his mother live in an apartment complex near the school Michael attends. Michael's father and mother are divorced, and he sees his father irregularly. His mother works full-time as a secretary and bookkeeper for an auto dealer.

Since the first grade, Michael has had a great deal of difficulty in school. His trouble began with the development of reading skills. He was unable to stay on task and had difficulty grasping basic reading concepts. By the third grade, Michael was exhibiting poor social skills, fighting with his classmates, and showing low impulse control. He repeated third grade but exhibited no significant gains by the end of the school year.

Prior to his entry into fourth grade, Michael was referred to the school psychologist for an evaluation. The results of this evaluation showed that Michael had a severe learning disability in reading comprehension. He also exhibited attention deficit disorder (ADD) tendencies that, according to the psychologist, might be the result of frustration over his inability to understand his schoolwork and his repeated failures in the classroom. Michael was placed in a resource room for help with his reading skills.

By the time Michael reached middle school, he had been placed in a self-contained special education classroom. He currently has a primary diagnosis of severe learning disability and a secondary diagnosis of emotional disability. His only mainstreamed classes are art, music, and gym.

On his last triennial psychological exam, Michael's full-scale IQ was 103. However, scores on the academic tests showed him to be 3 to 4 years behind his peers.

(continues)

Achievement testing showed that Michael has abilities and strengths in understanding mechanical principles, visualizing in three dimensions, and working rapidly and accurately with his hands. Michael also exhibited strength in basic math computational skills. These strength areas complement Michael's desire to work as an auto mechanic. Testing observations by the psychologist note that Michael has trouble concentrating and staying on task. Michael's teachers also note that he acts out in class, picks fights with his classmates, is a discipline problem, and has been placed on in-school suspension on several occasions. He does not complete assignments or bring required materials from home when directed to do so. Michael copes with discipline by lashing out when directly confronted. He will swear or start a fight with his classmates or brother.

During Michael's latest Individualized Education Program (IEP) conference, his mother said that Michael has been staying out late at night and experimenting with alcohol. She said he does not appear to have any friends, and she is afraid that he will drop out of school rather than face more failure at the high school level. She also said that Michael fights constantly with his younger brother, who is a high achiever and in the gifted class at the same middle school.

When interviewed by the school psychologist, Michael said he hated school and felt it was a waste of time. He was unwilling to accept any blame for his behavior and instead blamed his classmates for his discipline problems. He said that his classmates are "retards" and that he does not belong in that class. He also said that his mother and father like his brother better because he is smarter. Michael blames his mother for his parents' divorce and for the fact that his father does not visit regularly. When asked about his use of alcohol, Michael denied it and the use of any drugs.

Michael said that he would like to work on cars or maybe join the Army but was unable to articulate the requirements for either of these jobs. He also said he would quit school if he had to stay in that "retard" class when he goes to high school. When asked what he would do if he quit school, Michael said that he was not sure and that maybe he would get a job at a pizza place.

Based upon his observations and his interview with Michael, the school psychologist recommended that Michael receive individual counseling for disability awareness, self-esteem, and impulse control. He also recommended that Michael participate in group counseling for peer relationship and social skill development. Additionally, he recommended to Michael's mother that Michael and his family receive family counseling.

DESCRIPTION OF CURRICULUM

The ability to get along with others is strongly associated with success in many aspects of life (Elksnin & Elksnin, 1998; Gumpel, Tappe, & Araki, 2000). For most people, socialization skills develop as a normal part of maturation (Gaynor, Breland, Harlacher, Tondorf, & Zivkovich, 1992). Research and school records show that this process does not work for many students with disabilities. Failures in the area of socialization occur daily in the classroom. Some have noted that the "socially rejected" child is liked by few or no peers (Dodge, 1989; Gaynor et al.,

1992). Conversely, one accepting friend can help a student develop positive self-esteem (Kendrick, 1991). Attaining competence in social skills is not inevitable any more than it is in academics. Both require opportunities to learn (Gaynor et al., 1992). Students with disabilities may not learn these skills unless they are taught, and yet the teaching of social skills is often left to chance.

In some states, increased academic demands on schools have slowed efforts toward inclusion of students with disabilities with their same-age peers. Parents, special education professionals, and advocates have become concerned with the lessened opportunities for teaching and learning social skills. Social skills are important for inclusion to succeed, and they are often improved by being with same-age typical peers. Students in self-contained classes also need social skills so they can be successful when they go into society for recreation, leisure, and employment. Whether in self-contained or included classrooms, students need instruction in social skills.

Socialization

Socialization in the current context refers to how an individual interacts with others and participates in society. Along with the skills needed for positive peer relationships and good self-esteem, socialization addresses those skills, behaviors, and attitudes necessary for an individual to survive as a member of a group. The things a person learns in this area helps him or her become a better family member, worker, and citizen, regardless of culture or social status. Every culture (and subculture) establishes a set of minimum expectations. Individuals who ignore or violate these group expectations (or never acquire the skills and behaviors necessary to meet them) may be isolated, ostracized, or, at worst, punished.

The importance of socialization cannot be overstated, and the necessity of teaching basic social skills, behaviors, and attitudes is obvious. Teachers who teach students with disabilities have a particular need to become familiar with assessments and curricula that address these skills.

There are many curricula that address the general area of socialization. Some of them are listed with annotations in Appendix 7.A. This list is only a sample of the curricula available commercially and is intended to represent a cross section of approaches to teaching social skills, presentation modes, and target ages and groups. Some "classics" (e.g., Skillstreaming) as well as some relatively new and innovative approaches (e.g., *Nine Steps to Self-Esteem*) are included. For further discussion on assessing and teaching social skills, see those sections in this chapter.

Self-Esteem

There is an inextricable connection between self-esteem and achievement. People who feel good about themselves find it easier to feel good about things around them, including school. These positive feelings often lead to increased effort that results in praise, which, in turn, results in even better self-feelings. A very positive cycle. But what about people who do not have a history of success? They may have diminished feelings of self-worth and negative feelings about the world around them. They may, in fact, even blame the world for their failures. They do not approach school with much enthusiasm and therefore often are low achieving. Low achievement is met with criticism, which results in even lower self-esteem.

For low-achieving students, the classroom becomes a "breeding ground for feelings of inadequacy and worthlessness" (Curwin, 1993). Students who are continually confronted with failure have little opportunity to develop a positive self-esteem.

Many students with disabilities have low self-esteem. Whether this is the result of repeated failure and criticism or a cause of it, low self-esteem often leads to school failure or dropping out if not reversed or ameliorated. Students need to feel at least confident enough to make a reasonable effort if they are to make progress in school. Teachers can help them do this by setting high, yet reasonable, standards and by projecting a mind-set that students can attain these standards. Teachers, especially inclusion teachers, can also interact with students with disabilities in such a way as to provide a model for nondisabled student peers in the class.

The following are some principles of self-esteem that may help one understand the way it affects behavior:

- Students will act in ways that increase their sense of self-worth and satisfaction.

- Students will act in ways that confirm their self-concept.

- Students will act in ways so as to maintain a consistent self-image, regardless of changing circumstances.

These principles show, practically speaking, that it may be difficult to change a student's self-image once it has been ingrained and that a teacher should not be discouraged if first attempts at raising low self-esteem are met with a continuation of behaviors that lead to failure. The student may simply be trying to "correct" the teacher's misconception that he or she is a worthwhile individual. In time, this can change if the teacher provides enough opportunities for success and teaches coping skills. One of the most basic things a teacher can do to help students feel better about themselves is to give assignments or tasks early in the lesson (or the day) that are guaranteed to be successful. Other suggestions include praising effort, reinforcing successive approximations, and providing corrective feedback in such a way that it does not criticize the student but points out how the response falls short of the desired outcome. Teachers have found that using a student's strength areas to work toward academic goals leads to increased feelings of competence and self-esteem (Stringer, Morton, & Bonikowski, 1999).

Helping others has also been found to help certain students feel better about themselves (Curwin, 1993). For example, one student who was experiencing problems at school and at home was assigned by the school counselor to assist a first grader who was physically disabled. The student reported feeling good about the assistance he provided to the first grader, and his attitude toward school appeared to improve. Functioning in a helping role rather than in a needing role seemed to increase the student's feelings of control over his environment and improve his self-esteem.

School-based interventions can increase students' self-esteem and academic skills (Erlbaum & Vaughn, 1999; Slavin, 1991). Skill development and self-enhancement, which is a cognitive therapy approach in which the goal is for persons to rate themselves higher than they rate others in the areas of having control, being compared favorably to others, and having good things happen to them, were both found to improve self-concept in students. Cooperative learning, a method that involves learners of different ability levels working in small groups or teams to help one another, also increased students' self-esteem. Cooperative learning may be used as a supplement to direct teacher instruction in many settings and can be especially effective in included classrooms (Slavin, 1991).

Self-esteem is linked to achievement, but it is also closely related to peer acceptance, especially during the middle and high school years. Students who lack the skills necessary to make and keep friends will suffer greatly during these years. Although there are often gains noted in general adaptability, normalization, and socialization for students with disabilities in included settings, there are some possible disadvantages for students in the area of self-esteem. Students with disabilities in a mainstream setting may exhibit lower self-esteem than their nondisabled peers (Kauffman, Gerber, & Semmel, 1988). A possible reason for this is that these included students have few opportunities to associate with other people with disabilities (Stainback, Stainback, East, & Sapon-Shevin, 1994). This problem might be addressed by inviting role models to career days, showing films about people with disabilities who have succeeded in life, or giving a student with a disability opportunities to attend support meetings or social events for people with like disabilities.

The conditions that improve self-concept for all people, including people with disabilities, are

- feeling connected,
- feeling unique, and
- feeling empowered.

The more teachers do to see that these conditions exist in the classroom and throughout the school, the more likely that their students will have good feelings about themselves.

Peer Relationships

Peer relationships are the interactions an individual has with others of the same general age and life situation. Peer relationships differ from general socialization in that peer relationships are specifically those with a person's age and situational cohorts, rather than all the people and things in his or her environment. The precise correlation between good peer relationships and social skills is unclear. Many general social attributes (e.g., friendliness) as well as specific behaviors (e.g., sharing) appear to be related to peer acceptance, but it is still a mystery why some children are "popular" and some are neglected or overtly rejected by peers.

Students with disabilities are at risk for poor relationships with their peers. Peer rejection has been observed as early as the first 2 months of a preschool program, and it is estimated that as many as 75% of children with learning disabilities experience problems with social interaction and relationships (Hepler, 1997).

Although peer relationships are important at all ages, in developmental terms, they are probably most important during early adolescence. This is the time when being like one's peers takes on a special significance as young people struggle with separating their identity from that of their parents. A series of studies by Hughes (1999) has identified six empirically and socially validated conversational behaviors that are critical for appropriate social interaction between high school students with and without cognitive disabilities. They are (a) rate of initiating, (b) percentage of time initiating, (c) rate of responding, (d) percentage of time responding, (e) percentage of time attending to the person or social situation, and (f) percentage of time engaging in inappropriate or socially interfering motor behavior.

Good peer relationships do not just happen. Research in schools makes it clear that specific planning and intervention on the part of adults are required to teach and foster good peer relationships (Calloway, 1999; Hughes, 1999). In general, a teacher who wants to help a student be better accepted by his or her peers should (a) observe what the popular students do (and do not do) in particular situations; (b) compare this with what the target student does in similar situations; (c) identify the discrepancies, if any; and (d) teach the missing skills. (A note of caution: Sometimes popular students can engage in what might be considered inappropriate or unfriendly behaviors, and a "halo" effect will cover them. The same behaviors on the part of an unpopular child would probably not be condoned by the peer group.) The following is an example of teaching to the template (the model presented by the popular child):

➡ The teacher observes that popular students join activities in progress by praising one of the group members ("Nice throw, Jack! Can I toss one?"), whereas the unpopular student may push into the group and grab the ball away ("Watch me, I can throw way better than that."). The teacher would attempt to teach the target student how to use praise to enter a group.

One especially negative aspect of peer relationships is bullying. Bullying typically consists of intentional behaviors such as taunting, name-calling, threatening, hitting, and stealing that are initiated by one or more students against a victim or victims. Bullying may also take more indirect forms, such as gossip, that cause the subjects to be shunned or intentionally isolated. Boys who are bullies are more likely to take part in direct bullying methods, whereas their female counterparts are more likely to engage in subtle, indirect techniques, such as spreading rumors. Research indicates that approximately 15% of students are either bullied regularly or initiate bullying (Olweus, 1993). Students who are victims of bullying are typically insecure and have low self-esteem. They often lack social skills and friends and so may already be socially isolated. Victims tend to be close to their parents and may have parents who can be described as overprotective. The major physical characteristic of victims is that they tend to be weaker than their peers (Batsche & Knoff, 1994; Olweus, 1993). Unfortunately, students with disabilities often fit the description of those likely to be victims of abuse, and research shows them to be vulnerable (Bryan, Pearl, & Herzog, 1989; Doren, Bullis, & Benz, 1996; Halpern, Close, & Nelson, 1986).

Teachers can help with the problem of bullying at several levels. First, they can work with students at the classroom level to develop classroom rules against bullying. Special education teachers and behavior specialists can design and implement individualized interventions with the bullies and their victims. General and special education teachers can implement cooperative learning activities to help students who are socially isolated and provide adult supervision at times when bullying is likely (e.g., unstructured times such as lunch or between classes). Teachers can also work with school administration and parents to create and maintain a school climate in which bullying is not tolerated.

Of the social skills curricula presented in Appendix 7.A, most include peer relationships, and one, *Personal Power,* targets peer relationships for exceptional and at-risk students. *Steps to Respect* is a schoolwide program to address bullying.

No description of curriculum development in the area of social skills would be complete without examining two of the major areas that have emerged as problematic for students with disabilities: substance abuse and self-protection. Pressure to use or abuse alcohol and drugs and to have early and/or unprotected sex is a common occurrence for today's student. A student who is seeking to be accepted by his or her peers may succumb to this pressure.

Substance Abuse

Disability is correlated with several behavioral risk factors, including early school dropout, physical and sexual abuse, and drug and alcohol use and abuse. Most studies have found the rates of substance abuse among people with disabilities to be significantly higher than that of their nondisabled peers (Olkin, 1999). (The exception is with individuals with mental retardation, where the rates are actually lower than their nondisabled peers.) Possible reasons for this higher rate include stigma, social isolation, and frustration (Freeman, Ferreyra, & Calabrese, 1997; Greer, Roberts, & Jenkins, 1990). Unfortunately, there have been few studies on the prevalence of substance abuse among school-age students with disabilities.

The major barriers to treatment for persons from special populations are the lack of attention paid to the problem and the dearth of research on effective interventions (Olkin, 1999). Because of this denial and diagnostic overshadowing, which refers to symptoms being wrongly attributed to a person's disability, substance abuse is probably underidentified and underreported. Families and friends of people with disabilities may become codependent, viewing drugs or alcohol as an entitlement because the person with a disability has such a rough life and so should be excused for taking refuge in drugs (Cavaliere, 1995).

Though there is little information specifically related to students with disabilities, the general treatment approaches are similar. The long-term and probably the most effective approach is to deal with the stressors in the student's life. This would include teaching social, coping, life management, and self-advocacy skills. It might also include teaching academic and vocational skills when they would help the student become less stigmatized and socially isolated. Simultaneously, students with disabilities who also have substance abuse problems might benefit from programs that specifically target substance prevention and reduction. Due to increasing awareness of the problem, more materials for children and adults with disabilities and substance abuse problems are becoming available (Helwig & Holicky, 1994; Watson, Boros, & Zrimec, 1979–1980). Appendixes 7.A and C include some of the nationally recognized substance abuse programs.

Self-Protection

Students with disabilities also face problems of protecting themselves from physical, psychological, and sexual abuse from nonpeers. Despite the fact that there are few longitudinal, community-based studies (Martin, 1995) about this issue, there is enough documentation and anecdotal evidence to establish that children and adults with disabilities are more likely than their nondisabled peers to be victims (Boat & Sites, 2001).

One study found that children with disabilities were 2.1 times as likely to endure criminal physical abuse and 1.8 times more likely to experience sexual abuse than children without disabilities (Crosse, Kaye, & Ratnofsky, 1993; Sobsey, Lucardie, & Mansell, 1995).

Some have suggested that children with disabilities cause this increased likelihood by displaying certain behavioral characteristics such as tantrums and noncompliance that parents and caregivers perceive negatively, thus increasing the children's risk for abuse. Others argue that children with disabilities and their families display characteristics associated with abuse in the general population, including poverty, poor coping abilities, and parental history of abuse (Sobsey, 1994). Other reasons for the increased incidence of victimization among children and adults with cognitive disabilities may include desire for acceptance that leads them to agree to take part in behavior they do not like or do not want because of fear of losing social contact, feelings of powerlessness and dependency, little access to resources (e.g., transportation to the police station), and little education in self-protection (Petersilia, 2000). In addition, victims with cognitive disabilities often lack the vocabulary necessary to report the abuse, and even if they do report it, the victim is often not believed.

The psychological and emotional effects of child abuse are well known. Most child abusers were themselves abused as children. Less well known are the changes in the victims' brains that have been linked to abuse. There is now evidence that abuse causes changes in the anatomy of regions of the developing brains of traumatized children. This damage can lead to later behavioral manifestations that may be misdiagnosed as attention deficit disorder, disassociative behavior, or aggression (Cosmos, 2001). Appendixes 7.A and 7.B list curricula and training materials that teachers may find useful in teaching abuse prevention and in working with children who have been abused.

Sexual Abuse. Part of self-protection is protection from unwanted sexual contact. In one study, children with disabilities faced 1.8 times greater risk for sexual abuse than children without disabilities. Children who had been abused were 4.8 times as likely to have mental retardation. Only children with emotional disturbance were at greater risk (Mansell, Sobsey, & Moskal, 1998). Even though children with disabilities faced increased risk, there is little documented treatment for sexual abuse with this population. Indicators and problems associated with sexual abuse may be the same as with typical children, but the resulting social isolation, stigma, and loss of self-worth may be more acute. A child who is unable to process what is happening to himself or herself may exhibit anger, self-injurious behavior, and withdrawal as a result. Again, as with other forms of abuse, diagnostic overshadowing can prevent sexual abuse from being recognized (Mansell et al., 1998). Furthermore, some special education students can be at risk for sexual exploitation or may misuse their sexuality in a misguided attempt to attain popularity (Walker-Hirsch & Champagne, 1991).

Although there are numerous sex education programs for children and adults with developmental disabilities (Bambury, Wilton, & Boyd, 1999; Caspar & Glidden, 2001; Garwood & McCabe, 2000), they often do not contain information about self-protection. Many social skills curricula devote a portion of their training to teaching students how to resist peer pressure, but few specifically address the area of protection from inappropriate behavior by nonpeers. Students with developmental disabilities need personal safety training so they can learn the skills they need to avoid, recognize, and report crimes when they occur.

Circles (see Appendix 7.A) is a program that teaches students with limited cognitive and communication skills to distinguish different kinds of touching from people at different levels of intimacy in their lives (e.g., family, intimate friends, acquaintances). It also teaches students that it is okay to say "no" to inappropriate kinds of touch. Other curricula and materials that address the area of sexual abuse prevention are included in Appendix 7.A.

GENERAL APPROACHES TO ASSESSMENT

Assessment of students' social skills, self-esteem, or peer relationships may be done for a variety of reasons, including determining eligibility for services, identifying specific areas of need for training, tracking student progress during an intervention program, or providing a basis for educational decision making. In addition, a teacher, parent, or administrator may request an assessment because he or she believes the child has a problem such as excessive presence of an undesirable behavior or absence of prosocial behaviors. Table 7.1 displays the general approaches to the assessment of social skills, as well as their strengths and weaknesses. A list of some specific assessment instruments for social skill in the areas of self-esteem, peer relationships, and socialization may be found in Appendix 7.B.

The type and method of assessment used will depend primarily on its purpose. Although there are many commercially available instruments, many teachers find that direct observation is the shortest distance between a problem and its solution. Carter and Sugai (1989) pointed out that although it may be difficult, direct observation of student performance should be used as much as possible. For classroom interventions, direct observation is often the best method of assessment because it provides direct information about the frequency, duration, intensity, and context of the behavior.

An additional consideration regarding assessment, and ultimately intervention, is whether a student's problem is due to a skills deficit or a performance

TABLE 7.1
General Approaches to Social Skills Assessment

Approach	Description	Strengths	Limitations
Interview	Usually done face-to-face (or via telephone) and may use a structured instrument or an informal set of questions	Provides different perspectives May be informal (non-threatening) May identify skills important to interviewee	May contain interviewee bias Time-consuming to administer Requires structure to ensure validity and reliability
Rating Scale	Commercially available and may be standardized and normed for certain groups	Useful when a standardized assessment is needed May screen large numbers of students Can use multiple raters	May not pinpoint individual problems May be unreliable (if only one rater) May not support direct observation data
Self-Report	A set of questions to which students respond about their own feelings or performance in given situations	Useful when perception of student is desired	Unreliable
Direct Observation	Completed in real time (live or videotaped) and usually scored using an agreed-upon set of operational definitions	Precise information on current behaviors Provides comparison to social skills training performance	May require assistance Time-consuming to administer Not useful with low-incidence behaviors

deficit and whether the student has competing problem behaviors. One way of making this determination is to use the decision-making model in Table 7.2. This model helps teachers decide, after observing the student and reviewing pertinent records, whether a student has certain prosocial behaviors in his or her repertoire and, if so, what may be preventing the student from exhibiting the appropriate behaviors consistently. Once this determination has been made, appropriate interventions may be developed (Gresham, Sugai, & Horner, 2001).

Functional assessment has become a familiar term in the special education lexicon since the 1997 amendments to the Individuals with Disabilities Education Act (IDEA) required such assessments for students with disabilities under certain circumstances. A functional assessment (Foster-Johnson & Dunlap, 1993) helps teachers decide what type of intervention or training to use with students who display nonfunctional and even destructive behaviors for no apparent reason. The results of the assessment can be used to hypothesize what function the

TABLE 7.2
Social Skills Training Decision-Making Matrix

Acquisition	Performance	Competing Behaviors
If skill is present		
If student already knows this skill, work to attain fluency.	If student performs this skill consistently but poorly, provide opportunities to build fluency, maintenance, and generalization.	If competing behaviors are present, find a way to make desired behavior as efficient and effective as the competing behaviors.
If skill is absent		
If student does not know this skill, teach it.	If student performs the skill inconsistently, provide opportunities for performance with feedback (including correction or reinforcement).	If there are no overt competing behaviors, recheck for skill knowledge, fluency, and opportunity for reinforcement, then consider mental health evaluation.

behavior is serving for a student so that a meaningful program may be developed to replace the nonfunctional, challenging behaviors with more productive and prosocial behaviors (O'Neill et al., 1997).

The first step in conducting a functional assessment (after identifying and defining the target behavior) is to gather information about when, where, and under what conditions the student exhibits the behavior. The teacher should answer these two questions: (a) What happens right after the behavior? (b) What were the conditions in the classroom before, during, and after the behavior (e.g., which staff were present, what tasks were being presented, what were the other students doing, what was the teacher doing)? These questions focus on the classroom environment instead of on the student because one of the basic assumptions of the functional assessment approach is that *challenging behaviors are related to the context in which they occur.*

The next step of a functional assessment is to determine the purpose served by the behavior, based on the information gathered. This step addresses another basic assumption of this approach: *Challenging behaviors serve a purpose for the student.* Although teachers often assume that the purpose of challenging behaviors is to gain attention, which they do, one should consider other possibilities, such as (a) escape from an undesirable or difficult task, (b) avoidance of nonreinforcing activities or events, (c) need for more sensory stimulation, or (d) the desire for something for which the student has no words or way to communicate. Students with a limited repertoire of behaviors may use the same behavior to signal different things, and a certain behavior exhibited by one student may have an entirely different function when exhibited by another student.

The final step in a functional assessment is to develop an intervention based on the most likely reason for the behavior. This intervention may be as simple as attending to behaviors incompatible with the challenging behavior or as complex as developing a communication system that provides the student with an alternative way of asking for what she or he wants instead of acting out to obtain it.

The assessment of problem behaviors usually focuses on reducing or eliminating behaviors rather than on teaching needed skills. Students' IEPs would look much different if they were approached from such a perspective. For example, if a student's problem behavior is thought to be serving his need for attention, then teachers should find other ways to give attention in an academic (or social or physical) activity. If a student's intent is power or control, then teachers should find ways to give the student more control over her own learning environment, tasks, and response mode. The effectiveness of a functional assessment can only be evaluated by determining whether the problem behaviors decrease and the desired behaviors increase.

CURRICULUM DESIGN

Curriculum has been defined as how teachers and students spend their time in school (Wilcox & Thomas, 1980). This seems especially true in an area such as social skills, which pervades nearly every aspect of school life, as well as life at home, in the community, and at work. Because of this, the teaching of social skills does not lend itself to strict scheduling (e.g., every Tuesday and Thursday from 9 to 10) and is most effective when infused and embedded throughout the school day. Compared with academic areas, the scope and sequence of social skills are less well defined and more open to values interpretation.

Just because a social skills curriculum has a certain degree of flexibility, it does not mean that social skills should not be assessed and taught in a systematic manner. There is general agreement among parents and educators that the goals of social skills training should include teaching students to get along with authority figures and peers and to have feelings of self-worth that allow them to set and pursue positive life goals. There are also generally accepted methods for social skills instruction, and excellent examples of these models are available commercially. What teachers want to know are how to determine the specific social skills to teach individual students, when to teach these skills, and how to go about it. Some also want to know why.

The "whys" of social skills instruction are an indirect commentary on society. Educators are now expected to teach skills, behaviors, and attitudes that were previously taught at home or in churches and synagogues. And society is experiencing the following alarming trends that have direct implications for training in socialization, peer relationships, and self-esteem: increased amount of violence in society, increased incidents of bullying and pupil-to-pupil violence, and increased victimization of individuals with disabilities. These trends, along with the continued high rate of teen drug use, make it increasingly important to teach prosocial skills to students in school. In addition, the 1997 amendments to IDEA stressed the importance of meaningful and appropriate assessment and treatment of students with social control issues.

In answering the "what" and "when" questions, there are many factors that should be considered. Certain skills and behaviors are more appropriate than others for given developmental and chronological ages. Developmentally young students need the basics of social interaction, sharing, care of animals, and the environment. Middle school is a time of intense pressure to be like the group, so knowledge about how and when to be like the group and how and when to resist peer pressure is critical at this age. In high school, students are preparing to enter

TABLE 7.3
Social Skills List

Social Skills Training Project (Volusia County School Board, 1992)

I. Basic Interpersonal Skills

Body Language

1. Using good posture
2. Facing the person
3. Keeping a comfortable distance
4. Making eye contact

Contact Initiation
5. Using a pleasant voice
6. Greeting
7. Introducing yourself

II. Conversation Skills

Beginning and Ending
8. Beginning a conversation
9. Ending a conversation

Maintaining
10. Listening attentively
11. Making sense
12. Taking turns talking
13. Asking and answering questions
14. Sharing personal conversation

III. Participation Skills

Group Interaction
15. Joining an activity in progress
16. Inviting others
17. Performing introductions
18. Taking "no" for an answer

Cooperation and Competition
19. Asking for help
20. Offering help
21. Following rules
22. Showing sportsmanship
23. Dealing with losing

IV. Friendship Skills

Respect
24. Using polite words
25. Touching the right way
26. Giving a compliment
27. Receiving a compliment

Mutuality
28. Sharing
29. Asking a favor
30. Expressing affection
31. Apologizing

V. Conflict Skills

Assertiveness
32. Giving criticism
33. Resisting peer pressure

34. Standing up for a friend
35. Responding to teasing

Coping
36. Receiving criticism
37. Coping with your own anger
38. Dealing with anger of others
39. Negotiating

Skills of Handicapped Children (Walker, McConnell, Holmes, Todis, Walker, & Golden, 1983)

Area I: Classroom Skills

Listening to the teacher
Doing what the teacher asks
Doing your best work (work quietly and write neatly)
Following classroom rules

Area II: Basic Interaction Skills

Eye contact
Using the right voice
Starting a conversation
Listening
Answering
Making sense
Taking turns talking
Asking questions
Keeping the conversation going

Area III: Getting Along Skills

Using polite words
Sharing
Following rules
Assisting others
Touching the right way

Area IV: Making Friends

Good grooming
Smiling
Complimenting
Friendship making

Area V: Coping Skills

When someone says "no"
When you express anger
When someone teases
When someone tries to hurt you
When someone asks you to do something you can't do
When things don't go right

(*continues*)

TABLE 7.3 *Continued.*

Social Skills in the Classroom (Stephens, 1992)	**Environmental Behaviors**
Self-Related Behavior	Dealing with emergencies
Accepting consequences	Lunchroom behaviors
Ethical behavior	Movement around the environment
Expressing feelings	Care for the environment
Positive attitude toward self	**Interpersonal Behaviors**
Task-Related Behavior	Accepting authority
Asking and answering questions	Coping with conflict
Classroom discussion	Gaining attention
Completing tasks	Greeting others
Following directions	Helping others
Group activities	Making conversation
Independent work	Organized play
On-task behavior	Positive attitude toward others
Performing before others	Playing informally
Quality of work	Property: own and others

the real world of work or college. They need self-advocacy skills, appropriate workplace social skills, and, above all, the ability to solve complex social problems and make social decisions (see Table 7.3 for a more complete list of social skills).

Social skills programs for students with disabilities often have little impact on long-term behavior (Gresham et al., 2001). To help ensure that instruction will have a lasting effect, teachers should consider the following factors when teaching social skills:

- *Choice of instructional objectives.* There should be a match between the student's problem and the teacher's intervention. Too often, teachers use a one-size-fits-all approach, and the skills that are being taught do not address the primary deficit of some of the students.

- *Instruction methodology.* Students need opportunities to use and practice a newly learned skill (Elksnin & Elksnin, 1998). Teachers should provide frequent and useful feedback and reinforcement for performance, like they do with any other skill. Social skills instruction needs to be integrated into the entire school day. Just as teachers often grade spelling regardless of the subject area content, so they must take every opportunity to teach students social skills. Direct instruction and positive practice can be part of social studies, health, life management, or a learning strategies class. Whenever possible, social skills should be taught in the settings in which they will be used.

- *Student characteristics.* If the above two factors have been considered, and the student is not still not responding, he or she may need training in how to be more sensitive to environmental cues (Elksnin & Elksnin, 1998). For example, to teach a student to react appropriately in social situations, the teacher must first determine whether the student recognizes the feelings of others. If the student does not, then he or she will have to be taught to recognize and put names to certain feelings. There are programs that assist students in putting names to different feelings (e.g., anger, sadness, boredom) so students may learn to respond to them (Cartledge & Kleefeld, 1991).

Even when teachers do all the right things, social skills training still may not appear to be having much effect. In such cases, training may need to continue for a longer period of time (Gresham et al., 2001), or competing behaviors may persist, the causes of which must be discovered and eliminated. See Table 7.4 for a list of tips for teaching social skills.

Students with mild disabilities are able to learn social skills and generalize them to many settings and situations. For this reason, they can benefit from being taught social problem-solving strategies and social decision-making skills. Students with moderate to severe cognitive disabilities will probably need to be taught skills that will be useful to them in the environments in which they are most likely to be living, working, and playing.

TABLE 7.4
Hints for Working with Students Who Have Social Skill Deficits

1. Ask previous teachers about interactive techniques that have been effective with the student in the past.

2. Expose students with social skills deficits to other students who demonstrate the appropriate behaviors.

3. Use direct instruction on target behaviors.

4. Have preestablished consequences for appropriate and inappropriate behaviors.

5. Monitor behavior frequently and administer consequences immediately.

6. Determine whether the student is on medication, what the schedule is, and what the medication effects may be on his or her in-class demeanor, then adjust teaching strategies accordingly.

7. Use time-out sessions to cool off disruptive behavior and as a break if the student needs one for a disability-related reason.

8. Acknowledge the contributions of the student in group activities.

9. Develop a contingency plan (contract) with the student in which inappropriate forms of response are replaced by appropriate ones.

10. Treat the student with social skills deficits as an individual who deserves respect and consideration.

11. When appropriate, seek input from the student about his or her strengths, weaknesses, and goals.

12. Enforce classroom rules consistently.

13. Make sure discipline fits the "crime," without harshness.

14. Provide encouragement.

15. Reward more than you punish to build student self-esteem.

16. Change consequences if they are not effective for motivating behavioral change.

17. Develop a schedule for delivering positive reinforcement in all educational environments.

18. Ask others (students and staff) to be friendly to students who have social skills deficits.

19. Monitor student self-esteem and assist in modification as needed.

20. Point out role models with a disability similar to that of the student.

21. Be patient, sensitive, a good listener, fair, and consistent in your treatment of students with social skills deficits.

The answer to the "how" of teaching of social skills is both simple and complex. It is simple in that the methods used by most of the widely accepted social skills programs have many common elements. It is complex in that hardly anyone seems to agree on how much of which element goes into skill acquisition, mastery, maintenance, and generalization.

General Social Instruction

Some generally accepted practices for teaching almost any skill apply equally well to teaching social skills, such as direct instruction, prompting, coaching, positive reinforcement, shaping, fading, positive practice, and so on. A list and brief description of the most common general approaches to teaching social skills may be found in Table 7.5.

Social Skills Instruction for Students with Mild Disabilities

Cognitive behavior modification (i.e., the cognitive method) has been found particularly effective in teaching social problem solving to students with mild disabilities. This approach, based on the work of Donald Meichenbaum (1977) and others, approaches the task of solving social problems the same way as solving other types of problems, by (a) identifying the problem, (b) generating solutions, (c) determining the pros and cons of each solution, (d) picking a solution, (e) evaluating the efficacy, and (f) reinforcing self, if successful.

The distinguishing characteristic of cognitive behavior modification is how the student is taught the "self" component. The teacher, after having provided a rationale for the strategy by presenting reasons why the skill is important and discussing the consequences of not knowing the skill, talks aloud through the steps of the general problem-solving strategy (or the same steps using a specific situation). Then the student talks aloud through it until it is fairly certain that she or he knows it. The student then talks it through speaking softly, then subvocally, then to himself or herself. The student then practices enough specific situations using this technique until the problem-solving steps are second nature. An example of how a student might use the problem-solving strategy is as follows:

 Step 1: Student states the problem to himself or herself.

"This very large assistant principal has just told me to get to class, but if I don't go to my locker first to get my homework, I am toast in Ms. Gritz's class."

 Step 2: Student generates alternative solutions.

"I could just make a dash for it and yell out an explanation as I run past him; or I could tell him to get off my case, that I can tell time; or I could walk calmly up to him with my explanation and hope he lets me pass."

 Step 3: Student evaluates alternatives.

"The first one might work or it might tick him off. The second one would be stupid because he already thinks I'm a wise guy. The third one has a

TABLE 7.5
General Instructional Strategies for Social Skills

Strategy	Description
Direct Instruction	This strategy is a highly structured, teacher-centered approach to instruction. The basic components are *state, ask,* and *provide feedback and/or correction.* Direct instruction may be used to teach any skill or behavior. Its greatest strength is that it provides opportunities for practice and for immediate feedback. The steps in direct instruction are (a) review previously learned material, (b) state objective of current lesson, (c) present new material, (d) provide guided practice and corrective feedback, and (e) provide independent practice and periodic review.
Modeling	Modeling, or demonstration, is a technique that is especially useful with students who have limited receptive language abilities. The teacher (or other knowledgeable person) demonstrates the skill or behavior, often while talking through the steps involved.
Behavioral Rehearsal with Coaching	This strategy is especially useful when teaching social skills and is often used in conjunction with modeling. In this strategy, the student demonstrates a skill or behavior that has just been taught (often through modeling) while the teacher or other instructor provides ongoing prompts and feedback (like an athletic coach).
Role-Playing	Role-playing is a form of behavioral rehearsal. During role play, students are asked to "act out" responses to situations they have seen demonstrated. The skills taught during role-playing are usually those that might present a danger to the student or others if taught in vivo (e.g., avoiding a fight with a bully) or skills that are difficult to teach in the natural environment (e.g., how to deal with criticism). Role-playing is often used with special needs students to help them learn new social behaviors or to play out a situation in which the student is likely to be involved.
Cognitive Strategies (including Cognitive Behavior Modification)	The cognitive strategy approach has been used successfully to teach teach social skills to students with learning and behavior difficulties This approach often uses mnemonic devices to assist students in remembering the behavior steps. There are also specialized techniques in cognitive behavior modification that combine basic principles of applied behavior analysis (e.g., feedback and consequences) and cognitive approaches (e.g., self-talk).
Life Space Interview (LSI)	LSI a classroom counseling approach used to manage behavior and change behavior patterns of students. In this crisis intervention technique, a student's behavior is discussed with him or her, usually at the time of the problem behavior's occurrence.
PLISSIT	This is an acronym for a continuum of interventions that may be used by counselors and therapists with students who have been sexually mistreated. The letters stand for Permission, Limited Information, Specific Suggestions, and Intensive Therapy. Teachers and other school personnel are qualified to provide the first two interventions. If the student is still in distress, teachers make referrals to other appropriate professionals.

(continues)

TABLE 7.5 *Continued.*

Strategy	Description
Rational Emotive Behavior Therapy	This approach requires specific, intensive training to administer but consists mainly of helping students develop an understanding of the relationship between events in their lives and how the students feel about or react to these life events. This therapy is based on the following principles: (a) you are responsible for your own emotions and actions; (b) your upsetting emotions and nonfunctional behaviors are the product of your irrational thinking; (c) you can learn more realistic views and, with practice, make them a part of you; and (d) you will be able to accept yourself and derive greater satisfaction in life by developing a perspective that is reality based.
Peer Tutoring	Peer tutoring has been used extensively to improve academic skills, but its formal and systematic use in the area of social skills is increasing. In this strategy, same-age peers (with or without disabilities) provide or reinforce instruction, benefiting all who are involved. Tutors and peers experience growth in the target area, tutors gain self-confidence and self-esteem, and socially isolated students experience increased social acceptance.
Community-Based Instruction	Community-based instruction provides the opportunity for students to learn and practice practical social skills in the settings in which they will ultimately be used.

chance and is less likely to surprise him—and Mr. Holt (alias, The Hulk) does not like surprises!"

➔ **Step 4: Student selects an alternative.**

"I'd better take the third one."

➔ **Step 5: Student evaluates how well the solution worked.**

"That worked pretty well. He let me through and now maybe he gives me credit for being at least a semiserious student."

➔ **Step 6: Student reinforces himself or herself and considers other places this alternative might work.**

"Yessss! I'll have to try that with my dad the next time we get into it."

There are other, less instructionally intense methods for assisting students with social skills deficits, such as strategic placement. Strategic placement refers to the practice of putting a student who needs social skills training in situations with other students who are good role models. This strategy works particularly well for those students who learn incidentally but may be lost on some students unless the model students' behavior is praised specifically in the target student's presence.

Social Skills Instruction for Students with Mild to Moderate Disabilities

The basic steps for teaching a social skill are (a) present the skill: name it, define it, give a rationale for it, and model it, and (b) practice the skill: guided practice, talk through the skill, generalize the skill, assign its use to other settings, and reinforce its use in many settings. The following is an example of this strategy:

A teacher has assessed her students and found that they all need to learn (or improve upon) the skills required to enter a peer group appropriately. The teacher presents the skill (Step 1) to the class by naming it ("entering a peer group the right way") and describing what is meant by this. ("For example, students, when you see a group standing in the hall between classes and you want to be part of that group, how do you go about it in a way that will be accepted by most of that group?") The teacher then explains why she or he thinks this is an important skill and/or asks the students why they think this might be an important skill. The teacher then models the appropriate way to enter a group using a group of students, pretending that there are others there, or showing a video in which this skill is performed correctly. She or he talks aloud so the students recognize each step of the skill. "First, I come up to the outside of the group. I wait for a break in the conversation and then I greet someone in the group or address the group as a whole with some general comment or greeting." At this point, the teacher does *not* use nonexamples because when nonexamples are used during acquisition, they are often what students remember. Students are given the opportunity to practice the skill (Step 2) as the teacher talks them through it. Then they practice with each other, still getting feedback from the teacher. After this, it is a matter of students and teacher identifying various places where the skill can be practiced and the teacher asking for feedback on the usefulness of the skill.

More examples of this instructional sequence may be found in the Skill-streaming materials by Goldstein, Sprafkin, Geershaw, and Klein (1986) and McGinnis and Goldstein (1984).

Another method that has been used successfully for teaching social skills is peer teaching (Prater, Serna, & Nakamura, 1999). In this approach, students *with* disabilities were trained as peer coaches to address the skills of giving positive feedback, accepting negative feedback, and contributing to class discussion. They then modeled these behaviors and coached other students with disabilities in these skills.

Social Skills Instruction for Students with Severe Disabilities

The earliest social skills—those we hope to develop in early childhood—are linked inextricably to cognitive and communication skills. The baby who smiles and coos in response to interaction with a parent or who cries to get picked up is exhibiting early reciprocal social skills. Later, in play with parents such as peek-aboo or in social play with peers, the same skills (social, cognitive, communication) are linked.

There is a tendency to forget these linkages as children grow older and the three areas diverge and become more complex. Throughout life, however, cognitive and communication skills continue to play an important part in social skill development.

Students with severe disabilities are significantly delayed in the cognitive and communication abilities required to learn and perform the requisite social behaviors. For these students, the critical elements of functional curricula should be revisited with an eye to social skills. The general "rules" for functional curricula are that they

- are useful to the student immediately or in the foreseeable future,
- enhance the student's social value, and
- are age appropriate.

Teachers can use these same criteria as guidelines for determining which social skills to teach. Parental input is very important for social skills training; if parents value the skills that are being taught, they are more likely to prompt and reinforce them at home.

Instruction of social skills for students with severe disabilities will generally be carried out using the same instructional techniques as for other areas of instruction—a basic behavioral approach. Teachers should focus on teaching prosocial skills, rather than on the extinction of inappropriate ones. Teachers need "think replacement." Instead of taking away a behavior from a student who may have few skills, teacher should replace those that are not working for student and teacher with those that do. Instruction should focus on purposeful, active learning that involves the students in doing things that are incompatible with the interfering behaviors. For example, instead of a teacher spending a lot of time trying to get a student to stop a noisy repetitive movement, he or she should engage the student in an activity that is so interesting that the student chooses to be still. Or the student can be engaged in an activity that involves movement and noise in a positive way (e.g., clapping to music) but does not reinforce stereotypic behaviors. Teachers must always keep in mind that however nonfunctional and irritating the behavior seems, it is serving some function for the student. Understanding that function (probably by completing a functional asessment, as described earlier in this chapter) will put the teacher well on the way to finding a replacement behavior that is more useful for the student (and less annoying to the teacher).

Social Skills for Inclusion

Students with disabilities need opportunities for making friends with their same-age, nondisabled peers. Teachers and paraprofessionals in the schools can assist this process in a number of ways, including providing social opportunities, being open with children and adults about disabling conditions, and encouraging appropriate interactions (Calloway, 1999). Students who have been deemed inappropriate for the regular classroom due to problem behaviors need special and intense action. The behaviors most likely to result in exclusion are disruption, temper tantrums, aggression, fighting, destroying and damaging property, and overt defiance. The following plan outlines intervention for a troubled student who has been taken out of the included classroom due to one or several of the above indicators.

A teacher first chooses the behaviors to be targeted by (a) surveying the regular classroom and determining which behaviors are essential and useful, as well as the acceptable levels of performance of each, and (b) identifying behaviors that will be reinforced by peers and teachers (e.g., offering to share) and behaviors that can be used in many settings (e.g., smiling). Behaviors should be taught in a special class up to or above criterion. Direct instruction, prompting, modeling, rehearsal, and reinforcement can be used for initial acquisition; social script and role play can be used to attain fluency.

Nondesirable behaviors can be evaluated using the functional assessment procedures described earlier in this chapter. Teachers can develop a positive behavior support plan to address those challenging behaviors that are most likely to result in exclusion. *Positive behavior supports* are those people and events in the student's natural environment that prompt and sustain appropriate behavior (O'Neill et al., 1997). The following example shows how a functional assessment was used to change behavior in a student with severe disabilities:

> A student diagnosed with autism has severe disruptive behaviors, making inclusion with his typical peers in the regular classroom very difficult. His teachers conduct a functional assessment in the special and regular education classrooms and determine that sudden change in routine precipitates the student's outbursts in the regular education classroom. (In the special education classroom, due to the rigid structure, there had been few changes and outbursts occurred when he was asked to do tasks he did not choose.) The student had already learned the basic social skills required in a classroom such as sitting, working at his desk, and checking his schedule for the next assignment. The teachers determined that they would give the student a signal if an unexpected change was imminent by placing and switching red and black flags in a previously unused flag holder at the front of the room. All students were told what the flags meant (and it actually helped some other students who had difficulty handling change).

IEP DEVELOPMENT

For an IEP to truly meet the needs of the intended student, it should be predicated on certain basic values. One of the primary values is a family-oriented process focused on person-centered planning and choice. The development process must provide for coordination of services and interventions, with input from all relevant sources. Depending on the individual student, the activities and services should be community based, integrated within the general school program, or both. Specific resources and time commitments for services should be listed along with any modifications or accommodations that might be needed.

In this chapter, we are examining the components of the IEP that focus on skill development in the areas of socialization, peer relationships, and self-esteem. Figure 7.1 contains a list of possible IEP goals and short-term objectives in these areas. This list is intended to assist teachers in writing annual goals and

SOCIAL SKILLS GOALS

The following are some examples of annual goals and short-term objectives in the area of social skills. They are not intended to be exhaustive but to stimulate ideas for teachers. Each would, of course, need to be individualized and the elements of condition and criteria added for use in students' IEPs or behavior plans.

Note: Although self-esteem is often not explicitly included in listings of social skills, sample goals with accompanying short-term objectives in this area are provided for both the elementary and secondary levels.

Elementary Level

Classroom Survival Skills
Goal: The student will complete assignments in class.
Objective: Arrange assignments in a reasonable sequence.
Objective: Prioritize assignments.

Friendship Making
Goal: The student will introduce himself appropriately.
Objective: State the occasions when it is appropriate to introduce oneself.
Objective: Say, "Hello, my name is Henry," and extend hand for a handshake to three new people at school or in the community.

Dealing with Feelings
Goal: The student will be able to express her feelings without becoming upset.
Objective: Identify (name) feelings.
Objective: Describe her feelings to the teacher without crying, raising her voice, or throwing anything.

Alternatives to Aggression
Goal: The student will respond to teasing in a socially appropriate way.
Objective: Identify when other students are teasing in a playful way.
Objective: Develop and use three ways to divert teasers and respond without crying, hitting, or becoming verbally abusive.

Dealing with Stress
Goal: The student will deal with accusation by an authority figure in a socially appropriate way.
Objective: Identify when he is being accused of some misdeed (not just being corrected in class).
Objective: Use a problem-solving approach to respond to the accusation.

Self-Esteem
Goal: The student's self esteem will increase.
Objective: Make positive self-statements related to school, home, or personal appearance.
Objective: Identify three ways in which she will improve herself academically or personally.

Secondary Level

Problem Solving
Goal: The student will be able to determine a reasonable course of action in social situations using the ASSET problem-solving process.
Objective: Name the steps in the problem-solving process.
Objective: Demonstrate three in-class and one out-of-class uses of the problem-solving process.

Resisting Peer Pressure
Goal: The student will resist peer pressure to skip school.
Objective: Generate a list of reasons she should not skip school and keep them in her purse.
Objective: Use some or all of these reasons when responding to peer pressure to skip school.

Coping
Goal: The student will be able to protect herself if anyone tries to hurt her.
Objective: Identify the names and phone numbers of people to call for assistance in the event of potentially abusive situations.
Objective: Repeat three possible ways to remove herself from a potentially abusive situation.

(continues)

FIGURE 7.1. Examples of IEP goals and objectives for social skills development.

Secondary Level *Continued.*

Interpersonal Relationships
Goal: The student will be able to send an "I'm interested" message appropriately to another person.
Objective: Differentiate between appropriate and inappropriate ways of showing interest in another person.
Objective: Develop and use at least three ways of demonstrating interest (e.g., complimenting, sending a gift, extending an invitation).

Asking for Directions or Assistance
Goal: The student will ask for assistance with vocational assignments appropriately.
Objective: Identify the appropriate person to ask for assistance with a work task (e.g., when one task is finished and the next task is not clear).
Objective: Request assistance in classroom.

Self-Esteem
Goal: The student will participate actively and positively in his own transition IEP meeting.
Objective: Identify own strengths and weaknesses in academic areas.
Objective: Identify interests and aptitudes for one or more vocational areas.

FIGURE 7.1. *Continued.*

short-term objectives for students' IEPs. These examples for elementary and secondary students are not intended to be complete or exhaustive but to show goals and objectives that teachers might write after formal or informal assessment of the student. Although there are certain skills that all students need early and throughout their lives, it is never too late to begin teaching even the most basic skills. It is also important for teachers to model these skills and to reinforce them whenever they are practiced.

Teachers, family members, and the student should also answer the following questions as they develop this section of the IEP:

1. How does the student respond to different social situations?

2. What are the student's work habits?

3. How does the student respond to environmental stresses such as emergencies, deadlines, and pressure?

4. How does the student work as part of a group and alone, show leadership skills, give supervision, receive supervision, perform special tasks and duties, perform routine tasks and duties, and perform high-speed tasks and duties?

 MICHAEL

Michael is the 15-year-old student with a severe learning disability and an emotional disability who was introduced at the beginning of this chapter. Keeping the above questions mind and considering the information provided by Michael, his

(continues)

TABLE 7.6
IEP Goals and Objectives for Michael

Goal	Short-Term Objectives
I. Michael will demonstrate interpersonal skills necessary for successful participation in group activities.	1. When requested, Michael will verbalize the importance of getting along with others to counselor satisfaction. 2. Michael will accurately demonstrate appropriate peer social skills in a role-play situation. 3. Michael will verbalize his responsibilities when accepting and completing tasks in a learning group in 75% of opportunities. 4. Michael will consistently demonstrate appropriate behavior when participating in a group task.
II. Michael will use strategies for solving relationship problems in various settings.	1. When asked, Michael will identify at least three strategies for problem solving in personal relationships at home, at school, and in the community. 2. Michael will demonstrate use of problem-solving strategies during role-play situations to teacher satisfaction. 3. Michael will demonstrate use of problem-solving strategies during real-life situations at home, at school, and in the community.
III. Michael will make short- and long-term goals for academics, career, and relationships with others.	1. During his IEP meeting, Michael will state his desired in-school outcomes for the next 3 years in academics, career, and relationships with others. 2. Michael will develop specific goals in these three areas in his career planner. 3. Michael will write at least two strategies for achieving his goals in these three areas.
IV. Michael will demonstrate increased self-esteem.	1. When asked, Michael will be able to express three positive things about himself. 2. Michael will use behaviors that reflect self-esteem when carrying out productive activities in school 60% of the time. 3. When asked by his counselor, Michael will be able to describe his learning and behavior problems accurately.
V. Michael will demonstrate socially responsible behavior in the classroom and at home.	1. Michael will follow the instruction of adults with no outbursts in 75% of opportunities. 2. During 90% of structured classroom activities, Michael will demonstrate appropriate behavior. 3. In the community, Michael will demonstrate appropriate behavior on 75% of occasions.
VI. Michael will demonstrate good interpersonal skills. accuracy.	1. When asked, Michael will identify qualities of a positive relationship with a peer with 100% 2. Michael will identify appropriate and inappropriate behaviors for interacting with peers with 80% accuracy. 3. Michael will initiate interactions with peers.

family, and school personnel, the IEP team has developed several goals and objectives for Michael.

First, the team assessed his current level of performance. Michael reads with comprehension at a 3.7 grade level and is at a 5.2 grade level in math. Michael's areas of strength are in manipulating objects and understanding their mechanical functioning. He always volunteers to fix broken items in the classroom. Michael has expressed an interest in working on cars or joining the Army when he graduates from high school. Michael currently demonstrates poor impulse control and has difficulty interacting with authority figures and peers. He appears to be experimenting with alcohol.

Table 7.6 shows the list of long-term goals for Michael with specific objectives that will enable Michael to accomplish his goals. It is imperative to remember that the student should be a part of the goal development process to ensure success in achievement.

CONCLUSION

Teachers have the unusual opportunity to affect all areas of student development, including social development. Teachers must value themselves and model appropriate social behavior for their students. Socialization is more than the sum of the social skills students have acquired. It is also a reflection of how those students feel about themselves, their peers, their families, their community, and their environment.

APPENDIX 7.A
ANNOTATED LIST OF SOCIAL SKILLS CURRICULA

General Social Skills

The Walker Social Skills Curriculum: ACCEPTS
Authors: H. M. Walker, S. McConnell, D. Holmes, B. Todis, J. Walker, and N. Golden
Date: 1988
Publisher: PRO-ED
Comments: This curriculum is designed for elementary school students with mild to moderate disabilities and includes a teacher's manual, suggestions for activities, and videos.

The Walker Social Skills Curriculum: ACCESS
Authors: H. M. Walker, B. Todis, D. Holmes, and G. Horton
Date: 1987
Publisher: PRO-ED
Comments: This curriculum is designed for secondary students with mild to moderate disabilities and includes a teacher's manual, suggestions for activities, and videos.

ASSET
Authors: J. S. Hazel, J. B. Schumaker, J. A. Sherman, and J. Sheldon-Widgen
Date: 1981
Publisher: Research Press
Comments: This curriculum contains group activities for secondary students (ages 13–18) and includes a leader's guide, home notes, questionnaires, skill sheets, and audiotapes.

The Culture and Lifestyle-Appropriate Social Skills Intervention Curriculum (CLASSIC): A Program for Socially Valid Social Skills Training
Authors: J. A. Dygdon
Date: 1993
Publisher: Clinical Psychology
Comments: This program is available for both elementary- and secondary-age students.

Getting Along with Others
Authors: N. F. Jackson, D. A. Jackson, and C. Monroe
Date: 1983
Publisher: Research Press
Comments: This curriculum is designed for elementary school students and contains suggested modifications for other levels. It includes a list of suggested assessment tools, an activity notebook, and a program guide with teacher scripts. A secondary school–level version is also available.

Life Centered Career Education: A Competency-Based Approach
Author: D. E. Brolin
Date: 1997
Publisher: Council for Exceptional Children
Comments: This curriculum consists of three major components, 22 major competencies, four stages of career development, and three major instructional settings. It is designed primarily for students who will need continued support after graduation.

The Prepare Curriculum
Author: A. P. Goldstein
Date: 1999
Publisher: Research Press
Comments: This recently revised and expanded curriculum teaches prosocial competencies in the areas of reducing aggression, stress, and prejudice through games, role plays, reading and writing, drawing, brainstorming, group discussion, relaxation, tape recordings, photography, and other hands-on activities. It is designed for use with middle school and high school students.

Skillstreaming Series:
Skillstreaming the Adolescent
Authors: A. P. Goldstein, R. P. Sprafkin, N. J. Geershaw, and P. Klein
Date: 1980

Skillstreaming in Early Childhood
Authors: E. McGinnis and A. P. Goldstein
Date: 1980

Skillstreaming the Elementary School Child
Authors: E. McGinnis and A. P. Goldstein
Date: 1984
Publisher: Research Press
Comments: The Skillstreaming series is a classic. Some elements have been updated over time, such as the addition of videotaped demonstration. This comprehensive curriculum can be used with students with mild disabilities and typical students. The methodology and activity cards make the series teacher friendly.

Social Decision-Making Skills: Curriculum Guide for the Elementary Grades
Authors: M. J. Elias and J. F. Clabby
Date: 1989
Publisher: Aspen
Comments: This curriculum is designed for elementary school students (K–6) in regular and special education and includes a guide with scripted lessons and student worksheets.

Social Skills for Daily Living
Authors: J. Schumaker, J. B. Hazel, and C. S. Pederson
Date: 1988
Publisher: American Guidance Service
Comments: This curriculum is designed for individual and group instruction of secondary students (ages 12–21). Materials include a manual, student workbook, management forms, and a progress wall chart. The developers are from the University of Kansas Strategies Intervention Model team.

Social Skills in the School and Community
Author: L. R. Sargent
Date: 1991
Publisher: Council for Exceptional Children
Comments: This is less a curriculum than it is a collection of ideas for teaching social skills at all levels (elementary, middle, and high school). It is designed mostly for typical students and those with mild disabilities.

Social Skills on the Job
Author: American Guidance Service
Date: 1997
Publisher: American Guidance Service
Comments: This is a basic primer, providing a quick reference to basic social skills necessary for employment success.

Social Skills Strategies
Authors: N. Gajewski and P. Mayo
Date: 1989
Publisher: Thinking Publications
Comments: This is designed as a 2-year program for students with mild learning and behavioral problems or anyone with skill, performance, or self-control deficits.

Taking Part: Introducing Social Skills to Young Children
Authors: G. Cartledge and J. Kleefeld
Date: 1991
Publisher: American Guidance Service
Comments: This curriculum is designed for preschool to Grade 3 children, typical or exceptional, and includes a manual, puppets, stickers, posters, and activity sheets.

Thinking It Through
Authors: R. M. Foxx and R. G. Bittle
Date: 1989
Publisher: Research Press
Comments: This curriculum is designed for adolescent students. It has separate guides for teachers of students with developmental disabilities, mental illness, brain injuries, and emotional problems.

Thinking, Feeling, Behaving
Author: A. Vernon
Date: 1989
Publisher: Research Press
Comments: This curriculum is designed for small-group or individual instruction of students ages 1 through 6 years and 7 through 12 years (typical or with mild disabilities). The curriculum uses art, stories, games, and discussion.

Self-Esteem Curriculum

Esteem Builders: A K–12 Self-Esteem Curriculum for Improving Student Achievement and School Climate
Author: M. Borba
Date: 1989
Publisher: Jalmar Press
Comments: This curriculum is designed for students in Grades K through 8. The leader's manual outlines activities.

Peer Relationships Curricula

PEERS: A Program for Remediating Social Withdrawal in School
Authors: H. Hops, J. J. Guild, D. H. Fleishman, S. C. Paine, A. Street, H. M. Walker, et al.
Date: 1978

Publisher: Center at Oregon in the Behavioral Education of the Handicapped

Comments: This curriculum is designed for socially withdrawn students in the primary grades. It contains teacher and consultant guides, a student packet, and other program materials.

Personal Power: Peer Interaction Skills

Author: R. H. Wells

Date: 1983

Publisher: PRO-ED

Comments: This curriculum is designed for exceptional and at-risk students in Grades 4 through 12. It includes an instructor's guide, handouts, pretests, and a lesson plan manual.

Self-Protection (including physical and sexual abuse protection)

Circles I: Intimacy and Relationships

Authors: L. Walker-Hirsch and M. P. Champagne

Date: 1993

Publisher: Stanfield

Comments: This curriculum is designed to teach concepts of personal space, social distance, and appropriate social and sexual behavior. It clarifies circumstances for hugging, for shaking hands, and for ignoring people.

Life Horizons

Author: W. Kempton

Date: 1988

Publisher: Stanfield

Comments: This curriculum provides people who are developmentally immature with strategies to avoid sexual abuse and assault.

Old Me, New Me (formerly Peace, Harmony, Awareness)

Author: M. Lupin

Date: 1983

Publisher: Developmental Learning Materials

Comments: This is a relaxation program for children that includes an instructional manual and a series of audiotapes. Units emphasize self-concept, behavior problems, stress, and creativity.

Second Step

Author: Committee for Children

Date: 2001

Publisher: Committee for Children

Comments: This is a program for students in preschool through Grade 9 that develops students' social and emotional skills and teaches students to change the behaviors and attitudes that contribute to violence. It includes lessons that teach skills in empathy, impulse control, problem solving, and anger management. A family involvement component is available for the preschool and elementary levels of the program.

Steps to Respect: A Bullying Prevention Program

Author: Committee for Children

Date: 2001

Publisher: Committee for Children

Comments: This curriculum teaches students, staff, and parents skills to help students develop healthy relationships and decrease bullying at school. It is designed for schoolwide implementation, with lessons for the upper elementary grades (3–5 or 4–6).

Substance Abuse Prevention

Learning to Live Drug Free: A Curriculum Model for Prevention
Author: U.S. Department of Education
Date: 1992
Publisher: U.S. Government Printing Office (Available from National Clearinghouse for Alcohol and Drug Information, P.O. Box 2345, Rockville, MD, 20852)
Comments: This curriculum is designed for Grades K through 12 and contains a teacher's manual, teaching tips, activities, and a supplemental list of resources.

DISCOVER: Skills for Life
Authors: M. L. Thompson and J. F. Strange
Date: 1996
Publisher: American Guidance Service
Comments: A comprehensive violence prevention curriculum for Grades K through 12. Curriculum includes building self-esteem, drug and substance abuse prevention, decision-making skills, and violence prevention skills. The program provides students with knowledge, skills, and experiences to enhance their ability to make healthy choices about drugs and violence.

Drug Abuse Resistance Education (D.A.R.E.)
Date: 1997
Publisher: Laurel Glen
Comments: This is one of the oldest and best known of the drug prevention programs, but the long-term benefits have been debated.

LifeSkills Training
Author: G. J. Botvin
Date: 1996
Publisher: Princeton Health Press
Comments: This is one of nine programs designated as "exemplary" drug abuse and violence prevention programs by an expert panel for Safe and Drug-Free Schools (U.S. Department of Education).

APPENDIX 7.B
ANNOTATED LIST OF SOCIAL SKILLS
ASSESSMENT INSTRUMENTS

Interview Format

AAMR Adaptive Behavior Scale–School: Second Edition
Authors: N. Lambert, K. Nihira, and H. Leland
Publisher: PRO-ED
Date: 1993
Comments: This assessment is primarily for use with children with mental retardation ages 3 through 16, and it assesses social and daily living skills and behaviors.

Behavior Rating Profile–Second Edition
Authors: L. Brown and D. D. Hammill
Date: 1990
Publisher: PRO-ED
Comments: For Grades 1 through 12, this assessment includes self-report, school, home, and peer ratings and contains extensive validity measures.

Child Behavior Checklist
Authors: T. M. Achenbach and C. Edelbrock
Date: 2001
Publisher: Achenback System of Empirically Based Assessment (ASEBA)
Comments: For ages 4 through 16, this assessment uses multiple informants and environments, including self-report. It is useful for placement and programming.

Matson Evaluation of Social Skills
Authors: J. L. Matson, A. F. Rotatori, and W. J. Helsel
Date: 1983
Publisher: IDS
Comments: For ages 4 through 18, this instrument also uses self-report to assess observable socialization behaviors.

Self-Perception Profile for Children
Author: S. Harter
Date: 1985
Publisher: University of Denver
Comments: For preschool to adolescent students, this assessment uses parent reports to screen for developmental and emotional problems.

Scales of Independent Behavior–Revised
Authors: R. H. Bruininks, R. W. Woodcock, R. E. Weatherman, and B. K. Hill
Date: 1984
Publisher: Riverside
Comments: For infants to adults, this product assesses three major areas and provides a problem behavior scale. This assessment is statistically linked to the *Woodcock–Johnson Psycho-Educational Battery*.

Test of Pragmatic Language
Authors: D. Phelps-Terasaki and T. Phelps-Gunn
Date: 1992
Publisher: PRO-ED
Comments: For kindergarten through junior high students, this test assesses how students use language socially to achieve goals.

Vineland Adaptive Behavior Scales
Authors: S. S. Sparrow, D. A. Bella, and D. Cicchetti
Date: 1984
Publisher: American Guidance Service
Comments: Three versions of this assessment cover ages birth to adult (including a classroom version for ages 3–13). Examiner also may use direct observation in addition to, or instead of, interview.

Observation or Rater Format

Assessment of Interpersonal Relations
Author: B. A. Bracken
Date: 1993
Publisher: PRO-ED
Comments: This assessment is designed for use with adolescents and was conormed with the *Multi-Dimensional Self-Concept Scale.*

Burks' Behavior Rating Scales
Author: H. F. Burks
Date: 1977
Publisher: Western Psychological Services
Comments: For Grades 1 through 9, this assessment has 18 categories and 10-minute administration.

Social Skills Rating System
Authors: F. M. Gresham and S. N. Elliott
Date: 1990
Publisher: American Guidance Service
Comments: For preschool through high school students and normed for age, gender, and disability, this assessment uses multiple informants, including self-report, to rate both frequency and importance of social skills.

Social–Emotional Dimension Scale
Authors: J. B. Hutton and T. G. Roberts
Date: 1986
Publisher: PRO-ED
Comments: For ages 5-6 through 18-6, this scale covers six areas, including avoidance of peer and teacher interaction.

Self-Report Format

Coopersmith Self-Esteem Inventories
Author: S. Coopersmith
Date: 1990

Publisher: Consulting Psychologists Press
Comments: This assessment measures student attitudes in social, academic, and personal contexts.

Culture Free Self-Esteem Inventories–Second Edition
Author: J. Battle
Date: 2002
Publisher: PRO-ED
Comments: For children and adults, this product assesses five areas and has been standardized on special populations.

Multidimensional Self Concept Scale
Author: B. A. Bracken
Date: 1992
Publisher: PRO-ED
Comments: For ages 9 through 19, this scale assesses social affect, competence, and academic, family, and physical characteristics.

Personality Inventory for Children–Second Edition
Authors: D. Lachar and C. Gruber
Date: 2001
Publisher: Western Psychological Services
Comments: For elementary and junior high school students, this inventory assesses general self-worth and three subareas.

Piers Harris Children's Self-Concept Scale–Second Edition
Authors: E. V. Piers, D. B. Harris, and D. S. Herzberg
Date: 2002
Publisher: Western Psychological Services
Comments: For Grades 3 through 12, this scale assesses physical appearance, popularity, and happiness.

Self-Esteem Index
Authors: L. Brown and J. Alexander
Date: 1991
Publisher: PRO-ED
Comments: For ages 7 through 19, this assessment can be administered to a group or individual and results in a self-esteem quotient.

APPENDIX 7.C
INTERNET RESOURCES

Publishers of Curricula and Assessment Instruments

Academic Therapy Publications
http://www.academictherapy.com

Allyn & Bacon/Longman
http://www.ablongman.com

American Guidance Service
http://www.agsnet.com

ASEBA—Achenbach System of Empirically
Based Assessment
http://www.aseba.org/index.html

Aspen
http://www.aspenpublishers.com

Boys Town Press
http://www.girlsandboystown.org/products

Brookes
http://www.brookespublishing.com

Committee for Children
http://www.cfchildren.org/violence.htm

Consulting Psychologists Press
http://www.cpp-db.com

Council for Exceptional Children
http://www.cec.sped.org/bk

Exceptional Innovations
http://www.exinn.net/catalog.htm

Jalmar Press
http://www.jalmarpress.com

Life Skills Training
http://www.lifeskillstraining.com

Piney Mountain Press
http://www.pineymountain.com

PRO-ED
http://www.proedinc.com

Psychological Publications
http://www.tjta.com

Research Press
http://www.researchpress.com

Riverside Publishing
http://www.riverpub.com

Stanfield
http://www.stanfield.com

Thinking Publications
http://www.thinkingpublications.com

Western Psychological Services
http://www.wpspublish.com

Information on the Internet

Drug Abuse Resistance Education (D.A.R.E.)
http://www.dare-america.com

Learning Disabilities Information and Education Center
http://www.ldiec.net

National Clearinghouse for Alcohol and Drug Information
For Kids Only Section
http://www.health.org/features/kidsarea/kidsarea.htm

National Institute on Drug Abuse
Information about research-based drug prevention programs
http://www.nida.nih.gov/prevention/PROGRM.html

Safe and Drug-Free Schools Program
U.S. Department of Education Office of Elementary and Secondary Education
http://ojjdp.ncjrs.org/pubs/fedresources/ag-03.html

"Substance Abuse and Learning Disabilities: Peas in a Pod or Apples and Oranges?"
Article from Center on Addiction and Substance Abuse
http://www.casacolumbia.org/publications1456/publications_show.htm?doc_id=34846

"Virtual Reality Applications for Teaching Social Skills to Students with Emotional and Behavioral Disorders"
Article by Howard Muscott and Timothy Gifford
http://www.csun.edu/cod/conf/1994/proceedings/Tssts~1.htm

United States Center for Aggression Replacement Training
Source materials for children and youth with violence and impulse control issues
http://www.uscart.org

Software Packages

Relate
A three CD-ROM software package for teaching coping skills to children and teenagers.
Comment: These materials are very timely but expensive.
http://www.rippleeffects.com

Coolien Challenge
CD-based software program addressing violence and anger management for teens.
http://www.compu-teach.com/coolien.htm

REFERENCES

Achenbach, T. M., & Edelbrock, C. (2001). *Child Behavior Checklist.* Burlington, VT: Achenbach System of Empirically Based Assessment (ASEBA).

American Guidance Service. (1997). *Social skills on the job.* Circle Pines, MN: Author.

Bambury, J., Wilton, K., & Boyd, A. (1999). Effects of two experimental educational programs on the social-sexual knowledge and attitudes of adults with mild intellectual disability. *Education and Training in Mental Retardation and Developmental Disabilities, 34*(2), 207–211.

Batsche, G. M., & Knoff, H. M. (1994). Bullies and their victims: Understanding a pervasive problem in the schools. *School Psychology Review, 23*(2), 165–174.

Battle, J. (2002). *Culture Free Self-Esteem Inventories–Second Edition.* Austin, TX: PRO-ED.

Boat, B. W., & Sites, H. J. (2001). Assessment of trauma and maltreatment in children with special needs. In R. J. Simeonsson & S. L. Rosenthal (Eds.), *Psychological and developmental assessment: Children with disabilities and chronic conditions* (pp. 153–175). New York: Guilford.

Borba, M. (1989). *Esteem builders: A K–12 self-esteem curriculum for improving student achievement and school climate.* Torrance, CA: Jalmar Press.

Botvin, G. J. (1996). *LifeSkills training.* Princeton, NJ: Princeton Health Press.

Bracken, B. A. (1992). *Multidimensional Self Concept Scale.* Austin, TX: PRO-ED.

Bracken, B. A. (1993). *Assessment of Interpersonal Relations.* Austin, TX: PRO-ED.

Brolin, D. E. (1997). *Life centered career education: A competency-based approach.* Arlington, VA: Council for Exceptional Children.

Brown, L., & Alexander, J. (1991). *Self-Esteem Index.* Austin, TX: PRO-ED.

Brown, L., & Hammill, D. D. (1990). *Behavior Rating Profile–Second Edition.* Austin, TX: PRO-ED.

Bruininks, R. H., Woodcock, R. W., Weatherman, R. E., & Hill, B. K. (1984). *Scales of Independent Behavior–Revised.* Itasca, IL: Riverside.

Bryan, T., Pearl, R., & Herzog, A. (1989). Learning disabled adolescents' vulnerability to crime: Attitudes, anxieties, and experiences. *Learning Disabilities Research, 5,* 51–60.

Burks, H. F. (1977). *Burks' Behavior Rating Scales.* Los Angeles: Western Psychological Services.

Calloway, C. (1999). Promote friendship in the inclusive classroom. *Intervention in School and Clinic, 34*(3), 176–178.

Carter, J., & Sugai, G. (1989). Social skills curriculum analysis. *Teaching Exceptional Children, 22*(1), 36–39.

Cartledge, G., & Kleefeld, J. (1991). *Taking part: Introducing social skills to young children.* Circle Pines, MN: American Guidance Service.

Caspar, L. A., & Glidden, L. M. (2001). Sexuality education for adults with developmental disabilities. *Education and Training in Mental Retardation and Developmental Disabilities, 36*(2), 172–177.

Cavaliere, F. (1995, October). Substance abuse in the deaf community. *APA Monitor.*

Committee for Children. (2001). *Second step.* Seattle, WA: Author.

Committee for Children. (2001). *Steps to respect: A bullying prevention program.* Seattle, WA: Author.

Coopersmith, S. (1990). *Coopersmith Self-Esteem Inventories.* Palo Alto, CA: Consulting Psychologists Press.

Cosmos, C. (2001). Abuse of children with disabilities. *CEC Today, 8*(2), 1–15.

Crosse, S. B., Kaye, E., & Ratnofsky, A. C. (1993). *A report on the maltreatment of children with disabilities.* Washington, DC: U.S. Office on Child Abuse and Neglect.

Curwin, R. L. (1993, November). The healing power of altruism. *Educational Leadership, 50,* 36–39.

D.A.R.E. America. (1997). *D.A.R.E.* Inglewood, CA: Laurel Glen.

Dodge, K. A. (1989). Problems in social relationships. In E. J. Mash & R. A. Barkley (Eds.), *Treatment of childhood disorders* (pp. 223–241). New York: Guilford.

Doren, B., Bullis, M., & Benz, M. (1996). Predictors of victimization of adolescents with disabilities in transition. *Exceptional Children, 63*(1), 7–19.

Dygdon, J. A. (1993). *The culture and lifestyle-appropriate social skills intervention curriculum (CLASSIC): A program for socially valid social skills training.* Brandon, VT: Clinical Psychology.

Elias, M. J., & Clabby, J. F. (1989). *Social decision-making skills: Curriculum guide for the elementary grades.* Rockville, MD: Aspen.

Elksnin, L. K., & Elksnin, N. (1998). Teaching social skills to students with learning and behavior problems. *Intervention in School and Clinic, 33*(3), 131–141.

Erlbaum, B., & Vaughn, S. (1999). Can school-based interventions enhance the self-concept of students with learning disabilities? *Exceptional Parent, 29*(9), 92–94.

Foster-Johnson, L., & Dunlap, G. (1993). Using functional assessment to develop effective individualized interventions for challenging behaviors. *Teaching Exceptional Children, 25*(3), 44–57.

Foxx, R. M., & Bittle, R. G. (1989). *Thinking it through.* Champaign, IL: Research Press.

Freeman, A. C., Ferreyra, N., & Calabrese, C. (1997). *Fostering recovery for women with disabilities: Eliminating barriers to substance abuse programs.* Oakland, CA: Berkeley Planning Associates.

Gajewski, N., & Mayo, P. (1989). *Social skills strategies.* Eau Claire, WI: Thinking Publications.

Garwood, M., & McCabe, M. P. (2000). Impact of sex education programs on sexual knowledge and feelings of men with a mild intellectual disability. *Education and Training in Mental Retardation and Developmental Disabilities, 35*(3), 269–283.

Gaynor, J., Breland, J., Harlacher, S., Tondorf, N., & Zivkovich, M. (1992). *Social skills training project: Teacher handbook.* Daytona Beach, FL: Volusia County School District.

Goldstein, A. P. (1999). *The prepare curriculum.* Champaign, IL: Research Press.

Goldstein, A. P., Sprafkin, R. P., Geershaw, N. J., & Klein, P. (1980). *Skillstreaming the adolescent.* Champaign, IL: Research Press.

Goldstein, A. P., Sprafkin, R. P., Geershaw, N. J., & Klein, P. (1986). The adolescent: Social skills training through structured learning. In G. Cartledge & J. Milburn (Eds.), *Teaching social skills to children: Innovative approaches* (2nd ed., pp. 303–336). New York: Pergamon.

Greer, B. G., Roberts, D. E., & Jenkins, W. M. (1990). Substance abuse among clients with primary disabilities: Curricular implications for rehabilitation education. *Rehabilitation Education, 4,* 33–44.

Gresham, F., & Elliott, S. N. (1990). *Social Skills Rating System.* Circle Pines, MN: American Guidance Service.

Gresham, F., Sugai, G., & Horner, R. A. (2001). Interpreting outcomes of social skills training for students with high-incidence disabilities. *Exceptional Children, 67*(3), 331–344.

Gumpel, T. P., Tappe, P., & Araki, C. (2000). Comparison of social problem-solving abilities among adults with and without developmental disabilities. *Education and Training in Mental Retardation and Developmental Disabilities, 35*(3), 259–268.

Halpern, A. S., Close, D. W., & Nelson, D. J. (1986). *On my own: The impact of semi-independent living programs for adults with mental retardation.* Baltimore: Brookes.

Harter, S. (1985). *The Self-Perception Profile for Children.* Denver, CO: University of Denver.

Hazel, J. S., Schumaker, J. B., Sherman, J. A., & Sheldon-Widgen, J. (1981). *ASSET.* Champaign, IL: Research Press.

Helwig, A., & Holicky, R. (1994). Substance abuse in persons with disabilities: Treatment considerations. *Journal of Counseling and Development, 72,* 227–233.

Hepler, J. B. (1997). Evaluating a social skills program for children with learning disabilities. *Social Work with Groups, 20*(3), 21–37.

Hops, H., Guild, J. J., Fleishman, D. H., Paine, S. C., Street, A., Walker, H. M., et al. (1978). *PEERS: A program for remediating social withdrawal in school.* Washington, DC: Center at Oregon in the Behavioral Education of the Handicapped.

Hughes, C. (1999). Identifying critical social interaction behaviors among high school students with and without disabilities. *Behavior Modification, 23*(1), 41–60.

Hutton, J. B., & Roberts, T. G. (1986). *Social–Emotional Dimension Scale.* Austin, TX: PRO-ED.

Individuals with Disabilities Education Act Amendments of 1997, 20 U.S.C. § 1400 *et seq.*

Jackson, N. F., Jackson, D. A., & Monroe, C. (1983). *Getting along with others.* Champaign, IL: Research Press.

Kauffman, J. M., Gerber, M. M., & Semmel, M. I. (1988). Arguable assumptions underlying the Regular Education Initiative. *Journal of Learning Disabilities, 21*(1), 6–11.

Kempton, W. (1988). *Life horizons.* Santa Barbara, CA: Stanfield.

Kendrick, D. (1991, March 8). Special children need friends most. Alive and well. *The Cincinnati Enquirer,* p. E7.

Lachar, D., & Gruber, C. (2001). *Personality Inventory for Children–Second Edition.* Los Angeles: Western Psychological Services.

Lambert, N., Nihira, K., & Leland, H. (1993). *AAMR Adaptive Behavior Scale–School: Second Edition.* Austin, TX: PRO-ED.

Lupin, M. (1983). *Old me, new me.* Allen, TX: Developmental Learning Materials.

Mansell, S., Sobsey, D., & Moskal, R. (1998). Clinical findings among sexually abused children with and without developmental disabilities. *Mental Retardation, 36*(1), 12–22.

Martin, S. (1995, October). Are children with disabilities more likely to be abused? *APA Monitor.*

Matson, J. L., Rotatori, A. F., & Helsel, W. J. (1983). *Matson Evaluation of Social Skills.* Worthington, OH: IDS.

McGinnis, E., & Goldstein, A. P. (1980). *Skillstreaming in early childhood.* Champaign, IL: Research Press.

McGinnis, E., & Goldstein, A. P. (1984). *Skillstreaming the elementary school child.* Champaign, IL: Research Press.

Meichenbaum, D. (1977). *Cognitive-behavior modification: An integrative approach.* New York: Plenum.

Olkin, R. (1999). *What psychotherapists should know about disability.* New York: Guilford.

Olweus, D. (1993). *Bullying at school: What we know and what we can do.* Cambridge, MA: Blackwell.

O'Neill, R. E., Horner, R. H., Albin, R. W., Sprague, J. R., Storey, K., & Newton, J. S. (1997). *Functional assessment and program development for problem behavior.* Pacific Grove, CA: Brookes/Cole.

Petersilia, J. (2000). Invisible victims: Violence against persons with developmental disabilities. *Human Rights, 27*(1), 9–13.

Phelps-Terasaki, D., & Phelps-Gunn, T. (1992). *Test of Pragmatic Language.* Austin, TX: PRO-ED.

Piers, E. V., Harris, D. B., & Herzberg, D. S. (2002). *Piers Harris Children's Self-Concept Scale.* Los Angeles: Western Psychological Services.

Prater, M. A., Serna, L., & Nakamura, K. K. (1999). Impact of peer teaching on acquisition of social skills by adolescents with learning disabilities. *Education and Treatment of Children, 22*(1), 19–36.

Sargent, L. R. (1991). *Social skills in the school and community.* Reston, VA: Council for Exceptional Children.

Schumaker, J., Hazel, J. B., & Pederson, C. S. (1988). *Social skills for daily living.* Circle Pines, MN: American Guidance Service.

Slavin, R. E. (1991). Synthesis of research on cooperative learning. *Educational Leadership, 48,* 71–82.

Sobsey, D. (1994). *Violence and abuse in the lives of people with disabilities.* Baltimore: Brookes.

Sobsey, D., Lucardie, R., & Mansell, S. (1995). *Violence and disability: An annotated bibliography.* Baltimore: Brookes.

Sparrow, S. S., Balla, D. A., & Cicchetti, D. (1984). *Vineland Adaptive Behavior Scales.* Circle Pines, MN: American Guidance Service.

Stainback, S., Stainback, W., East, K., & Sapon-Shavin, M. (1994). A commentary on inclusion and the development of a positive self-identity by persons with disabilities. *Exceptional Children, 60*(6), 486–490.

Stephens, T. M. (1992). *Social skills in the classroom.* Odessa, FL: Psychological Assessment Resources.

Stringer, S. J., Morton, R. C., & Bonikowski, M. H. (1999). Self-esteem in children. *Journal of Instructional Psychology, 26*(3), 196–201.

Thompson, M. L., & Strange, J. F. (1996). *DISCOVER: Skills for life.* Circle Pines, MN: American Guidance Service.

U.S. Department of Education. (1992). *Learning to live drug free: A curriculum model for prevention.* Rockville, MD: Government Printing Office.

Vernon, A. (1989). *Thinking, feeling, behaving.* Champaign, IL: Research Press.

Volusia County School Board. (1992). *Social skills training project.* Daytona Beach, FL: Author.

Walker, H. M., McConnell, S., Holmes, D., Todis, B., Walker, J., & Golden, N. (1983). *The Walker social skills curriculum: ACCEPTS.* Austin, TX: PRO-ED.

Walker, H. M., Todis, B., Holmes, D., & Horton, G. (1987). *The Walker social skills curriculum: ACCESS.* Austin, TX: PRO-ED.

Walker-Hirsch, L., & Champagne, M. P. (1991, September). The circles concept: Social competence in special education. *Educational Leadership, 48,* 65–67.

Walker-Hirsch, L., & Champagne, M. P. (1993). *Circles I: Intimacy and relationships* [Videotape series]. Santa Barbara, CA: Stanfield.

Watson, E. W., Boros, A., & Zrimec, G. (1979–1980). Mobilization of services for deaf alcoholics. *Alcohol, Health, and Research World, 4,* 33–38.

Wells, R. H. (1983). *Personal power: Peer interaction skills.* Austin, TX: PRO-ED.

Wilcox, B., & Thomas, A. (1980). *Critical issues in educating autistic children and youth.* Washington, DC: U.S. Department of Education.

CHAPTER 8

Preparing Students for Employment

Cheryl Hanley-Maxwell and Lana Collet-Klingenberg

Throughout the history of American education, schools have been the means of educating children to be productive members of society. And one way to be a productive member of society is to have a paid job. Workers with paid employment contribute to the economy through the taxes they pay, the goods they buy, and their lessened reliance on government subsidies. Moreover, being a productive member of society through paid employment enhances an individual's sense of self-worth and connection to the larger community in which he or she lives.

Federal laws and initiatives reflect society's awareness of the role that schooling plays in enhancing or diminishing the employability of former students. Vocational training legislation since the 1970s has focused on the development of employment skills for people who meet the federal definitions of disadvantaged or disabled. Some of the legislation from the past 20 years includes the Job Training Partnership Act of 1982 (P.L. 97-300), Carl D. Perkins Vocational and Technical Education Act of 1998, and the Workforce Investment Partnership Act of 1998 (P.L. 105-220). Legislation about rehabilitation also ties schooling to work by directly addressing the role of rehabilitation in the vocational preparation of students with disabilities (e.g., Rehabilitation Act Amendments of 1992 [P.L. 102-569] and 1998 [P.L. 105-220]). Finally, education law has explicitly addressed the role of schooling in preparing students for the world of work. Legislation, including Goals 2000: Educate America Act of 1994 (P.L. 103-227) and the School to Work Opportunities Act of 1994 (P.L. 103-239), has targeted the development of employability skills in all students in the public education system. Furthermore, starting with the 1984 Office of Special Education and Rehabilitation Service's transition initiative (Will, 1984), transition, and thus employment preparation, has become a part of special education law (i.e., the Individuals with Disabilities Act [IDEA] of 1990 [P.L. 101-476] and the 1997 amendments to IDEA [P.L. 105-17]).

These laws reflect concerns about postschool outcomes for former students and, especially, student with disabilities. Employers lament the lack of employment preparation on the part of all former students, and researchers and advocates decry the particularly poor employment outcomes for former students with disabilities (Phelps & Hanley-Maxwell, 1997). Studies indicate that just graduating may be a problem for many students with disabilities (Benz & Halpern, 1987; Edgar, 1987; "Where We Are in Special Education Today," 2001), and graduating does not necessarily lead to vastly improved postschool outcomes. For instance, as many as 19% of youth with disabilities are still seeking employment months after leaving school (Colley & Jamison, 1998), and few are earning more than minimum wage (Edgar, 1987). Although percentages and specific outcomes vary with each study, most postschool data reflect poor outcomes for former special education students (Phelps & Hanley-Maxwell, 1997). Despite the vocational emphases of federal law, these statistics have not appreciably changed in the past 15 years. Thus, educators need to give renewed attention to the issues that surround the vocational education of students with disabilities.

One area to which one can turn for more information is research. Results from a variety of studies reveal that postschool outcomes are positively influenced by paid or unpaid work experiences during high school (e.g., Benz, Lindstrom, & Yovanoff, 2000; Colley & Jamison, 1998; Eisenman, 2000; Kohler, 1993; Luecking & Fabian, 2000; Wagner, Blackorby, Cameto, & Newman, 1993). However, "work is a necessary, but not sufficient, factor in predicting subsequent employment" (Luecking & Fabian, 2000, p. 218). Attention to the development of appropriate work behavior (Luecking & Fabian, 2000) and related skills (e.g., academics, self-determination, social skills) also appears to be critical (Benz et al., 2000; Eisenman, 2000; Wehmeyer & Schwartz, 1997).

Including the above experiences and skills in the schooling of students with disabilities, as well as other skills and experiences discussed in later sections of this chapter, will enhance but not ensure better employment outcomes for students with disabilities. Unfortunately, students with disabilities face other barriers to achieving successful employment outcomes, including (a) lack of power to control their own destinies, (b) restrictive health care and Social Security policies, (c) employer biases, (d) poor or no transportation services (Wehman, Brooke, & Inge, 2001), and (e) the erroneous beliefs of gatekeepers that restrict access to certain types of experiences and training (Szymanski, Enright, & Hershenson, 2003). These barriers indicate that educators need to work to change curricular content and the context in which students with disabilities are educated and employed.

The purposes of this chapter are (a) to introduce issues related to the construction of vocationally relevant curricular content and experiences for students with disabilities and (b) to provide an organizing structure for infusion of this content into K through 12 curricula. To construct and integrate such content, educators must be familiar with four topics: career development, assessment, content organization, and skills development across all the school years.

CAREER DEVELOPMENT

Career development is a vital factor in a life span approach to transition from school to work. Various theories attempt to describe the process of career development. One of these theories, work adjustment theory, is based on the constructs of work personality, work competencies, and work goals (Hershenson, 1984). Skills in these three areas develop throughout a person's life in combination with each other and in conjunction with environmental influences. There are, however, "primary periods" (Szymanski, 1994) during which each of these foundation pieces tends to develop.

"Work personality develops during the preschool years, work competencies during the school years, and work goals develop during the later school years" (Szymanski, 1994, p. 403). More specifically, play enhances the development of work personality, home and school work responsibilities assist in the development of work personality and work competency, and career fantasy and exposure to work role models provide for the development of work goals, which are further refined by career-related experiences and learning opportunities. Additionally, work adjustment in general is further influenced by the expectations of family, culture, and community (Szymanski, 1994). In other words, career development theory emphasizes the breadth of vocational planning considerations and the longitudinal nature of the vocational development process.

In recent work, Szymanski et al. (2003) reviewed career development theories and their implications for people with disabilities. They focused on an ecological theory of career development based on five interrelated constructs or concepts and seven processes. The constructs include individual attributes and aspects (e.g., gender, abilities, interests, values), contextual aspects (e.g., socioeconomic status, educational opportunities, legislation, unusual events such as winning the lottery), mediating factors (e.g., individual or personal beliefs about self, cultural and societal beliefs about an individual's identity), environmental influences (e.g., work environment characteristics and conditions), and outcomes (e.g., satisfaction, productivity, tenure, stress).

Of the seven processes of the ecological theory, three are related to the characteristics, beliefs, and conditions or states of the individual: (a) congruence, which is the match or mismatch of the individual and his or her environment; (b) decision making, which is the consideration of career alternatives and acting on those considerations; and (c) development, which is the growth or change of the individual over time. The remaining four processes of the ecological theory interact with a person's internal processes but are external to the person: (a) socialization, which is the teaching of work and life roles; (b) allocation, which is the use of criteria to include or exclude individuals from opportunities or directions; (c) chance, which is the experience of unpredictable events; and (d) labor market forces, which is the influence of economic or business factors. The inclusion of labor market forces as the seventh process reflects the growing understanding that the concept of career is dramatically changing (Szymanski et al., 2003). Future careers can no longer be thought of as advancement through a profession or an employer; a one-career career path is no longer readily available (Gorden, 2000). Instead, future employees will need to identify their own needs and goals, as well as obtain and organize their own developmental experiences to pursue their goals across many employers or organizations (Hall & Mirvis, 1996; Ochs & Roessler, 2001). Furthermore, future employees will need to focus on recognizing opportunities, adapting to change, and working from general knowledge in arts, science, and technology (Gorden, 2000).

The expanded ecological theory of career development (Szymanski et al., 2003) has curricular content, experience, and service implications for students with disabilities. This theory suggests that relevant curricular content would include developing skills in recognizing one's own abilities, interests, limitations, values, work expectations, self as a worker, and accommodation and adaptation needs. Relevant content would also include topics such as work values and attitudes, self-advocacy, problem solving, decision making (within the context of cultural expectations), social skills, knowledge of work environments, stress reduction, and job flexibility. Essential experiences for career development include self-assessment activities, exposure to role models, work experiences, a variety of life experiences, chores and other responsibilities, creation of a career portfolio, and mentoring. Finally, students with disabilities need a variety of services to enhance their career development. These include advocacy, assistive technology, support and accommodation, education and training, career counseling, ecological assessment, social skills training, and planning (considering incentives and disincentives, familial cultural and religious concerns). Services would also include basing job training and job match on job analyses that consider the organizational culture, stresses and pressures, opportunities for career advancement, and reinforcers in potential occupations and work sites (Szymanski et al., 2003).

Additional career development theories and their impact on curricular choices are discussed within the context of the design and application of the curricular model proposed in this chapter. However, career development theories are only one source to explore when attempting to identify important vocational content. Educators should also consider what assessment reveals about the skill and knowledge needs of each student.

ASSESSMENT

Individualized curriculum that facilitates the development of work-related skills is determined through an ongoing and thorough process of ecological assessment and functional vocational assessment. Ecological assessment is broad based and geared toward a greater understanding of a student within all of the ecologies or environments of his or her life. Functional vocational assessment is more specific and focuses on the needs, skills, and interests of a student within the context of potential or targeted work environments. Both forms of assessment are presented in this chapter so that the reader may determine which assessment would be most useful for the age and needs of a particular student.

Ecological Assessment

In ecological assessment, a student's skills and skill needs are evaluated within the context of current and potential future education, employment, residential, and community setting demands (Browder & King, 1987). According to Brown-Glover (1992), this results in "a true set of individualized goals" (p. 243). The student's strengths and limitations in specific tasks are assessed along with existing and potential support systems (Pancsofar, 1986). In addition, the personal interests and goals of the student and his or her family are considered. Thus, ecological assessment involves (a) assessment of potential skill needs, (b) assessment of the student's skill use in real-life settings and the student's and his or her family's interests and goals, and (c) assessment of support needs and systems. Each of these areas are discussed next.

Potential Skill Analysis

A vital part of a thorough assessment, potential skill analysis includes both task-specific analysis and the analysis of social skills needed for survival in possible or targeted settings. Additionally, the analysis should include process skills, or those "integrative" skills needed in various target situations (i.e., known and potential future work and living environments). Observations at the potential or targeted sites, interviews with knowledgeable individuals (e.g., coworkers and supervisors), and reviews of existing curricular materials in the targeted skill area are used to identify potential skill needs. The identified skills then form the basic content of the assessment and instructional components and the basis for consideration of possible adaptation and accommodation needs. Aspects of possible content for assessment may also be adapted from some of the commercially available products designed to measure life skills (e.g., *Street Survival Skills Questionnaire*, Linkenhoker & McCarron, 1980; *Test for Everyday Living*, Halpern, Irvin, & Landman, 1979; *National Independent Living Skills Screening Instrument*, Sands, Woolsey, & Dunlap, 1985) and curriculum-based measures that accompany some functional curricula (e.g., *Life Centered Career Education Competency Rating Scale*, Brolin, 1997).

Individual Assessment

Not to be confused with readiness testing, tests of eligibility, or the myriad interest inventories available, assessment of the student is used to determine programmatic needs (Hanley-Maxwell, Owens-Johnson & Fabian, 2003; Hanley-Maxwell, Szymanski, & Owens-Johnson, 1998). This determination is accomplished through a systematic examination of the student's performance of essential skills and the examination of information about the student's learning history, future goals and aspirations, and interests. Assessment of the student also includes the identification of assistive technology and adaptation needs (e.g., partial participation, materials adaptation, setting adaptation, task resequencing). A related form of assessment, curriculum-based assessment (CBA), is similar in process to the individual needs assessment. However, CBA is typically tied to predetermined curricula. Here, skills that are taught within a targeted curriculum form the core of the assessment content. Students are assessed in relation to their performance of various examples of those skills within the targeted curriculum. It is important to note that good individual assessment along with vocational assessment is related to better postschool outcomes for students with disabilities (Asselin, Tood-Allen, & deFur; Benz, Yovanoff, & Doren, 1997; Kohler, Kohler, Field, Izzo, & Johnson; and Wagner et al., as cited in Izzo, Cartledge, Miller, Growick, & Rutkowski, 2000). Each of these forms of assessment is also part of the recommended practices endorsed by the Council for Exceptional Children's Division of Career Development and Transition (Sitlington, Neubert, & LeConte, 1997).

Support System Assessment

This portion of the assessment process identifies potential facilitating and inhibiting relationships that may affect successful adult outcomes. Support systems examined include friends, family, and potential relationships in future jobs or residences (Hanley-Maxwell & Bordieri, 1989). A student's self-efficacy is also considered here because it will affect the level of support needed in employment settings. Available supports and potential support sources are matched to the current and projected support needs and wishes of the student. Assessment (and planning) for supports should always consider the use of natural supports.

> Natural supports are described as any assistance, relationships, or interactions that allow a person with disabilities to secure, maintain, and advance in a community job of his or her choosing in a way that corresponds to the typical

work routines and social interactions of other employees and that enhances that individual's social relationships. (Test & Wood, 1996, p. 155)

Natural supports do not replace the need for professional intervention or support. When needed, professional support can be used to provide needed or supplementary supports. Furthermore, natural supports do not replace the use of assistive technology, compensatory strategies, job modification, or any other support strategy (Unger, Parent, Gibson, Kane-Johnston, & Kregel, 1998).

Unger et al. (1998) provide a model for identifying and organizing needed supports. They designed this model for use in supported employment planning, but it has direct applicability to planning support needs for students who will be leaving the K through 12 school system. There are seven steps in this model:

1. Determine individual needs and preferences
2. Brainstorm potential options
3. Assess job and community supports
4. Identify individual choices
5. Develop strategies for accessing supports
6. Evaluate support effectiveness
7. Arrange provision for ongoing monitoring (Unger et al., 1998, p. 3)

No matter what supports are identified and used, the determination of appropriateness centers on the effectiveness or success of the supports. Lastly, the educator is reminded that, as with all other services and programs, natural supports must be individualized. Thus, they will vary from one student and one setting to another (Inge & Tilson, 1997).

Functional Vocational Assessment

Functional vocational assessment helps to determine what skills and capabilities a student has and how those skills are used across work and work-related environments (Kellogg, 1995). Subjects for a functional vocational assessment include vocational aptitudes, specific abilities, and skills, interests, work attitudes, and knowledge about work (Hanley-Maxwell, Bordieri, & Merz, 1996). The type and levels of necessary work-related supports needed and available are also determined through this kind of assessment, and natural supports must be part of this consideration. Although the potential listing of content areas is infinite, a number of areas are universal to most students. The following two sections provide a discussion of (a) potential content areas and (b) accessing information in these content areas.

Content Areas

Potential content areas for a functional vocational assessment include information on the student's work and school history, including learning style, work-related skills and concerns, work endurance and stamina, use of academic skills, and the ability to follow directions. Information about the student's communication skills, social skills, interaction style, and behavior also is regarded as important for job training and placement. Additional information should be collected regarding the student's mobility and orientation skills, medical needs and management, fine and gross motor skills, transportation needs, and any other special needs or considerations for employment. Current and future financial information, goals, and needs must also be addressed. Finally, and most important, the strengths and preferences of the student must be taken into consideration across all these content areas.

Accessing Information

Information in each of the content areas is sought from a variety of sources, including the students, his or her significant others, and written documents. Observations and interactions with the student are considered first and foremost. For an assessment to be fair and accurate, the individual conducting it must know or get to know the student being assessed (Hanley-Maxwell et al., 1998; Hanley-Maxwell et al., 2003). Additional and confirming information may be gathered through interviews and discussions with other people who play significant roles in the student's life. Finally, documents such as written reports, case histories, and education and work records may be reviewed to further supplement the information gathered through the other means discussed above. All information is then compiled into a plan for further training or education, job development, or placement of the student into an already-identified job.

Summary

The process of ecological assessment and functional vocational assessment includes identifying current and future environments, the skills necessary for successful functioning in those environments, the abilities of the student in performing those skills, and the supports available and needed by the student to function as independently as possible. Thorough and ongoing (i.e., longitudinal and varied in skills, settings, and materials) assessment helps to identify curricular content that is individualized and that focuses on preparing students for adult life. Used together, ecological and functional vocational assessment ensure "goodness of fit" between the realities of a student's life (in terms of skills, needs, goals) and the instruction provided (via the Individualized Evaluation Program [IEP] and a well-planned curriculum). It cannot be stressed enough that "moment-in-time" assessment provides little usable information for making curricular decisions. Students' lives are not static events to be probed once and permanently plotted. They are fluid, ongoing experiences that involve many factors. Only through continual assessment and reassessment, combined with the construction and use of the IEP, can educators begin to address real-life issues and needs in the curricula that they design and implement. Recommendations by the Council for Exceptional Children's Division of Career Development and Transition (Sitlington et al., 1997) provide an excellent summary of the issues related to effective assessment. The first recommendation is for educators to use four guiding questions when planning a vocational or transitional assessment:

1. What do I already know?
2. What do I need to know?

3. How can I get this information?
4. How will I collect and use it in IEP process? (Sitlington et al., 1997, p. 75)

Once educators have answered these questions, the Division of Career Development and Transition recommends that they follow seven guidelines in conducting an assessment:

1. individualize
2. consider assistive technology and accommodation
3. use natural or actual environments
4. use methods that will produce needed and functional information
5. assess in varied formats and over time
6. assess using multiple methods and multiple people
7. use results in planning (Sitlington et al., 1997, p. 75)

Educators must know what to do with the information they receive from assessment. Some of the assessment methods discussed previously in this section will identify lists of potential skill needs, whereas others will yield information about student performances in relation to those skills. In the end, educators must know how to prioritize the skills and information from these lists. Johnson and Wehman (2001) provide a process for prioritizing content for instruction, from the initial identification of potential skill needs to the selection of instructional objectives. The first step is to work in collaboration with the student and his or her family to identify potential occupations and job sites (if appropriate) and to complete potential skills analyses in relation to these occupations and job sites. Once skill analyses are completed, the individual student can be assessed in relation to these skills. Assessment should also identify skills that occur in two or more areas of the student's life that are appropriate skill targets (in terms of being age appropriate) and rank those skills in order of frequency of occurrence (most to least). This list should also be used to identify skills that play the greatest role in the safety of the student, now and in the future. Finally, the educator should determine which of these skills are most critical to the student's independence. The educator can now select the skills to target for first instruction, based on the following two factors: (a) the skills are essential to the safety of the student in current environments, and (b) "the student must perform [these skills] frequently in order to function independently within his or her current and identified future environments" (Johnson & Wehman, 2001, p. 150). The remaining skills on the list should be prioritized for instruction based on frequency of need.

ORGANIZING CONTENT

Although existing curricula offer comprehensive listings of skill domains, skill clusters, and specific skills needed for work, none of them are all-inclusive, nor could they ever be. An effective vocational curriculum is one that teaches the student the skills that she or he will need to function in his or her adult world, and this adult world will be different for every student. Because there is no way to exaustively list the ideal skills for inclusion in vocation-related curricula, we will not replicate the work done by many authors in compiling skill listings. However, it is important to list those domains and skill clusters identified in many curricular materials. These are woven within the curricular areas of the model used in this chapter. This section includes a description of the model and a discussion of the design and use of this model.

Successful movement from school to work requires that the student receive a solid educational foundation that prepares him or her for various adult roles, careful longitudinal planning, and the provision of postschool supports and services identified in the planning process (Wehman et al., 2001). Locating and linking with those postschool services are also critical aspects of transition. Much of the current conception of work preparation and related best practices appears to focus on the secondary and postsecondary years. In fact, Michaels (1994) equates transition with adolescence as he describes the life events of that time period. "Adolescence (and transition) is a time of . . . taking responsibility for one's self, separating from parental control and values, separating from the control of the school system, and developing an internal locus of control" (p. 12). However, understanding the basic premises of the entire preparation process provides a guide for evaluating decisions related to what, why, when, where, and how teachers assess, plan, and teach (Stodden & Leake, 1994) throughout the educational years.

Students must be provided instruction throughout their school careers on the options, skills, and outcomes that are selected by representatives from four perspectives: student, family, community, and society. This emphasis on the importance of all aspects of a student's life is called the life-space perspective by Szymanski (1994). When life-space issues are combined with life span issues, which include career development, the result is a curricular model that teaches skills that fall into two general areas. The first area is basic skills and processes, which are taught within the context of providing the student with generalizable skills to use in making independent and meaningful life decisions. The second general area is career and work options, which are taught throughout the schooling process. Students must receive specific instruction, however, as needed in critical skill areas. The "skills needed for job success need to be infused into the curriculum throughout the grades but also need to be taught on an individualized basis" (Izzo et al., 2000, p. 153).

The curricular structure presented in this chapter organizes skills to be taught from the primary grades and higher. It does not incorporate skills by traditional domains (e.g., academic, social, vocational, and independent living areas). This model represents these domains and proposes a different way of identifying and organizing critical skills. In addition, it is designed to be used with curricula already in place in the classroom. It is also based on the premise that students with disabilities receive the bulk of their education in integrated environments. Research indicates that students who are in integrated educational environments experience better postschool outcomes (Phelps & Hanley-Maxwell, 1997).

The organizing structure is intended as a working model to make identification and incorporation of targeted skills into the classroom curriculum more manageable and thus more successful. In this model, the skills that make up the areas or domains fall into three categories: (a) foundation or fundamental skills, (b) integrative skills, and (c) application skills, or those skills that are needed by a student for specific reasons having to do with the community in which he or she lives, the job he or she desires, or his or her abilities and limitations. These skills, depicted in Figure 8.1, are introduced to students in a semisequential manner beginning in preschool and elementary school and continuing through high school and into adult services.

Foundation or Fundamental Skills

The foundation level of skill development includes those skills that have been identified as being the most basic and essential for school and postschool functioning. These skills provide the foundation for more complex skill development and for a variety of occupations later in life, and they span a continuum from simple to complex (Ford et al., 1989; Gajar, Goodman, & McAfee, 1993). Fundamental skills include those in the following general areas: academics, technology, personal care, communication, and behavior.

Academic Skills

Academic skills critical to adult functioning are those identified in the SCANS report (U.S. Department of Labor, 1991), current professional texts and curricular materials, and research including the results of the National Longitudinal Transition Study (Wagner et al., 1993). They include reading, math, and writing (Cronin & Patton, as cited in Johnson & Wehman, 2001). Each of the academic areas represents a continuum of performance demands that range from basic survival to meaningful use to highly technical use. Interestingly, although special education has traditionally focused on functional use of these academic areas, recent research indicates that when teachers hold high expectations for achievement (Benz et al., 1997; Benz et al., 2000; Ochs & Roessler, 2001), students have better postschool outcomes. The development of higher order thinking skills (e.g., thinking independently, interpreting and manipulating information, being creative, taking initiative) and of more advanced academic skills appears to be essential in the job markets of the future (Gorden, 2000). Finally, the rapid changes in the uses of technology mean that future workers will need to be able to be flexible and adaptable in their learning (National Career Development Associates, as cited in Luecking & Fabian, 2000).

Reading skills encompass understanding the meaning of pictures, figures, symbols, and words. Basic reading skills include identification of sounds, performance skills, and ability to define word meanings. More advanced skills include prediction, synthesis, and analysis. Examples of practical applications of reading skills include reading universal signs, single-word signs, newspaper want ads, job listings, job applications, maps, phone books, and instructions.

Math skills that are useful in work settings include the application of basic skills and operations to everyday tasks. Basic skills include whole-number use, addition, subtraction, money use, time telling, measurement, and estimation. More advanced skills include multiplication, division, decimals, fractions, percent, mixed operations, word problems, and mathematical reasoning. Practical skills include measuring liquids and solids, using a calculator, using money, balancing a checkbook, and using simple math operations in everyday tasks.

Elementary School	Middle School	High School	Adult Life

Foundation Skills ————————————————————————————→
Academic (reading, writing, math)
Personal Care
Behavior
Communication
Technology

      Integrative Skills ————————————————————————→
      Self-Determination Skills
        Decision making
        Choice making
        Problem solving
        Goal setting and attainment
        Self-awareness and knowledge
        Self-regulation
        Risk taking and safety
        Self-advocacy and leadership
      Personal values (including work values and attitudes)
      Social skills

            Application Skills —————————————————————→
            Career Skills
              Self-determination
              Career planning
              Occupational knowledge
              Job seeking and search
                Finding jobs
                Applying for jobs
                Interviewing
                Selecting jobs
              Job tasks in common occupations
              Job-specific skills

FIGURE 8.1. Curricular time line for vocational skills.

Writing skills are important components in a variety of work-related tasks. At a minimal level, writing includes signing contracts, checks, tax forms, or other legal agreements. Writing is also necessary for completing job applications and generating information for written materials, such as résumés, letters of interest, and job-specific requirements such as correspondence memos and billing. More sophisticated forms of writing are used for specific jobs and careers (e.g., journalist, editor, writer).

Technology

For most students, the use of technology is now considered a fundamental skill. For any individual planning to work (and, to a lesser extent, live) in the future, understanding the use of computers and other technology (e.g., video and audio devices) is critical. Although most jobs in the future will not require a college degree, general knowledge in technology is essential (Gorden, 2000). Additionally, students who use assistive technology must know about and be proficient with their assistive tools.

Personal-Care Skills

Personal-care skills include activities of daily living, dressing, grooming, hygiene, eating, mobility, and other activities needed to function in everyday life, as well as to prepare for work. These skills, although not directly related to the job, affect an individual's success in the employment community (Gajar et al., 1993; Karge, Patton, & de la Garza, 1992; McCrae, 1991).

Communication Skills

Communication skills include listening and speaking (verbally and nonverbally) and are essential to success in postschool environments (Eisenman, 2001). Communicating basic needs, following instructions, answering questions, asking for help, giving instructions, asking questions, offering assistance, asking for a raise, interviewing, giving criticism and feedback, and decoding nonverbal messages are critical communication skills on the job (Carnevale et al., cited in White, 1992; Karge et al., 1992; McCrae, 1991; U.S. Department of Labor, 1991).

Behavioral Skills

Behavioral skills, at the fundamental level, are the foundation to the social and self-determination skills targeted at the integrative level. At their most basic, these skills focus on external management of appropriate and inappropriate social behaviors. This would include, but not be limited to, responding to directions, prompts, and consequences; having appropriate verbal or physical contact with other people; and seeking attention in appropriate ways and at appropriate times. More advanced levels would include students moving toward an internal locus of control and toward self-management skills at the integrative level.

All learners must have these fundamental skills. The level of achievement in any one skill area, however, is dependent on the characteristics of the student and the end goals as determined through thorough and ongoing assessment as a part of the IEP process.

Earlier curricular models attended to individual skills, such as fundamental skills, rather than the processes of learning and problem solving (i.e., generalization and maintenance; Hanley-Maxwell & Collet-Klingenberg, 1996). Michaels (1994) called this the "basic skills approach" (p. 135) and expressed concern that too little attention was given to "higher level skill areas" (p. 135). He proposed an expanded basic skills approach that includes process skills of task approach and problem solving, self-efficacy (e.g., self-monitoring), and social skills as critical fundamental skills for all students (Michaels, 1994). Newer curricular models provide more attention to teaching these higher order skills. In concert with Michaels's approach and trends for including these skills, the second category of skills described in this model, integrative skills, emphasizes the acquisition of learning processes that will allow the student to acquire new skills, perform variations of old skills, and be flexible under new demands.

Integrative Skills

Although still considered important for postschool success, the skills at this level are more complex and will enable an individual to be adaptable to changes in work and living settings. The skills presented in this section are grouped only for the purpose of this discussion. As will become clear, many of these skills are interrelated. Furthermore, most of these skills are taught within the context of other learning activities (e.g., some self-determination skills are taught within the context of career exploration). The skill groupings include social skills, self-determination, and personal values. Most of the skills at this level reflect various combinations of foundation skills and the covert cognitive skills that underlie functional skill usage.

Social Skills

Social skills have been consistently shown to be related to success on the job (Benz et al., 1997; Benz et al., 2000; Cronin & Patton, as cited in Johnson & Wehman, 2001; Hughes et al., 1997; Ochs & Roessler, 2001). Research has shown that social skills or the lack thereof can have a dramatic impact on the success of any individual in any adult role (Chadsey-Rusch, 1986; Chadsey-Rusch & Gonzalez, 1988; Greenspan & Shoultz, 1981; Hanley-Maxwell, Rusch, Chadsey-Rusch, & Renzaglia, 1986), especially in employment roles as demonstrated by the following facts: The most common reason for job termination is inappropriate social skills (Hanley-Maxwell et al., 1986), the most commonly reported problems in the work environment are related to interpersonal communication (Chadsey-Rusch & Gonzalez, 1988), and the most common interaction in the work environment is joking and teasing (Chadsey-Rusch & Gonzalez, 1988). Critical social skills identified in the SCANS report (U.S. Department of Labor, 1991) include cooperating, negotiating conflict, understanding others' perspectives, and working as a team. Minskoff and Demoss (1994) asked employers to the identify workplace social skills needs. More than 70% of the employer respondents identified 10 skills: accepts supervision, follows directions, asks for information or assistance when needed, accepts constructive criticism, accepts help from coworkers, helps others when appropriate, does not bully or boss, speaks appropriately to supervisors, does not use profanity in workplace conversations, and listens to other person when involved in conversations.

Self-Determination

Self-determination, being a causal agent in one's own life, has been consistently cited as a critical aspect of adult-life success. Field, Martin, Miller, Ward, and Wehmeyer (1998) identified a variety of curricula that can be used to teach self-determination skills. The eight overlapping areas typically covered in self-determination curricula include the following: (a) choice making, (b) problem solving, (c) decision making, (d) goal setting and attainment, (e) risk taking and safety, (f) self-regulation, (g) self-advocacy and leadership, and (h) self-awareness and self-knowledge (Wehmeyer & Schwartz, 1998). Wehmeyer and Schwartz (1998) caution that these areas cannot be thought of as a listing of curricular content. However, they provide a framework to discuss the development of essential skills. Because the first four skill areas are interwoven, they are discussed first.

In choice making, students must be able to identify their own interests and preferences, select options, and act on the selection (Hughes et al., 1997; Wehmeyer & Schwartz, 1998). Choice making also requires decision-making skills. Choice-making skills should not be taught separately or out of context but incorporated into daily activities at school and at home. Furthermore, students need to be provided with many opportunities and rewards for using these skills (Eisenman, 2001).

Problem solving also requires decision-making skills. When problem solving, a student must be able to identify and define the problem, generate potential solutions, and use decision-making skills to take action (Wehmeyer & Schwartz, 1998). Problem-solving skills have been the center of discussions about the preparation of students for adult work roles. Specifically mentioned in the SCANS report (U.S. Department of Labor, 1991) and other employer research, problem-solving skills have taken on a new level of importance in recent literature about the transition process. Problem-solving skills include identifying the problem, potential solutions, potentially needed resources, and potential outcomes; selecting one solution; and assessing the solution's success (Chadsey-Rusch, 1986). Mithaug, Martin, and Agran (1987) recommend teaching students the following steps to enhance students' adaptability through problem solving: (a) identify the problem, (b) define alternate solutions, (c) determine action, (d) take action, (e) evaluate the consequences, and (f) determine the need for adjustment. Although problem-solving skills can be taught out of context, they must be quickly incorporated into daily activities and learning experiences.

Decision-making skills include the use of problem-solving skills. To make decisions, one must identify one's own needs, interests, and abilities. Then he or she must use problem-solving skills to consider and prioritize alternatives. When making decisions, a student also has to select goals based on current performance, identify barriers to the completion of the goals, and identify steps to take and their time line. Finally, the student must act, trying various solutions, evaluating the results, and choosing the next steps (Hughes et al., 1997; Ochs & Roessler, 2001; Wehmeyer, Palmer, Agran, Mithaug, & Martin, 2000). Because self-knowledge and planning are part of decision-making skills, these skills can be developed jointly through various assessment and planning activities, including IEP development and daily and long-term project planning activities.

As seen above, to make a decision, a student also needs skills in goal setting and attainment. Wehmeyer (1994) sees this as the most important component of self-determination. Goal setting and attainment involves two general steps (Hughes et al., 1997; Wehmeyer & Schwartz, 1998). The first is setting goals based on interests, skills, and limitations. The second step is developing an action plan and taking action (Martin, Huber Marshall, & DePry, as cited in German, Martin, Marshall, & Sale, 2000). These two general steps can be broken into a series of more discreet steps: (a) define and describe goal; (b) set performance standard; (c) identify skills and needs in relation to goals; (d) identify motivation and supports for reaching the goal; (e) develop an action plan to address needs (by breaking the goals into smaller steps); (f) identify what strategies will be used to achieve the goal, get feedback, and obtain support; (g) develop a performance schedule; (h) act; and (i) evaluate and choose next step. Evaluation should result in adjusting actions and goals by using past performances to guide future steps. Evaluation also includes reviewing past feedback, developing new goals, and making new action plans (Wehmeyer et al., 2000). *Take Action: Making Goals Happen* (Huber Marshall et al., as cited in German et al., 2000) is a program that teaches these skills; it is a module from the ChoiceMaker Self-Determination Curriculum, which includes an assessment tool and instruction modules (Martin & Huber Marshall, as cited in German et al., 2000).

Another key area of self-determination skills is risk taking and safety, or identifying potential hazards and acting to minimize danger (Wehmeyer & Schwartz, 1998). Agran, Swaner, and Snow (1998) detailed essential safety skills within the context of two larger areas: practicing safe behaviors and responding appropriately to accidents, threats, and so on. Skills within these two areas include recognizing unsafe conditions, using protective clothing and devices, using equipment appropriately, lifting properly, engaging in safe work behaviors, recognizing unsafe acts, preventing accidents, reporting accidents, knowing first aid and CPR, and practicing good housekeeping.

The sixth self-determination skill is self-regulation (Hughes et al., 1997; Wehmeyer & Schwartz, 1998). Individuals can self-regulate, solve problems, manage their own behavior, and evaluate their performances through monitoring and sometimes recording their behavior (Wehmeyer et al., 2000). The skills of self-regulation are similar to those found in problem solving and are often considered part of the larger constellation of skills known as self-efficacy, which include self-knowledge, including interests and abilities; self-consequation, including reinforcement and correction; self-monitoring; self-control; and self-assertion (Martin, Marshall, & Maxson, 1991; Mithaug et al., 1987). These skills are required if the student is to become a flexible, responsible, and independently functioning adult. As in problem solving, being able to identify and respond to natural cues and consequences is an important component of self-efficacy and a critical part of building independence for adulthood (Berg, Wacker, & Flynn, 1990; Renzaglia & Hutchins, 1988). Responding to natural consequences requires a student to (a) identify potential consequences, (b) identify and respond to natural reinforcers, and (c) use feedback to guide future behavior.

Also essential to self-determination is the ability to be a self-advocate and a leader. Skills in this area include knowing one's own rights and responsibilities, using self-advocacy appropriately, and knowing when and how to be a member of a team (Wehmeyer & Schwartz, 1998). Self-advocacy skills are considered important from both employer and employee perspectives. Initiating contact, convincing others, and being self-assertive integrate the fundamental skills in the areas of communication and behavior with the skills of problem solving and decision making. Responding to the behavior of others is also an important part of self-advocacy, including skills such as avoiding victimizing situations, letting one's needs and desires be known, and responding to and offering criticism.

The final self-determination skill students need is self-awareness or self-knowledge. Self-determined individuals know and understand the psychological and physical needs of people, including themselves. They understand that there are differences in these needs among people (other than themselves). And they understand their own behavior and needs affect others (Wehmeyer & Schwartz, 1998). Implicit in this area is that self-determined individuals can apply these understandings to their own situation and their own needs. Self-awareness is developed though self-assessment activities that can be incorporated into other lessons or conducted as separate events (e.g., completing self-interest inventories, working with career exploration software).

Self-determination skills are combined in planning a common activity in adulthood. There are many avenues for students to learn to combine and then apply these combined skills in formulating and enacting plans. For example, planning is demonstrated in such tasks as IEP participation, stress management, and time management, and it is critical to the development of long-term career goals and the identification of personal needs as they relate to work. Planning and problem solving are often combined in the decision-making process. The IEP plays a pivotal role in long-range planning. But if the IEP process does not progressively enhance the control that individual students exert over their lives, then these students become victims of the process (Michaels, 1994). The IEP should be viewed as a tool that can be used to assist students in learning planning, self-advocacy, and responsibility skills. Students should not have IEPs completed for them "or to them" (Michaels, 1994, p. 14); instead, students should be vitally involved in all aspects of the process, especially during adolescence. "Adolescence is a critical period for the development of skills related to self-determination" (Wehmeyer, 1992, p. 308). During this period, students learn the skills necessary to develop realistic expectations. These skills include identifying physical and psychological needs, planning ways to meet those needs, gathering necessary resources, and taking action as required to meet those needs (Wehmeyer, 1992). The IEP process provides the vehicle for learning how to perform these self-determination skills.

Students and parents should be considered and treated as active and important members of the multidisciplinary team, not as passive participants whose role is to okay a plan of action decided in advance by school staff. Strategies for home–school collaboration and active parent involvement are provided in a number of sources (e.g., Wehman, Moon, Everson, Wood, & Barcus, 1988). Additionally, using life planning strategies (e.g., McGill Action Planning System, Vandercook, York, & Forest, 1989; Lifestyles Planning Process, O'Brien & Lyle, 1987; Personal Futures Planning, O'Brien, 1987; Choosing Options and Accommodations for Children [COACH], Giangreco, Cloninger, & Iverson, 1998) can enhance the involvement and direction of the planning process by students and their families. These strategies are designed to help parents and students create a vision for the future and to help ensure that planning is viewed as a lifelong process and that students are provided with the vehicle to take charge of their own lives.

Research has raised clear questions about the ability of 17- and 18-year-old students to make career decisions in high school that will dictate the students' actual path after high school (Shapiro & Lentz, 1991). The results of this research support the notion that student involvement in planning must take place throughout the school career, not just in the later high school stages of transition planning, if students are to learn to make choices, follow through with choices, and revise their plans accordingly. Furthermore, these research results support the career development literature that suggests no student (disabled or not) is ready to make long-term career decisions at the age of 17 or 18. Any plans that students and their families make must be flexible enough to accommodate the real changes that will occur in the postschool environment. The skills of planning, problem solving, and decision making are central to successful flexibility. If a student has the skills and the opportunities to make decisions from a very young age, then involvement in the planning process itself becomes the key to success—not what career choices are actually made upon leaving high school. With the acquisition and use of foundation and integrative skills, the student will leave the school environment with the tools to make ongoing and flexible career and life plans.

Personal Values

Personal values are seen by employers as critical for current and future employees (Carnevale et al., cited in White, 1992; Gorden, 2000; Karge et al., 1992; U.S. Department of Labor, 1991). Personal values refer to self-esteem, responsibility and dependability, quality of work, personal ethics, and response to peer pressure. The personal values area tends to be problematic for many educators, who ask, "Whose values do I teach?" Although this is a complicated question that is worthy of exploration, suffice it to say that educators should provide opportunities and experiences for all students (regardless of race, ethnicity, socioeconomic status, or gender) to explore their personal values as they move through school. This provides students with the background they need to form their own values.

Application Skills

The third level of the proposed curricular model is the most difficult group of skills to precisely define. Specific application skills should be targeted to a student's interests, abilities, and needs, as well as the idiosyncrasies of the community in which he or she will work. This set of skills currently receives the most attention at the secondary and postsecondary levels (Halpern, 1992). Application skills are the academic and specific technical skills required for targeted jobs or further academic training and include those skills needed to get and keep jobs.

In general, application skills are made up of fundamental and integrative skills. Whereas fundamental and integrative skills can be considered generic, application skills tend to be specific to the student and the community in which she or he lives. Application skills build on the first two levels of the curricular model to support successful and meaningful outcomes. The first two levels of the model, fundamental and integrative skills, are the crux of the model, whereas application skills bridge the gap between those critical foundation skills and the realities of employment settings. Without a solid foundation of fundamental and integrative skills, application instruction will ultimately fail.

Although application skills are usually community and career specific, some are essential for all learners. This section addresses two skill areas common to all students (i.e., career skills, job-seeking skills) and discusses types of jobs frequently available in all communities.

Career Skills

Career skills include self-knowledge, knowledge about occupations, and career planning. Farley and Johnson (1999) explored one strategy to help students develop these skills: the occupational choice strategy (Roessler & Schriner, 1988). This strategy focuses on developing knowledge about self, work, and career planning and includes a host of subskills. Vocational self-knowledge includes interests, aptitudes, work values, personal strengths, and limitations (Ochs & Roessler, 2001; Roessler & Schriner, 1988). Knowledge about work includes knowing about available jobs, requirements of various occupations, and labor market trends (Benz et al., 2000; Benz et al., 1997; Eisenman, 2001; Ochs & Roessler, 2001; Roessler & Schriner, 1988; Saunders, Stoney, & Weston, as cited in Eisenman, 2001). And career planning (Benz et al., 2000; Eisenman, 2001) requires self-determination skills (Wehmeyer & Schwartz, 1998).

Job-Seeking Skills

Research reveals that students also need to acquire job-seeking or job search skills (Benz et al., 1997; Benz et al., 2000). Skills that fall within this area are finding job vacancies, filling out applications, interviewing, and selecting a job. Furthermore, students need to know specific interviewing skills such as how to start the interview; how to represent relevant experience, education, work history, and disability information; how to seek information about the job; how to address topics that need to be addressed, even if the interviewer does not ask; how to present one's self in a positive light; and how to close the interview. Farley and Johnson (1999) suggest two programs that teach the skills listed above: *Job Application Training* (Means, 1989) and *Gettting Employed Through Interview Training* (Roessler, Hinman, & Lewis, 1986).

Common Occupations

Some skills are common to many occupations. Johnson and Wehman (2001) cite work done by Sowers and Powers that identify skill clusters found in a variety of jobs, including typing, computer data entry, word processing, filing, telephone answering, photo copying, collating and stapling, mail preparation, packaging, unpackaging and pricing, delivery, light assembly, light cleaning, and microfilming.

Another way to begin to identify potential job-specific skill needs is to look at the current areas of employment for individuals with disabilities and the growing industries that may provide employment opportunities in the future. The most frequent jobs held by individuals with disabilities include jobs in restaurant and food services, janitorial services, housekeeping and maintenance, construction, retail and sales (Colley & Jamison, 1998; Morgan, Ellerd, Jensen, & Taylor, 2000), production and stocking, and, in urban areas, office work (Morgan et al., 2000). Future job opportunities may be found in tourism, casinos (Morgan et al., 2000), and service, craft, or technical industries (Gorden, 2000). However, the reader is cautioned to understand that "[these jobs] probably reflect job placement as a protocol, not career aspirations of job seekers" (Morgan et al., 2000, p. 84). Thus, educators must be careful not to assume that these are the occupations desired by their students. Additionally, educators should remember that schooling must prepare students to be flexible enough to follow multiple career paths.

Although this curriculum presents skills in sequential order, skills within and across the three levels of the curricular model do not have to be acquired in sequential order. Many skills will be taught and learned simultaneously (e.g., social and communication skills, problem solving and job seeking). But, when the number of skills taught must be cut down because of time constraints or learner-related issues, the skills sacrificed must not be those in the fundamental or integrative categories: the personal skills, communication skills, social skills, and integrative cognitive or self-determination skills. The reason for this is simple: Early goals and plans (those identified in school) are reworked, revised, and often discarded as self-understanding increases. The experiences of childhood, adolescence, and even young adulthood reveal more about what is not wanted in adult life than what is wanted. In fact, many individuals change jobs several times in their adult lives. Thus, if only job- and career-specific skills are learned, students are trapped into predetermined targets, and their flexibility as adults is reduced.

CURRICULUM ACROSS THE SCHOOL AGES

Vocationally related curricular content, including fundamental, integrative, and application skills, lends itself to an organized and logical time line for instruction, if following a sequential plan for the introduction of these skills. Fundamental skills can and should be infused into the regular (functional or academic) curriculum beginning during the preschool and elementary years. Integrative skills should be introduced during the early elementary years and refined during junior high and high school. Finally, application skills should be explored and identified during the later elementary grades, continued into the junior high school years, and targeted intensively during high school. As might be apparent when reviewing the three categories of skills, each category builds on the previous one(s). Specifically, foundation skills (e.g., completing tasks, working cooperatively, sharing tasks and materials, asking for assistance, offering assistance) are combined and augmented, considering generalization and maintenance issues, to form integrative skills (e.g., time management, problem solving, conflict resolution). Combined foundation and integrative skills then become the basis from which goal-specific skills (e.g., job search skills, specific job or job-related skills) are taught. Thus, skills within each level are not taught and then abandoned (i.e., assumed to be part of the student's repertoire) but continually retaught (often at greater or more complex levels) throughout the schooling process. Tables 8.1 through 8.3 summarize the relevant content, experiences, and services identified in the research and according to career development theories as essential to successful vocational outcomes for students with disabilities. These summaries do not list the skills, experiences, and services according to grade level because these specifics vary with the student and the context in which the student finds himself or herself. However, we have included general guidelines according to grade level in the following sections.

TABLE 8.1
Summary of Essential Vocational Skills for Students,
Derived from Career Development Theories and Disability-Related Research

1. Academics: functional and higher order thinking, and reading, writing, math
2. Communication: speaking and listening
3. Social skills
4. Personal care
5. Self-determination: problem solving, decision making, self-advocacy
6. Self-knowledge regarding abilities, interests, limitations, values, work expectations, self as worker, accommodation and adaptation needs
7. Vocational safety
8. Career awareness and planning
9. Job seeking and search
10. Skills in common occupational areas
11. Work values and attitudes
12. Knowledge of work environments
13. Stress reduction
14. Flexibility: generalizable skills and generalization skill

TABLE 8.2
Summary of Essential Experiences for Students,
Derived from Career Development Theories and Disability-Related Research

1. Variety of life experiences
2. Self-assessment activities
3. Work role models
4. Work experiences
5. Chores and other responsibilities
6. Career portfolio
7. Mentoring
8. Life planning strategies
9. IEP participation
10. Environments that encourage and reward self-determination
11. Job exploration
12. Paid employment

TABLE 8.3
Summary of Essential Services for Students,
Derived from Career Development Theories and Disability-Related Research

1. Instruction in academics, social skills, self-determination skills, job seeking and search, job interviewing, safety
2. Advocacy
3. Assistive technology: adaptation and accommodation
4. Ecological assessment: vocational assessment and job analyses
5. Career counseling
6. Culturally sensitive planning

Elementary School

The elementary school years are critical to acquisition of the foundational skills and beginning acquisition of the integrative skills necessary for later flexibility. Krumboltz's (1979) theory highlights the importance of all life's activities in career development. Based in social learning, this theory describes career development as an interaction between genetics, past learning experiences, current tasks, environmental conditions, and events. The combination of early learning experiences, role models, and the acquisition and reinforcement of self-concept and work concepts builds a solid foundation for such critical career skills as self-observation, self-determination, and basic work behaviors (e.g., attendance, punctuality, work completion).

The elementary years fall within the first stage of Super's (1957, 1974) career development model, the growth stage. Super's model reinforces the need for students to have early and frequent opportunities to explore career alternatives as part of their early learning experiences. Career development results from the interaction between the student and his or her various learning experiences as he or she synthesizes and compromises along the way. The result of this interactive and dynamic process is occupational self-concept. The growth stage ends with the student's development of (a) work attitudes and behaviors and (b) a progressive narrowing of career options. Critical activities during the elementary years include exploratory behavior that develops the concepts of self and careers and the development of autonomy, time management, and self-esteem.

Translating career theory and desired exit skills into elementary curriculum is somewhat difficult. However, there are target skills, evolving knowledge, and specific activities, summarized in Table 8.4 and discussed in this section, that are consistently identified as important. Example IEP goals and objectives for selected skills are provided in Table 8.5.

No current literature recommends work experiences during the elementary years. However, home chores and neighborhood jobs (similar to those of nondisabled peers) and participation in youth groups and clubs provide important foundation experiences for students to learn work attitudes and related behaviors (Banks & Renzaglia, 1993; Hershenson, 1981; Szymanski, 1994). Additionally, elementary school is the time to begin fostering students' vocational awareness through exposure to a variety of career opportunities. Initial efforts should use fantasy (e.g., "What do you want to be when you grow up?") to focus on the awareness of work as an adult outcome and the variety of occupations available.

Work-related skills learned at this time should cut across traditional and academic curricular domains. Skill development should include the fundamental skills of grooming and hygiene, mobility, interpersonal interaction, direction following, task completion, punctuality, attendance, communication, math, reading, writing, and behavioral control. Elementary curriculum should also include initial phases of development of newly emerging integrative skills such as time management; organization of resources; independence; decision making; self-esteem; reasoning; awareness of personal familial, and cultural values; and self-awareness/appraisal.

TABLE 8.4
Essential Vocational Components of an Elementary School Curriculum

Target Activities	Target Skills	Evolving Knowledge
Career fantasy	Grooming and hygiene	Self-awareness
Home chores	Mobility	Self-appraisal
Neighborhood jobs	Interpersonal interaction	Self, familial, and cultural values
Work role models	Direction following	Autonomy
Career exploration	Task completion	Time perspective
Clubs	Punctuality	Careers
Youth activities	Attendance	Self-esteem
Assistive technology	Communication	Independence
	Math	
	Reading	
	Writing	
	Behavior control	
	Introduction to:	
	Time management	
	Organization of resources	
	Decision making	
	Reasoning	
	Self-efficacy	
	Self-determination	
	Technology use	

TABLE 8.5
Example Elementary School IEP Goals and Objectives

Goal	Objectives
To improve grooming and hygiene skills	a. After using the restroom, the student will wash her hands with 100% accuracy for 4 out of 5 days. b. The student will arrive at school dressed in clothes appropriate for the weather with 100% accuracy for 4 out of 5 days. c. Given the task of setting the table for snack or meal time, the student will initiate and complete washing her hands prior to the task 5 out of 5 times.
To improve time management and punctuality skills	a. When the morning bell rings, the student will be in his seat in the classroom, with the proper materials, and ready to begin instruction for 4 out of 5 days. b. Given in-class activities and assignments, the student will complete her work in the allotted time period 75% of the time for a 2-week period. c. When allowed to choose an activity for free period, the student will choose an activity that can be completed within the allotted time period for 3 out of 4 activities for 2 consecutive weeks. (He may ask for information regarding the time required for a chosen activity.)
To improve behavior and interaction with peers	a. When faced with a conflict involving a peer, the student will talk to the peer about possible ways to resolve the situation before getting a teacher to intervene for 2 out of 3 situations for a 3-week period. b. When feeling angry with a peer, the student will talk to the peer or a teacher about how she feels and will refrain from hitting the peer for 2 out of 3 situations for at least a 2-week period. c. The student will initiate an activity of her choice with a group of two to three peers during recess time for 3 out of 5 days across 2 consecutive weeks.
To increase career awareness skills	a. The student will participate in all career awareness week activities at school. b. The student will ask a guest speaker at least one question related to work during career awareness week. c. The student will participate in an in-class activity related to career awareness week. d. The student and his parents will take part in take-your-child-to-work day.

Middle School

Super (1957, 1974) sees the exploration stage of his career development model starting during the middle school years, when the student progressively and naturally narrows the occupational options. During this stage, which continues into high school, students move from the career fantasies they have carried over from the growth stage to tentative career options to initial career choices. They do this in a circular manner that includes exploration of the breadth of occupations to depth in an occupational area, then back to breadth and into depth until the student finds the "right" occupation. Students also continue to work on self-appraisal skills and acquisition of knowledge about work environments (Holland, 1985). Other skills that are targeted for continued refinement are those fundamental and integrative skills started during the elementary years. Special focus should be given to self-knowledge, values clarification, problem solving, decision making, social skills, and applied academics. Middle school is the time to start work on application behaviors, including career awareness, work support behaviors (e.g., attendance, punctuality, work quality, time management, independence), self-efficacy skills, and career exploration. During middle school, students should focus on acquiring generalizable core skills (e.g., social skills, communication), technology, and integrative skills that will ensure flexibility in preparing and accessing any given occupation. Some students can begin trying out different types of jobs during middle school.

Table 8.6 summarizes the middle school curriculum in relation to target activities, target skills, and evolving knowledge. Table 8.7 presents IEP examples of skills selected from the middle school years.

High School

Because the end goals of career interventions are career development, decision-making skills, career choice making, increased self-concept, appropriate work attitudes, and increased competence in locating and securing employment (Rojewski, 1994), high school experiences need to attend to the development of these skills. Wehmeyer (1992) also reminds us that adolescence is the time that students typically develop the self-appraisal skills needed to identify their physical and psychological needs (Roe, 1956; Roe & Lunneborg, cited in Rojewski, 1994), make plans for meeting those needs, and gather the necessary resources

TABLE 8.6
Essential Vocational Components of a Middle School Curriculum

Target Activities	Target Skills	Evolving Knowledge
Home jobs	Social skills	Career awareness
Neighborhood jobs	Academics	Values clarification
Volunteer work	Attendance	Self-appraisal
Career exploration	Punctuality	Self-awareness
Specific skill training in the community (for certain students)	Work quality	
	Time management	
	Decision making	
Clubs	Self-efficacy	
Youth activities	Choice making	
Mentoring	Option identification	
Assistive technology	Goal setting	
	Responsibility	
	Communication	
	Preferences and needs	
	Self-monitoring	
	Self-evaluating	
	Technology use	
	Introduction to:	
	Career selections	
	Job searching	

TABLE 8.7
Example Middle School IEP Goals and Objectives

Goal	Objectives
To improve career awareness skills	a. Given access to and instruction on using a career exploration computer program in the school library, the student will complete a self-assessment on career interests, choose three careers to explore, and complete a one-page report on each one. b. Given a job (e.g., home, neighborhood, community, or school—if nondisabled peers are doing similar jobs; can be paid or volunteer) that he helped to choose, the student will be punctual in arriving at work and will complete the tasks required with minimal assistance (i.e., by asking questions if needed, but completing tasks independently) and with 90% accuracy for at least 3 consecutive weeks. c. During career awareness week, the student will choose four careers to explore via attendance at talks, tours of businesses, and job shadowing. He will document this exploration by submitting a one-page written report on the careers at the beginning of the following week.
To improve problem-solving and decision-making skills	a. When confronted with the opportunity to make a decision regarding what to work on during academic resource period, the student will verbally list to the teacher what her options are (i.e., her assignments), when the assignments are due, which are the most difficult, and what she would like to work on. She will then choose an assignment and review her decision with the teacher. After discussing it with the teacher, she will have the option to revise her decision one time. The student will do this for each resource period and, with the teacher, will rate her decisions based on completion of work in a timely fashion. b. When given a choice of activities during class time, the student will independently (i.e., without input from peers or teachers) choose an activity and stay with that activity for the required period of time for 4 out of 5 periods for 2 consecutive weeks. c. When faced with a conflict of interests for use of free time (at home and at school), the student will evaluate the situation by verbally listing her options with a peer or adult, talking about the pros and cons of each option, choosing an option, and following through with it. She will later evaluate the outcome of her choice with a peer or adult and talk about whether she would make the same choice in the future. She will do this at least 2 times a week.

to do so. Educators should assist students in the development of these skills and in making career selections that match their interests, needs, and abilities with targeted work environments (Dawis & Lofquist, cited in Rojewski, 1994; Holland, 1985). Matching these variables will result in higher job satisfaction (Holland, 1985). High school programs should ensure training in specific work skills, if appropriate, based on the functioning level of the student. High school experiences related to the development of specific work skills include participation in job clubs offered by local rehabilitation agencies (Johnson & Wehman, 2001), participation in occupationally related school clubs, development of career portfolios, and participation in work experiences, self-assessment activities, and mentoring (Szymanski et al., 2003).

Banks and Renzaglia (1993) make recommendations related to specific skill training. They recommend that students be given opportunities to gather enough information about themselves and potential work environments to make career choices (Rojewski, 1994), instead on focusing on specific skills. Keeping these issues in mind, Mithaug et al.'s (1987) focus on curricula designed to promote generalization and adaptation seems particularly appropriate. Skills emphasized in this type of curriculum include decision making, independence, self-evaluation, and adjustment based on feedback. When these skills are added to the specific vocational skills of seeking, securing, and maintaining employment through generalizing foundation skills and integrative skills, a comprehensive vocational curriculum begins to emerge. The reader is cautioned to remember the importance of academic skills in job success. Although continuation of reading, math, and writing skill programs that are showing little success in skill acquisition is not recommended (Gajar et al., 1993), many students with special needs will need or want to continue to focus on the acquisition of these skills within a functional context or within an academic context for those students going on to postsecondary education. Again, this decision is to be made with the student and his or her family in relation to postschool goals.

Benz et al. (2000) found that vocational training is correlated with postschool success. Vocational training can occur as a specific site-based experience, vocational education classes and programs, and blended occupational–academic programs. Blended academic–occupational programs are an alternative to traditional academic-only or vocational-only educational approaches in secondary education. Blended programs usually teach students skills by integrating basic academics into industrial trade courses or by teaching applied academics within the context of various occupations. These programs teach general work-related skills and knowledge, academic principles, and real-world practices, problem solving, and teamwork (Eisenman, 2000). Blended curricula appear to be more successful than traditional vocational or academic programs in teaching a variety of critical work-related skills (e.g, self-detemination, academic skills; Eisenman, 2000, 2001; Benz et al., 1997).

Finally, research has been abundantly clear that work experience during high school is essential (Luecking & Fabian, 2000) for postschool success, especially two or more work experiences during the last 2 years (Benz et al., 1997) of high school and paid experiences (Benz et al., 2000). All researchers agree that real work is needed for students to build vocational competence behaviors (Luecking & Fabian, 2000) and appropriate work behaviors (i.e., competencies, social skills, higher order thinking). Work experiences can come in the forms of structured work experience (Luecking & Fabian, 2000), work-based training (Blackorby & Wagner, 1996; Colley & Jamison, 1998), community service, job shadowing, school-based enterprises, and youth apprenticeship. However, it must be stressed that paid work appears to yield the most postschool success (Benz & Lindstrom, 1997). Although follow-up research has shown that early job choices rarely match later career choices (Shapiro & Lentz, 1991), the importance of early work experience to making career choices and having ultimate success in obtaining and keeping employment is clear (Rojewski, 1994). These skills, activities, and knowledge for high school students are listed in Table 8.8. Selected IEP examples are presented in Table 8.9, with a full example of an IEP for a student, Donna, presented in Figure 8.2.

TABLE 8.8
Essential Vocational Components of a High School Curriculum

Target Activities	Target Skills	Evolving Knowledge
Part-time or summer employment	Self-appraisal	Self-concept
Work experiences (two or more)	needs identification	Specific work skills
Locating and securing employment (job club)	psychological	Work attitudes
Occupational clubs	physical	
Youth activities	needs planning	
Career portfolio	resource identification	
Mentoring	resource planning	
Internships	resource gathering	
IEP participation	Job seeking	
Career counseling	Job securing	
Ecological assessment	Job maintaining	
Job analysis and placement	Career choice making	
(for some students)	interests	
Vocational training	needs	
	abilities	
	Specific job skills	
	(when appropriate)	
	Decision making	
	Self-efficacy	
	Choice making	
	Option identification	
	Goal setting	
	Responsibility	
	Communication	
	Preferences and needs	
	Self-monitoring	
	Self-evaluation	
	Academics	
	Technology	
	Stress reduction	
	Vocational safety	
	Risk taking	

Clearly, high school is a time of concentrated activity related to vocational preparation. Transition planning is part of every IEP, and students continue to develop work-related skills, actively explore occupations, and begin making career decisions. Furthermore, students and their families become acquainted and make connections with postschool programs and service. For some students, this is also the time they begin the jobs they will have when they leave school. In fact, for students moving immediately to the world of work, it is important that they secure a job prior to leaving school, which prevents unnecessary service gaps and waiting lists (Johnson & Wehman, 2001; Wehman et al., 2001). The placement of students in jobs prior to leaving school raises issues for the educator in relation to job development and placement. Although this chapter is not about these issues, a brief mention of each is important for any vocational curriculum discussion. Additionally, it is important that the educator know that research in supported employment has shown that certain styles of job development and placement yield better results (in terms of wages, integration, benefits) for the employee with disabilities. This research clearly demonstrates that the more the

TABLE 8.9
Example High School IEP Goals and Objectives

Goal	Objectives
To gain work-related knowledge via coursework	a. The student will register for, attend, and pass (C or better) at least two vocational education classes per semester. b. The student will register for, attend, and pass (C or better) the course, "Work Experience in the Classroom," while involved in the work experience setting.
To gain direct work-related skills via work experience	a. Having worked with the teacher to identify at least two potential work experience sites, the student will choose a site, apply for the job, and interview for the job. b. Given a work experience opportunity, the student will attend work for the required hours per week. c. Given a work experience opportunity, the student will learn the skills required of the job with 95% accuracy.
To gain experience finding, applying for, and interviewing for jobs	a. Using such resources as the newspaper, employment services, and word of mouth, the student will identify at least three part-time jobs that interest her. She will do this by the middle of the second week of the first semester. b. Upon identifying at least three part-time jobs of interest, the student will ask for, fill out, and submit applications for each. She will do this by the end of the second week of the first semester. c. Upon being notified by potential employers for an interview, the student will arrive for the interview at the scheduled time and participate in the interview. She will also follow up the interview with a phone call within 3 to 5 days.
To practice work-related time management skills	a. Within the context of a work experience or part-time work, the student will arrive to work on time every day for a 3-week period. b. Within the context of a work experience or part-time work, the student will complete all of his assigned duties within the time allotted by the employer. He will do this with 75% accuracy for 2 consecutive weeks (criterion to be raised as student gains experience). c. Within the context of a work experience or part-time work, the student will sign out and sign in at the correct times for beginning and ending work and for all breaks and lunches. He will do this with 90% accuracy for 2 consecutive weeks (criterion to be raised as student gains experience).
To continue to build on the academic skills necessary for entry into postsecondary education	a. The student will enroll in a freshman prealgebra course, complete all of the coursework (with assistance and adaptations from the resource teacher), and pass the course (C or better). b. The student will enroll in an English composition course, complete all of the coursework (with assistance and adaptations from the resource teacher), and pass the course (C or better).

worker with disabilities is like the typical employee in job acquisition, training, and support, the better the outcomes (Mank, Cioffi, & Yovanoff, 1997). As a result, educators should consider the use of one-stop job centers (Hanley-Maxwell et al., 2003) for many of these activities. One-stop job centers are federally mandated centers that provide locally accessible, comprehensive employment services with no eligibility requirements. These services are a blend of those traditionally provided by various state job service agencies.

(*text continues on p. 239*)

INDIVIDUALIZED EDUCATION PROGRAM

Meeting Date: 5/21/03

Beginning Date of IEP: 8/20/03

Ending Date of IEP: 5/20/04

Student Name: Donna Ray

Birth Date: 11/27/89

Sex: F

Parent/Guardian: John and Joan Ray

Address: 201 Chestnut Way

Phone: 555-5555

District of Residence: River Hill

District of Placement: River Hill

Amount of Special Education (amount/percentage of time): 25%

Extent to which student will participate in regular education programs (describe any modifications required): 75%; resource room for math, reading, vocational education activities, and related services specified below

Related Services (specify amount of time for each service):

___ assistive technology	___ parent counseling/training	___ recreation	___ social work services
___ audiology	___ physical therapy	5% rehabilitation counseling	___ transportation services
___ counseling	5% psychological services (assertion trng.)	5% school health services (sex ed.,	___ other (specify) ___
___ medical services	___ occupational therapy	birth control counseling)	___ other (specify) ___

Physical Education: ☒ Regular ☐ Specially Designed   Vocational Education: ☐ Regular ☒ Specially Designed

Standardized Testing Participation

Eighth/tenth-grade testing: ☐ Yes ☐ No ☒ With modifications   Competency-based testing: ☐ Yes ☐ No ☒ With modifications   Achievement testing: ☐ Yes ☒ No ☐ With modifications
resource provided oral testing

Justification for removal from regular education or regular education environment (include nature and severity of disability and any potential harmful effects on the child or on the quality of services): Moderate mental retardation. Student needs extra assistance with basic academics, as well as an increased emphasis on postsecondary vocational needs. Parents have requested assertion training, sex education, and a consult with Division of Vocational Rehabilitation.

Special Education Teacher:	Local Education Agency Representative:
Parents/Guardians:	Student:
Agency Representative: none	Other (specify):
Efforts to involve parents: Phone call to set date; letter of invitation to meeting	

(continues)

FIGURE 8.2. Sample IEP for Donna.

INDIVIDUALIZED EDUCATION PROGRAM

Student Name: Donna Ray   **Date:** 5/21/03

Annual Goal: To maintain and expand functional reading and writing skills as they relate to work

Present Levels of Performance: Donna can complete simple forms with minimal assistance, filling in her name, address, phone number, Social Security number, birth date, and so on. She often needs assistance in filling in essay-type information (e.g., What are your goals? What do you like? Where have you worked?). She can read simple signs (e.g., "men," "women," "bus," "exit") but has trouble with nonroutine reading of maps, instructions, directions, and so on.

EVALUATION

Short-Term Objectives	Objective Criteria	Methods of Measurement	Schedule
Donna will complete a variety (at least 5) of job applications independently.	Completed applications with fewer than 3 errors	Career education teacher review of completed applications	Fall semester
Donna will travel to businesses in the community, acquire, and complete a variety of job applications (at least 3) independently.	Completed applications turned in to employers	Employer feedback (follow-up phone call)	Spring semester
Donna will read signs in the community so she can move about independently.	Read and responded appropriately to all signs encountered in community	Teacher and parent monitoring; self-monitoring	Fall and spring semesters
Donna will construct a grocery list and shop from that list at the store.	All items on list bought or accounted for with 100% accuracy for 4 out of 5 trips	Teacher and parent monitoring	Fall and spring semesters

Specific special education and related services needed to achieve this goal: Community instruction and travel time

Action taken on this goal at IEP review (continue as is, continue with modifications, discontinue—met, discontinue—revised/replaced):

(continues)

FIGURE 8.2. Continued.

233

INDIVIDUALIZED EDUCATION PROGRAM

Student Name: Donna Ray

Date: 5/21/03

Annual Goal: To maintain and expand functional math skills

Present Levels of Performance: Donna can tell time on an analog (traditional) clock or watch. She can use money appropriately (e.g., make change, round up to the nearest dollar to pay), although she sometimes takes a while to do so. She sometimes has difficulty estimating the cost of items and whether she has enough money. She can compute basic math problems, but has difficulty applying the concepts to real-life situations.

EVALUATION

Short-Term Objectives	Objective Criteria	Methods of Measurement	Schedule
Donna will use a calculator while shopping at the grocery store to add up her total and estimate how much she has spent.	100% accuracy for 4 out of 5 trips	Self-recording of total from calculator compared to total on receipt; teacher and parent monitoring	Fall and spring semesters
Donna will count out to the nearest dollar the total requested by the cashier; hand it to the cashier; and wait for change.	100% accuracy for 4 out of 5 trips	Self-report; teacher and parent monitoring	Fall and spring semesters
Donna will take a basic accounting class to learn how to use checking and savings accounts.	Enrollment in class; passing grade of C or above	Self-report to resource teacher; reports from accounting teacher to resource teacher	Beginning, middle, and end of spring semester
Donna will open a savings account at her parents' bank in her name. She will deposit her weekly allowance (from chores) in the account.	Account opened; passbook in Donna's possession	Parent report to resource teacher	Spring semester
Donna will be listed on her parents' checking account and will use checks to pay for some purchases (e.g., large grocery trips, items for home, clothing).	Checks will be written with 100% accuracy	Checks with Donna's name on them; self- and parent report to resource teacher	Monthly reports
Using a calculator, task analysis, and the reconciliation form provided by the bank, Donna will balance the family checkbook.	2 out of 3 months with 100% accuracy	Completed reconciliation form to be reviewed by parents or resource teacher	Monthly

Specific special education and related services needed to achieve this goal: Community instruction and travel time

Action taken on this goal at IEP review (continue as is, continue with modifications, discontinue—met, discontinue—revised/replaced):

(continues)

FIGURE 8.2. Continued.

INDIVIDUALIZED EDUCATION PROGRAM

Student Name: Donna Ray   **Date:** 5/21/03

Annual Goal: To increase awareness of career options for after high school

Present Levels of Performance: Donna does not seem particularly concerned about the kind of work she will be involved in after she finishes high school. She has a variety of interests that need to be explored further.

EVALUATION

Short-Term Objectives	Objective Criteria	Methods of Measurement	Schedule
Donna will take the Careers class (open to freshman, sophomores, and juniors).	Enrollment in class; passing grade of C or above	Careers class teacher report	Beginning, middle, and end of fall semester
Donna will complete career-related activities on the Career Options computer software package available in the school library.	Printouts of self-interest inventory, computer matches to careers, and brief reports on at least 3 careers	Self monitoring and report to resource teacher; printouts to be reviewed with Careers class teacher and resource teacher	Fall and spring semesters
Donna will participate in Career Week activities at the high school. This will include attending at least 3 presentations, going on at least 1 tour, and participating in 1 job shadow.	Donna will complete reaction sheets on each of these experiences	Reaction sheets to be reviewed with Careers class teacher and resource teacher	Spring semester

Specific special education and related services needed to achieve this goal: Resource time and teacher for assistance with written documentation (e.g., reaction sheets)

Action taken on this goal at IEP review (i.e., continue as is, continue with modifications, discontinue—met, discontinue—revised/replaced):

(continues)

FIGURE 8.2. *Continued.*

235

INDIVIDUALIZED EDUCATION PROGRAM

Student Name: Donna Ray

Date: 5/21/03

Annual Goal: To increase and improve employment-related skills

Present Levels of Performance: Donna has no work history. In addition, she has had few responsibilities at home. While eager to please, she shows little initiation to find or complete tasks, and needs supervision to stay on task in the academic setting. However, the tasks that she does complete are usually done quite well.

Short-Term Objectives	Objective Criteria	EVALUATION		
		Methods of Measurement	Schedule	
Donna will initiate and complete 2 daily chores (making bed and doing dinner dishes) and 3 weekly chores at home (taking out garbage, cleaning upstairs bath, cleaning room).	Daily chores will be completed 4 out of 5 days; weekly chores, 3 out of 4 weeks	Both Donna and her mom will check off tasks on a chart to be hung in the kitchen at home; reports via Donna and her mom to resource teacher	Reports between home and school 3 times a semester; fall and spring semesters	
Donna will work in the local public library, reshelving returns, for 3 hours a week.	Attendance at job	Librarian and self-report	Fall semester	
Donna will work in a local grocery store, restocking shelves and assisting customers for 5 to 10 hours a week.	Attendance at job	Employer, teacher supervisor (varies), and self-report	Spring semester	

Specific special education and related services needed to achieve this goal: None

Action taken on this goal at IEP review (i.e., continue as is, continue with modifications, discontinue—met, discontinue—revised/replaced):

(continues)

FIGURE 8.2. *Continued.*

236

INDIVIDUALIZED EDUCATION PROGRAM

Student Name: Donna Ray

Date: 5/21/03

Annual Goal: To improve social interaction skills, especially regarding assertiveness and sexual responsibility

Present Levels of Performance: Donna appears to get along well with others (adults and peers), and reports that she enjoys being with her friends. However, her teachers and parents are concerned that Donna is too passive and is often taken advantage of—to the point of being sexually promiscuous.

Short-Term Objectives	EVALUATION		
	Objective Criteria	Methods of Measurement	Schedule
Donna will take an after-school assertiveness training class with a small group of students and the school guidance counselor.	Attendance in and completion of course	Report by counselor; self-report to resource teacher	First 6 weeks of fall semester
Donna will take an after-school sex education class with a small group of students and the school nurse/health educator.	Attendance in and completion of course	Report by nurse/health educator; self-report to resource teacher	Second 6 weeks of fall semester

Specific special education and related services needed to achieve this goal: Involvement of related services staff (i.e., school counselor, school nurse/health educator); waiver of enrollment fees due to family's economic status

Action taken on this goal at IEP review (i.e., continue as is, continue with modifications, discontinue—met, discontinue—revised/replaced):

(continues)

FIGURE 8.2. *Continued.*

237

TRANSITION PLANNING SUMMARY PAGE

Yes	No	Transition Services Included in the IEP (indicate location in IEP)
X		Transition-related instruction*: pp. 2-6
X		Community experiences*: pp. 2, 3, 5
X		Employment objectives*: pp. 2, 4, 5
X		Postschool adult living objectives*: pp. 2, 3-6
X		Acquisition of daily living skills**: pp. 7, 8
	X	Functional vocational evaluation**: To be conducted during fall of junior year

* If not included as annual goals and short-term objectives in the IEP, write an annual statement of needed services. If not needed, write a statement regarding the basis upon which the services were excluded.
** If not included as goals and objectives in the IEP, these require an annual statement of needed services, if appropriate.

If the student did not attend the IEP meeting, what steps were taken to ensure that the student's interests and preferences were considered in the planning? NA

Participating Transition Service Agencies and Name of Representative	Date Agency Representative Invited and Method of Invitation	Statement of Agency Responsibilities/Linkages Related to Each of the Needed Transition Skill Areas
Division of Vocational Rehabilitation: *Scott Hall—DID NOT ATTEND MEETING*	*4/1/03: phone call* *4/15/03: letter* *5/15/03: phone call*	*Has agreed to consult with the family at the school at the end of the school year regarding services available to Donna*

If an invited agency representative did not attend the IEP meeting, what steps were taken to obtain the participation of the agency in the planning of transition services? *See above*

FIGURE 8.2. *Continued.*

Job development includes three aspects: identifying jobs, refining available options, and expanding options (in terms of job type and number; Hanley-Maxwell et al., 2003; Owens-Johnson & Hanley-Maxwell, 1999). Some jobs may be developed for experiential reasons, and others may be selected as placement options for students prior to leaving school. Educators who develop jobs may do so for specific students or may create a bank of jobs from which students can choose. Regardless of the approach to job development, the student must be actively involved in the process (Rogan, Banks, & Howard, 2000).

Job placement follows job development and results in the optimal job position for the student, based on her or his existing abilities and interests (Geist & Calzaretta, 1982). Job placement can be done by a variety of people beyond educators, including rehabilitation counselors, job placement specialists, individual contractors, and supported employment providers. All placements processes should match the future employee with potential jobs based on the results from assessments of the student and job analyses (Hanley-Maxwell et al., 2003).

CONCLUSION

As seen in Donna's IEP (see Figure 8.2), work-related curriculum crosses traditional curricular domains (both academic and functional), "borrows" skills from each of these domains, and supplements those skills with work-targeted content. Work-related curriculum should lead the student to acquire skills in decision making and career choice making, increase his or her self-concept, develop appropriate work attitudes, increase his or her competence in locating and securing employment, develop skills that support job maintenance (e.g., social skills, communication, problem solving), and develop skills that lead to lifelong learning and flexibility. Early and varied learning experiences contribute to each of these areas, and career fantasy, informal and formal work experiences, and part-time jobs provide the vehicle for the development of career-specific skills and interests. The goal of work-related curricular content should not be to prepare a student for a particular occupation but to prepare him or her to make relevant career decisions throughout life. Without thoughtful, ongoing assessment and planning, individualized work-related curricula cannot be adequately developed. Thus, as intended from the outset, the IEP becomes the critical planning tool for effective education.

REFERENCES

Agran, M., Swaner, J., & Snow, K. (1998). Work safety skills: A neglected curricular area. *Career Development for Exceptional Individuals, 21,* 33–44.

Banks, R., & Renzaglia, A. (1993). Longitudinal vocational programs: A review of current recommended practices for individuals with moderate to severe disabilities. *Journal of Vocational Rehabilitation, 3*(2), 5–16.

Benz, M. R., & Halpern, A. S. (1987). Transition services for secondary students with mild disabilities: A statewide perspective. *Exceptional Children, 53,* 507–514.

Benz, M. R., & Lindstrom, L. E. (1997). *Building school-to-work programs: Strategies for youth with special needs.* Austin, TX: PRO-ED.

Benz, M. R., Lindstrom, L., & Yovanoff, P. (2000). Improving graduation and employment outcomes of students with disabilities: Predictive factors and student perspectives. *Exceptional Children, 66,* 509–529.

Benz, M. R., Yovanoff, P., & Doren, B. (1997). School-to-work components that predict postschool success for student with disabilities. *Exceptional Children, 63,* 151–165.

Berg, W. K., Wacker, D. P., & Flynn, T. H. (1990). Teaching generalization and maintenance of work behavior. In F. R. Rusch (Ed.), *Supported employment: Models, methods, and issues* (pp. 145–160). Sycamore, IL: Sycamore.

Blackorby, J., & Wagner, M. (1996). Longitudinal postschool outcomes of youth with disabilities: Findings from the National Longitudinal Transition Study. *Exceptional Children, 62,* 399–413.

Brolin, D. (1997). *Life centered career education: A competency-based approach.* Reston, VA: Council for Exceptional Children.

Browder, D. M., & King D. (1987). Comprehensive assessment for longitudinal curriculum development. In D. M. Browder (Ed.), *Assessment of individuals with severe handicaps* (pp. 25–53). Baltimore: Brookes.

Brown-Glover, P. (1992). Applications for youth with mild mental retardation. In P. Wehman (Ed.), *Life beyond the classroom: Transition strategies for young people with disabilities* (pp. 237–260). Baltimore: Brookes.

Carl D. Perkins Vocational and Technical Education Act of 1998, 20 U.S.C. § 2301 *et seq.*

Chadsey-Rusch, J. (1986). Identifying and teaching valued social skills. In F. R. Rusch (Ed.), *Competitive employment: Service delivery models, methods, and issues* (pp. 273–287). Baltimore: Brookes.

Chadsey-Rusch, J., & Gonzalez, P. (1988). Social ecology of the workplace: Employers' perceptions versus direct observation. *Research in Developmental Disabilities, 9,* 229–245.

Colley, D. A., & Jamison, D. (1998). Postschool results for youth with disabilities: Key indicators and policy implications. *Career Development for Exceptional Individuals, 21,* 145–160.

Edgar, E. (1987). Secondary programs in special education: Are many of them justifiable? *Exceptional Children, 26,* 555–561.

Eisenman, L. (2000). Characteristics and effects of integrated academic and occupational curricula for students with disabilities: A literature review. *Career Development for Exceptional Individuals, 23,* 105–119.

Eisenman, L. (2001). Conceptualizing the contribution of career-oriented schooling on self-determination. *Career Development for Exceptional Individuals, 24,* 3–17.

Farley, R. C., & Johnson, V. A. (1999). Enhancing career exploration and job seeking of secondary students with disabilities. *Career Development for Exceptional Individuals, 22,* 43–54.

Field, S., Martin, J., Miller, R., Ward, M., & Wehmeyer, M. (1998). *A practical guide to teaching self-determination.* Reston, VA: Council for Exceptional Children, Division on Career Development and Transition.

Ford, A., Schnorr, R., Meyer, L., Davern, L., Black, J., & Dempsey, P. (1989). *The Syracuse community-referenced curriculum guide for students with moderate and severe disabilities.* Baltimore: Brookes.

Gajar, A., Goodman, L., & McAfee, J. (1993). *Secondary schools and beyond: Transition of individuals with mild disabilities.* New York: Macmillan.

Geist, C., & Calzaretta, W. (1982). *Placement handbook for counseling disabled persons.* Springfield, IL: Charles C Thomas.

German, S. L., Martin, J. E., Marshall, L. H., & Sale, R. P. (2000). Promoting self-determination: Using Take Action to teach goal attainment. *Career Development for Exceptional Individuals, 23,* 27–38.

Giangreco, M. F., Cloninger, C. J., & Iverson, V. (1998). *Choosing options and accommodations for children (COACH): A guide to educational planning for students with disabilities.* Baltimore: Brookes.

Goals 2000: Educate America Act of 1994, 20 U.S.C. § 5801 *et seq.*

Gorden, E. E. (2000). Help wanted: Creating tomorrow's work force. *Futurist, 34*(4), 48–52.

Greenspan, S., & Shoultz, B. (1981). Why mentally retarded adults lose their jobs: Social competence as a factor in work adjustment. *Applied Research in Mental Retardation, 2,* 23–38.

Hall, D. T., & Mirvis, P. H. (1996). The new protean career: Psychological success and the path with a heart. In D. T. Hall (Ed.), *The career is dead: Long live the career* (pp. 15–45). San Francisco: Jossey-Bass.

Halpern, A., Irvin, L., & Landman, J. (1979). *Test for everyday living.* Monterey, CA: CTB/McGraw-Hill.

Halpern, A. S. (1992). Transition: Old wine in new bottles. *Exceptional Children, 58,* 202–211.

Hanley-Maxwell, C., & Bordieri, J. (1989, Fall). Purchasing supported employment: Evaluating the service. *Journal of Applied Rehabilitation Counseling, 20*(3), 4–11.

Hanley-Maxwell, C., Bordieri, J., & Merz, M. A. (1996). Supporting placement. In E. M. Szymanski & R. M. Parker (Eds.), *Work and disability: Issues in career counseling and job placement* (pp. 341–364). Austin, TX: PRO-ED.

Hanley-Maxwell, C., & Collet-Klingenberg, L. (1996). Curricular choices related to work. In P. Wehman & J. Kregel (Eds.), *Functional curriculum for elementary, middle, and secondary age students with special needs* (pp. 155–183). Austin, TX: PRO-ED.

Hanley-Maxwell, C., Owens-Johnson, L., & Fabian, E. (2003). Supported employment. In E. M. Szymanski & R. M. Parker (Eds.), *Work and disability: Issues in career counseling and job placement* (2nd ed.). Austin, TX: PRO-ED.

Hanley-Maxwell, C., Rusch, F. R., Chadsey-Rusch, J., & Renzaglia, A. (1986). Reported factors contributing to job terminations of individuals with severe disabilities. *Journal of the Association for Persons with Severe Handicaps, 11*(1), 45–52.

Hanley-Maxwell, C., Szymanski, E. M., & Owens-Johnson, L. (1998). Supported employment and transition. In R. M. Parker & E. M. Szymanski (Eds.), *Rehabilitation counseling: Basics and beyond* (2nd ed.). Austin, TX: PRO-ED.

Hershenson, D. B. (1981). Work adjustment, disability, and the three R's of vocational rehabilitation: A conceptual model. *Rehabilitation Counseling Bulletin, 25,* 91–97.

Hershenson, D. B. (1984). Vocational counseling with learning disabled adults. *Journal of Rehabilitation, 50,* 40–44.

Holland, J. L. (1985). *Making vocational choices: A theory of vocational personalities and work environments* (2nd ed.). Englewood Cliffs, NJ: Prentice Hall.

Hughes, C., Bogseon, H., Kim, J., Killian, D. J., Harmer, M. L., & Alcantara, P. R. (1997). A preliminary validation of strategies that support the transition from school to adult life. *Career Development for Exceptional Individuals, 20,* 1–14.

Individuals with Disabilities Education Act of 1990, 20 U.S.C. § 1400 *et seq.*

Individuals with Disabilities Education Act Amendments of 1997, 20 U.S.C. § 1400 *et seq.*

Inge, K., & Tilson, G. P. (1997). Ensuring support systems that work: Getting beyond the natural supports versus job coach controversy. *Journal of Vocational Rehabilitation, 9*(2), 133–142.

Izzo, M. V., Cartledge, G., Miller, L., Growick, B., & Rutkowski, S. (2000). Increasing employment earnings: Extended transition services that make a difference. *Career Development for Exceptional Individuals, 23,* 139–156.

Job Training Partnership Act of 1982, 19 U.S.C. § 1501 *et seq.*

Johnson, S., & Wehman, P. (2001). Teaching for transition. In P. Wehman (Ed.), *Life beyond the classroom* (3rd ed., pp. 145–170). Baltimore: Brookes.

Karge, D. B., Patton, P., & de la Garza, B. (1992). Transition services for youth with mild disabilities: Do they exist, are they needed? *Career Development for Exceptional Individuals, 15,* 47–68.

Kellogg, A. (1995). *Guidelines for conducting functional vocational evaluations.* Madison: State of Wisconsin, Department of Public Instruction.

Kohler, P. D. (1993). Best practices in transition: Substantiated or implied? *Career Development for Exceptional Individuals, 16,* 107–121.

Krumboltz, J. D. (1979). A social learning theory of career decision making. In A. M. Mitchell, G. B. Jones, & J. D. Krumboltz (Eds.), *Social learning and career decision making.* Cranston, RI: Carroll.

Linkenhoker, D., & McCarron, L. (1980). *Street Survival Skills Questionnaire.* Dallas, TX: McCarron-Dial Systems.

Luecking, R. G., & Fabian, E. S. (2000). Paid internship and employment success for youth in transition. *Career Development for Exceptional Individuals, 23,* 205–219.

Mank, D., Cioffi, A., & Yovanoff, P. (1997). Analysis of the typicalness of supported jobs, natural supports, wages, and integration outcomes. *Mental Retardation, 35,* 185–197.

Martin, J. E., Marshall, L. H., & Maxson, L. L. (1991). Transition policy: Infusing self-determination and self-advocacy into transition programs. *Career Development of Exceptional Individuals, 16*(1), 53–61.

McCrae, L. (1991). A comparison between the perceptions of special educators and employers: What factors are critical for job success? *Career Development for Exceptional Individuals, 14,* 121–130.

Means, B. (1989). *Job application training.* Fayetteville: University of Arkansas, Research and Training Center in Vocational Rehabilitation.

Michaels, C. A. (1994). *Transition strategies for persons with learning disabilities.* San Diego, CA: Singular.

Minskoff, E. H., & Demoss, S. (1994). Workplace social skills and individuals with learning disabilities. *Journal of Vocational Rehabilitation, 4,* 113–121.

Mithaug, D. E., Martin, J. E., & Agran, M. (1987). Adaptability instruction: The goal of transition programming. *Exceptional Children, 53,* 500–505.

Morgan, R. L., Ellerd, D. A., Jensen, K., & Taylor, M. J. (2000). A survey of community employment placements: Where are youth and adults with disabilities working? *Career Development for Exceptional Individuals, 23,* 73–86.

O'Brien, J. (1987). A guide to lifestyle planning. In T. Bellamy & B. Wilcox (Eds.), *The activity catalogue: A programming guide for youth and adults with severe disability* (pp. 75–89). Baltimore: Brookes.

O'Brien, J., & Lyle, C. (1987). *Framework for accomplishment.* Decatur, GA: Responsive Systems Associates.

Ochs, L. A., & Roessler, R. T. (2001). Students with disabilities: How ready are they for the 21st century? *Rehabilitation Counseling Bulletin, 44,* 170–176.

Owens-Johnson, L., & Hanley-Maxwell, C. (1999). Employer views on job development strategies for marketing supported employment. *Vocational Rehabilitation, 12,* 113–123.

Pancsofar, E. (1986). Assessing work behavior. In F. R. Rusch (Ed.), *Competitive employment: Issues and strategies* (pp. 93–102). Baltimore: Brookes.

Phelps, L. A., & Hanley-Maxwell, C. (1997). School to work transition for youth with disability: A review of outcomes and practices. *Review of Education Research, 67,* 197–226.

Rehabilitation Act Amendments of 1992, 29 U.S.C. § 706(8), 794, 794a, 794b.

Rehabilitation Act Amendments of 1998, 29 U.S.C. § 798 *et seq.*

Renzaglia, A., & Hutchins, M. (1988). A community-referenced approach to preparing persons with disabilities for employment. In P. Wehman & M. S. Moon (Eds.), *Vocational rehabilitation and supported employment* (pp. 91–110). Baltimore: Brookes.

Roe, A. (1956). Early determinants of vocational choice. *Journal of Counseling Psychology, 4,* 212–217.

Roessler, R., Hinman, S., & Lewis, F. (1986). *Getting employed through interview training (GET-IT).* Fayetteville: University of Arkansas, Research and Training Center in Vocational Rehabilitation.

Roessler, R., & Schriner, K. (1988). *Occupational choice strategy.* Fayetteville: University of Arkansas, Research and Training Center in Vocational Rehabilitation.

Rogan, P., Banks, B., & Howard, M. (2000). Work place supports in practice: As little as possible, as much as necessary. *Focus on Autism and Other Developmental Disabilities, 15*(1), 2–11.

Rojewski, J. W. (1994). Applying theories of career behavior to special populations: Implications for secondary vocational transition programming. *Issues in Special Education and Rehabilitation, 9*(1), 7–26.

Sands, D. J., Woolsey, T., & Dunlap, W. R. (1985). *National Independent Living Skills Screening Instrument.* Tuscaloosa: University of Alabama.

School to Work Opportunities Act of 1994, 20 U.S.C. § 6101 *et seq.*

Shapiro, E. S., & Lentz, F. E. (1991). Vocational–technical programs: Follow-up of students with learning disabilities. *Exceptional Children, 58,* 47–59.

Sitlington, P. L., Neubert, D. A., & LeConte, P. J. (1997). Transition assessment: The position statement of the Division of Career Development and Transition. *Career Development for Exceptional Individuals, 20,* 69–79.

Stodden, R. A., & Leake, D. W. (1994). Getting to the core of transition: A reassessment of old wine in new bottles. *Career Development for Exceptional Individuals, 17,* 65–76.

Super, D. E. (1957). *The psychology of careers.* New York: Harper & Row.

Super, D. E. (1974). Vocational maturity theory: Toward implementing a psychology of career education and guidance. In D. E. Super (Ed.), *Measuring vocational maturity for counseling and evaluation* (pp. 9–24). Washington, DC: American Personnel and Guidance Association.

Szymanski, E. M. (1994). Transition: Life-span, life-space considerations for empowerment. *Exceptional Children, 60,* 402–410.

Szymanski, E. M., Enright, M., & Hershenson, D. B. (2003). Career development theories, constructs, and research: Implications for people with disabilities. In E. M. Szymanski & R. M. Parker (Eds.), *Work and disability: Issues in career counseling and job placement* (2nd ed.). Austin, TX: PRO-ED.

Test, D. W., & Wood, W. M. (1996). Natural supports in the workplace: The jury is still out. *Journal of the Association for Persons with Severe Handicaps, 21*(4), 155–173.

Unger, D., Parent, W., Gibson, K., Kane-Johnston, K., & Kregel, J. (1998). An analysis of the activities of employment specialists in natural support approach to supported employment. *Focus on Autism and Other Developmental Disabilities, 13*(1), 27–38.

U.S. Department of Labor. (1991). *What work requires of schools: A SCANS report for America 2000.* Washington, DC: Author.

Vandercook, T., York, J., & Forest, M. (1989). McGill Action Planning System (MAPS): A strategy for building the vision. *Journal of the Association for Persons with Severe Handicaps, 14*(3), 205–215.

Wagner, M., Blackorby, J., Cameto, R., & Newman, L. (1993). *What makes a difference? Influences on postschool outcomes of youth with disabilities.* Menlo Park, CA: SRI.

Wehman, P., Brooke, V., & Inge, K. J. (2001). Vocational placements and careers. In P. Wehman (Ed.), *Life beyond the classroom* (3rd ed., pp. 211–246). Baltimore: Brookes.

Wehman, P., Moon, M. S., Everson, J. M., Wood, W., & Barcus, J. M. (1988). *Transition from school to work: New challenges for youth with severe disabilities.* Baltimore: Brookes.

Wehmeyer, M. L. (1992). Self-determination and the education of students with mental retardation. *Education and Training in Mental Retardation, 27,* 302–314.

Wehmeyer, M. L. (1994). Employment status and perceptions of control of adults with cognitive and developmental disabilities. *Research in Developmental Disabilities, 15*(2), 119–131.

Wehmeyer, M. L., Palmer, S. B., Agran, M., Mithaug, D. E., & Martin, J. E. (2000). Promoting causal agency: The self-determined learning model of instruction. *Exceptional Children, 66,* 439–453.

Wehmeyer, M. L., & Schwartz, M. (1997). Self-determination and positive adult outcomes: A follow-up study of youth with mental retardation of learning disabilities. *Exceptional Children, 63,* 245–255.

Wehmeyer, M. L., & Schwartz, M. (1998). The self-determination focus of transition goals for students with mental retardation. *Career Development for Exceptional Individuals, 21,* 75–86.

Where we are in special education today. (2001, September). *CEC Today, 8*(3), 1, 5.

White, W. J. (1992). The postschool adjustment of persons with learning disabilities: Current status and future projections. *Journal of Learning Disabilities, 25,* 448–456.

Will, M. (1984). *OSERS programming for the transition of youth with severe disabilities: Bridges from school to working life.* Washington, DC: Office of Special Education and Rehabilitative Services, U.S. Department of Education.

Workforce Investment Partnership Act of 1998, 29 U.S.C. § 2801 *et seq.*

CHAPTER 9

Travel and Mobility Training

Michael D. West, Katherine Wittig, and Victoria Dowdy

  ALEX

Alex is a 16-year-old male with mild mental retardation who also experiences moderate levels of depression. He is ambulatory, highly verbal, and reads at the second-grade level. Alex can do simple math such as counting and making change to $1.00. He lives with an older brother in a government-subsidized apartment in a rural town. Alex's parents live in a large midwestern city. They do not wish for Alex to live with them there because when the family had lived together in another large city, Alex had become fascinated with gang-related activities, particularly drug running. Since moving out of his parents' home about a year ago, Alex has missed his parents a great deal and has been dejected and morose about his perceived rejection by them.

Alex is enrolled in a local high school and participates in supported employment training services. His Individualized Education Program (IEP) and Individual Transition Plan (ITP) place a strong emphasis on work-related activities. Alex currently works in a small restaurant as a busboy and dishwasher and hopes to continue there after graduation, perhaps taking on additional duties. This job site is 4 miles from Alex's apartment and 10 miles from his school. Although there is an effective public transportation system in Alex's area, he currently depends on others to provide transportation. How can Alex's school personnel plan for him to independently get to his job and to his apartment, before and after he graduates?

On February 1, 2001, President George W. Bush launched the New Freedom Initiative (Bush, 2001), a set of targeted policy directives to increase the participation of citizens with disabilities in work, school, and community. Those directives included increased access to education, assistive technology, telecommuting opportunities, and transportation. Regarding transportation, President Bush wrote,

Transportation can be a particularly difficult barrier to work for Americans with disabilities. In 1997, the Director of Project Action stated that "access to transportation is often the critical factor in obtaining employment for the nation's 25 million transit dependent people with disabilities." Today, the lack of adequate transportation remains a primary barrier to work for people with disabilities: one-third of people with disabilities report that inadequate transportation is a significant problem.

Through formula grant programs and the enforcement of the ADA [Americans with Disabilities Act of 1990], the Federal Government has helped make our mass transit systems more accessible. More must be done, however, to

245

test new transportation ideas and to increase access to alternate means of transportation, such as vans with specialty lifts, modified automobiles, and ride-share programs for those who cannot get to buses or other forms of mass transit.

On a daily basis, many non-profit groups and businesses are working hard to help people with disabilities live and work independently. These organizations often lack the funds to get people with disabilities to job interviews, to job training, and to work.

The Federal Government should support the development of innovative transportation initiatives and partner with local organizations to promote access to alternate methods of transportation. (Bush, 2001, p. 18)

President Bush's (2001) New Freedom Initiative is a welcome and much-needed step toward increasing the workforce and community participation of citizens with disabilities. In this chapter, we address travel and mobility issues and alternatives for students and adults with disabilities.

DESCRIPTION OF CURRICULUM

Mobility and travel mean movement *within* and *between* environments. Mobility within environments refers to a person moving about in one environment, such as a school, workplace, home, store, or other public area. Mobility between environments refers to a person moving from one environment to another, such as from home to school, work, or a shopping center.

Both aspects of student mobility are essential components of educational planning and instruction. Increasing a student's mobility within environments increases the likelihood that he or she will achieve successful educational outcomes. The student's ability to maneuver about and locate specific areas within an environment increases the student's competencies and independence in that particular setting, improving the chances that the student will be successful there (McGregor, 1995). For example, instructing a student in work-related skills will more likely result in successful employment if the student is also able to move about within the building, locate work areas, or access common areas such as restrooms, cafeterias, break rooms, and conference areas.

Attention to student mobility is an important educational goal for a second reason: Increasing mobility between environments has a positive effect on student self-determination. Student self-determination is a concept that has received much attention in educational research and policy in recent years and is increasingly being promoted as both a means and an outcome in special education programs. The following section provide background information for understanding self-determination and the role that mobility plays in it.

Self-Determination

What Is Self-Determination?

Most people value their ability to make decisions about the style of clothing they wear, the individuals with whom they live, the decor of their home, the place they work, the job they perform, and many other facets of life. Such decisions are the expressions of personal autonomy by which individuals define themselves. The ability to make choices that are meaningful is self-determination. The two key components of self-determination are *choice* and *control* (Deci & Ryan, 1985; Lovett, 1991; Price, 1990). Self-determination can be found whenever individuals are free to exercise choice and to have those choices be the prevailing controlling factors in their lives, free from coercion or artificial constraints.

In recent years, choice and self-determination have been recognized as expressions of dignity and autonomy for people with disabilities and have become a focus of educational and habilitative programs (Guess, Benson, & Siegel-Causey, 1985; Shevin & Klein, 1984; West & Parent, 1992). A number of strategies have been demonstrated for enabling choice for persons with even severe and multiple disabilities (Reid & Parsons, 1990, 1991; Wacker, Wiggins, Fowler, & Berg, 1988). In general, choice and self-determination lead to improved service outcomes, and in the particular case of vocational rehabilitation services, they lead to more satisfying and successful employment, with decreased social and economic dependence.

Why Is Self-Determination a Critical Issue for Students with Disabilities?

Research over the past two decades indicates that individuals, disabled or not, tend to participate more in and receive greater benefit from activities in which they exercise choice and control. Dattilo and Rusch (1985) found that students with disabilities engaged in a leisure activity more when given the choice of participation than when the choice was eliminated. Children with autism have been found to exhibit fewer antisocial or challenging behaviors when they are allowed choices from among activities (Dyer, Dunlap, & Winterling, 1990; Koegel, Dyer, & Bell, 1987). There have been similar findings about adults with cognitive disabilities (Ip, Szymanski, Johnston-Rodriguez, & Karls, 1994). Parsons, Reid, and Baumgartner (1990) studied clients of a sheltered workshop and found that attendance improved when participants were allowed to choose their own jobs, rather than being assigned to a particular job by workshop staff.

As students approach transition, self-determination becomes even more critical (Ward, 1989). For most students, the end of high school brings decisions about college, careers, housing, social outlets, and other adult concerns—decisions in which the students are active participants. For many students with disabilities, however, the end of schooling means being placed on waiting lists for residential or vocational services and lifelong dependence on family, friends, and service agencies. Teaching students with disabilities to be self-directed and self-determined increases the likelihood of successful transition to a more independent life as an adult (Gerber, Ginsberg, & Reiff, 1992; West, Barcus, Brooke, & Rayfield, 1995).

The Individuals with Disabilities Education Act of 1990 (IDEA) requires that students' goals and preferences be considered in transition planning. New strategies for promoting student self-determination in the transition process have been developed in recent years, including the Life Centered Career Education model (Brolin, 1993) and student-directed transitional planning models (Wehmeyer & Kelchner, 1995).

How Does Mobility Increase Self-Determination?

In a study of self-determined adults with disabilities conducted by West et al. (1995), availability of transportation and independent mobility in the community were major factors in promoting self-determination. Having a means of accessing different environments increased individuals' range of options for work, socialization, recreation, and housing. Individuals who were mobile were able to decide where and how they lived, rather than having to relinquish control to service agencies, family members, or others.

As they approach the transition to adult life, students who are dependent on family or social service agencies for transportation will be functionally limited in the jobs and housing options that are available to them, as well as the friends with whom they can socialize and the types of social, community, and recreational outlets they can enjoy as adults. Increasing students' mobility and transportation skills and resources therefore increases the amount of choice and control that they experience.

Adaptations and Support

Many students with disabilities can be taught to drive or bicycle, negotiate a large and complex building, use public transportation, cross streets safely, and meet other mobility and transportation needs independently. If students can learn to use these skills independently, then certainly they should be taught to do so. But if a student is not able to move within or between environments independently because of cognitive or physical limitations, then the teacher must plan to provide for either *adaptations* or *support* to assist the student in meeting his or her mobility and transportation needs (Sharpton & West, 1996).

Mobility and transportation adaptations refer to redesigning an existing option so that a student is able to use it. When this redesign involves the use of mechanical or electronic devices, it is often termed *assistive technology* (Carr, 1994). Adaptations can also be made to the ways in which tasks or skills are performed, maximizing the physical or cognitive skills of the student, or in the cues to which the student must attend, such as substituting color or pictorial cues for written words. Often, students must receive training in how to use an adaptation. Possible mobility adaptations include the following:

1. Modifying an automobile or van so that a student can learn to drive it

2. Providing a student who has problems with balance with a three-wheel bicycle

3. Using a wheelchair, motorized cart, walker, or other mobility aid

4. Modifying the environment for wheelchair or walker accessibility, such as widening aisles, installing ramps or electronic doors, and raising worktables

5. Installing handrails along walkways to provide support for students with orthopedic or health impairments that cause imbalance or lessened stamina

6. Placing markers, such as signs or color-coded lines, strategically to assist a student in locating target destinations

7. Providing a student with a map of an area, or written or taped directions

8. Developing templates with different coin combinations for assisting students in identifying correct change for bus fares and transfers

To select a method of adaptation or assistive technology and to evaluate its effectiveness in meeting a student's mobility needs, teachers should use the following questions, presented by Sharpton and West (1996) and The Arc (1994):

1. Will the adaptation be effective in meeting the student's needs?

2. Will the adaptation be convenient and easy to use?

3. Is the adaptation safe, durable, and reliable?

4. What are the repair and maintenance needs for the assistive device?

5. Can the adaptation be used in multiple environments?

6. Does an adaptation draw unnecessary attention to the student?

7. Is the student happy with the adaptation? Are there alternative methods that make him or her feel more comfortable?

If an appropriate adaptation is not available to meet a student's identified need, then the teacher must look for other ways to support the student, that is, identify alternative means for enabling the student to travel within or between environments (Sharpton & West, 1996). Support options typically involve the assistance of another person or organization. Some examples include the following:

1. Using a personal assistant, friend, or family member to assist a student in moving within work or community environments

2. Identifying students without disabilities to serve as buddies or helpers to assist students with cognitive or orthopedic disabilities in reaching target destinations, such as the library, cafeteria, and classrooms, or to assist with such chores as reaching library books on high shelves

3. Locating other workers within an employment setting or, in the case of recreational outings, persons having similar interests, with whom a student can ride and who can assist the student with scheduling and reimbursement

4. Aiding a student in making contacts with coworkers within employment sites who can assist the student with reaching common areas, such as restrooms or cafeterias

5. Arranging for transportation through paratransit services or human service agencies

Locating mobility and transportation supports often requires the teacher to explore creative alternatives. When using support options, teachers should identify both main support options and backup options (Parent, Unger, Gibson, & Clements, 1994). If a student uses a ride-share to get to work, there will be days when the coworker is unable to drive to work due to illness, vacation, car problems, or time conflicts. If the student worker is totally dependent on the coworker, then the student would be absent or late those days, which would reflect poorly on the student. One backup plan would be to have the student's parent or sibling provide transportation when ride sharing is unavailable. The same principle applies for assisting students with mobility within the school setting.

APPROACH TO ASSESSMENT

Regardless of a student's age, the assessment of mobility and transportation needs should take a functional approach, first identifying the environments that the student wants or needs to reach and those in which the student is expected to function. Once the student's environments have been identified, an assessment of the student's capacities and resources will help determine if the necessary skills can be taught or if adaptations and support options are more appropriate (McGregor, 1995). It would be a waste of precious instructional time to teach a student to use public transportation if the student will not live in an area with bus service; likewise, mobility and transportation supports used in the school setting will not necessarily be feasible or available in community settings. These situations underscore the need for the instruction of functional mobility and transportation within *natural environments* and *ecological assessment* of mobility needs and resources (Bailey & Head, 1993; Everson, 1993).

Natural environments are those in which the student currently engages or is likely to engage in the future. For students in elementary grades, school-based activities are generally limited to the classroom and a few other settings, such as the library, cafeteria, and music classroom. Students in a classroom typically travel to these settings as a group (disregarding resource rooms, communication training, and other therapeutic settings for students with disabilities). Middle schools typically schedule classes so that students in the same homeroom take different courses or attend the same course at different times. For students with disabilities, this method of scheduling increases the complexity and difficulty of getting from one area of the school to another and of identifying mobility needs and potential support persons. In high school, additional complexity arises with community-based training, such as work experience and job training programs, training in shopping and money-handling skills, and so on. Following exit from school, students will enter diverse work, social, and residential environments.

No two students will have identical needs and solutions during any of these stages. The most effective means of identifying a student's mobility and transportation needs is through an individualized assessment of the mobility requirements of the environments into which he or she functions or is expected to function (e.g., ecological assessment) and matching those requirements to training, adaptation, or support options that are available (Bailey & Head, 1993).

CURRICULUM DESIGN

This section presents three case studies of instructional objectives plans for students with disabilities, one each in elementary, middle, and high school. These case studies illustrate combinations of training and support services that can be used to increase students' mobility and the use of instruction and support in natural environments based on real needs.

Before proceeding, we should address a key concern of instructors, schools, and parents of students with disabilities with regard to travel and mobility training—safety. Although most would agree that travel and mobility are essential skills for survival in the community, instructors must consider and plan for risks to the student or adult with disabilities. Such behaviors as delayed response to verbal instructions, fleeing from the training situation, or lack of inhibition would all indicate an increased need for vigilance on the part of the instructor and perhaps the use of highly intrusive instructional strategies such as gradual guidance or maximum prompts. Groce (1997) has suggested that students or adults have a minimal level of skills before proceeding with travel training, such as

1. an awareness of personal space, meaning a clear idea of where their personal space ends and that of others begins;

2. an awareness of their environment; and

3. the ability to recognize and respond to danger.

On Our Own, a project designed to introduce high school students with physical disabilities to public transportation in New York City, developed a set of quality assurance standards (COACH/Academy for Educational Development, n.d.) for travel training programs. Funded by Project ACTION, an Easter Seals Society initiative, the On Our Own project created the list of standards to help organizations, including schools and adult service providers, design a travel skills curriculum for individuals with disabilities that is safe for the learners and that has a high quality of instruction. The following is the list of standards for travel skills programs recommended by On Our Own and Project ACTION:

- The organization has established the need for transportation training for their students or clients based on an assessment of their needs, public transportation available, and the organization's mission.

- The organization has defined transportation-related skills which are acceptable by the Board of Directors or Board of Education, and is prepared to implement a transportation skills program to achieve the goals inherent in the definition.

- The organization has established training time for management personnel to assure commitment to the goals of the transportation skills program and to assist personnel in identifying schedule or programmatic changes which may be necessary.

- The organization has established the number of personnel required for implementation of the transportation skills program, the professional qualifications required for the staff, and the corresponding job descriptions.

- The organization has committed professional staff to administer and support the program and has scheduled adequate time for daily supervision of program staff.

- The organization has dedicated sufficient training time for the staff prior to the implementation of the program.

- The organization has accepted guidelines which affirm a student's or client's successful completion of the transportation skills program.

- The organization has an established liaison with the transit system, police department, and department of transportation in the operating area.

- Management has introduced the transportation related skills program to all the employees of the organization and affirmed the organization's commitment to the philosophy of using and teaching the use of accessible public transportation.

- Management has established goals for the transportation skills program.

- The transportation skills program staff has established an assessment tool to identify the transportation-related needs and abilities of the clients.

- The transportation program staff has established a system for reviewing the clients' activities in the organization, reviewing the goals for the clients, and interacting with the direct care providers.

- The transportation program staff has established procedures for maintaining appropriate records and data on all activities with clients to be shared with the management and relevant staff on a periodic basis.

- Transportation program staff has established guidelines for routes that are suitable for clients' needs and abilities.

- Transportation program staff has established a system of informing the clients, their families or primary care providers, and the organization of the clients' participation in the program and the results of that participation.

- An annual report on the transportation skills program is prepared and submitted to management by the program staff. (COACH/Academy for Educational Development, n.d., ¶ 2)

Additional information on safety in travel training and commercially available training programs can be obtained from National Information Center for Children and Youth with Disabilities (www.nichcy.org) and Project ACTION (www.projectaction.org).

AMY, AN ELEMENTARY SCHOOL STUDENT

Amy is a second-grader enrolled in a suburban elementary school in Virginia. Amy sustained a spinal cord injury during an accident when she was 2 years old. Amy's spinal column was injured at the fifth vertebrae, resulting in complete paralysis of her lower extremities. Amy uses a motorized wheelchair controlled by a touch-control mechanism located on a small laptray. Amy's parents are very interested in her special education program and in increasing her mobility and independence. They have requested that Amy's full-time instructional assistant be faded as much as possible. Amy's IEP team developed the plan presented in Figure 9.1.

The instructional method used by Amy's teachers and aides was to develop task analyses for getting to each destination (see Chapter 2 and Figure 9.2) and, using a system of least prompts, give Amy verbal or gestural prompts to assist her in deciding which routes to take to her destinations. During initial training sessions, Amy's teachers and aides pointed out directional signs and landmarks in the hallways that she could use. When Amy took a wrong turn, they corrected her with either verbal prompts ("Try it again, Amy") or by pointing in the correct direction. Using the task analysis, they will be able to monitor her progress, pinpoint the areas in which she is having difficulty, and determine when she reaches the instructional criterion for each objective. After Amy reaches these criteria, she will be informally monitored to ensure that she continues to reach each destination independently.

Current Skill Level: Amy independently navigates her electric wheelchair down one corridor of her school.

Travel/Mobility Goal: Amy will independently travel from her classroom to at least three school-based destinations.

Instructional Objectives:
1. Amy's teacher will develop a mobility plan with assistance from Amy's occupational and physical therapists by 10/2/03.
2. Amy will use her wheelchair independently to reach the cafeteria on 5 of 5 trials, by 11/1/03.
3. Amy will use her wheelchair independently to reach the library on 5 of 5 trials, by 12/6/03.
4. Amy will use her wheelchair independently to reach the gym on 5 of 5 trials, by 2/1/04.

FIGURE 9.1. Mobility training portion of IEP for Amy.

Objective: Amy will use her wheelchair independently to reach the cafeteria on 5 of 5 trials, by 11/1/03.

Instructional Method: Use least prompts for correction—gestural prompts (pointing in correct direction) or verbal prompts ("Try it again, Amy"). Record V for verbal prompt required; G for gestural; ✔ for correct performance.

Date										
1. Exit classroom door.										
2. Make right turn.										
3. Proceed to second hallway intersection.										
4. Turn left.										
5. Proceed to third door on right (cafeteria sign).										
6. Turn right.										
7. If door is shut, push open with wheelchair.										
8. Enter cafeteria.										

FIGURE 9.2. Sample task analysis for Amy.

 DeJuan, a Middle School Student

DeJuan is a 12-year-old boy with severe visual impairment. He recently transferred to his local middle school after attending a private school for persons with visual impairments. Academically, DeJuan is on the same grade level as his peers in all subjects. DeJuan's parents are anxious for him to assimilate into the seeing world.

DeJuan's case manager is a resource room special education teacher whose caseload comprises students with learning disabilities. She has expressed concern that she lacks the knowledge and experience to "work with blind kids." A meeting was scheduled to develop DeJuan's IEP. Participants included DeJuan, his parents, the IEP case manager, school occupational therapist, assistant principal, school guidance

(continues)

counselor, and DeJuan's counselor from the state department for visual impairments. The mobility plan that was developed for DeJuan is presented in Figure 9.3.

Because DeJuan's difficulties were related to the time required to get from one place to another and his fear, and not necessarily his learning routes, his teachers and aides focused on training the walker buddies how to ease DeJuan's fears and provide encouragement. His teachers and aides also used a stopwatch to time him on each route during the instructional period and tracked the amount of travel time he required on a daily basis. This charting enabled his teachers to see when DeJuan had reached the 15-minute criterion they had established.

TIM, A HIGH SCHOOL STUDENT

Tim is an 18-year-old student with mild mental retardation and behavior disorders. He is ambulatory and very articulate. Tim has had various community-based work experiences, including working at a local grocery store. With the support of his parents, Tim has obtained a part-time job bagging groceries at a grocery store in his neighborhood. Tim's parents and teachers are concerned about his safety during the frequent traveling in the parking lot required by the job. At Tim's IEP meeting, the mobility plan presented in Figure 9.4 was developed.

Because of the potential danger to Tim in this training, the IEP team felt that every effort should be taken to ensure error-free learning. This is why the instructional objectives require 100% performance criteria on 5 consecutive days (see a sample task analysis in Figure 9.5). This level of mastery should ensure that Tim has safe mobility ingrained into his work routine before supervision is reduced. The team also felt that a teacher or aide should accompany Tim until complete mastery is attained.

(continues)

Current Skill Level: DeJuan is able to locate classrooms within his homeroom wing only. He is somewhat fearful of crowds between classes but has indicated a strong interest in using some of his new friends as "walker buddies."

Travel/Mobility Goal: Given a time frame of not more than 15 minutes, DeJuan will independently ambulate from one end of the school to the other (from the gym to his homeroom) by June 2004.

Instructional Objectives:
1. The school will allow early release time for long-distance classes for DeJuan and two identified "walker buddies" from each class during mobility training (October–December). The state agency counselor will provide supervision and program development.
2. DeJuan will ambulate from the gym to the B-wing with a buddy within arm's reach, in 15 minutes or less, by 12/20/03.
3. DeJuan will ambulate from the gym to his English class with early release time only, in 15 minutes or less, by 2/15/04.
4. DeJuan will ambulate from the gym to his homeroom, in 15 minutes or less, by 6/1/04.

FIGURE 9.3. Mobility support and training portion of IEP for DeJuan.

The instruction methods include task analyses of the correct behaviors for initial skill instruction, a daily charting form for recording the number of attempts for one of the objectives (which should vary daily) and the times Tim performs correctly, and immediate cessation of incorrect behavior through either a verbal warning or a physical prompt (e.g., putting an arm in front of him to block him from moving forward). After Tim reaches the instructional criteria, the teacher will fade her presence, first by observing him from a conspicuous position, then by surreptitious monitoring, and finally by random observations.

Current Skill Level: Tim can ambulate from one place to another but does not appear to do so safely. He has been observed walking across a road without looking and must be reminded to look for oncoming cars.

Travel/Mobility Goal: Tim will exhibit safe travel at all times during the 2-hour training session as a grocery bagger.

Instructional Objectives:
1. Tim will look both ways before crossing the street adjacent to the grocery store and correctly judge when safe to cross, 5 consecutive work sessions, 100% of attempts, under teacher supervision.
2. Tim will exhibit safe travel in the grocery store parking lot while pushing carts to and from the store, 5 consecutive work sessions, 100% of attempts, under teacher supervision.

FIGURE 9.4. Mobility training portion of IEP for Tim.

Objective: Tim will exhibit safe travel in the grocery store parking lot while pushing carts to and from the store, 5 consecutive work sessions, 100% of attempts, under teacher supervision.

Instructional Method: Record performance for *each* opportunity; use additional sheets if necessary. Record ✔ for performed correctly; X for correction by verbal warning or physical interruption.

Task Analysis: Returning Carts to Store	1	2	3	4	5	6	7	8	9	10
1. Exit store to front drive.										
2. Look both ways prior to crossing.										
3. Cross when clear.										
4. Walk along car row to cart return area.										
5. Push together carts (up to 20).										
6. Connect carts with strap and clip harness.										
7. Check for oncoming cars.										
8. Maneuver carts to center of aisle.										
9. Push toward store.										
10. If car approaches, move to one side.										
11. Stop at front drive, check for traffic.										
12. Cross when clear.										
13. Push carts into store to cart rows.										
14. Undo harness.										

FIGURE 9.5. Sample task analysis for Tim.

SAMPLE IEP FOR ALEX

We began this chapter with a case study of Alex, who had a personal and educational goal for full-time employment in the restaurant industry. The IEP in this section (see Figure 9.6) shows how Alex's IEP team addressed that goal and its related mobility and transportation issues.

Alex's IEP shows the integration of postschool environments and transportation needs and resources. Because it is available in Alex's area and because Alex is capable of learning to access it, bus service was selected as Alex's method for for getting him to his place of employment.

I. Postsecondary Education

Current Skill Level: Alex is currently enrolled in a vocational special needs program at his school. He is not earning Carnegie units toward a regular diploma; rather, Alex will earn a Vocational Certificate in Supported Employment.

Postsecondary Education Goal: Alex will explore available options in his area.

Objective: Alex will explore postsecondary options with his teacher, including the following:

  a. Job Corps
  b. Project Work and Education at Franklin Pierce College
  c. Adult education programs offered through the school system

II. Postsecondary Employment Goal

Current Skill Level: Alex is part of a small enclave of students with vocational special needs who work in a shopping mall. Alex works in a small restaurant as a busboy and dishwasher. Another student from his class shares these duties. A job coach monitors progress for 15 minutes during each of the 3 hours they are working at the site. Wages are paid by the restaurant.

Postsecondary Employment Goal: Full-time supported employment in an individual job placement in the restaurant industry.

Objective: Alex will work independently for up to 2 hours a day by June 2004.

  a. Alex will load and unload the dishwasher independently by December 2003.
  b. Alex will bus tables independently by February 2004.
  c. Alex will clean and sanitize his workstation independently by May 2004.

III. Postsecondary Adult Living

Current Skill Level: Alex is dependent on others for transportation.

Postsecondary Adult Living Goal: Alex will increase his independent mobility skills.

Objective: Alex's special education teacher will develop a daily bus training program by October 19, 2003. The program will include the following:

  a. Procurement of bus schedule
  b. 1:1 training for the initial 3 weeks, with Alex and teacher riding bus together, fading to teacher following in car
  c. Independent bus travel for supervised trip within 4 weeks
  d. Independent bus travel, including one transfer at Main Street depot, within 8 weeks
  e. Independent bus travel from school to work within 12 weeks

---

FIGURE 9.6. IEP for Alex.

CONCLUSION

This chapter has examined mobility and transportation skills within the context of increasing student success and self-determination and ultimately the quality of the student's school experiences and adult life. Instruction in mobility and transportation can be most effectively conducted in natural environments, guided by ecological assessment of each student's individual abilities and mobility needs. Instruction in mobility and transportation is but one option; adaptation and support can be used when a student is unlikely to be able to attain independence through instruction alone.

REFERENCES

The Arc. (1994). *How to evaluate and select assistive technology.* Arlington, TX: Author.

Bailey, B. R., & Head, D. N. (1993). Providing O&M services to children and youth with severe multiple disabilities. *RE:view, 25,* 57–66.

Brolin, D. (1993). *Life centered career education:* A *competency-based approach.* Reston, VA: Council for Exceptional Children.

Bush, G. W. (2001). *New Freedom Initiative* [Online]. Retrieved from http://www.whitehouse.gov/news/freedominitiative/freedominitiative.pdf

Carr, T. (Ed.). (1994). Assistive technology: Enhancement for daily living [Special issue]. *HKNC-TAC News, 7*(2).

COACH/Academy for Educational Development (n.d.). *Quality assurance standards in travel training* [Online]. Retrieved October 28, 2002, from http://projectaction.org/coach/standard.htm

Dattilo, J., & Rusch, F. R. (1985). Effects of choice on leisure participation for persons with severe handicaps. *Journal of the Association for Persons with Severe Handicaps, 10,* 194–199.

Deci, E. L., & Ryan, R. M. (1985). *Intrinsic motivation and self-determination in human behavior.* New York: Plenum.

Dyer, K., Dunlap, G., & Winterling, V. (1990). Effects of choice making on the serious problem behaviors of students with severe handicaps. *Journal of Applied Behavior Analysis, 23,* 515–524.

Everson, J. M. (1993). *Youth with disabilities: Strategies for interagency transition programs.* Boston: Andover Medical.

Gerber, P. J., Ginsberg, R., & Reiff, H. B. (1992). Identifying alterable patterns in employment success for highly successful adults with learning disabilities. *Journal of Learning Disabilities, 25,* 475–487.

Groce, M. M. (1997). *An introduction to travel training* [Online]. Available: http://www.nichcy.org/pubs/transum/ts9txt.htm.

Guess, D., Benson, H. A., & Siegel-Causey, E. (1985). Concepts and issues related to choice-making and autonomy among persons with severe disabilities. *Journal of the Association for Persons with Severe Handicaps, 10,* 79–86.

Individuals with Disabilities Education Act of 1990, 20 U.S.C. § 1400 *et seq.*

Ip, S. M. V., Szymanski, E. M., Johnston-Rodriguez, S., & Karls, S. F. (1994). Effects of staff implementation of a choice program on challenging behaviors in persons with developmental disabilities. *Rehabilitation Counseling Bulletin, 37,* 347–357.

Koegel, R. L., Dyer, K., & Bell, L. K. (1987). The influence of child-preferred activities on autistic children's social behavior. *Journal of Applied Behavior Analysis, 20,* 243–252.

Lovett, H. (1991). Empowerment and choices. In L. H. Meyer, C. A. Peck, & L. Brown (Eds.), *Critical issues in the lives of people with severe disabilities* (pp. 625–626). Baltimore: Brookes.

McGregor, M. L. (1995, April). *Orientation and mobility for students with multiple severe disabilities.*

Paper presented at the 73rd Annual International Convention of the Council for Exceptional Children, Indianapolis, IN.

Parent, W., Unger, D., Gibson, K., & Clements, C. (1994). The role of the job coach: Orchestrating community and workplace supports. *American Rehabilitation, 20*(3), 2–11.

Parsons, M. B., Reid, D. H., & Baumgartner, M. (1990). Effects of choice versus assigned jobs on the work performance of persons with severe handicaps. *Journal of Applied Behavior Analysis, 23,* 253–260.

Price, F. B. (1990). Independence and the individual with disabilities. *Journal of Rehabilitation, 56,* 15–18.

Reid, D. H., & Parsons, M. B. (1990). Assessing food preferences among persons with profound mental retardation: Providing opportunities to make choices. *Journal of Applied Behavior Analysis, 23,* 183–195.

Reid, D. H., & Parsons, M. B. (1991). Making choice a routine part of mealtimes for persons with profound mental retardation. *Behavioral Residential Treatment, 6,* 249–261.

Sharpton, W., & West, M. (1996). Severe and profound mental retardation. In P. J. McLaughlin & P. Wehman (Eds.), *Mental retardation and developmental disabilities* (2nd ed., pp. 131–145). Austin, TX: PRO-ED.

Shevin, M., & Klein, N. (1984). The importance of choice-making skills for students with severe disabilities. *Journal of the Association for Persons with Severe Handicaps, 9,* 159–166.

Wacker, D. P., Wiggins, B., Fowler, M., & Berg, W. (1988). Training students with profound or multiple handicaps to make requests via microswitches. *Journal of Applied Behavior Analysis, 21,* 331–343.

Ward, M. J. (1989). The many facets of self-determination. *National Information Center for Children and Youth with Handicaps: Transition Summary, 5,* 2–3.

Wehmeyer, M., & Kelchner, K. (1995). *Whose future is it anyway? A student-directed transition planning process.* Arlington, TX: The Arc.

West, M., Barcus, J. M., Brooke, V., & Rayfield, R. G. (1995). An exploratory analysis of self-determination of persons with disabilities. *Journal of Vocational Rehabilitation, 5,* 357–364.

West, M., & Parent, W. S. (1992). Consumer choice and empowerment in supported employment services: Issues and strategies. *Journal of the Association for Persons with Severe Handicaps, 17,* 47–52.

CHAPTER 10

Community Participation

Stacy K. Dymond

ERIKA

Erika is 13 years old and attends the eighth grade at the middle school. Her classes consist of home economics, technology education, science, social studies, art, adaptive physical education, and computer science (some are scheduled daily for the school year, others for only a quarter). Erika's extracurricular activities include participation in the Breakfast Club (a group that meets once a week at school to eat breakfast, socialize, and receive help with homework) and in intramural sports. She also receives instruction in a variety of other environments throughout the school building and local community. In the school, she is sampling office, cafeteria, laundry, and maintenance jobs, and in the community, she is learning to use stores, restaurants, and public recreation facilities.

Erika is identified as having severe mental retardation and mild cerebral palsy. A variety of staff with expertise in special education, physical therapy, occupational therapy, and speech therapy provide supports that ensure her participation and inclusion in the school and community. These individuals, along with a paraprofessional, work closely with the eighth-grade teachers to embed Erika's Individualized Education Program (IEP) objectives into the curriculum and make appropriate adaptations when necessary. As a team, they provide direct instruction to Erika in her eighth-grade classes, extracurricular activities, school-based jobs, and community activities.

During the past couple of years, Erika's IEP team has begun to shift the focus of her instruction from classroom-based activities to school- and community-based options. Erika's parents would like their daughter to maintain her current level of involvement at school; however, they recognize that increasing attention must be placed on teaching skills that will enhance her transition to adulthood. In addition to developing social relationships with peers, Erika's parents' priorities for instruction include building independent self-care, domestic, and community skills; expanding vocational exploration in the school building; and increasing Erika's ability to communicate her wants and needs. Due to the severity of Erika's disability, a transition plan has been established as part of the IEP to ensure appropriate planning for her transition from school to adulthood.

This year, Erika's community skills instruction will focus on locating items in a store, purchasing items, and ordering food at a fast-food restaurant. Stores and restaurants have been targeted based on Erika's preferences and the frequency with which her family uses these businesses. Whenever possible, situations have been arranged that allow Erika to participate in community activities with her

(continues)

259

peers. Table 10.1 lists each of Erika's community objectives, the environments and frequency in which they will be addressed, and strategies for involving peers in each activity. Because the school is also an important "community" within which Erika must function, IEP objectives will be targeted within the context of two extracurricular activities—Breakfast Club and intramural sports. These activities provide natural opportunities within the school setting to teach skills that will enhance her participation in the school community. Table 10.2 illustrates how Erika will address several IEP objectives while participating in these activities.

Because Erika has a difficult time generalizing the things she learns in one setting to other similar environments, the IEP team has decided to address each of Erika's community skills objectives in the community environments where the skills are normally performed. When possible, these objectives will also be taught during functional school routines (e.g., in the school cafeteria, Erika will use pictures to choose which lunch she wants and pay for her lunch as stated in her community objectives). The team has also identified strategies for incorporating many of Erika's other IEP objectives into her community skills activities (see Table 10.3). A copy of her complete IEP is included at the end of this chapter.

Through community-based instruction, Erika is learning skills that will increase her participation and inclusion in the community. As in many schools today, her IEP team is struggling to determine the appropriate amount of time that she should spend in general education classes with her peers versus in the community. Whereas the majority of her day was spent in activities with her same-age peers during elementary school, instructional time in community environments has become increasingly important as she prepares for adulthood. Balancing the need for school inclusion with that of community inclusion will be an issue that Erika's IEP team will continue to address as she approaches graduation.

COMPATIBILITY OF SCHOOL AND COMMUNITY INCLUSION

During the past decade, research on inclusive education has expanded to provide promising evidence of its effectiveness as a service delivery model for educating students with disabilities (Dymond, 2001; Hunt, Farron-Davis, Beckstead, Curtis, & Goetz, 1994; Kennedy & Itkonen, 1994; Mortweet et al., 1999; Ryndak, Morrison, & Sommerstein, 1999; Waldron & McLeskey, 1998). Interestingly, inclusion remains an elusive concept, in that its definition is not uniformly agreed upon in the field. Some believe that students with disabilities must spend all of their time in general education activities with their peers who do not have disabilities in order to be included. Others believe that inclusion can occur if students spend only a portion of their day with nondisabled peers. Recently, this discussion has been extended to focus on the appropriateness of community-based instruction for students with disabilities. Questions have arisen as to whether community-based instruction is compatible with an inclusive approach (Dymond & Orelove, 2001).

Arguments against the use of community-based instruction have raised concerns about the opportunities that students miss for interacting with their peers when they participate in community-based instruction (Schuh, Tashie, Lamb,

(text continues on p. 263)

TABLE 10.1
Erika's Community-Based Activities

Objective	Activities	Environments	Instructors	Frequency	Peer Involvement
When provided with a coupon picture (or other picture) of an item in a store, Erika will pick up the item that matches the picture and release it in her cart or basket within 20 seconds. (Erika will be positioned 2 to 3 feet in front of the item before she is asked to locate it.)	Purchase items for cooking class	Ukrops Grocery, Kmart	Home economics teacher	Mondays (first two semesters)	A small group of home economics students accompany Erika and the teacher to work on comparison shopping and/or to learn about nutrients and calories contained in the food purchased.
Given the checkout line of a store or restaurant and money to cover the cost of the purchase, Erika will hand the cashier the money, wait for change, and deposit the change in her purse, with no more than 1 gestural cue. (The instructor will provide Erika with the appropriate amount of money prior to reaching the checkout line.)	Purchase and deliver groceries to a homebound senior citizen	Ukrops Grocery, CVS Drugstore	Special education teacher	Wednesdays (first two semesters)	Students participate in service learning by accompanying Erika to purchase groceries for homebound seniors living in the same apartment building. In health class, students use the experience to discuss nutrition.
	Purchase food for making lunch	Ukrops Grocery	Speech therapist, peer	Fridays (last two semesters)	One of the high school students from Erika's neighborhood is a cashier at the store and provides natural prompts when Erika makes purchases.
In a fast-food restaurant, Erika will hand the cashier pictures of the items she wishes to order, 100% of the time.	Eat lunch at a fast-food restaurant	Burger King, Wendy's, Ukrops Cafeteria	Paraprofessional	Tuesdays (all four semesters)	Peers from Erika's homeroom sign up (with parental permission) to go out to lunch with Erika during their normal lunch period.
	Order a drink at a fast-food restaurant	Burger King, Wendy's, Ukrops Cafeteria	P.E. teacher, paraprofessional, or speech therapist	Once every other week (all four semesters)	Members of adaptive P.E. class purchase a soda with Erika on the way home from a community outing.

TABLE 10.2
Erika's Extracurricular School Activities

Objective	Activities	Environments	Instructors	Frequency	Peer Involvement
Given a functional task or activity that requires one-to-one correspondence, Erika will pick up and distribute one item to each person or place, with 100% accuracy.	Breakfast Club (setting the table, passing out food)	School	Teacher in charge of Breakfast Club	Mondays (all four semesters)	All students are involved with setting the table and passing out food. Erika will work with a partner to set one of the tables.
	Intramural sports (handing out practice jerseys and equipment)	School	P.E. teacher, peers	Thursdays (all four semesters)	Peers will assist Erika in handing out one practice jersey to each player and distribute one set of equipment to each team.
When initiating a greeting with a friend or stranger (not a relative), Erika will wave, shake hands, say "hello," and/or give "high fives" 100% of the time.	Breakfast Club (greeting peers and teacher)	School	Teacher in charge of Breakfast Club	Mondays (all four semesters)	Peers naturally greet each other upon entering the room and as additional students come in the room.
	Intramural sports (greeting peers and teacher)	School	P.E. teacher, peers	Thursdays (all four semesters)	Peers will greet Erika upon entering the gym or sports field and when obtaining equipment.
Given an activity that requires bilateral hand usage, Erika will use both hands to complete the task 100% of the time.	Intramural sports (zipping coat, throwing ball)	School	P.E. teacher	Thursdays (all four semesters)	All students may need to put on a coat to participate in outdoor intramural sports. Erika will throw a new ball to a player when one goes off the playing field.

TABLE 10.3
Objectives Embedded into Community Activities for Erika

Domain	Objective	Community Skills Activity
Domestic	Making a sandwich	Using supplies purchased in the community to make lunch 2 to 3 times a week at school
Domestic	Wiping face with a napkin	During lunch in the school cafeteria; during lunch or when stopping for a soda at a restaurant
Functional Academics	Using a picture schedule	Pictures of community activities will be placed in the schedule
Communication	Making picture choices	Choosing school cafeteria lunches; choosing type of soda or meal to purchase at a restaurant
Communication	Requesting a break	Signing break, as needed, during all community activities
Communication	Requesting the bathroom	Pointing to picture of bathroom, as needed, during all community activities
Social	Greeting others	Greeting the cashier at a restaurant or grocery store; greeting another shopper in the store; greeting the bus driver
Social	Saying "thank you"	After receiving change from a cashier; when someone holds a door open
Motor	Bilateral hand usage	Pushing a grocery cart; carrying a bag of groceries; carrying a lunch tray in the cafeteria or restaurant; zipping coat
Motor	Alternating legs when climbing stairs	Exiting and entering the school building, stores, and restaurants; getting on and off the bus

Bang, & Jorgensen, 1998; Tashie, Jorgensen, Shapiro-Barnard, Martin, & Schuh, 1996). Proponents of this view believe that students with disabilities should receive their instruction in general education settings during their school years because this is the environment where their same-age peers are engaged in learning. It has been suggested that community-based instruction, if needed, should occur after school or on weekends. If students receive special education services after age 18, instruction during school hours would be appropriate because the students' same-age peers would no longer be at school (Fisher & Sax, 1999; Schuh et al., 1998; Tashie et al., 1996).

Those who support the continuation of community-based instruction believe that it is compatible with an inclusive approach to schooling (Agran, Snow, & Swaner, 1999; Dymond & Orelove, 2001; McDonnell, 1997). Middle and high school teachers have supported the use of both community-based instruction and school inclusion as effective in teaching students social skills and preparing them for postschool outcomes (Agran et al., 1999). Although school is the preferred environment for instruction, there are some skills that can only be taught in the community. Simulating them in a school environment without providing opportunities for instruction in the community may not ensure that the student is able to perform the skill within the natural environment.

Dymond and Orelove (2001), in their discussion of what constitutes effective curricula for students with severe disabilities, suggest that it may be time to redefine the concept of community-based instruction. They argue that community-based instruction should not be viewed as a segregated activity for students with disabilities, but rather as an opportunity to engage all students in real-life applications in their communities. Numerous examples show how students with and without disabilities can pursue learning together in the community (Beck, Broers, Hogue, Shipstead, & Knowlton, 1994; Longwill & Kleinert, 1998; Yoder, Retish, & Wade, 1996).

Inclusion refers to the membership of all students (both with and without disabilities) in their schools and communities (Ferguson, 1995). To say that it can only take place when students are located in a general education classroom with their peers is misleading. Inclusion can easily occur in both school and community environments. School personnel and parents can choose both of these types of service; a choice of one does not exclude the other. Equally important, community-based instruction can and should include students without disabilities when the experience will assist all students in meeting their educational goals. (Table 10.1 illustrates how Erika's community objectives were structured to promote peer involvement.)

The desired outcome of education is for all students to become productive, independent, and contributing members of society (Everson, 1988). Many skills can and should be taught within the school setting; however, others are better learned in the community. Although community skills instruction is traditionally emphasized at the high school level, elementary and middle school personnel should consider its appropriateness for the students they serve (Dymond & Orelove, 2001). One certainty in the field of education is that there is no one best way of educating all students. To say that all students should receive inclusive education or all students should receive community-based instruction is inappropriate. For some students, a given educational program may not be suitable at a particular age or during a particular year; for others it may conflict with a student's or a parent's preferences. This chapter is designed to assist teams of school personnel, families, and community members in determining when and where community skills instruction is appropriate by describing the content and components of instruction, providing strategies for student assessment and the selection of objectives, and outlining steps for developing inclusive community-based opportunities for students with and without disabilities.

DESCRIPTION OF FUNCTIONAL COMMUNITY SKILLS

Functional skills are skills that are immediately applicable to daily life. Some of the key qualities that define a functional skill include the following:

- It is performed within the context of a "real" activity.
- The activity is meaningful to the student.
- People without disabilities believe the activity serves a purpose.
- If the student is unable to perform the skill for himself or herself, it will need to be completed by another individual.
- The skill will be used throughout the student's life.

Functional skills also include those activities that teach students to participate in future environments (Brown et al., 1979). By focusing on skills that will be needed in the near future, teachers can encourage a smooth and successful transition between current and subsequent environments (e.g., elementary to middle school, high school to adulthood). Curricula that address functional community skills teach students of all ages to actively participate as valued members of their school and community.

Content of Instruction

The definition of community skills has evolved with time. Like many other functional skills, community skills are not identified as one set of curricula that all students must learn. The skills that are addressed with a student depend on the activities available in the community and the individual needs and preferences of the student and his or her family. As a result, most discussions regarding the content of community skills instruction focus on the types of environments or activities where skills may be addressed to facilitate participation in the community. In the late 1980s, Ford et al. (1989) defined the major goal areas of community skills instruction to include travel, community safety, grocery shopping, general shopping, eating out, and using services. These goal areas remain important today, yet they fail to fully reflect our current understanding of the term *community*.

Table 10.4 provides an updated and expanded view of the types of nonwork activities in which individuals engage in their communities. The first three categories (*restaurants/eateries, grocery stores, retail stores*) focus on places individuals go to purchase tangible items such as food, clothing, and other necessities. The *services* category refers to assistance individuals purchase from specially trained persons, and the *public facilities* category lists services typically provided by the government or nonprofit organizations. The *recreation facilities* category describes the places where individuals may choose to spend leisure time. Activities that allow individuals to give back to their community through helping others are categorized as *volunteer work*. The last category, *transportation*, addresses the methods individuals might use to access the activities in their community.

In the past, community has generally been construed as any location outside of the school building or home. This emphasis is reflected in Table 10.4. With the movement toward inclusive schooling, there has been increased recognition of the need to extend our interpretation of community to include the school environment (Sands, Kozleski, & French, 2000; Stainback, Stainback, & Ayres, 1996). Students spend a large amount of time in school. For them, this is one portion of the greater community in which they must learn to function during their school years. Table 10.5 identifies some of the many nonacademic activities associated with the school community. These activities have been grouped according to special events, clubs/organizations, school jobs, athletics, and the arts.

If functional skills help students participate in current and future environments (Brown et al., 1979), then the definition of community skills must be broadened to incorporate a more comprehensive view of community. Instruction must focus on skills that students need to function within both the general community (i.e., outside the home and school setting) and the school community. Teaching students the requisite skills they need to participate in these activities enhances their inclusion within the multiple communities they access. For

TABLE 10.4
Activities in the General Community

Restaurants/Eateries	Grocery Stores	Retail Stores	Services	Public Facilities	Recreation Facilities	Volunteer Work	Transportation
Fast-food restaurant	Convenience grocery store (e.g., 7-Eleven, small stores associated with gas stations)	Clothing store	Bank	Library	YMCA	Meals on Wheels	School buses
Sit-down restaurant (informal)	Stand-alone grocery stores (e.g, IGA, Kroger)	Drug store	Barbershop/hair salon	Church	Recreation center/fitness center	Red Cross	Public buses
Sit-down restaurant (formal)	Grocery stores within large stores (e.g., Wal-Mart, Kmart)	Sporting goods store	Nail salon	Recycling center	Museum	United Way	Taxis
Food court		Music store	Dry cleaner	Post office	Skating rink	Food bank	Train/subway
Sidewalk cart (i.e., mobile food stands that set up on the street to sell hotdogs, sandwiches, etc.)		Video store	Laundromat	Department of Motor Vehicles	Movie theater	Nursing home	Bicycle
Restaurant that delivers		Pet store	Doctor/dentist	Social Security office	Arcade	Humane Society	Walking
		Toy and hobby store	Veterinarian	County offices (e.g., voter registration office)		Salvation Army	Riding/driving a car
		Mail-order shopping					

TABLE 10.5
Activities in the School Community

Special Events	Clubs/ Organizations	School Jobs	Athletics	Arts
Field day	Breakfast Club	Office assistant	Participate on a sports team	Participate in school plays and musicals
School dance (e.g., attend the dance, decorate, sell tickets)	Drama club	Classroom helper	Play intramural sports	Attend concerts
	School newspaper	Lunch monitor		Participate in choir or band
	Yearbook staff	Safety patrol	Attend school sporting events	
Prom night	Student council	Library assistant		Contribute to art show
Talent show			Assist with sporting events (e.g., keep score, sell tickets, serve as team manager, man the concession stand)	
	Dance Team	School store worker		Post artwork in school hallways
Beauty pageant	Art club			
Field trip	Girl Scouts/ Boy Scouts	Attendance collection		Assist with events (e.g., hand out programs, sell tickets, usher people to their seats, manage costumes)
Spelling bee		Mail or newsletter delivery	Help organize sports banquet	
School assembly	4-H club			
	JROTC			

purposes of this chapter, the term *school* will be used to refer to the school community and the term *community* will be used to refer to all environments outside the home and school.

Location of Instruction

Functional community skills are typically taught in the community, in the school, or in a combination of school and community settings. Instruction that occurs in the community is known as community-based instruction. Research has repeatedly demonstrated that systematic instruction in the community leads to skill acquisition (see Gee, Graham, Sailor, & Goetz, 1995; Inge & Dymond, 1994; McDonnell, Hardman, Hightower, Keifer-O'Donnell, Drew, 1993; Sowers & Powers, 1995). Learning skills in the community allows students to use the actual materials involved with the activity and to learn skills within the context of the normal sights, sounds, smells, lighting, and distractions that are associated with the natural environment. Many students are unable to generalize skills learned under simulated conditions (i.e., ones that use artificial materials and settings that approximate the real thing) to the actual environments and situations where they are normally performed. For example, a teacher in a classroom that houses a mock grocery store may find that students learn to shop appropriately in the classroom but fail to use the skill correctly when taken to an actual grocery store. Community-based instruction overcomes this problem by teaching skills in the location where they are expected to be performed. Other benefits of community-based instruction are listed in Table 10.6.

TABLE 10.6
Benefits of Community-Based Instruction

1. Teaches skills that allow the student to more fully participate in activities outside the school setting with peers and family members

2. Exposes students to a variety of experiences, thus broadening the choices available to them and increasing their ability to affect their environment

3. Provides opportunities for students to learn social skills with members of the greater community (not just family, school staff, and other students)

4. Enhances students' quality of life by increasing community inclusion, independence, and participation

5. Prepares students for adulthood by teaching skills that will have longitudinal usage

6. Raises families' expectations for their children

7. Increases the community's expectations for individuals with disabilities

8. Helps school staff and other IEP members to determine student preferences and plan for postschool opportunities that reflect those preferences

Often, skills that are needed in the community can be embedded within functional school-based routines. This is known as community-referenced instruction. Unlike simulations that seek to approximate the materials and conditions of the community environment, community-referenced instruction references the community by addressing skills that have joint applicability within the school and community environments. Both methods (community-referenced instruction and simulations) been used when there are barriers (e.g., costs, scheduling, transportation) to community-based instruction (Branham, Collins, Schuster, & Kleinert, 1999). Community-referenced instruction and simulations are most effective when used in combination with community-based instruction rather than as sole instructional methods (see Bock, 1999; Branham et al., 1999; Morse & Schuster, 2000). Examples of how community-based instruction, community-referenced instruction, and simulated instruction differ are provided in Table 10.7.

Given the broader definition of community that was previously discussed, it is evident that the location of community skills instruction depends on the activity selected for instruction. The school is the natural environment for developing skills that promote school inclusion and enhance participation in valued activities that are associated with school. When the goal is to teach students to participate in nonschool settings, the natural environment for instruction is the community.

Students Who Benefit

In the past, functional skills, particularly those taught in the community, have sometimes been conceptualized as a separate type of curriculum specifically for students with disabilities. Yet if one considers that the central premise of functional skills is to teach students skills in the settings where they are needed, one can easily see how teaching that incorporates functional, community-based applications can benefit both students with and without disabilities. The definition of the specific skill to be learned may differ depending on the unique needs of

TABLE 10.7
Differences Among Community-Based Instruction,
Community-Referenced Instruction, and Simulation

Skill	Community-Based Instruction	Community-Referenced Instruction	Simulation
Dressing	Putting on a coat to go into the community; taking off coat after arriving at the community location (if appropriate); trying on clothes in a department store; changing clothes at the YMCA to participate in swimming or aerobics	Changing clothes for gym; putting on and taking off a coat during school arrival and departure; changing shirts after lunch (if the current one becomes soiled); putting on a smock for painting in art class	Five trials of putting on and taking off a shirt in the classroom during a dressing program; tying shoelaces on a dressing board; buttoning clothes on a doll
Purchasing	Purchasing items at the drugstore; paying for a game of bowling; purchasing a soda at a restaurant; buying stamps at the post office	Purchasing lunch in the cafeteria; buying a drink from the soda machine; purchasing a ticket to a school basketball game; buying school buttons or ribbons to wear on school colors day	Counting money in the classroom (e.g., "Show me $6.25"); pretending to shop and pay for items in a classroom grocery store; sorting coins (nickels, dimes, and quarters)
Communicating/ Understanding Pictures	Locating items in the store from a picture grocery list; ordering in restaurant using a picture menu; presenting a picture to a store clerk to determine the location of a bathroom	Reviewing the school lunch choices and selecting pictures of the items desired; choosing a leisure activity from a series of picture choices; using a picture schedule throughout the school day	Matching pictures of various foods with their plastic replicas; identifying a picture by pointing to it when the teacher verbally requests, "Show me the _____"

each student, but the need for application of the skill to real settings, activities, and problems remains the same. Functional skills are designed to teach students to actively participate in valued, real-life activities. Teaching these skills alongside peers who do not have disabilities will enhance the learning of all students.

Core Components

Instruction in community skills enhances students' participation in school and community activities. Although this chapter will focus primarily on how to provide instruction for students with and without disabilities through community-based instruction, one should not forget the importance of teaching skills in the school setting that reference the same skills being taught in the community. The more opportunities students have to use a new skill and apply it across multiple settings, the greater the probability of skill acquisition. The following identifies and explains some of the core components of community skills instruction.

Instruction Reflects Local School and Community Opportunities

Community instruction emphasizes skills and activities that are valued by students, their parents, and the community. Because schools and communities differ from location to location, instruction should focus on the opportunities available in the student's local community. For example, using public transportation might be an appropriate instructional objective for many students living in urban environments; however, it has limited applicability in rural areas where the primary method of transportation may be a family member's or friend's car. Likewise, JROTC may be a highly visible activity that includes a large number of students in one school setting, yet not be available in other schools.

In addition to reflecting the opportunities available in the community, instruction should also take place in each student's community of residence. Students with disabilities are increasingly being served in their home school (i.e., the school they would attend if they did not have a disability). Community-based instruction for these students naturally occurs in their local community. In rural areas where two or three centrally located schools serve all students in the county or urban areas where all students (regardless of disability) attend regional high schools, many schools find it necessary to transport students to their own neighborhoods so that instruction can occur in the businesses the family normally frequents.

Age Appropriateness

Choosing skills that reflect a student's school and community and teaching the skills in the environments where they are normally performed will do little to ensure functionality if the activities in which the skills are taught are not age appropriate. An activity is age appropriate if a person of the same age without a disability would find the activity acceptable. Instruction and participation in the school and community increase with student age and should parallel the opportunities available to students without disabilities. Children in elementary school, for example, may accompany their parents to the grocery store and participate by choosing a favorite cereal or snack item. In contrast, a high school student may be responsible for traveling to the store independently and picking up several grocery items needed for dinner. In the school community, young children may be responsible for removing trash from the area where they eat lunch, whereas a teenager might sample a job in the cafeteria that involves restocking trays and silverware.

Independence Versus Participation

The ideal goal of functional programming is for students to acquire independent life skills. Many students, however, will always require some level of assistance and may not reach full independence in the activities in which they participate. For these students, partial participation (Baumgart et al., 1982) may be an appropriate instructional method. In this strategy, a student participates in (and receives instruction on) a portion of a task, and an adult or peer assists the student in performing all other skills. For example, when using the post office, a student with a significant motor impairment may need assistance with placing a stamp on the correct location of an envelope. Once this assistance is provided, the student would participate by dropping the envelope in the mail slot. At a school music concert, this same student may need assistance from a peer to grasp one program (i.e., a listing of the order of the music performances) but then participate by independently handing the program to a patron. Although the student may never reach full independence in these activities, partial participation enables him or her to exert control over the environment and participate to the maximum extent possible.

Omission of the Readiness Theory

According to the readiness theory, students must learn certain prerequisite skills before they will be "ready" to go into the community (Wilcox, 1987). School personnel subscribing to this theory often use it to justify why students with severe disabilities or challenging behaviors should not be included in general education settings or receive community-based instruction. They believe that if students exhibit challenging behaviors in the classroom, they will also exhibit these challenging behaviors in other school and community settings. As a result, these school personnel list school inclusion and community-based instruction as future objectives and spend the present year trying to teach the student appropriate behaviors.

One of the major problems with the readiness theory is that some students may spend their entire lives "getting ready" without ever arriving at the place they are trying to reach. By preventing students from accessing integrated settings, teachers may in fact be promoting the challenging behaviors they are trying to change. Teaching age-appropriate, functional skills in normalized school and community environments contributes to positive behaviors. It provides natural opportunities for students to learn appropriate behaviors in the settings where they are needed. It also enhances the student's quality of life by promoting independence, providing opportunities to develop relationships, and increasing the variety of activities and number of choices available to the student.

Collaboration

Skills are selected for instruction using a team approach. Parents and students are key participants in determining which goals and objectives should be targeted. Other members of the team may include general and special educators, paraprofessionals, therapists, and peers. Because there are numerous activities that occur in the school and community, team members must spend time up front to determine priority areas for instruction that will maximize the student's participation in current and future environments (see assessment section that follows). These team members will play an important role in coordinating, implementing, and evaluating instruction.

Systematic Instruction

Most community skills for students with disabilities are taught in the community rather than the school. Unlike field trips, which occur sporadically, community-based instruction involves regular, repeated instruction on specific IEP objectives. Systematic instructional procedures (e.g., task analyses, specific teaching strategies, natural cues and corrections, reinforcement, data collection) are used to teach each skill.

Community skills have been successfully taught through a variety of systematic approaches, including constant time delay (Branham et el., 1999; Morse & Schuster, 2000), progressive time delay (Frederick-Dugan, Test, & Varn, 1991; Gee et al., 1995), and prompt-and-fade procedures (Bock, 1999; Gee et al., 1995). In addition, when instruction is provided primarily in simulated or community-referenced situations, generalization strategies should be used to ensure that students can perform previously learned skills in the actual community settings where they are needed (Bock, 1999; Branham et al., 1999).

Heterogeneous Grouping of Students

To maximize inclusion and participation, instruction in school and community settings should emulate natural heterogeneous groups. For example, rather than integrating a large group of students with disabilities into one school club, the students should be dispersed across multiple clubs. In the community, teachers might instruct students with and without disabilities in small groups (e.g., 3 to 4 students), rather than instruct all students with disabilities in one special education class. Small-group instruction ensures that the needs of each student will be adequately met while maintaining the natural proportion of students with disabilities to students without disabilities that is characteristic of the population in the community. When transportation availability dictates that a large group of students receive community-based instruction at the same time, the group can be split up to receive instruction at different locations.

Frequency of Instruction

The amount of time devoted to teaching community skills depends primarily on the preferences of the family and the goals they have for their child. Other factors that the IEP team may wish to consider include the student's age and severity of disability. In general, as a student grows older, the need for instruction in the community increases. For students who have severe disabilities and do not easily generalize what they learn in one setting to another setting, community skills instruction (whether it be community based, community referenced, or a combination of these) may be a priority throughout the student's entire school career.

GENERAL APPROACHES TO ASSESSMENT

To maximize the benefits of functional community skills instruction, goals and objectives should be chosen for each student based on the student's interests, preferences, and needs. Traditional models of assessment and service delivery for students with disabilities have focused on a systems-centered approach (Bradley, 1994), where a student's deficits are assessed, and services are chosen based on the programs offered by the school. Recognizing that this model prevents students from obtaining access to opportunities not offered by "the system," many schools are now creating services and supports based on the preferences of the student. Known as person-centered planning, this approach seeks to understand a student's hopes, needs, and dreams for the future. Control for developing appropriate student objectives shifts from the teacher to a team that includes the student with a disability, family members, friends, and professionals who can assist the student in achieving his or her goals. Services and supports are created for the person based on his or her vision for the future, rather than being based on programs currently offered by the school.

In Erika's team, members used a variety of assessment tools to learn about her skills and preferences, her parents' priorities for instruction, and the dreams she and her family had for the future. The team's knowledge about the businesses and agencies in the community and about the activities available through school were then combined with the assessment information to identify instructional priorities. This section suggests four steps for completing a person-centered assessment that focuses on a student's skills and talents rather than his or her deficits. The steps are as follows: (a) inventory the school and community, (b) determine student and parent preferences, (c) gather information about student skills, and (d) prioritize student goals and objectives.

Step 1: Inventory the School and Community

Community skills instruction should reflect the activities and opportunities available in the student's school and community. For many students, families, and school personnel, the assessment process begins by determining all the possibilities for activities and opportunities that exist. Sitting around a table and discussing options rarely reveals the true realm of opportunities in the student's school and community. Ecological inventories are one way to obtain this information prior to beginning a student's individualized planning process.

An ecological inventory involves canvassing the community to identify all the environments (e.g., agencies, organizations, businesses, schools) where activities take place (Brown et al., 1979). One of the best ways to complete an ecological inventory is by walking or driving around the community. Because most people access only a portion of their community, they often have difficulty trying to recall from memory all the community has to offer. A teacher conducting his first ecological inventory once commented that he thought his community was so rural that it had little opportunity for his students. When he took his inventory that he completed at school into the community and compared it with the businesses and agencies he saw, he was amazed at the wealth of opportunities that were available for his students.

After the environments in the community have been identified, the next step in an ecological inventory is to determine the subenvironments. The subenvironments are the different physical areas of a business, agency, or school. For example, within a grocery store, some of the subenvironments might include the cart area, the canned goods aisle, the meat section, the dairy case, the bakery, the deli, the salad bar, and the checkout lines. At school, some of the subenvironments might include the office, gymnasium, library, auditorium, sports fields, and cafeteria. These subenvironments can be broken down further into the activities that occur in each area and the skills required to participate in these activities. An example of a partial ecological inventory that Erika's team developed for Wendy's fast-food restaurant is shown in Table 10.8.

Many schools find it helpful to organize the results of their ecological inventory into a file that can be accessed by various team members. Periodically, the file can be updated to add new businesses and remove ones that have left the

TABLE 10.8
Partial Ecological Inventory for a Fast-Food Restaurant

DOMAIN: *Community*
ENVIRONMENT: *Wendy's*

Subenvironment	Activity	Skills
Food counter	Ordering food	Waiting in line, looking at the menu, greeting cashier, making a choice, placing order, waiting for food
	Paying for food	Obtaining money, handing money to cashier, receiving change, putting change in wallet, saying thank you
Condiments section	Obtaining condiments	Obtaining a straw, ketchup, napkins, and silverware
Seating area	Obtaining a table	Carrying tray, locating a table, sitting down, removing coat
	Eating lunch	Unwrapping food, unwrapping silverware, putting straw in drink, putting ketchup on burger, using a napkin, eating
	Socializing with others	Greeting friends, asking for help or helping others, commenting on food, talking with friends about shared interests

area. Other helpful information to include with the inventory results are the location of the business, its distance from the school building, its proximity to other businesses where instruction could occur, and environmental aspects that may affect students (e.g., noise, temperature, visual distractions, walking distance, long lines at the checkout counter). This file can be particularly helpful to new school personnel, staff who live in a different community from that of the school, and families who are trying to evaluate different instructional possibilities for their child.

The second part of assessing the community involves taking the information from the ecological inventory and defining the types of activities and skills that are most often performed at each age level (elementary, middle, and high school) so that the skills selected for instruction will be age appropriate. One way to find out which activities are appropriate for which age is by observing students without disabilities as they engage in activities in their school and community, noting their age and level of participation. Another effective strategy is to interview parents of children without disabilities and students without disabilities. Parents can identify the variety of activities and skills that their child performs at a certain age, whereas students without disabilities will be able to define the activities that are most valued by their peer group.

Step 2: Determine Student and Parent Preferences

In addition to reflecting the opportunities available in one's locality, community skills instruction should also be based on student and parent preferences for instruction. This information can be gathered through questionnaires, interviews, observations, community sampling, and personal futures planning. Multiple methods are often needed to obtain an accurate understanding of each party's interests and preferences.

Questionnaires are one of the most frequently used strategies for assessment. Parent questionnaires often include a series of questions about the child's current level of participation and skills in the school and community, areas where the child experiences difficulty, activities the child seems to enjoy, and the parents' priorities for skill instruction. Student questionnaires generally seek to identify the student's personal interests and previous experiences in the school and community. Questionnaires are helpful in that they allow people to think privately before responding. However, because questionnaires sometimes neglect to obtain complete or accurate information, they are often most beneficial when used in combination with an interview.

Interviews can occur by phone or face-to-face. In some cases, an interview can be used to review the results of a questionnaire and clarify parent or student responses. In other cases, interviews may involve the use of pictures of school and community activities or a copy of the school's ecological inventory file. Using pictures and lists allows parents and students to look at a variety of options for potential community skills instruction without having to recall specific examples in their minds. This option can be especially helpful when obtaining information from parents who have a disability or are unable to read.

Observation is a particularly effective assessment strategy for students who have severe disabilities and may not be able to respond to questionnaires or picture choices. The person conducting the assessment observes the student in a variety of activities at home and school, then, based on the observations, develops a list of activities and activity qualities that the student likes and dislikes. Next, the list is compared with opportunities in the school and community that reflect the qualities of activities that the student most enjoys. For example, if a student enjoys participating in activities that involve music (a quality of an activity), instruction might occur in environments that naturally involve music. In the community, these environments might include a music store, skating rink, or department store. School activities might include pep club, cheerleading, or choir.

Community sampling, an extension of the observation process, involves taking students into the community to observe their reactions to various environments and activities. This method is helpful when a student's team is trying to decide among a number of possibilities or when logistical arrangements (e.g., length of the activity, amount of walking involved) may affect the student's perception of an activity. By visiting the environment, additional information can be gathered before a decision is made about the appropriateness of the environment for instruction.

Personal futures planning is a method for assisting an individual with a disability in planning for their future and in taking steps toward achieving their goals (Mount, 1994). Although there are many ways of conducting personal futures planning, one of the tools most frequently used with school-age students is the Making Action Plans System, also known as MAPS (Forest, Pearpoint, & O'Brien, 1996; Furney, 1993). Unlike the other models of assessment profiled in this section, the MAPS process assists team members in structuring community instruction within the context of how it will help the student reach overall life goals.

Step 3: Gather Information About Student Skills

When completed, Step 2 should result in a list of community environments and activities that reflect the preferences of the student and parent. In Step 3, these activities are explored in greater detail, and information is gathered about the student's skills and abilities in each activity. Much of this information can be obtained by interviewing people who know the student well and have observed him or her in the environments of interest. In some cases, this information may be sufficient for the team to move to the prioritization process in Step 4. In cases where a student may not have had previous opportunities for participation (e.g., the student accompanies a parent to the post office but has not actively engaged in any activities), further assessment of the student's skills may be warranted.

Informal assessments of student skills are most accurate when they occur in the environment where the activity is typically performed. One method for conducting an informal assessment is to develop a task analysis for each of the activities in question, observe the student performing the skills (without teacher instruction), and record which steps the student performs correctly or incorrectly or does not attempt. By allowing the student to sample the activity, the team may find that the student already has many of the needed skills and that instructional time would be better spent in another area. The team might also determine that a number of skills could be targeted for instruction and that the team needs to identify which skills should receive primary focus during the upcoming year. Step 3 should result in a list of specific skills and activities from which the team will select goals and objectives for the student.

Step 4: Prioritize Student Goals and Objectives

Organizing the assessment results to determine priority areas for instruction is one of the most difficult, yet most essential, steps for identifying student objectives. The team must evaluate each of the proposed areas for instruction and determine which ones have the greatest potential value for the student. There are a number of factors to consider when prioritizing objectives (see Falvey, 1989; Giangreco, Cloninger, & Iverson, 1993). Table 10.9 shows a list of questions that a team may wish to consider as it weighs the value of each potential community skill.

Erika's team followed the preceding four steps to assess her skills and her interests.

TABLE 10.9
Questions To Consider When Prioritizing Community Skills Objectives

1. Does the skill reflect the student's strengths and interests?

2. Has the student's family identified the skill as a priority?

3. Is the skill chronologically age appropriate? Do students without disabilities of the same age participate in this activity?

4. Will learning this skill increase the student's level of participation in the community with family and friends during nonschool hours?

5. Can the skill be taught and applied in a variety of community environments?

6. Is it possible to embed the skill into natural school-based routines (community-referenced instruction)?

7. Is the skill reasonable for the student to achieve?

8. Will acquiring this skill help the student function more independently in future environments?

ERIKA'S ASSESSMENT

Step 1: Inventory the School and Community

Erika lives within 5 miles of the middle school, and her parents frequently use the businesses within that area. Because the school district had previously completed an ecological inventory of the area, Erika's teacher began the assessment process by reviewing the inventory results so that she could share the existing possibilities with Erika's parents and other team members. The inventory showed that a variety of restaurants, stores, and other businesses (e.g., skating rink, bowling alley) were located in the community and that transportation would require a school bus or car because public transportation was not available. The team also reviewed the nonacademic activities that occur at the middle school during the after-school hours.

Step 2: Determine Student and Parent Preferences

Erika's parents decided to participate in a MAPS planning process to help them determine some long-range goals for her future. They invited several of Erika's friends, teachers, and therapists to attend. Two of the dreams Erika's parents have for her future are that she participate in meaningful activities in the school and community and that she have friends and family who are actively involved in her life. Although Erika was not able to articulate these goals, she smiled and nodded when asked what she thought about them. As a result of MAPS, a number of steps were identified that the group could take to help Erika achieve these goals. Because Erika has limited methods for expressing herself, the team assessed her preferences by developing a list of activities and qualities of activities that they knew she liked. Her preferred activities involved being with other people, eating, preparing food, keeping things in and retrieving things from her book bag, and walking. In the school environment, the team thought Erika might enjoy joining the Breakfast Club, which meets once a week at school to eat breakfast, work on homework, and socialize. They also thought she might enjoy being a manager for one of the after-school intramural sports teams (e.g., retrieving balls, getting out equipment, interacting with and cheering on peers). In the community, the team decided that possible environments of interest to Erika would be the grocery store and a fast-food restaurant because both encourage social interactions, center around food, and provide opportunities for walking. Additionally, Erika could learn to retrieve money from a purse instead of a book bag to purchase items in each environment.

Step 3: Gather Information About Student Skills

Erika's parents involve her in most activities; however, she has never actively participated in the community environments they frequent. As a result, the team decided to take Erika into a grocery store and a fast-food restaurant to observe her reactions and any attempts she made to participate. The team also provided Erika with opportunities to sample the two school activities (i.e., Breakfast Club, after-school intramurals) to gather information about her interest and skills. Erika responded favorably to all activities, as evidenced by smiling and social interactions with others. Team members found that Erika possessed few skills that were needed in each activity.

(continues)

Step 4: Prioritize Student Goals and Objectives

After Erika sampled each activity, her IEP team reconvened to review the assessment results and identify specific community skills objectives. Erika's parents thought that instruction in all of the activities would help her to participate in the school and community and enhance her inclusion with peers. They also thought the community experiences would expose her to different jobs that she might be able to sample in the future. Because Erika demonstrated limited skills in the community environments, the team targeted three objectives that would allow her to partially participate in five different activities (see Table 10.1). Three IEP objectives currently addressed in other school activities were selected for incorporation during Breakfast Club and intramural sports (see Table 10.2). The team felt that addressing these skills in new environments would broaden Erika's generalization of the skills to more settings.

CURRICULUM DESIGN

At a time when the field of education is working to increase the inclusion of students with disabilities into general education settings, how can one teach community skills in a functional manner? This section discusses several strategies for making community skills instruction "inclusive" and "functional" for students with and without disabilities. Particular attention is given to methods for overcoming obstacles to teaching in the community and applications for students across different ages.

Structuring Heterogeneous Groups

Students with and without disabilities can benefit from community skills instruction (Beck et al., 1994; Gent & Gurecka, 1998; Longwill & Kleinert, 1998). Learning functional skills helps all students apply concepts from school to real-life problems and activities. Three methods for incorporating heterogeneous groups into instruction include providing community-referenced instruction in school settings, including peers in community-based instruction, and developing volunteer work and service learning opportunities.

Provide Community-Referenced Instruction in School Settings

Community-referenced instruction involves finding functional applications in the school setting for skills that are traditionally taught in the community. This method is frequently used when limitations exist to providing instruction in the community. At one high school, the teacher of a building maintenance class collaborated with a special education teacher to identify ways that students could apply community skills in the school setting. They identified several projects that enabled the students to learn specific skills related to building maintenance while simultaneously completing tasks that benefited the school community. For example, students worked together to fix and paint bleachers around the football field, to design and build a new sign for the school to announce upcoming events, and to repair furniture that was sitting in storage. All of these activities could also be taught in the community through volunteer work, service learning, or paid employment.

Include Peers in Community-Based Instruction

A number of schools have developed strategies for providing community-based instruction to students both with and without disabilities (e.g., see Beck et al., 1994; "Team Your Students," 1996). For students without disabilities, community-based instruction can be a method for applying what has been learned in the classroom (e.g., triple-digit addition) to the real world (e.g., figuring the cost of groceries to make sure that one does not overspend a budget). Because peers without disabilities may not need to participate in community skills instruction as frequently as students with disabilities, a teacher may decide to rotate small groups of peers without disabilities through the experience. For example, Joe, a student with a disability, may need community-based instruction three times a week. Each day Joe goes into the community, his teacher schedules a group of three peers without disabilities to participate in instruction. These groups rotate on each day of instruction so that all students receive community-based instruction at least once a month. While Joe and his peers may complete the activity (e.g., grocery shopping) together, Joe may be working on learning to locate items in the store while his peers address a math class objective (e.g., using a calculator, comparing unit prices of items, figuring the total of the grocery bill).

Develop Volunteer Work and Service Learning Opportunities

As students grow older, they are expected to increasingly participate in their communities by helping others. Burns, Storey, and Certo (1999) define *community service* as a form of volunteer work that occurs in the community and is designed to foster civic responsibility. When this service simultaneously enables students to achieve specific learning objectives, it is termed *service learning*. Multiple opportunities exist within the community for students with and without disabilities to participate in volunteer work and service learning (for examples, see Gent & Gurecka, 1998; Longwill & Kleinert, 1998; Yoder et al., 1996). Service learning has been found to have a positive effect on the attitudes of students without disabilities toward peers with disabilities (Burns et al., 1999).

In the opening case study (see Table 10.1), Erika and her classmates participated in service learning at the grocery store. This activity was structured so that Erika could address a specific IEP objective while participating with her peers, who were working on other learning objectives related to health and nutrition. By completing grocery shopping for homebound senior citizens, the students performed a service that benefited members of their community. At the same time, they were using information gained from the experience to further their own educational goals.

Overcoming Obstacles to Community-Based Instruction

Despite the benefits of community-based instruction for students with and without disabilities, a number of questions often arise about the feasibility of providing instruction in the community, including liability, transportation, staffing, and program expense issues. Several strategies for addressing these issues are now widely accepted and practiced in the field. In addition to considering the ideas offered in this chapter, school personnel would be wise to consult with professionals from other school districts in their region to discover other strategies.

Liability

Because students participate in community-based instruction to address objectives in their IEP or the general education curriculum, the school system is responsible for students while they are in the community in the same way that they are responsible for them when they are on school grounds. Many schools initially fear that the risks involved with providing students community-based instruction may increase their susceptibility to claims of liability and, in particular, negligence. Liability refers to who is responsible if a student is injured in the community or if property is damaged. An individual can be deemed liable on the basis of negligence (i.e., not providing appropriate supervision or care). To protect staff from liability and claims of negligence, schools should consider the following steps before implementing community-based instruction:

1. Present the program to the school board and obtain its approval.

2. Contact the school's insurance carrier and review the current policy to make sure that it covers all students and staff engaged in community-based instruction. In some cases, a clause may need to be added if staff will be providing instruction outside normal school hours.

3. Develop a manual that identifies professional conduct during instruction and discusses procedures for handling emergencies.

4. Make sure that all staff are trained in CPR and basic first aid.

5. Obtain written parental permission for instruction in the community.

6. Verify that each student is covered by a parent's or guardian's health insurance or a school insurance policy.

7. Include all community-based instruction objectives in the IEP of a student with a disability or provide written documentation of the objectives students are addressing in the general curriculum.

Transportation

Depending on the community and the location of its schools, transportation can be a logistical nightmare. In one school district, both the elementary and high school are located at a rural crossroads centrally located for three towns. Within a 5-mile radius, the schools have access to two convenience stores, a small "mom-and-pop" grocery store, and a church. Although instruction occurs in these environments, staff and students also regularly travel a minimum of 20 miles one way to provide instruction in the three towns where most of the students live. A school car that was donated to the driver education program (by a car dealership) is used to transport students.

A number of options exist for transporting students to and from the community. These include the following:

- *Walking.* Walking helps students work on mobility goals and street-crossing skills. In many urban areas, it may also be the most convenient method for accessing the community.
- *School Buses.* Teachers, paraprofessionals, and other school staff who have a bus driver's license may be able to use a school bus during the day to transport students. In addition, scheduling community outings to coincide with the current school bus schedule (e.g., dropping students in the community on the way to school, picking up students from the community on the way home, riding with other students traveling to work–study programs) can maximize school resources.
- *School Cars and Driver Education Vehicles.* More economical than a school bus, these vehicles can often be stationed at the school and designated specifically for students receiving community-based instruction.
- *Private Vehicles.* Use of staff's and volunteers' cars provides maximum flexibility when scheduling community instruction; however, care should be taken to make sure that the school's insurance covers this transportation option.
- *Public Transportation.* In urban areas, public buses, subways, taxis, and specialized transportation (e.g., buses for people with disabilities) all provide excellent methods for accessing the community throughout the day.
- *Transportation Provided by Other Agencies.* In some instances, schools can access transportation provided by adult service agencies (e.g., The Arc, Office of Mental Retardation/Developmental Disabilities) when additional seats are available on their vans.

Staffing

Community-based instruction should occur with small heterogeneous groups of students (no more than three or four per instructor). Most schools rarely have the luxury of such high staffing ratios; however, creative ways do exist for maximizing existing resources. The following arrangements can be made for other staff, in addition to the special education teacher, to provide community-based instruction:

- Therapists who normally schedule time during a student's classes can provide therapy goals as part of a student's community instruction.
- Peer tutors, adult volunteers, and college students can assist school staff with instruction.
- Job descriptions for paraprofessionals can be changed to include the provision of community instruction. (Although paraprofessionals work under the general supervision of a teacher, there is no reason they cannot independently provide instruction in the community once they have received appropriate training.)
- Team teaching among special education teachers or between special and general education teachers promotes a shared responsibility for all students. Small-group instruction in the school or community is possible while other students receive large-group instruction.
- General education teachers can provide instruction in the community to a small group of students both with and without disabilities to address individual needs.

Program Expenses

Although the most cost-effective method for providing community-based instruction is to access environments and activities that do not require money (e.g., public library, window shopping, music store "listening library," community center, street crossing, mall walking), many students' objectives cannot be completed without some level of funds. Parents have frequently been requested to contribute money for their son's or daughter's instruction in the community. Not all families, however, are financially able to offer assistance, and lack of money should not prohibit any student from receiving community-based instruction. Instead, the following alternatives should be considered:

- Convert a portion of the classroom supply budget for community-based instruction. Obtain permission for staff to procure cash advances so that students can use real money to make purchases.

- Have students use their lunch money to purchase lunch supplies at the grocery store. Provide instruction on meal preparation during the week.

- Conduct fund-raisers (e.g., bake and sell cookies during lunch hour, sell coffee and muffins to teachers throughout the school day, obtain orders for cakes and cookies from school staff, grow plants for the holidays, hold car washes). Involve students with and without disabilities in the fund-raiser. Funds raised can be used to support community-based instruction for all students.

- Have families send in a list of purchases they need and the money to pay for them. Obtain similar lists from school staff or elderly people in the community who need assistance.

Developing Guidelines and Procedures for Implementing Community-Based Instruction

Providing students with quality instruction in the community requires extensive upfront planning. School personnel should develop procedures and guidelines for implementing community-based instruction prior to actually teaching students in the community. Many school systems have found it helpful to compile a manual or handbook documenting the decisions that have been made. The development of a manual has several benefits. First, it reinforces the school district's commitment to providing students with instruction in the community. Second, it provides staff with specific procedures for implementing instruction. Third, it helps maintain consistency in the delivery of services throughout the school district.

Although a community-based instruction manual may have many components, the following areas should be emphasized:

- *School Philosophy or Mission Statement.* This might include the importance of preparing students to enter the adult world, the benefits of teaching in real settings where students need to perform the skills they learn, and the school system's commitment to teaching students to live as independently as possible.

- *Liability.* The school's liability for students who are receiving instruction in the community should be explained, as should the strategies the school district has taken to prevent claims of negligence. Information about school insurance coverage of staff and students during instruction in the community should be explicitly stated.

- *Handling Emergencies.* Specific procedures for handling emergencies in the community should be identified. Requirements for students to carry personal identification cards and for staff to carry important phone numbers might also be included.

- *Transportation.* This section should identify the types of transportation that are acceptable (e.g., school bus, public transit, personal vehicle, walking) and indentify the person who is responsible for making travel arrangements.

- *Instructional Expenses.* Identify how community-based instruction will be funded. For example, families might be requested to fund all activities where the child performs a service for the family while the school covers the cost of all other expenses. Describe how funds will be accessed and by whom.

- *Staff Responsibilities.* Clearly define which school personnel will be responsible for setting up community sites, analyzing the tasks, teaching students, supervising paraprofessionals, and providing instruction to students who remain at school. Guidelines might be provided on how to write IEP goals for community environments.

- *Release Forms.* Parental permission forms should be obtained for transportation to and participation at each new instructional site. Although community-based instruction goals will be included in the IEP of a student with a disability or documented in writing for a student who is addressing objectives from the general curriculum, parents should be informed and agree to the specific skills to be taught, activity location, and instructional dates and times.

DESIGNING THE CURRICULUM FOR DIFFERENT AGE LEVELS

Although students of all ages access the community, the types of activities in which they engage often depend on student age. For example, a 6-year-old child may accompany his parents to the food court of a mall and choose the type of food he wants to eat (e.g., hamburger); a 12-year-old may decide the specific eatery in the food court at which she wishes to eat and order a meal with money provided by the parent; an 18-year-old will choose the time of day he goes to the mall to eat, the amount of money he will spend, and the friends or family members with whom he will eat. As a person grows older, his or her number of choices and responsibilities increases.

The selection of community skills for instruction should reflect the natural range of choices and responsibilities available to most students as they mature. Although some students with disabilities may require adaptations or assistance to participate in an activity, the types of activities they access should be determined by their preferences and chronological age rather than their ability to independently perform the skills involved with the activity. Naturally, a variety of other considerations will influence the type of community skills instruction any one student receives.

Elementary School

Community skills instruction is provided primarily in the school building during the elementary years. Skills are selected that reference those needed to participate in the community at that age. For example, learning to carry a tray in the cafeteria can be applied in fast-food restaurants or other cafeterias in the community. Instruction also prepares students to function in future environments. Students who are taught to board and exit a school bus during arrival and departure from school will use these same skills when traveling to a business in the community when they are older. Although providing instruction in the school setting does not guarantee that the student will be able to apply the skill in the community, it does provide natural opportunities for students to learn functional skills with their peers.

Occasionally, there may be situations that require regular instruction in the community. A student's behavior may be so difficult that it precludes the family from accessing the community with their child, the severity of a student's disability may prevent him or her from generalizing the skills learned at school to similar community settings, or the parent may simply prefer that instruction occur in the community environments that the family frequents. The type of instruction provided (community referenced or community based) should reflect the individual needs of the student.

Middle School

For many students, middle school is the time when instruction begins to focus on learning skills in community environments. Although community-referenced instruction remains an important component of a student's in-school experiences, many age-appropriate skills become increasingly difficult to reference in the school setting. For instance, teaching a student to locate personal care items in a drugstore can only be taught in the community drugstore. To approximate these skills in the school setting would entail the creation of artificial simulations that have limited meaning for most students. Certainly many skills can still be referenced in the school setting; however, the goal at this age is to provide students with increasing opportunities to perform skills in the actual environments where they will be used.

During middle school, the amount of time devoted to community skills instruction gradually increases. By being exposed to a number of community environments and receiving instruction in critical areas, students can begin to acquire the skills for adulthood. These opportunities can also help students identify preferred community activities and potential options for future employment. For some individuals, community skills objectives may be included in the transition component of the IEP at this time.

High School

During high school, all students begin to make curriculum choices based on the goals they have for their life as adults. Some focus on advanced academics that will prepare them for college, others pursue training in a vocational trade, and still others participate in a shortened school day so that they can maintain a part-time job outside of school.

Community skills instruction during the high school years builds on skills learned at the elementary and middle school levels. Instruction in community environments continues to take on increased importance as the length of time devoted to community skills, and community functioning in general, expands. Once a student graduates with his or her peers at age 18, special education services may focus exclusively on instruction in community environments (across all instructional domain areas) to ensure that the services and supports the student needs are in place by age 21.

CONCLUSION

Learning community skills is essential for students of all ages and all abilities and ensures that students learn skills that enhance their participation in the school and community. Where instruction takes place (e.g., school, community, or a combination of both settings) depends on the nature of the activity and the needs and preferences of the student and his or her family. Clearly there are numerous benefits to receiving instruction in the community. In addition, strategies exist for enabling students with and without disabilities to address their diverse needs for learning within the context of functional, community activities. By extending the view of inclusive education to include school and community settings, school personnel can provide opportunities for all students to benefit from instruction that emphasizes real-life applications.

APPENDIX 10.A:
ERIKA'S IEP GOALS AND OBJECTIVES

Domestic

⊒ Goal

To increase independence in dressing, food preparation, eating, and cleaning activities

1. Given a shirt and an activity that necessitates changing clothes, Erika will independently put on the shirt within 3 minutes.

   Note. Examples include the following: changing for gym class; changing from bathing suit to regular clothes at the YMCA; changing shirt after lunch if it becomes soiled during eating; changing into home economics uniform, which is a shirt to protect clothes during cooking.

2. Given bread, cold cuts, a knife, and mayonnaise or mustard, Erika will make a sandwich for lunch 2 to 3 days a week with 90% accuracy.

   Note. Erika will bring her sandwich to the lunchroom in a lunch bag and eat with her peers as usual on the days this objective is addressed.

3. Given a paper napkin during lunch or snacks, Erika will wipe her mouth without prompts 90% of the time.

   Note. Environments where this objective will be addressed include the school cafeteria, the classroom, Wendy's, Ukrops Cafeteria, and Burger King.

Recreation and Leisure

⊒ Goal

To expand Erika's leisure skills in integrated school and community environments

1. Given free time, Erika will participate in board games with her peers 2 times a week.

2. Given pictures of leisure activities in the community, Erika will point to 1 picture and participate in that activity for at least 15 minutes 1 time a week.

   Note. Leisure choices will include bowling, swimming, aerobics, arcade games, exercise machines, browsing in stores, movie rentals, movie theaters, and the public library.

3. Given breaks between activities, Erika will select an age-appropriate free-time activity and engage in the activity independently for 5 minutes 90% of the time.

Community

→ **Goal**

To develop skills in the community that will promote increased independence and inclusion

1. When provided with a coupon picture (or other picture) of an item in a store, Erika will pick up the item that matches the picture and release it in her cart or basket within 20 seconds.

   Note. Stores will include Ukrops Grocery, Kmart, and CVS Pharmacy. Erika will be positioned 2 to 3 feet in front of the item before she is asked to locate it.

2. Given the checkout line of a store or restaurant and money to cover the cost of the purchase, Erika will hand the cashier the money, wait for change, and deposit the change in her purse, with no more than 1 gestural cue.

   Note. The instructor will provide Erika with the appropriate amount of money prior to her reaching the checkout line.

3. In a fast-food restaurant, Erika will hand the cashier pictures of the items she wishes to order 100% of the time.

Vocational

→ **Goal**

To sample four different jobs within the school building during the year (Erika will sample only one job each semester. Each objective will be targeted for 30 minutes, 3 to 5 times per week.)

1. Given the school cafeteria dishwasher, Erika will stack dirty plates, cups, and silverware in the dish rack with 90% accuracy.

   Note. Erika will partially participate in all aspects of running the dishwasher; however, instruction in this environment will focus only on this objective.

2. Given a maintenance cart and a job duties checklist, Erika will clean the teachers' lounge with 100% accuracy.

   Note. Cleaning the teachers' lounge will consist of emptying the trash, wiping down the vending machines, and washing the worktable.

3. Given clean towels and aprons in the home economics room, Erika will fold each item with 90% accuracy.

   Note. Erika will partially participate in washing dirty towels and aprons and drying them. This objective will be targeted once Erika takes the items out of the dryer.

4. Given the daily announcement printouts, Erika will insert one announcement into each teacher's mailbox 100% of the time.

   Note. Erika and another office assistant who does not have a disability will work together to complete this task.

Functional Academics

⮊ Goal

To improve math, time management, and money skills within the context of functional routines

1. Given a functional task or activity that requires one-to-one correspondence, Erika will pick up and distribute one item to each person or place with 100% accuracy.

   Note. Examples include the following: inserting one copy of the daily announcement printouts in each teacher's mailbox; passing out one set of pastel chalks to each student in art class; dealing one card to each player during a free-time board game; inserting one new handout or other material into students' social studies or science folders; passing out jerseys during gym class.

2. Given a picture schedule in a notebook, Erika will open her notebook, pick up the first picture, attach it with Velcro to the outside of her notebook, and walk to the location of that activity with a peer, with no more than 1 gestural prompt.

   Note. One picture will be attached with Velcro to each page of Erika's notebook, and pictures will be sequenced according to the order in which they occur. Once Erika has arrived at the next activity, the picture on the cover of her notebook will be placed in a "discard" pocket in the back of the notebook.

3. Given coins and a change card, Erika will match the correct coins to the card to purchase a drink or snack from a vending machine with 90% accuracy.

   Note. A change card will be developed that shows pictures of each snack in the school vending machines and the corresponding coins necessary to purchase each item.

Communication

⮊ Goal

To increase Erika's ability to influence and control the events in her environment

1. Given a choice of 3 pictures, Erika will point to 1 picture and obtain the item or activity chosen 90% of the time.

   Note. Examples include the following: choosing a leisure activity; choosing a peer with whom to work; indicating which job to perform first; making choices among cafeteria lunch options; determining a soda choice for break time.

2. Given a difficult task and the need to take a break, Erika will sign "break" to request a break in instruction 80% of the time.

3. Given the need to use the bathroom, Erika will initiate pointing to a picture of a toilet 100% of the time.

Social

⮕ Goal

To develop socially appropriate methods for interacting with others

1. When initiating a greeting with a friend or stranger (not a relative), Erika will wave, shake hands, say "hello," or give "high fives" 100% of the time.

2. After receiving assistance with a task or activity, Erika will look at the individual who provided the assistance and say "thank you" 90% of the time.

   Note. Examples include the following: receiving change from a school cafeteria or store cashier; receiving assistance from a peer or teacher; receiving medication from the nurse.

Motor

⮕ Goal

To maximize Erika's strength and use of both sides of her body to perform daily routines

1. Given an activity that requires bilateral hand usage, Erika will use both hands to complete the task 100% of the time.

   Note. Examples include the following: rolling a maintenance or grocery cart; catching, holding, or rolling a ball during gym class; carrying a tray in the cafeteria or a restaurant; zipping pants or coat; opening a can of soda; folding towels; putting on a shirt.

2. When going up or down stairs, Erika will alternate right and left legs for at least 6 consecutive steps.

   Note. Examples include the following: entering and exiting the school building; walking to the cafeteria; walking from the cafeteria to the nurse's office.

REFERENCES

Agran, M., Snow, K., & Swaner, J. (1999). A survey of secondary level teachers' opinions on community-based instruction and inclusive education. *Journal of the Association for Persons with Severe Handicaps, 24,* 58–62.

Baumgart, D., Brown, L., Pumpian, I., Nisbet, J., Ford, A., Sweet, M., et al. (1982). Principle of partial participation and individualized adaptations in educational programs for severely handicapped students. *Journal of the Association for the Severely Handicapped, 7,* 17–27.

Beck, J., Broers, J., Hogue, E., Shipstead, J., & Knowlton, E. (1994). Strategies for functional community-based instruction and inclusion for children with mental retardation. *Teaching Exceptional Children, 26*(2), 44–48.

Bock, M. A. (1999). Sorting laundry: Categorization strategy application to an authentic learning activity by children with autism. *Focus on Autism and Other Developmental Disabilities, 14,* 220–230.

Bradley, V. J. (1994). Evolution of a new service paradigm. In V. J. Bradley, J. W. Ashbaugh, & B. C. Blaney (Eds.), *Creating individual supports for people with developmental disabilities: A mandate for change at many levels* (pp. 11–32). Baltimore: Brookes.

Branham, R. S., Collins, B. C., Schuster, J. W., & Kleinert, H. (1999). Teaching community skills to students with moderate disabilities: Comparing combined techniques of classroom simulation, videotape modeling, and community-based instruction. *Education and Training in Mental Retardation and Developmental Disabilities, 34,* 170–181.

Brown, L., Branston, M. B., Hamre-Nietupski, S., Pumpian, I., Certo, N., & Gruenewald, L. (1979). A strategy for developing chronological age appropriate and functional curricular content for severely handicapped adolescents and young adults. *Journal of Special Education, 13*(1), 81–90.

Burns, M., Storey, K., & Certo, N. J. (1999). Effect of service learning on attitudes towards students with severe disabilities. *Education and Training in Mental Retardation and Developmental Disabilities, 34,* 58–65.

Dymond, S. K. (2001). A participatory action research approach to evaluating inclusive school programs. *Focus on Autism and Other Developmental Disabilities, 16,* 54–63.

Dymond, S. K., & Orelove, F. P. (2001). What constitutes effective curricula for students with severe disabilities? *Exceptionality, 9,* 109–122.

Everson, J. M. (1988). An analysis of federal and state policy on transition from school to adult life for youth with disabilities. In P. Wehman & M. S. Moon (Eds.), *Vocational rehabilitation and supported employment* (pp. 67–78). Baltimore: Brookes.

Falvey, M. A. (1989). *Community-based curriculum: Instructional strategies for students with severe handicaps* (2nd ed.). Baltimore: Brookes.

Ferguson, D. L. (1995). The real challenge of inclusion: Confessions of a "rabid inclusionist." *Phi Delta Kappan, 77,* 281–287.

Fisher, D., & Sax, C. (1999). Noticing differences between secondary and postsecondary education: Extending Agran, Snow, and Swaner's discussion. *Journal of the Association for Persons with Severe Handicaps, 24,* 303–305.

Ford, A., Schnorr, R., Meyer, L., Davern, L., Black, J., & Dempsey, P. (Eds.). (1989). *The Syracuse community-referenced curriculum guide for students with moderate and severe disabilities.* Baltimore: Brookes.

Forest, M., Pearpoint, J., & O'Brien, J. (1996). MAPS, circles of friends, and PATH: Powerful tools to help build caring communities. In S. Stainback & W. Stainback (Eds.), *Inclusion: A guide for educators* (pp. 67–86). Baltimore: Brookes.

Frederick-Dugan, A., Test, D. W., & Varn, L. (1991). Acquisition and generalization of purchasing skills using a calculator by students who are mentally retarded. *Education and Training in Mental Retardation, 26,* 381–387.

Furney, K. S. (1993). *Making dreams happen: How to facilitate the MAPS process.* Burlington: University of Vermont, Center for Transition Policy and Development.

Gee, K., Graham, N., Sailor, W., & Goetz, L. (1995). Use of integrated, general education, and community settings as primary contexts for skill instruction for students with severe, multiple disabilities. *Behavior Modification, 19,* 33–58.

Gent, P. J., & Gurecka, L. E. (1998). Service learning: A creative strategy for inclusive classrooms. *Journal of the Association for Persons with Severe Handicaps, 23,* 261–271.

Giangreco, M. F., Cloninger, C. J., & Iverson, V. S. (1993). *Choosing options and accommodations for children: A guide to planning inclusive education.* Baltimore: Brookes.

Hunt, P., Farron-Davis, F., Beckstead, S., Curtis, D., & Goetz, L. (1994). Evaluating the effects of placement of students with severe disabilities in general education versus special classes. *Journal of the Association for Persons with Severe Handicaps, 19,* 200–214.

Inge, K. J., & Dymond, S. (1994). Challenging behaviors in the workplace: Increasing a student's access to community-based vocational instruction. *Journal of Vocational Rehabilitation, 4,* 272–284.

Kennedy, C. H., & Itkonen, T. (1994). Some effects of regular class participation on the social contacts and social networks of high school students with severe disabilities. *Journal of the Association for Persons with Severe Handicaps, 19,* 1–10.

Longwill, A. W., & Kleinert, H. L. (1998). The unexpected benefits of high school peer tutoring. *Teaching Exceptional Children, 30,* 60–65.

McDonnell, J. (1997, February). Participation in content-area classes and community-based instruction in secondary schools: Isn't it about achieving a balance? *TASH Newsletter, 23*(2), 23–24, 29.

McDonnell, J., Hardman, M. L., Hightower, J., Keifer-O'Donnell, R., & Drew, C. (1993). Impact of community-based instruction on the development of adaptive behavior of secondary-level students with mental retardation. *American Journal on Mental Retardation, 97,* 575–584.

Morse, T. E., & Schuster, J. W. (2000). Teaching elementary students with moderate intellectual disabilities how to shop for groceries. *Exceptional Children, 66,* 273–288.

Mortweet, S. L., Utley, C. A., Walker, D., Dawson, H. L., Delquadri, J. C., Reddy, S. S., et al. (1999). Classroom peer tutoring: Teaching students with mild mental retardation in inclusive classrooms. *Exceptional Children, 65,* 524–536.

Mount, B. (1994). Benefits and limitations of personal futures planning. In V. I. Bradley, J. W. Ashbaugh, & B. C. Blaney (Eds.), *Creating individual supports for people with developmental disabilities: A mandate for change at many levels* (pp. 97–108). Baltimore: Brookes.

Ryndak, D. L., Morrison, A. P., & Sommerstein, L. (1999). Literacy before and after inclusion in general education settings: A case study. *Journal of the Association for Persons with Severe Handicaps, 24,* 5–22.

Sands, D. J., Kozleski, E. B., & French, N. K. (2000). *Inclusive education for the 21st century.* Stamford, CT: Wadsworth.

Schuh, M. C., Tashie, C., Lamb, P., Bang, M., & Jorgensen, C. M. (1998). Community-based learning for all students. In C. M. Jorgensen (Ed.), *Restructuring high schools for all students: Taking inclusion to the next level* (pp. 209–231). Baltimore: Brookes.

Sowers, J., & Powers, L. (1995). Enhancing the participation and independence of students with severe physical and multiple disabilities in performing community activities. *Mental Retardation, 33,* 209–220.

Stainback, S., Stainback, W., & Ayres, B. (1996). Schools as inclusive communities. In W. Stainback & S. Stainback (Eds.), *Controversial issues confronting special education: Divergent perspectives* (2nd ed., pp. 31–43). Boston: Allyn & Bacon.

Tashie, C., Jorgensen, C., Shapiro-Barnard, S., Martin, J., & Schuh, M. (1996, September). High school inclusion strategies and barriers. *TASH Newsletter, 22*(9), 19–22.

Team your students for inclusive research outside of school. (1996, August). *Inclusive Education Programs: Advice on Educating Students with Disabilities in Regular Settings, 3,* 1, 10.

Waldron, N. L., & McLeskey, J. (1998). The effects of an inclusive school program on students with mild and severe learning disabilities. *Exceptional Children, 64,* 395–406.

Wilcox, B. (1987). Why a new curriculum? In B. Wilcox & G. T. Bellamy (Eds.), *A comprehensive guide to The Activities Catalog: An alternative curriculum for youth and adults with severe disabilities* (pp. 1–10). Baltimore: Brookes.

Yoder, D. I., Retish, E., & Wade, R. (1996). Service learning: Meeting student and community needs. *Teaching Exceptional Children, 28,* 14–18.

CHAPTER 11

Living at Home
Skills for Independence

Daniel E. Steere and Teri L. Burcroff

One's home is a unique environment. It is a place of privacy where one can relax at the end of a work day, spend time with family, or simply be alone. A home is unlike any other environment in that it provides safety, privacy, comfort, and a haven. O'Brien (1994) characterized a home as having three key dimensions: (a) a sense of place that allows comfort and personalization; (b) a sense of control, including the selection of the home and with whom to live; and (c) a sense of security by being the homeowner or tenant who controls the terms of the lease. The establishment of one's home is a major achievement and indicator of success in adult life.

A home is therefore a place that in some ways has fewer demands than places of employment or other community environments. Without the ability to complete a number of complex activities, however, one may have difficulty in the home. Consider the importance of the following activities:

- planning and preparing a balanced, nutritional menu of meals
- cleaning one's home or apartment
- cleaning one's clothes
- bathing and maintaining appropriate hygiene
- using electrical appliances safely
- using the telephone
- engaging in leisure activities at home
- getting along with family or roommates, unless one lives alone
- knowing what to do in an emergency
- caring for oneself if ill
- interacting with neighbors
- managing finances to maintain one's home

This list illustrates the complexity and importance of skill development related to living at home. An underlying concern with all of these areas is the need for individuals to plan and manage their time effectively to complete all of these activities. Consequently, the development of effective self-management skills (Agran, Fodor-Davis, Moore, & Deer, 1989; Hughes & Agran, 1993) is a common thread running through all of the activities described in this chapter. In addition, because most individuals have more than one home during their lifetime, home living skills must be able to be generalized. For example, a person who can operate more than one type of vacuum cleaner, stove, or telephone will be more likely to be successful in a new house or apartment. For this reason, teachers should systematically provide multiple examples of activities throughout the years of instruction to enhance student generalization (Horner, Sprague, & Wilcox, 1982; Steere, 1997).

The stakes for learning home living skills are high. In recent years, a supported living approach, in which individuals live where they want with necessary support, has been developed as an alternative to the traditional residential services continuum (Racino & Walker, 1993). Supported living services are based on the presumption that individuals of differing needs can live where and how they want when flexible and individualized supports are provided (West, 2001). This approach has allowed individuals with a range of support needs to live on their own without having to earn this status by meeting vague readiness criteria. Despite the development of the supported living movement, however, individuals with disabilities continue to enter restrictive residential programs that do not meet O'Brien's (1994) dimensions of home. Too often, skill deficit continues to be equated with the need for more restrictive or structured programs, thus perpetuating the traditional continuum of residential services (Taylor, 1988). Although all students should be able to live where and how they want after leaving school, those who learn home living skills may in fact have a greater chance to establish a home of their own in adulthood. When the development of these skills is neglected, students are more likely to spend their adult lives with little choice or control over where and how they live. The importance of home living skills is further highlighted by recent research indicating that individuals who live in small, community-based settings of their choosing are more likely to be more autonomous (Wehmeyer & Bolding, 1999) and to engage in more varied community activities of their own choosing (Howe, Horner, & Newton, 1998).

We believe that instruction in living at home should be based on the presumption that all students, including those with severe disabilities, can master many of the skills required for success. In addition, all individuals should have opportunity to live where and how they want without having to demonstrate readiness. Certainly, many students will continue to require support for some areas of home living well into adulthood (Racino & Walker, 1993). However, instruction during the school years should prepare students for maximum independence in home living. This chapter addresses the major skill areas that need to be mastered for success in living at home. Some activities that are completed in part at home (e.g., financial management, leisure activities) are addressed elsewhere in this book, and readers should refer to those chapters for additional ideas.

In the remainder of this chapter, we describe nine key activity areas that are needed for success in the home and that should be included in a curriculum. We then describe four considerations for assessment of home living activities. We provide specific considerations in curriculum development at the elementary, middle, and high school levels and sample objectives. Finally, we discuss additional considerations for teaching home living skills. First, however, the following case study is provided as a point of reference for our discussion of the development of home living activities. We will return to this case study later in the chapter to discuss the development of appropriate Individualized Education Program (IEP) objectives for home living.

MARK

Mark is 13 years old and lives with his family. He has autism and requires extensive support. Mark has many skills, including the ability to dress himself, to brush his teeth, and to wash himself if the shower is prepared for him. In addition, Mark can operate the toaster and prepare himself a bowl of cold cereal with milk. He is able to operate the television and enjoys watching it. He can also operate the stereo system to play CDs and tapes, which is another of his favorite leisure activities. Mark is able to feed his pet cat without assistance. Mark is verbal and can greet visitors to his family's home, although his rapid speech, awkward syntax, and limited vocabulary make it difficult for visitors to understand him. Mark's parents know he needs to develop greater independence and have developed a system of chores for him to complete every day. Mark is responsible for setting the dinner table, feeding his cat, making his bed, and brushing his teeth. On weekends, he is also responsible for vacuuming the living room floor and sweeping the kitchen. He accompanies his family for grocery shopping and helps pick out items from a list. He also assists them at the Laundromat, where he loads laundry into the washing machines and inserts the coins. He checks off completed activities on a job chart. Mark's parents provide him with an allowance that is paid when he completes a designated series of chores. Mark uses his earnings to purchase additional tapes and CDs for his collection.

Despite his many abilities and his parents' active efforts to teach and support him, Mark lacks skills in many areas. For example, he cannot cook a meal other than toast or cereal. He can clean the dishes but requires verbal and gestural prompting to do so. Mark is not able to plan a balanced diet for shopping and, if left by himself, would rely on potato chips and other preferred snack food. He can speak on the telephone but would not know what to do if an emergency required him to call 911 or a neighbor. Although Mark can shower and dress himself, he requires prompting to initiate these activities. In fact, he is often resistant to changing his clothing, particularly during changes of the seasons from cold to warm weather. Mark has not been taught to regulate the heat or air conditioning in his home. Finally, Mark requires considerable prompting from his family to stop one activity and begin another. For example, unless prompted by his parents to begin his chores or get dressed, he would remain in his pajamas and watch television for hours. Clearly, Mark needs continued instruction in a number of areas to become more independent in his family's home and to increase the likelihood of success in future homes away from his family.

GENERAL DESCRIPTION OF CURRICULUM CONTENT

As illustrated above, numerous activities need to be completed at home. In this section, we describe nine general activity areas necessary for success in most homes. The areas addressed in this section are (a) planning and preparing meals within a balanced diet; (b) self-care, bathing, and hygiene; (c) cleaning and care of the home; (d) cleaning and care of clothing; (e) telephone use; (f) leisure activities; (g) safety procedures for emergencies in the home; (h) time management and scheduling activities at home; and (i) negotiating with others and self-advocacy for successful home living. Under each of the nine areas, key activities that should be considered for inclusion in the curriculum are highlighted. The nine areas and key activities are shown in Table 11.1.

Planning and Preparing Meals

A major activity that is completed at home is planning, preparing, and eating meals. A key consideration for this set of activities is that the meals be nutritious and balanced. There is a danger that, without active instruction, people with disabilities may eat only foods that are high in calories and low in nutritional value. Therefore, it is essential that students learn that meals must have variety and include foods from the major food groups. This can be taught creatively by designing menu planning forms that are organized by meals, as shown in Figure 11.1. Such menu planners can then be used as shopping lists to increase the likelihood that the student will purchase health foods.

A second consideration is the student's ability to prepare both simple meals, such as making a sandwich, and meals that require cooking, such as a dinner with meat, vegetables, and rice or potatoes. Such skills should be taught systematically over the years, so that the student's ability to prepare increasingly complex meals develops as the student becomes older. Some students who learn to read will be able to follow recipes from food packages or from cookbooks. Others will require adaptations such as picture recipes or recipes recorded onto audiotapes. An underlying skill in meal preparation is the ability to follow a set of directions and to sequence steps within a more complex set of activities. As a result, one important instructional strategy is to develop simple task analyses of cooking activities in written or pictorial form.

A third consideration for this curriculum area is the student's ability to use cooking equipment correctly and safely, including the use of simple utensils, such as a cutting knife, and of appliances such as a stove, oven, microwave, coffeemaker, or toaster. Teachers should introduce appliances systematically to increase the likelihood that the student will generalize the skills to new appliances. In addition, because the preparation of different foods requires the ability to time the length of cooking, the student's ability to use a watch or a simple kitchen timer is another important component skill.

Finally, students must learn how to store food appropriately. Because food that is left out or stored improperly can present a danger, students should be taught how to correctly freeze or refrigerate perishable foods. A chart such as the one in Table 11.2 can help students who have difficulty in this area.

Self-Care, Bathing, and Hygiene

Self-care, bathing, and hygiene are a key part of the home living curriculum that can affect many other areas, including success in employment and in general community environments. Students must learn to master a number of key skills in this area, including the ability to shower or bathe on a regular basis. Hair and nail care are also essential.

TABLE 11.1
Curriculum Areas and Activities for Living at Home

Curriculum Area	Key Activities
1. Planning and preparing meals	Planning a menu Preparing meals Using cooking equipment Storing food safely
2. Self-care, bathing, and hygiene	Showering or bathing Caring for hair Caring for nails Caring for teeth Toileting Washing hands and face
3. Cleaning and care of the home	Vacuuming Dusting and wiping surfaces Neatening and organizing
4. Cleaning and care of clothing	Washing and drying clothes Changing clothes as needed Folding and storing clothes
5. Telephone use	Calling for appointments or services Calling friends and acquaintances Calling in emergencies Answering calls from others
6. Leisure activities	Watching television Listening to music Performing hobbies Entertaining visitors
7. Safety procedures	Calling 911 in an emergency Evacuating during a fire Responding to smoke detectors Using a fire extinguisher Calling an ambulance or doctor if one becomes very sick Safely answering the door
8. Time management and scheduling activities	Adhering to a daily schedule Following a calendar Using alarm clocks
9. Negotiating with others and self-advocacy	Negotiating responsibilities with roommates Negotiating communal versus private property and areas within the home Negotiating with neighbors regarding issues such as noise, external lights, and so on Speaking up to ensure that important responsibilities are carried out by roommates or others Speaking up on one's behalf to ensure that needed supports are obtained

Dental care is an important consideration for self-care. Students must learn to brush and floss their teeth regularly. In addition, some students may need to learn to use mouthwashes or fluoride supplements.

Appropriate hygiene skills include toileting and washing hands and face. The use of deodorant becomes important as students enter adolescence.

FIGURE 11.1.
Sample menu planner
for a nutritious diet.

MENU PLANNER Menu for *Monday*	What I Need to Buy (Put These on the Shopping List!)
Breakfast	
Toast and butter	Bread
Cereal and milk	Milk
Banana	
Orange juice	Orange juice
Coffee	
Lunch	
Bologna sandwich	
Apple	Apples
Chips	
Soda	
Dinner	
Frozen fish fillets	
Frozen French fries	
Canned corn with butter	Canned corn
Milk	
Coffee	
Ice cream	Ice cream

Cleaning and Care of the Home

A home that is not cared for can become unsanitary. In addition, visitors are less likely to return to a home that is dirty or smells. Therefore, students must learn to care for their home correctly and then do so on a frequent and regular basis.

Cleaning and care of the home entails activities such as vacuuming, dusting, and wiping surfaces, particularly in the kitchen and bathroom areas. To complete these activities, students will need to learn how to use equipment such as vacuum cleaners, carpet sweepers, brooms, and mops and how to use spray bottles and other dispensers for chemical cleaners. An additional cleaning activity is the use of an automatic dishwasher or hand washing of dirty dishes.

In addition to cleaning, another important skill is the ability to neaten and organize one's living environment. Although personal choice in the degree of neatness is a consideration, the ability to make one's bed, put away dishes and dirty clothing, or clear off chairs and tables is important, particularly when other people live in the home or are visiting. These skills require one to know where and when to put things away.

Cleaning and Care of Clothing

Students need to learn to change their clothing regularly and frequently. For example, Mark's desire to keep winter clothing on in warm weather results in hygiene problems that make people want to keep their distance. For students who lack judgment in this area, one effective strategy is to make a simple rule that all clothing must be changed after a daily shower.

TABLE 11.2
Sample Reminder Sheet for Where To Store Food Correctly

Where to Put the Food
Put These in the Freezer
Frozen waffles
Frozen orange juice concentrate
Meat (unless you will use it today)
Ice cream
Vegetables (frozen)
French fries
Put These in the Refrigerator
Apple juice in jars and boxes
Butter
Milk
Lettuce, tomato
Cheese
Soda
Jelly
Put These in the Cabinet
Granola bars
Rice
Potatoes
Vegetables in cans
Cookies

Students must also learn to wash soiled clothing. If a washing machine is available within a home, then students can learn to use it on a regular basis. For others, the use of coin-operated machines at a Laundromat will be necessary. In either case, skills in this area include separating clothes into lights and darks, measuring detergent and fabric softener, and selecting correct wash cycles. Finally, students need to learn to fold or hang clothes correctly and put them away.

Telephone Use

Telephones have multiple uses at home. First, telephones are used for personal management activities such as calling for a doctor's appointment or for a repair person. Second, telephones are used to make calls to family and friends. Third, telephones are used to receive incoming calls from others. Finally, telephones are essential during an emergency.

Component skills of telephone use include dialing and speaking clearly into the receiver and sometimes operating an answering machine.

Leisure Activities

A variety of leisure and recreational activities may be completed at home, such as watching television, listening to music, and reading or looking at books and magazines. Additional leisure activities may include hobbies, such as collecting coins, building models, and making crafts. As with other areas of home living, many of these leisure activities involve the use of electronic equipment such as stereos, televisions, and their associated remote controls.

A second major category of leisure activities involves visitors to the home, such as inviting a friend over for dinner or lunch. Although this activity requires many of the skills previously discussed, it also involves making greetings, interacting appropriately, and providing food or beverages. Scheduling and time management, discussed below, are also important to the success of hosting leisure activities at home.

Safety Procedures

Although emergencies rarely arise, individuals must be prepared to handle them quickly when necessary. Generally, emergencies in the home often involve fire, illness, or unwanted visitors. To respond to a fire, a student must be able to dial 911 and report the emergency. For students with little verbal language, adaptations such as a direct emergency line to the fire or police department may be appropriate. In addition, students should learn to use a home fire extinguisher and know how to evacuate the home.

An additional safety issue concerns sudden or extreme illness, especially for individuals who live on their own. Again, the ability to contact emergency personnel is essential.

Knowledge about interacting with strangers is an important safety skill for students in many curriculum areas. In the home, individuals need to know whom they can let in and how to answer the door when a stranger calls.

Unforeseen events are another safety concern for individuals with disabilities. Although such events may not constitute emergencies if tended to, emergencies may result if they are not. Examples of unforeseen events include a clogged drain, ants in the kitchen, or an electrical storm that interrupts electricity service. Although these events occur infrequently, students with disabilities should be taught problem-solving skills to handle such situations. For individuals who live in apartments in urban settings, this will involve calling a landlord or a building manager, whereas those living in rural areas may need to learn to handle unforeseen events themselves.

Time Management and Scheduling Activities

Although self-management skills are addressed elsewhere in this book, it is important to reiterate that all of the above home living activities rely on an individual's ability to manage time and schedule activities effectively. For example, the ability to cook a healthy dinner is not useful unless one remembers to make it. Knowing how to wash clothes is insufficient if a person fails to make time to do so. Consequently, careful scheduling of chores, menus, and other self-management or leisure activities is an important skill area for successful home living. Many individuals remember to plan when a calendar is hung near the telephone. Others may require written menus that can be hung on the refrigerator. Additional planning aides include date books and handheld tape recorders for recording important activities. One of the best ways to teach time management is to keep students on a regular schedule so they can establish routines, such as always getting up at 6:00 A.M. with an alarm clock, always eating dinner at 6:30 P.M., or always doing laundry on Saturday mornings.

Negotiation and Self-Advocacy

Successful home living frequently requires negotiation skills. Consider, for example, the negotiations that need to take place with roommates and others who share the home, such as access to specific spaces within the home, ownership of property within, and distribution of responsibilities for upkeep of the home. Even individuals who live alone may have to negotiate with others, such as neighbors, who may be an important source of support. Some of the negotiation skills students should learn include sharing responsibilities, listening to others' points of view, and stating clearly one's own needs.

Closely related to negotiation is self-advocacy. Frequently, one's actions in a home affect the other people living there. For example, all residents may recognize that a task needs to be completed, but the urgency with which it is initiated may vary from person to person. Negotiation may determine whose turn it is to complete important tasks, and self-advocacy is essential to ensure the fair distribution of responsibilities. Once responsibilities are established, lack of action may become a factor and, again, self-advocacy is important for communicating the need for activities to be completed in a timely manner. Being able to speak for one's self ensures that all residents remain satisfied with their responsibilities.

CONSIDERATIONS FOR ASSESSMENT OF HOME LIVING SKILLS

Assessment of home living skills should provide an instructor with useful information that will assist in instructional decision making. In particular, instructors need to know what activities to teach, what steps need to be practiced, what materials should be incorporated into instruction, and when and where to teach. To determine the answers to these key questions, instructors should use the four approaches to assessment discussed in this section: ecological inventory, task-analytic assessment, assessment of student and family choices, and social validation. These approaches are not mutually exclusive, and all four should be incorporated into an assessment plan.

Ecological Inventory

As discussed in Chapter 1, ecological inventories are an essential element in longitudinal curriculum design (Brown, Branston-McClean, Baumgart, et al., 1979). Within the context of teaching living home skills, instructors must conduct careful inventories of each student's current home environment and potential future environments. For younger students, more emphasis may be placed on teaching skills needed within their current family home. For older students, however, skills needed for potential new homes, such as apartments within likely neighborhoods, should be considered.

The use of ecological inventories is particularly important in identifying activities that may be unique to particular environments. For example, removal of trash from containers will vary from one home to another, particularly because of specific recycling requirements in different areas. Although this is just one activity that is important to the maintenance of a clean and healthy home environment, the variations in ways it can be completed illustrates the need for instructors to conduct careful ecological inventories of current and likely future environments.

When the likely future environment for a student is not known, the instructor and the student's family can conduct inventories of apartments or homes that represent possible options. For example, they could conduct inventories of three apartments that are within the likely geographic area and price range that the student would be likely to afford. By analyzing more than one such apartment or home, instructors can develop variations in activities and incorporate them into instruction using a general case programming strategy (Horner et al., 1982). See Table 11.3 for a list of activities common to most homes but that could be performed differently from home to home. Instructors who are aware of such potential generalization challenges can incorporate a variety of examples into their teaching, such as teaching a student with severe disabilities to use different types of faucets or cabinet latches.

Task-Analytic Assessment

Once important activities are identified via ecological inventories, specific assessment of students' abilities to complete important activities should be conducted. The task-analytic assessment approach recommended by Pancsofar (1986), in which the natural cue for the performance of each step in a task analysis is provided, is recommended for this purpose. In using this approach, the instructor first develops a task analysis of a particular activity identified through an ecological inventory. Next, the instructor identifies the natural cue that sets the occasion for each step in the task analysis. For example, Table 11.4 shows a task analysis of operating a home dishwasher. The natural cues that are identified for each step in this task are also shown in Table 11.4. These natural cues

TABLE 11.3
Common Home Activities that May Be Performed in Multiple Ways

Opening cabinet latches	Operating lock mechanisms, doorknobs, and latches
Turning on water faucets	Turning light switches on and off
Operating microwave ovens	Using alarm clocks
Using stoves and ovens	Opening refrigerators and freezers
Operating television sets	Disposing of garbage
Operating DVD players	Putting on and fastening different articles of clothing
Operating telephones	Obtaining mail from a mailbox
Operating tape or CD players	

TABLE 11.4
Task Analysis of Operating a Dishwasher

Natural Cue	Step in the Task Analysis
Dishwasher door closed	Open dishwasher door
Door opened; soap receptacle in open position	Pour in liquid soap to fill the soap receptacle
Receptacle filled with soap	Close the soap receptacle
Receptacle closed	Close the dishwasher door
Door closed	Set temperature cycle
Cycle button depressed	Turn knob to "on" position to start the wash cycle

describe how the materials and environment look just before the completion of the next step. These cues become clues for the learner to perform the next step (Pancsofar, 1993). The instructor then assesses a student's ability to complete the activity by noting his or her response to the salient natural cues. If the student performs a step correctly, then it is recorded in the assessment data. If, however, the student does not perform a particular step correctly, then the instructor can stop the student and arrange the natural cues for the next step in the activity. This strategy allows the instructor to pinpoint steps that need to be taught, thereby increasing the efficiency of instruction. In addition, the instructor can also assess the type of assistance that is required for a student to perform a step correctly.

Assessment of Student and Family Choices

A third aspect of assessment is the analysis of choices made by both students and their family. Because so many activities that are performed in the home are based on choices (e.g., types of food, music, television programs, clothing), it is essential that the preferences of students be known. Students' choices and preferences clearly need to be balanced with those of the family members who serve as primary advocates for students. For example, a student's preferences for food should be balanced with the parents' interest in a healthy diet for their son or daughter.

Because this is such an important aspect of assessment, we suggest that an ongoing profile of student and parent choices be maintained and updated regularly. Such a profile should include not only a list of the preferences that have been expressed but also those preferences that have been acted upon (Pancsofar, 1993). Table 11.5 shows an example section of a choice profile for a student's home living activities. A number of materials are available that provide structured inventories of choices, including those by Allen (1989) and by Butterworth et al. (1993).

The direct teaching of choice-making skills has been identified as important for people with disabilities (Guess, Benson, & Siegel-Causey, 1985; Schloss, Alper, & Jayne, 1993). This implies not only that students are taught to make choices but also that they have opportunities to exercise choices (Bambara, Koger, Katzer, & Davenport, 1995) and reflect upon their experiences in choice making

TABLE 11.5
Sample Section of Choice Profile

Favorite Things To Eat and Drink	*Preferred Times To Go to Bed and Get Up*
Ice cream for dessert!	Weekdays: up at 7:00 A.M.; in bed by 10:00 P.M.
Chicken casserole and chicken potpie	Weekends: up at 8:30 A.M.; in bed by 11:30 P.M.
Mexican dinners (frozen)	
Apples	*Preferred Times for Chores*
Grilled cheese sandwiches	Clean house on Saturday mornings
Tuna sandwiches	Make bed and clean dishes daily
Apple juice	·Do laundry on Sunday mornings
Favorite Things To Watch on TV	*Preferred Times for Shopping*
Music videos	Saturday afternoons
Half-hour sitcom reruns (*Seinfeld, Friends*)	
Favorite Music	*Favorite People To Invite Over*
Michael Jackson	Rob and Liz (neighbors)
Madonna	Teresa (sister)
Favorite Leisure Time Activities	
Look at *TV Guide*	
Watch TV	
Call friends or family members on the telephone	

(Pancsofar, 1993). Clearly, assessment in this area should be as systematic as the other approaches.

Social Validation

Social validity refers to the degree to which behavior change is socially meaningful as assessed by the reactions of others or by comparison to the performance of others (Wolf, 1978). Increasingly, we recommend a social validation component to assessment, particularly for the development of home living skills.

The importance of assessing social validation is perhaps best illustrated by the following situation. An individual with severe disabilities lived in an apartment by himself with support for specific activities through a supported living program. His support professionals reported to his family that he was doing well and that the support professionals were satisfied with his performance of home activities. A friend of the family, however, stopped by the individual's apartment one afternoon to visit and noted that the bathroom was dirty and smelled. She also noted that there was little healthy food in the refrigerator. Clearly, what the supported living staff felt was acceptable was not acceptable to this close friend. This situation illustrates the importance of social validity in assessment. Questions such as those listed in Table 11.6 should be incorporated into assessment of skill development on an ongoing basis. A negative response to any of these questions would indicate the need for additional instruction or support.

TABLE 11.6
Social Validation Questions

1. Is the student able to plan a healthy diet?
2. Can the student prepare meals in a safe manner?
3. Can the student safely store and handle food?
4. Is the student able to keep the home clean, sanitary, and odor free?
5. Is the student able to operate equipment in the home safely?
6. Can the student occupy his or her free time?
7. Does the student know how to respond in an emergency or when the smoke detector sounds?
8. Does the student know how to call for help using 911?
9. Does the student have any friends with whom to spend free time?
10. Does the student have acceptable personal cleanliness and hygiene?
11. Can the student dress himself or herself?
12. Can the student care for his or her own toileting needs?
13. Can the student manage his or her own time effectively?
14. For any of the above questions to which the answer is "no," what type of instruction or support needs to be provided?

CURRICULUM DESIGN

A general overview of the recommended components of a curriculum for home living activities is provided in the following section. Readers should note that there are several available curriculum materials that contain excellent ideas for home living skills development. Table 11.7 lists four sample curriculum models that contain objectives for home living. We recommend that instructors consult all available material, including those shown in Table 11.7, as they develop IEP objectives for specific students.

In this section, we describe important considerations for addressing the curriculum areas at the elementary, middle, and secondary levels. Readers should be aware that the considerations that we offer in this section are general and that all curricular decisions should be based on the unique profiles of students with the active input of their families. The assessment strategies described above are key approaches to targeting objectives that will be tailored to each student.

One of the major challenges to teaching the skills needed for success within the home is determining when and where to teach these skills. Teachers rarely have regular access to the student's current home as a teaching environment, and families cannot be expected to assume the additional challenge of becoming full-time instructors within their own homes. Consequently, teachers must use creativity at all levels in teaching home living activities within the context of naturally occurring opportunities throughout the day. Table 11.8 illustrates some of the naturally occurring opportunities that could be used for teaching skills related to home living at the elementary, middle, and secondary levels.

TABLE 11.7
Sample of Currently Available Curriculum Materials

	COACH: Choosing Options and Accommodations for Children (Giangreco, Cloninger, & Iverson, 1998)[1]	Syracuse Community-Referenced Curriculum Guide (Ford et al, 1989)[2]	Community-Based Curriculum (Falvey, 1989)[3]	Community Living Skills (Dever, 1988)[4]
Domains/Areas Covered	Communication *Socialization *Personal management *Leisure and recreation Applied academics *Home School Community Vocational	Self-management and home living Vocational *Recreation and leisure General community functioning Functional academics Embedded social, communication, and motor skills	Community *Domestic Recreation Employment Motor Communication Functional academics	*Personal maintenance and development *Homemaking and community life Vocational and leisure Travel

* An asterisk indicates curricular areas directly related to goals and objectives for living at home.

[1] *COACH: Choosing Options and Accommodations for Children,* by M. Giangreco, C. Cloninger, and V. Iverson, 1998, Baltimore: Brookes.

[2] *Syracuse Community-Referenced Curriculum Guide for Students with Moderate and Severe Disabilities: A Guide for Educational Planning for Students with Disabilities* (2nd ed.), by A. Ford, R. Schnorr, L. Meyer, L. Davern, J. Black, and P. Dempsey, 1989, Baltimore: Brookes.

[3] *Community-Based Curriculum: Instructional Strategies for Students with Severe Handicaps,* by M. Falvey, 1989, Baltimore: Brookes.

[4] "Community Living Skills: A Taxonomy," by R. Dever, in *Monograph of the American Association on Mental Retardation 10,* edited by M. J. Begab, 1988, Washington, DC: American Association on Mental Retardation.

Much of what occurs within a home setting happens within the context of routines, such as daily routines, like meal preparation, or weekly routines, like taking out the trash. Each day of the week may have its own routines, depending on an individual's interests and obligations. Although task analysis is an essential aspect of curriculum design, the development of task analyses without considering broader routines may result in important skills being ignored, particularly at the beginning and ending of a task analysis (Brown, Evans, Weed, & Owen, 1987). For example, a task analysis for washing a load of laundry may omit the important first step of determining when this needs to occur (e.g., day of the week, fullness of laundry hamper) or the important last steps of folding the laundry and putting it away. An analysis of routines helps to identify these important aspects of home activities. Stremel et al. (1992) suggest identifying high- and low-preference routines based on each student and his or her family. For example, a high-preference routine for a student might be dinner time, whereas a low-preference routine might be toothbrushing before bedtime. Brown et al. (1987) recommend that analysis of routines include the following steps:

1. Determine the frequency of important routines (e.g., daily, weekly, or less frequently).

2. Determine if other routines can be substituted for those identified (e.g., substituting a different leisure activity for watching a favorite TV program) so that students can learn new routines.

3. Identify the core steps leading to the end result of the routine, recognizing that any given task may result in teaching more than one routine (e.g., preparing the laundry for washing may be one routine, washing it may be another, and folding and putting it away may be a third).

4. Identify extension steps or components of routines, including initiation, preparation, performance and rate of completion monitoring, difficulties in problem solving, and completion.

Table 11.9 shows a sample routine analysis for Mark.

An additional consideration across the span of the educational years is the gradual and subtle shift of teachers from focusing only on teaching students to also putting necessary supports and adaptations into place (Steere, Pancsofar, Wood, & Hecimovic, 1990). Although teachers should attempt to teach important skills throughout students' educational years, some students with severe disabilities may never fully master some activities and may require adaptations and supports to be successful. By determining the needed supports and adaptations and putting them into place prior to the end of educational services, teachers can contribute to students' increased likelihood of success in adulthood.

The remainder of this section addresses considerations at the elementary, middle, and high school levels. Sample objectives are included in Table 11.10 to illustrate how these considerations are included in curriculum design.

Elementary Level

The elementary school years, from approximately ages 5 through 11 years, form the foundation for future learning throughout a student's educational career.

TABLE 11.8
Naturally Occurring Opportunities To Teach Home-Related Skills in School

Skill Areas	Elementary School Years	Middle School Years	Secondary School Years
Planning and Preparing Meals	Making lunch request in cafeteria Setup and cleanup for snack and lunch	Making lunch request to cafeteria Going on community outings for fast food Health class unit on nutrition	Preparing meal for lunch (lunchbox) Working with kitchen staff Reading newspaper food sections for recipes
Self-Care, Bathing, and Hygiene	Taking off jacket or coat in morning on arrival Putting on coat in afternoon for dismissal Dressing aspects of toileting	Cleaning teeth after meals Responding to medical emergencies Washing hands after restroom Using tissues for nose blowing	Using restrooms at community work sites Using restrooms in community restaurants
Cleaning and Care of the Home	Cleaning up after each activity Washing chalkboards Washing desktops Watering plants Care of classroom pets	Cleaning up after meals in cafeteria Organizing materials for cleaning up Changing light bulbs, towels, and other disposable items	Assist in cleaning the chemistry lab Cleaning up work area at community work site
Care and Cleaning of Clothing	Wearing paint smocks during art	Sewing on buttons Sorting objects by color Folding clothes after dressing for gym	Caring for uniforms and other work clothing Using Laundromats
Telephone Use	Calling friends for homework assignments Calling home from school Calling the office from the classroom Dialing 911	Performing receptionist activities in school office Using telephone book to order supplies for a project	Using telephones as part of job duties at community work sites
Leisure Activities in the Home	Cooperative classroom games Reading time Computer games	Performing reading activities Using VCR Using CD player	Engaging in conversations in school cafeteria
Safety Procedures in the Home	Responding to fire drills Helping with first aid in class Pairing up with another student to walk to the nurse	Responding to fire drills Using extension cords Checking for placement of objects near heat sources	Learning safety procedures in roles at community work sites
Time Management and Scheduling	Taking responsibility for homework folder Calendar activities Self-responsibility for homework Stating schedule for day	Following transportation schedules Following class schedules Writing important calendar dates Reading television program schedules	Maintaining a personal calendar Assuming responsibility for following a work schedule
Negotiation and Self-Advocacy	Working with a partner on a classroom assignment Speaking up when others infringe on rights	Working with members of a cooperative group on an outside assignment Speaking up when others infringe on rights	Negotiating with co-workers at a community work site about duties and responsibilities Speaking up when others infringe on right

TABLE 11.9
Sample Routine Analysis for Mark

ROUTINE: *Preparation of simple dinner*
DOMAIN: *Home*
FREQUENCY: *Daily*

Component	Behavior
Initiation	Indicates mealtime or hunger
Preparation	Finds and chooses a meat, vegetable, starch, dessert, and beverage
Core action	Prepares the meal
Monitoring	Checks each item for doneness and seasoning
Rate of completion	Completes preparation of each item at approximately the same time and within a reasonable time frame
Problem solving	If problems occur, such as potatoes boiling over, steps are taken to remedy situation
Completion	Puts food on serving plate and enjoys the meal

TABLE 11.10
Sample IEP Objectives at the Elementary, Middle, and High School Levels

Level	Objective
Elementary	Given two slices of bread, jelly, and peanut butter, the student will correctly make a peanut butter and jelly sandwich, without assistance, for 3 consecutive opportunities.
Middle School	During the preparation for gym class, the student will change into her gym clothes without assistance on 5 consecutive opportunities.
High School	Given a weekly menu planner, the student will develop a written menu for each meal of the week. In addition, the student will make a checkmark next to those items for which he needs to shop. The completeness and accuracy of the menu planner will be assessed by his parents. Criterion will be met when 3 consecutive menu planners are completed to the parents' satisfaction.

Curriculum planning during this time, therefore, is a multifaceted set of activities that enables the teacher to prepare a student for later learning experiences. Many factors affect the planning of appropriate goals and objectives for a student at a given point in time. Teachers are, in most cases, responsible for selecting curriculum materials that can be used with relative ease to meet the instructional needs of their students. The purpose of this section is not to describe available curriculum materials and models, as that has been done elsewhere (Snell, 1993; Spooner & Test, 1994), but to provide a conceptual framework that teachers can use in selecting goals and objectives.

Factors to consider within the context of this conceptual framework include the student's present and future living circumstances, the needs of the family, the use of naturally occurring opportunities for instruction, the age appropriateness of skills, and the introduction of choice making and its consequences.

Brown, Branston, Hamre-Nietupski, et al. (1979) refer to the necessity of identifying a student's current and future environments to ensure that the goals and objectives selected are functional and relevant to that student's life. For a child living at home, the current environment is obvious, but potential future living environments may not be so clear. Will the child live with his or her family after high school or in a supported or independent living arrangement in the community? During the elementary years, this question may not be easily answered, but it should be considered within the context of providing multiple opportunities to practice skills in a range of naturally occurring situations, conditions, and settings (Brown & Snell, 1993).

During this time, the needs and desires of family members, especially within their own home, are of critical significance because siblings and parents spend more time with the student than anyone else (Giangreco, Cloninger, & Iverson, 1998). Family needs, desires, and aspirations must be identified and prioritized in a respectful, nonjudgmental, and supportive manner (Forest & Pearpoint, 1992). Expectations of parents as teachers should be tempered with the knowledge that most parents work outside the home and barely have enough time to prepare meals, do laundry, and keep up with the cleaning. It is realistic, however, to teach parents specific instructional strategies to help them make the most of naturally occurring opportunities for teaching within their homes.

Selection of individualized educational goals and objectives must also be guided by the concept of chronological age appropriateness (Brown, Branston, Hamre-Nietupski, et al., 1979), which involves assessing the skills, activities, and level of independent performance of chronological age peers. Once a teacher has examined the skills of age peers, he or she can identify the critical elements of a task and decide which, if not all, of the components are appropriate for inclusion in a student's curriculum. For example, what would one expect of a 5-year-old, 8-year-old, or 10-year-old child without a disability in the area of meal planning and preparation? For a 5-year-old, assistance and supervision in spreading peanut butter onto one slice of bread and jelly onto another would be a reasonable expectation. As students grow older, they would be expected to complete the task with increasing independence.

Another important aspect of this conceptual framework is the introduction of choice and the consequences of making choices (Houghton, Bronicki, & Guess, 1987). During the elementary school years, opportunities to teach children about making choices are provided with guidance and supervision from adults. In the home environment, choice is incorporated into many activities, such as choosing what to eat for breakfast or selecting a television program. A student without a disability makes many choices throughout the course of the day, and a student with disabilities should be afforded these same opportunities.

Naturally occurring opportunities, conditions, and settings for teaching should be used to their full advantage, especially when one considers that more and more students with disabilities are included in regular education classes for a major portion of their school day. Teachers need to make every teachable moment count.

Middle School Level

During later elementary years and the beginning of middle school, the focus of the curriculum should shift toward the future needs of students once they are more independent of their families. Preparation for transition from school to adulthood begins for many students at age 14 or younger. Planning during the middle school years, therefore, entails a broader examination of the future potential home environments for students. Students' independent performance of many tasks becomes more of a focus than in previous years, and more complex activity sequences are introduced. An increasing emphasis is placed on the inclusion of more community-based activities and the preparation for life as an adult (Clark, Field, Patton, Brolin, & Sitlington, 1994; Halpern, 1994). All components of the conceptual framework discussed for the elementary school level continue to be considered in curriculum planning at the middle school level. In fact, many of the activities taught in the elementary school years will continue, but with a focus on increasing complexity and independence. For example, the complexity of meal preparation increases from making a simple sandwich to making an entire lunch or learning how to make a simple dinner. In addition, adaptations and supportive environments that allow student participation are designed for students who are not expected to be completely independent.

The partnership between families and teachers must be maintained during the middle school years because this is the time when many parents first begin to think about their children's life after the end of educational services. Teachers can assume the role of supporter and consultant to families during the transition planning process. Likewise, families are essential partners to teachers in identifying important teaching activities that can happen during naturally occurring opportunities within the school.

Secondary Level

At the secondary level, finding time for direct instruction in home living activities becomes a major challenge. At this level, particularly as students approach the end of educational services, they should be spending a major portion of their day in natural community environments, particularly work sites (Wehman, 2001). Teachers, therefore, need to be extremely creative in finding opportunities to teach home living skills within different contexts. For example, as shown in Table 11.8, dressing and grooming skills can be taught within the context of preparing to go to work or gym class. Similarly, lunch planning and preparation can occur as students prepare their own lunch to take to a work site. Finally, students can assume greater responsibility for following a schedule to meet all of their obligations throughout the school day.

A second consideration is that students should have experiences in which they complete more complex activity sequences. For example, students may be expected to plan and prepare their own lunch, or they may clean an entire area at a work site, if appropriate. It is particularly important that these activities be completed with less direct instruction from teachers and that students extend their abilities to follow pictorial or written checklists.

Well-designed classroom activities can augment, but not replace, community-based instruction. For example, menu planning and other similar activities could well be taught within a classroom, particularly during home economics or English classes. In addition, the use of videotapes allows teachers to expose students to different home living skills that may not otherwise be available for teaching. For example, a teacher could videotape different ways of making a telephone call or could use videotapes to demonstrate the use of different types of ranges for cooking. With creativity, teachers can use this type of classroom instruction to expand the range of examples to which students are exposed. Experience and instruction in natural community environments, including students' homes, should be included on a frequent and regular basis and will allow teachers to assess the effectiveness of classroom-based instruction.

At the secondary level, students and their families should be actively involved in transition planning and therefore should be considering carefully the home environments in which students will live after the end of educational services. Some students will remain in their family homes, whereas others may wish to rent or even to purchase their own homes. These decisions will affect students' instruction, and professionals and families must work together to focus on skills that will be needed for future success.

Finally, the continued development of home leisure activities should not be neglected at the secondary level. Secondary-level students with specific areas of interest can develop a number of leisure activities. For example, a student who enjoyed stock car racing subscribed to racing magazines and looked at the pictures. In addition, he watched races on television. The student also worked on scrapbooks of stock car pictures and models of famous cars. By building several leisure activities around an existing area of interest, as in this example, instructors increase the likelihood that students will engage in, and perhaps expand, a range of leisure activities. In addition, building upon areas of interest in a home setting can lead to community-based leisure activities, such as going to the library, joining a club, or attending a sporting event such as a real race.

Mark's IEP

In this section, we provide a sample section of an IEP related to activities needed for success in living at home. This sample IEP was developed for Mark, the 13-year-old student with autism who was profiled at the beginning of this chapter. Mark's IEP for home living activities is shown in Table 11.11.

Mark's IEP is based on him learning more complex activities, such as planning and preparing a meal and following a schedule of daily activities. In addition, Mark will learn to complete current activities with increasing independence. Objectives such as learning how to regulate his home's temperature and how to respond to a home emergency will clearly extend Mark's competence in home living activities. At age 13, Mark has the opportunity to master the necessary skills so that, by the time he leaves school, he is able to perform most activities in the home with far less support.

Additional Considerations

There are several additional considerations for effective instruction in home living activities. First, the selection of environments for teaching is an important consideration. Although some skills related to home living can be taught in a school setting, instruction in natural settings is ideal and essential. Although this presents a major challenge for many educators, a variety of strategies can address it. Some special education programs rent actual apartments that can be used for instruction. Additionally, actual materials and equipment that are found in most homes should be used for instruction in school, such as a microwave oven

TABLE 11.11
Mark's IEP for Home Living Skills

Goal 1.0	**Mark will develop his ability to complete all washing, grooming, and hygiene activities according to a written schedule.**
Objective 1.1	When provided with a written daily schedule with specific times written on it for washing his hands for lunch and changing his clothes before going to his work site, Mark will initiate these activities without additional prompts for 7 consecutive days, within no more than 3 minutes of the time listed on the daily schedule.
Goal 2.0	**Mark will learn to prepare shopping lists and make simple dinners.**
Objective 2.1	When given a preprinted menu template with food categories listed on it, Mark will prepare written menus for two dinners for himself. Each dinner must contain a meat, vegetable, potato or rice, dessert, and a beverage.
Objective 2.2	When provided with a frozen dinner, Mark will correctly read the directions, set the microwave, and cook his meal for 3 different meals over 3 consecutive opportunities.
Goal 3.0	**Mark will learn to respond to home emergencies.**
Objective 3.1	Upon hearing the sound of a home smoke alarm without prior notice, Mark will correctly follow the steps of (a) notifying his parents (or teacher in school) that he hears the alarm and then (b) going outside to the front lawn of his home or school. All steps must be correctly followed within 15 seconds of hearing the alarm over 5 consecutive opportunities at different times of the day. This objective will be taught at the school and generalization will be assessed at his home.
Objective 3.2	Given a home-style telephone, Mark will demonstrate how to call 911 and state his name, address, and the nature of the emergency (e.g., fire, illness). This objective will be accomplished using a simulated situation in which Mark can speak to an instructor via the school telephone. He will have met this objective when 3 new school personnel who do not know him well are able to understand his request for assistance.
Goal 4.0	**Mark will learn to regulate the temperature in his home.**
Objective 4.1	Given photographs of a variety of home thermostats, Mark will correctly state the current temperature on each thermostat over 3 consecutive occasions.
Objective 4.2	When provided with a thermostat in a home or apartment setting, Mark will correctly and accurately set the thermostat as requested by the instructor. He will demonstrate mastery by setting temperatures from 65 to 70 degrees over 3 consecutive sessions.

placed in a central location. Conducting instruction in a real apartment or home can be implemented on a regular basis to assess skill development and generalization of skills learned in school. The key point is that instruction must not rely entirely upon simulations of home living environments, but instead must incorporate real materials and settings. Of course, effective simulations can increase students' exposure to home living activities, particularly if slides or videotapes show the range of environments to which students are expected to generalize.

A second consideration for instruction is that it occur within logical and appropriate contexts. For example, meals should be prepared at mealtimes, and dressing skills should be taught when students are going to gym or changing to go to a community job. This strategy requires instructors to be organized in their scheduling so that activities can be taught within appropriate situations.

A third consideration is the need for close collaboration with families. Family members provide ongoing support within the home and can provide valuable information about skill development in the activities described in this chapter.

Educators should not view home skills development as the sole province of families, however; families should instead be seen as essential partners in the curriculum design and instruction process. The importance of this partnership is highlighted by Szymanski's (1995) description of the importance of home chores in establishing a work ethic and work habits, which are important not only in later employment settings but also in completing necessary activities at home.

A fourth consideration is the need to identify skill areas in which a student may need additional support over time. Although active and systematic instruction in home living skills should continue throughout a student's education, not all students will master all activities necessary for success in living at home. However, as described by Racino and Walker (1993), people with disabilities can live successfully in their own homes if support is provided, and many people aspire to owning their own homes with support from others (O'Brien, 1994). Educators can play a key role in helping to identify the minimal level of support that is necessary for success.

The need for developing strong self-management skills in students must be reiterated. Individuals can be successful in their homes if they are able to manage their time and remember to complete necessary activities. The mastery of self-management skills, as described elsewhere in this book, will have a major impact on successful home living.

Finally, it is important to note that an individual's ability to get along with others in a home setting is another important aspect of success. Even individuals who choose to live with others do not get along with them at all times. Although this issue is addressed in Chapter 7, readers should note the importance of applying the concepts described there to the home setting.

SUMMARY

In this chapter we have described curriculum development for activities necessary for successful home living. Although the home is a place for relaxation and private time, individuals still must perform numerous activities successfully to live as independently as possible. Many home living skills have a direct impact not only on an individual's success in other environments, such as work, but on his or her general health and safety. In this chapter, we have focused on nine key activity areas. Each area requires careful, systematic, and longitudinal instruction for students to master it. In addition, we have described four key approaches to the assessment of home living skills. Finally, we have provided suggestions for the development of a home living curriculum during the elementary, middle, and secondary levels.

As a final consideration in this chapter, we suggest that Szymanski's (1994) assertion that longitudinal and early experiences make a positive impact on transition outcomes is most relevant to the topic of living at home. Skill development that is carefully and systematically structured is more likely to result in generalized and durable skills. Close, collaborative partnerships between educators and family members are essential to this effort and can have a substantial positive impact on the abilities of people with disabilities to live successfully in their future homes.

REFERENCES

Agran, M., Fodor-Davis, J., Moore, S., & Deer, M. (1989). The application of a self-management program on instruction-following skills. *Journal of the Association for Persons with Severe Handicaps, 14,* 147–154.

Allen, W. (1989). *Read my lips: It's my choice.* St. Paul, MN: Governor's Planning Council on Developmental Disabilities.

Bambara, L., Koger, F., Katzer, T., & Davenport, T. (1995). Embedding choice in the context of daily living routines: An experimental case study. *Journal of the Association for Persons with Severe Handicaps, 20,* 185–195.

Brown, F., Evans, I., Weed, K., & Owen, V. (1987). Delineating functional competencies: A component model. *Journal of the Association for Persons with Severe Handicaps, 12,* 117–124.

Brown, F., & Snell, M. (1993). Meaningful assessment. In M. E. Snell (Ed.), *Instruction of students with severe disabilities* (pp. 61–98). New York: Merrill.

Brown, L., Branston, M. B., Hamre-Nietupski, S., Pumpian, I., Certo, N., & Gruenewald, L. (1979). A strategy for developing chronological-age-appropriate and functional curricular content for severely handicapped adolescents and young adults. *Journal of Special Education, 13,* 81–90.

Brown, L., Branston-McClean, M., Baumgart, D., Vincent, L., Falvey, M., & Schroeder, J. (1979). Using the characteristics of current and subsequent least restrictive environments in the development of curricular content for severely handicapped students. *AAESPH Review, 4,* 407–434.

Butterworth, J., Hagner, D., Heikkinen, B., Farris, S., DeMello, S., & McDonough, K. (1993). *Whole life planning: A guide for organizers and facilitators.* Boston: Institute for Community Inclusion.

Clark, G., Field, S., Patton, J., Brolin, D., & Sitlington, P. (1994). Life skills instruction: A necessary component for all students with disabilities; A position statement of the Division of Career Development and Transition. *Career Development for Exceptional Individuals, 17,* 125–134.

Dever, R. (1988). Community living skills: A taxonomy. In M. J. Begab (Ed.), *Monograph of the American Association on Mental Retardation.* Washington, DC: American Association on Mental Retardation.

Falvey, M. (1989). *Community-based curriculum: Instructional strategies for students with severe handicaps.* Baltimore: Brookes.

Ford, A., Schnorr, R., Meyer, L., Davern, L., Black, J., & Dempsey, P. (1989). *The Syracuse community-referenced curriculum guide for students with moderate and severe disabilities: A guide for educational planning for students with disabilities* (2nd ed.). Baltimore: Brookes.

Forest, M., & Pearpoint, J. (1992). Putting all kids on the MAP. *Educational Leadership, 50*(2), 26–31.

Giangreco, M., Cloninger, C., & Iverson, V. (1998). *COACH: Choosing outcomes and accommodations for children.* Baltimore: Brookes.

Guess, D., Benson, H., & Siegel-Causey, E. (1985). Concepts and issues related to choice-making and autonomy among persons with severe disabilities. *Journal of the Association for Persons with Severe Handicaps, 10,* 79–86.

Halpern, A. (1994). The transition of youth with disabilities to adult life: A position statement of the Division of Career Development and Transition. *Career Development for Exceptional Individuals, 17,* 115–124.

Horner, R. H., Sprague, J., & Wilcox, B. (1982). General case programming for community activities. In B. Wilcox & G. T. Bellamy (Eds.), *Design of high school programs for severely handicapped students* (pp. 61–98). Baltimore: Brookes.

Houghton, J., Bronicki, G., & Guess, D. (1987). Opportunities to express preferences and make choices among students with severe disabilities in classroom settings. *Journal of the Association for Persons with Severe Handicaps, 12,* 18–27.

Howe, J., Horner, R., & Newton, S. (1998). Comparison of supported living and traditional residential services in the state of Oregon. *Mental Retardation, 36,* 1–11.

Hughes, C., & Agran, M. (1993). Teaching persons with severe disabilities to use self-instruction in community settings: An analysis of applications. *Journal of the Association for Persons with Severe Handicaps, 18,* 261–274.

O'Brien, J. (1994). Down stairs that are never your own: Supporting people with developmental disabilities in their own homes. *Mental Retardation, 32,* 1–6.

Pancsofar, E. (1986). Assessing work behavior. In F. R. Rusch (Ed.), *Supported employment issues and strategies* (pp. 93–102). Baltimore: Brookes.

Pancsofar, E. (1993). *Community connections.* Manchester, CT: Communitas.

Racino, J., & Walker, P. (1993). "Whose life is it anyway?": Life planning, choices, and decision making. In J. Racino, P. Walker, S. O'Connor, & S. Taylor (Eds.), *Housing, support, and community: Choices and strategies for adults with disabilities* (pp. 57–80). Baltimore: Brookes.

Schloss, P., Alper, S., & Jayne, D. (1993). Self-determination for persons with disabilities: Choice, risk, and dignity. *Exceptional Children, 60,* 215–225.

Snell, M. (1993). *Instruction of students with severe disabilities* (4th ed.). New York: Merrill.

Spooner, F., & Test, D. (1994). Domestic and community living skills. In E. C. Cipani & F. Spooner (Eds.), *Curricular and instructional approaches for persons with severe disabilities* (pp. 149–183). Boston: Allyn & Bacon.

Steere, D. (1997). *Increasing competence for more variety in adult life: A general case approach* (Innovations, AAMR's Research to Practice Series). Washington, DC: American Association on Mental Retardation.

Steere, D., Pancsofar, E., Wood, R., & Hecimovic, A. (1990). Principles of shared responsibility. *Career Development for Exceptional Individuals,13,* 143–153.

Stremel, K., Matthews, P., Wilson, R., Molden, V., Yates, C., Busbea, B., et al. (1992, December). *Facilitating infant/toddler skills in family–child routines.* Paper presented at the Council for Exceptional Children/Division of Early Childhood International Conference on Children with Special Needs, Washington, DC. (ERIC Document Reproduction Service No. ED353736)

Szymanski, E. (1994). Transition: Life span and life space considerations for empowerment. *Exceptional Children, 60,* 402–410.

Szymanski, E. (1995, September). *Transition from school to adulthood.* Presentation at the Statewide Conference on Transition from School to Work, Montana State University–Billings.

Taylor, S. (1988). Caught in the continuum: A critical analysis of the principle of least restrictive environment. *Journal of the Association for Persons with Severe Handicaps, 13,* 41–53.

Wehman, P. (2001). *Life beyond the classroom: Transition strategies for young people with disabilities* (3rd ed.). Baltimore: Brookes.

Wehmeyer, M., & Bolding, N. (1999). Self-determination across living and working environments: A matched-samples study of adults with mental retardation. *Mental Retardation, 37,* 353–363.

West, M. (2001). Independent living. In P. Wehman (Ed.), *Life beyond the classroom: Transition strategies for young people with disabilities* (3rd ed., pp. 261–274). Baltimore: Brookes.

Wolf, M. (1978). Social validity: The case for subjective information or how applied behavior analysis is finding its heart. *Journal of Applied Behavior Analysis, 11,* 203–214.

CHAPTER 12

Teaching Personal Care and Hygiene Skills

Fred Spooner and Wendy M. Wood

Cleanliness, good health, and the ability to handle one's personal needs such as toileting, eating, and dressing are highly valued in American culture. In many ways, these basic skills are viewed as essential, evidenced by the emphasis placed on personal care and hygiene skills by parents of infants and toddlers (e.g., toileting, independent eating), children ages 5 to 12 (e.g., independent bathing, dressing, toothbrushing), adolescents (e.g., independent personal hygiene, including shaving, menstrual care, deodorant use), to adulthood (e.g., meal preparation, clothing care and maintenance, medication management, nutrition). As children grow, they are expected to become more independent with these basic tasks. The degree to which students with disabilities can acquire these skills will affect their lives in many ways.

The greater one's independence with basic tasks of daily living, the less one will have to depend on others for support (Epps & Myers, 1989; Spooner & Test, 1994). With greater independence comes more choices, more freedom to participate in community settings and activities, and more decision-making control over when, where, and with whom one lives, works, recreates, and otherwise participates in society. Unlike public education services, some adult service organizations are not operating under entitlement mandates (i.e., they are without a public law requiring that all individuals identified with a disability be served regardless of severity or financial means). Therefore, some adult service programs may set limits on who will be served or may establish eligibility criteria that restrict participation of certain individuals (e.g., individuals who are not toilet trained, individuals who cannot eat independently). In other settings, individuals who do not follow a routine of regular bathing and who do not use deodorant may be rejected by peers in social situations or by coworkers in employment settings because they smell bad or are perceived to be dirty. Individuals who can independently eat, toilet, shower and dress, shop for groceries, plan and prepare meals, and work in a real job for real pay (i.e., not sheltered employment) will likely be able to live in community settings with less supervision or support. A general rule might be that the more a person can do without the involvement of another person in a supervisory or assistance role, the more an individual can enact his or her choices.

WHAT SKILLS COMPRISE PERSONAL CARE AND HYGIENE?

Working Americans typically start their day with a quick breakfast, a shower, and a routine of various steps to get ready (e.g., dressing, primping) to leave for the day. Each of these activities includes a subset of activities that must be completed. For example, a quick breakfast might also include taking prescribed medications or vitamins; after showering, an individual will typically need to brush and floss his or her teeth, use mouthwash, dress in clean clothes, and style her or his hair. At some point during the aforementioned routine, many women may want to apply makeup and most men will need to shave. Other daily activities might include meal planning, food storage and disposal, selection of clothing, and laundry and clothing maintenance.

During the day, most individuals eat a midday meal, and use the bathroom and wash their hands several times throughout the day. In the evening after returning from work, individuals typically undress from their work clothes and redress into more comfortable clothes, prepare and eat an evening meal, perform some household chores, enjoy some leisure activities, and end the evening by undressing from evening leisure clothes into bed clothes, brushing and flossing teeth, and washing face and hands before bed. In addition, one may want to check that appropriate clothing is clean and available for the next day. Of course, the sequence varies from person to person (e.g., some people prefer to shower or bathe in the evenings before bed, some individuals' work clothes are just as comfortable for evening leisure clothes, some people do not require hairstyling on a daily basis, and many individuals work on schedules other than 8 A.M. to 5 P.M.).

Although the above daylong scenario has not been tested on a representative sample of adult Americans, the personal care and hygiene tasks listed approximate what would be included in a daily routine for many adult Americans. Based on this assumption, this chapter addresses the topics listed above and other personal care and hygiene tasks that occur less frequently, such as cutting hair, cutting fingernails and toenails, painting fingernails, cleaning ears, and, for women, handling menstrual care and shaving legs and underarms. Instructional strategies and content in this area span across the school years for students ages 5 through 21 years with varying levels of disability. Strategies include provisions for training students to perform skills to full independence and to various levels of partial participation (Baumgart et al., 1982; Ferguson & Baumgart, 1991; Snell, 1993).

The above tasks were listed in an approximate order of when during the day and in what relation to each other they may occur to establish the context of what might be a *typical* person's daily schedule. When planning a program for a particular student, teachers should accommodate the student's situation and preferences.

WHO WILL NEED ASSISTANCE WITH PERSONAL CARE AND HYGIENE?

Almost by definition, most people with special needs will require some assistance in the area of personal hygiene, whether it be a few of the finer, more advanced points of hygiene, like flossing teeth and using mouthwash and picking out seasonally appropriate clothing, or some of the more basic skills, like independent toileting and showering. Because it is likely that students with the most severe deficits will require the most systematic instruction in personal care and hygiene skills over an extended period of time, we now turn to a discussion of this particular group.

Although several different definitions of severe disabilities have been posited in the professional literature (e.g., ABT Associates, 1974; Justin, 1976; Meyer, Peck, & Brown, 1991; Sailor & Haring, 1977; Snell, 1987, 1991), there appear to be two perspectives on the strategies that one uses to formulate a definition. The first perspective is based on a deficit model (e.g., ABT Associates, 1974; Justin, 1976). That is, people with severe disabilities have traditionally been explained by their paucity of skills (e.g., severe intellectual deficits, self-injurious behavior, stereotypic behavior, not toilet trained). In some cases, the litany of problems was so great that an automatic mind-set was formed that people who functioned at such a level could not learn.

A second, more recent, perspective is based on the supports needed to participate in a meaningful lifestyle (e.g., McDonnell, Hardman, McDonnell, & Keifer-O'Donnell, 1995; Meyer et al., 1991; Sailor & Haring, 1977). Sailor and Haring (1977) were probably among the first authors to identify the supports necessary to promote successful community participation based on primary service need. They indicated that if a student's needs were of an academic nature, then referral to a program for students with severe disabilities would be inappropriate. If, on the other hand, the student's needs were assessed to be basic, then placement in a program for students with severe disabilities would be suitable. Meyer et al. (1991) continued to refine the "supports necessary" notion by indicating that

> individuals of all ages . . . require ongoing support in more than one major life activity in order to participate in integrated community settings and to enjoy a quality of life that is available to citizens with fewer or more disabilities. Support may be required for life activities such as mobility, communication, self-care, . . . and self-sufficiency. (p. 19)

The second perspective is the one that clearly identifies people with severe disabilities in a positive light and also continues to suggest that these people will require extensive support, in most cases, to participate in integrated community settings with a lifestyle that is commensurate with their chronological-age peers. These are individuals who, as Brimer (1990) suggests, have a heterogeneity of etiologies. Individuals with severe disabilities likely will not acquire most functional skills such as personal hygiene unless extensive systematic and longitudinal training is implemented. If skills such as independent toileting, dressing, hair washing, menstrual care, and shaving are not part of a person's skill repertoire, then these skills will need to be performed by someone else for the person, thus decreasing the person's independence and self-sufficiency. Skills in the area of personal hygiene are essential building blocks of personal autonomy, giving the person who increasingly masters these skills more freedom and greater personal choice.

DECREASED FOCUS ON CURRICULUM-RELATED RESEARCH

Although curriculum and training of skills related to personal care and hygiene have remained extremely important to persons with severe disabilities, other topics have been featured in recent years in many journals devoted to developmental disabilities. The focus appears to have shifted from curriculum (e.g., leisure recreation, community functional skills) to context and setting (e.g., interactions, integration, and inclusion; Nietupski, Hamre-Nietupski, Curtin, & Shrikanth, 1997). Nietupski et al. (1997) reviewed curricular research in severe disabilities from 1976 to 1995 in six major journals in the field (e.g., *Journal of the Association for Persons with Severe Handicaps, Education and Training in Mental Retardation and Developmental Disabilities,* and *Journal of Applied Behavior Analysis*). Through this 20-year period, the percentage of total articles on curricular research increased from 1976 to 1980 and from 1981 to 1985 but decreased for the next 10 years, from 1986 to 1995. On the other hand, the average annual frequency of articles focusing on interactions, integration, and inclusion and documenting the impact of inclusion on students with disabilities (e.g., Evans, Salisbury, Palombaro, & Goldberg, 1994) and on outcomes for students without disabilities (e.g., Helmstetter, Peck, & Giangreco, 1994) has significantly increased. It would appear that investigators have shifted their focus from creating opportunities through teaching to crafting opportunities through advocacy and alteration of the environment in which educational services are delivered.

Despite this research trend, functional living skills (e.g., personal care and hygiene) are still important to people with severe disabilities and their parents (Westling, 1996). If these skills are not taught to persons with severe disabilities, then they will likely not acquire them. Although current published research is not documenting skill acquisition of functional living skills, issues in this area still need to be explored, such as the use of self-management strategies in training hygiene skills (Garff & Storey, 1998; Pierce & Schreibman, 1994) and the application of prompting procedures in teaching dressing skills (Sewell, Collins, Hemmeter, & Schuster, 1998).

CURRICULUM BASED ON COMPETENT PEERS IN FUTURE ENVIRONMENTS

In this chapter, the personal care and hygiene curriculum is based on activities that are typical for working adults in American culture. By focusing on work-ing adults, we are designing these curricular components around competent individuals (i.e., competent peers; Haring, 1991; Haring, Roger, Lee, Breen, & Gaylord-Ross, 1986; Wolf, 1978) in future environments (Brown, Nietupski, & Hamre-Nietupski, 1976; Polloway, Patton, Smith, & Roderique, 1991; Test & Spooner, 1996; Vincent, Salisbury, Walter, Gruenwald, & Powers, 1980). As such, content is focused on developing personal cure and hygiene skills in the context of a daily routine of the activities necessary for an individual to participate in paid and integrated employment.

TABLE 12.1
Levels of Independence and Related Support Needs and Community Support Options

Total Independence	Independent on Some Tasks, Partial Support Needed on Others	Partial Participation with Support Needed on All Tasks	Full Care Needed
Can live independently in private home or apartment	Can live in community with natural supports from family and friends, case management support, long-term follow-along support through a supported living or employment program, or personal care assistant part-time support	Can live in community with natural supports from family and friends, long-term follow-along support through a supported living program, or personal care assistant part-time support	Can live in community with ongoing support from family and friends, in a supervised apartment program with full-time staff, in a group home, with full-time personal care assistant services, or with in-home nursing care

We do not present content in "cookbook" fashion in this chapter. Rather, we discuss a process of identifying and analyzing the current and future environments of a particular student (i.e., ecological analysis) while also gathering information on a student's individual skills. This is followed by an assessment of the student's skills level in relation to the skills deemed necessary for functioning in the current and future environments (Ysseldyke, Christenson, & Kovaleski, 1994). We then discuss how members of a transdisciplinary team can use this information to formulate an Individualized Educational Program (IEP) that will build the necessary repertoire of personal care and hygiene skills for the student to achieve maximum independence in current and future environments where competent peers live and work. We also examine the process of teaching students with special needs to attain partial independence or partial participation in conjunction with arranged public or natural supports. For these students, the IEP process will involve working with family members of young children and with adult community service agencies for students nearing transition to determine the degree of independence a student can achieve with her or his personal care and hygiene skills. Table 12.1 delineates approximate levels of support available for varying degrees of personal indepedence.

We have provided two longitudinal case studies in this chapter. Both cases begin with each student at age 5 and continue through secondary school. The cases are used to illustrate how teams of concerned educators should work together with parents to focus on current needs and future environments and goals for students with special needs. For the purpose of these case studies, the process of planning for the development of personal care and hygiene skills in the student's IEP is framed by discussions of what skills are (a) important for increasing independence in current environments (effectively serving to reduce the burden on the primary caregivers), (b) important for increasing independence in future environments, and (c) important for enhancing integration with current and future age peers. The first case study is of Sharice, a young girl with severe intellectual disability and physical disability caused by cerebral palsy. The second case study is of Michael, a student with mild to moderate intellectual disability and a difficult home life.

SHARICE

Sharice is a 5-year-old girl scheduled to attend a regular elementary school in the fall. At the request of her parents, she will be served in a regular kindergarten classroom with collaborative support from a special education teacher. Sharice has severe and multiple disabilities, including severe intellectual (IQ = 30) and physical disability. She uses a manual wheelchair for mobility, has good use of her right hand and arm, and has limited use of her left. She can stand for brief periods if supported by another person. Sharice has not yet demonstrated an ability to pull herself up with a handrail, but her physical therapist indicated that she should be capable of this with practice. She has some functional receptive language and uses some one-word utterances. Sharice enjoys being around people, evidenced by her smiles when her sister or her sister's friends include her in their activities. Sharice's older sister, Yolanda, lets Sharice come in her room when Yolanda has friends over because many of her friends appreciate Sharice's friendliness. Yolanda and her friends help Sharice eat, take her for walks around the neighborhood, and help her change clothes.

Sharice is not yet toilet trained even though her doctor says that she is physically capable (i.e., she has bladder and bowel control) of accomplishing this objective. Her mother explained to the two new teachers that Sharice has not been able to access the bathroom at home because the room and the doorway are too small for her wheelchair. Sometimes, she and Sharice's father ask Sharice if she needs to go, and they lift and carry her into the bathroom even when they are uncertain about her indication. Sometimes she goes and sometimes she does not. "Most of the time we keep a diaper on her because we never know when she is going to need to go," Sharice's mother explained.

Recently, however, Sharice and her family moved into a new house. Her mother said that the large bathroom was a big selling point of the house. Sharice's father is installing a wide door that swings into the hallway instead of into the bathroom to allow Sharice to get through the doorway and pull the door closed behind her for privacy—something she has never had. Now she needs to know how and when to respond to her bodily sensations indicating when she needs to go to the bathroom and how to transfer from her wheelchair to the toilet without assistance.

In addition to not being toilet trained, Sharice eats most foods with her fingers. She has not been able to hold a spoon and transfer food from the plate or bowl to her mouth without spilling all or most of the food. She has not learned to use a fork because of poor handgrip. Sharice also needs help to brush her teeth, brush her hair, and get dressed, and her mother provides total assistance with bathing. Sharice's other areas of need involve language and communication, functional reading, and socialization and participation with age peers without disabilities.

MICHAEL

Michael is a 5-year-old boy with moderate intellectual disability (IQ = 45) caused by Down syndrome. Although small in stature, Michael is physically capable and

(*continues*)

strong. He is very vocal about what he wants or needs, although his vocabulary is limited. His preschool teacher says that she suspects he may be somewhat selective in his receptive language in that he seems to have trouble understanding her directions, particularly when she instructs him to change from an activity he likes.

In the area of personal care and hygiene skills, Michael can eat independently with a spoon, although his mother says that she wishes he did not spill so much food. He can dress himself but needs help zipping and snapping his jeans, and he cannot tie his shoes. He is toilet trained, but his mother reports that he still wets his bed two to three times per week. Michael participates in brushing his teeth but is very slow. His mother puts toothpaste on his toothbrush every morning and helps him with brushing. His preschool teacher said that he does not have any pattern established for brushing his teeth and that he seems to move the brush around inside his mouth randomly. Michael does not know how to wash his face without assistance and must be told to wash his hands after each visit to the bathroom.

Michael lives alone with his mother, and his father is not present in his life. His mother works full-time for the local newspaper as a clerical support person and waitresses as a second job on Saturday and Sunday mornings. She says that the extra money is critical because Michael's father does not contribute support for Michael's care. She works from 7:00 A.M. to 3:30 P.M. Monday through Friday at the newspaper office and from 6:30 A.M. to 2:30 P.M. Saturday and Sunday at her waitress job. Michael's grandmother takes care of him until his mother comes home from work. According to his mother, his grandmother has a difficult time "controlling" Michael, so to help "keep him busy," she lets him watch videos or play with his toy cars until his mother gets home from work. His grandmother places very few demands on Michael, but she does have him put his toy cars away after he finishes playing with them and sometimes lets him help her set the dinner table.

Planning for Sharice's Elementary School Years

At the end of Sharice's preschool program for students with disabilities, a meeting was held to facilitate her transition to elementary school. The preschool teacher and occupational therapist whom Sharice was leaving met with the K–5 special education teacher, the regular education kindergarten teachers, the special education coordinator, Sharice, her mother and father, her two sisters, a neighbor who is a friend of the family, a physical therapist, an occupational therapist, and other members of the school transdisciplinary team near the end of the year before Sharice was to enter kindergarten. The team looked at Sharice's current strengths and needs and worked together to determine Sharice's IEP goals for her year in kindergarten. Because Sharice will be served in the regular classroom, the regular education teacher will be the person who has primary contact with Sharice for instruction. In addition to determining goals, the team needed to design an optimum service delivery and support system to enable Sharice to participate as fully as possible in the regular classroom with her age peers and to achieve the goals that are most essential to her current and future needs in the classroom and other environments.

The special education teacher facilitated the meeting and encouraged Sharice's family to talk about goals and objectives they felt would be important for Sharice. The teacher also asked Sharice, her parents, and her older sister to talk about what types of things Sharice liked to do in her free time and what things might be important to her. The special education teacher also initiated planning with the general education teacher and the special services support staff to design the optimum service and support system for Sharice in the general education classroom. The special education teacher asked for members of the IEP team to discuss and prioritize Sharice's needs with regard to the following: (a) current environments, (b) near future environments (for the next 2–4 years), and (c) skills and behaviors that would enhance Sharice's acceptance by her current and future age peers (Fredericks & Brodsky, 1994).

Understandably, some basic needs in personal care and hygiene were discussed by all because improving these skills would enhance Sharice's ability to participate in classroom activities. All agreed that independent toileting was the highest priority, followed by independent eating, hand washing, and toothbrushing. Because this was kindergarten, the general education teacher said that she could very easily include a unit on dental care for her class that would benefit all of her students. At the conclusion of the unit, toothbrushing practice could be moved home with continued practice and monitoring from Sharice's parents and older sister. The occupational therapist was asked to suggest the best way to position Sharice for toothbrushing and set up the task so that Sharice could most easily reach and manipulate the materials (e.g., toothbrush, toothpaste, glass, water faucet, towel). In addition, the general education teacher said that teaching her students to wash their hands after leaving the bathroom and before lunch was a regular activity for her kindergarten students. Correct positioning for Sharice to brush her teeth would also be appropriate for washing her hands and face.

For Sharice to toilet independently, she will initially need the intensive involvement of the special education teacher and the occupational therapist because teaching her this skill will involve having her (a) indicate her need to go to the bathroom, (b) learn the optimal positions for her to wheel her chair up to the toilet, (c) learn to hold on to the handrail and pull herself up, and so forth. Training in this skill will need to be approached in a well-planned sequence with cooperative teaming between the special education teacher and the occupational therapist before her performance of the skill can be transferred to the classroom teacher to support. Additionally, the occupational therapist will visit Sharice's new home to assess the bathroom and give Sharice's father guidance on how best to install the handrail in the bathroom and Sharice's mother advice on how best to assist Sharice in practicing her transfer from her chair to the toilet seat and back again. As Sharice meets objectives of the in-school training, the special education teacher or the occupational therapist will contact Sharice's parents to assist in generalizing her independent toileting skills to her home environment. Working on this difficult skill while Sharice is young takes advantage of her small body weight for lifting and transferring herself and encourages development of the necessary muscle groups early in life. Table 12.2 lists the goals and objectives that the IEP team delineated for Sharice for her year in kindergarten and the service design created to achieve those goals and objectives.

TABLE 12.2

Sharice's Goals and Objectives for Kindergarten

Instructional Goal	Objectives	Person Responsible	Projected Completion Date
1. The student will toilet herself independently.	1.1. During class, lunchroom, and recess activities, Sharice will indicate her need to go to the bathroom by saying, "Bathroom, please," to the teacher or classroom assistant for 95% of the opportunities for 7 consecutive days.	GE teacher and SE teacher	11/1/03
	1.2. When wearing pants with an elastic band, Sharice will slide her outer pants and underpants down around her knees while holding onto the side handrail without assistance for 7 consecutive days.	PT and OT	1/1/04
	1.3. Given a toilet with a side handrail, Sharice will transfer to the toilet seat without assistance for 7 consecutive days.	PT and OT	3/1/04
	1.4. After urinating or defecating, Sharice will wipe herself without assistance for 7 consecutive days.	PT and classroom assistant; OT and SE teacher	3/1/04 4/1/04
2. The student will eat independently.	2.1. Given an adaptive spoon, a bowl of food appropriate for eating with a spoon (e.g., oatmeal, stew, cereal, baked beans, Jell-O), Sharice will eat using a spoon with less than 5% spillage for 5 consecutive days.	OT and classroom assistant	11/15/03
	2.2. Given bite-sized pieces of food on a plate, Sharice will eat 10 out of 10 pieces with a fork on 5 consecutive days.	Classroom assistant and peer tutors	12/15/04
	2.3. Given a plate of food, Sharice will eat using a spoon or a fork with less than 5% spillage for 5 consecutive days.	SE teacher with transfer home to parent	4/1/04
3. The student will wash her hands and face independently.	3.1. At appropriate times during the day, Sharice will wash her hands with 100% accuracy within a 3-minute period for 5 consecutive days.	GE teacher and peer tutors	11/1/03
	3.2. After brushing her teeth, Sharice will wash her face using a washcloth and warm water within a 3-minute period for 5 consecutive days.	SE teacher with transfer home to parent	2/1/04
	3.3. After brushing her teeth, Sharice will wash her face using a washcloth, warm water, and no-tears soap within a 3-minute period for 5 consecutive days.	Parent at home	4/1/04
4. The student will brush her teeth independently.	4.1. Given a toothbrush with an adapted handle and toothpaste in an adapted dispenser, Sharice will put toothpaste on her toothbrush with 95% accuracy for 5 consecutive days.	OT	11/1/03
	4.2. After lunch, Sharice will brush her teeth with 85% accuracy for 5 consecutive days.	SE teacher	2/1/04
	4.3. After breakfast and before bed, Sharice will brush her teeth with 95% accuracy for 5 consecutive days.	Parent with SE teacher in consulting role; home visit initially	4/1/04

Note. GE = general education, SE = special education, PT = physical therapist, OT = occupational therapist.

Arranging Peer Tutoring for Sharice

Because Sharice is receiving her education in a general education classroom, the team must devise effective and efficient ways to unobtrusively provide instruction to Sharice in the skills she needs within the general education classroom routine. The team decides that, after some initial training by the general education teacher, some of Sharice's classmates can work with her as peer tutors on washing her hands at the natural times of the day, namely, before lunch, in the bathroom, after art class, and before the afternoon snack. Those students in class who show an interest in helping Sharice (e.g., those who ask the teacher if they can push Sharice's wheelchair, help her eat her lunch, or otherwise assist her during the school day) will be selected as peer tutors. Because it is natural for all kindergartners to wash their hands, Sharice will be put in a group with the peer tutors for hand washing. The general education teacher will work with Sharice on learning to wash her hands within this group. The general education teacher plans to let the students' natural curiosity about Sharice and their interest in helping her lead them through observing the teacher or classroom assistant working with her and then volunteering to help her themselves. After allowing the peer tutors to observe Sharice's instruction, the general education teacher gradually will let the peer tutors play a role in Sharice's instruction. The special education teacher developed a simple task analysis in the form of a peer tutor guide sheet (see Figure 12.1).

During Sharice's kindergarten year, at her annual IEP meeting, her team met to plan what goals and objectives should be addressed for the next several years in school in an attempt to design her IEP to maximize her independence in current and future environments and to enhance her participation with her age peers. The list in Table 12.3 represents the skills to be taught and the approximate schedule for these to be included across Sharice's elementary school years.

Planning for Michael's Elementary School Years

Prior to his enrollment in kindergarten, Michael attended a preschool program for 3 days each week. The month before he transitioned out of preschool, Michael, his mother, his preschool teachers, and the district special education coordinator met to discuss what goals and objectives would be important for Michael to have on his IEP for the coming year and what goals might be appropriate for the next several years. Because the team was looking at what skills Michael would need in future environments, it was apparent that all goals could not be accomplished in any one year.

The team worked with Michael's mother to identify her needs for Michael. Because she was a single parent to a child with a disability and worked two jobs, she did not have much assistance in caring for Michael and had even less free time for herself or quality time with Michael. She said that getting Michael ready for school in the morning was a real challenge, and, because of her early morning work schedule, she wished Michael could do more to get himself ready for school in the morning. The team decided that the special education teacher would analyze the activities required for Michael to get ready to leave for school in the morning and begin instructional planning and implementation to increase Michael's independence in a morning "get ready for school" routine. Table 12.4

HAND WASHING

Peer tutor instructions: In the box, write

    I if she does a step by herself (*independent*)

    H if you *help* her do a given step

Task Steps

To begin the task, please say to Sharice, "Let's wash our hands." Then, wait about 4 seconds to allow her time to complete the first step herself. If she does not, then prompt her on the first step. Continue through the steps below using the same procedure of waiting, then prompting.

Task Steps	Tutoring Session Date								
1. Pull up under the sink.									
2. Turn on the cold water (rotate handle 1/4).									
3. Turn on the hot water (rotate handle 1/4).									
4. Wet both hands.									
5. Rub hands on soap.									
6. Rub hands together.									
7. Rinse hands in water.									
8. Turn off cold water.									
9. Turn off hot water.									
10. Dry hands with paper towel.									
11. Put paper towel in trash.									
Number of steps correct									
Percentage of task correct									

FIGURE 12.1. Peer tutor task analysis for hand washing.

shows a tentative plan for addressing personal care and hygiene skills during Michael's elementary school years. This plan was developed based on an analysis of Michael's home life and his mother's schedule.

Making Personal Care and Hygiene Skills Development Meaningful

For the most part, personal care and hygiene competence needs to be evident in the home setting (e.g., bathing, brushing teeth, dressing, hair care) and other settings outside of the classroom (e.g., the work setting, public restrooms). Although skills training can be carried out in the school setting, provisions must be made

TABLE 12.3
Sharice's Elementary School Goals in Personal Care and Hygiene

Goals for K–2nd Grade	Goals for 3rd–4th Grade	Goals for 5th Grade
Goals for Kindergarten	**Goals for 3rd Grade**	**Goals for 5th Grade**
IST on: *Walking to alarm. Transferring from bed to wheelchair. Independent toileting. Washing hands and face. Eating using a spoon and fork. Brushing teeth independently.*	*Extend and Maintain Morning Routine* 1. GTH waking to alarm. 2. *IST on transferring from bed to chair—PP.* 3. Independent toileting. 4. Eating breakfast independently. 5. Go to bathroom for brushing teeth, *washing face,* washing hands. 6. *IST on putting on a pullover shirt, at home—dressing with PP.* 7. GTH combing hair. 8. *Putting bathroom materials away.* 9. GTH putting on coat to leave for school. 10. *Leaving for bus stop.*	*Maintain Morning Routine and Improve Proficiency* Maintain 1, 2, 3, 4, 5, 7. 6. GTH putting on shirt and pants, remainder dressing—PP. 8. GTH putting on a hair band. 9. Leave for bus stop. *Build Evening Routine* 1. *IST on selecting outfit for next day.* 2. *CWP on training bathing skills.* 3. *CWP dressing for bed.* 4. Brushing teeth.
Goals for 1st Grade		
IST on: Improving proficiency with toileting. Improving proficiency with eating skills. Improving proficiency brushing teeth. GTH of independent toileting skills, independent eating, hand and face washing across three target environments (home, fast-food restaurant, grandmother's house). *IST on combing hair. IST on putting on and taking off coat.*	**Goals for 4th Grade** 1, 3, 4, 5, 7 maintain skills. 2. GTH transferring from bed to chair. 6. Dressing: *In-school training on putting on jeans; GTH pullover shirt to home; remainder dressing—PP.* 8. *IST putting on a hair band.* 9. *Leaving for bus stop.*	
Goals for 2nd Grade		
Build Morning Routine 1. GTH waking to alarm. 2. GTH independent toileting. 3. GTH eating breakfast independently. 4. Go to bathroom for brushing teeth, washing face and hands, combing hair (mother will assist and/or supervise for remainder of morning routine—dressing, etc.). 5. *Leaving for bus stop.*		

Note. PP = partial participation; IST = in-school training; GTH = generalize to home; CWP = consultation with parent; *italicized print* = new skills.

for generalizing the learned skills to their more natural settings. In Sharice's and Michael's cases, the school staff would work on skills development in the school setting and then work with Sharice's parents and Michael's mother to generalize those skills to the home setting in a routine that would fit their particular schedule and activities. In almost all cases, in-school training followed by generalization to the home setting would require a good consultative effort between the school staff and the student's family. Tables 12.3 and 12.4 include tentative plans

TABLE 12.4

Michael's Elementary School Goals in Personal Care and Hygiene

Goals for K–2nd Grade	Goals for 3rd–4th Grade	Goals for 5th Grade
Goals for Kindergarten	**Goals for 3rd Grade**	**Goals for 5th Grade**
IST on:	*Extend and Maintain Morning Routine*	*Maintain Morning Routine and Improve Proficiency*
Waking to alarm.	1. Wake to alarm.	1. Wake to alarm.
Independent toileting.	2. Go to bathroom.	2. Go to bathroom.
Washing hands and face.	3. *Fixing breakfast (PP:*	3. Go to kitchen:
Eating using a fork.	*Get glass from cabinet.*	Get glass from cabinet.
Brushing teeth in reasonable time frame.	*Get orange juice from refrigerator.*	Get orange juice from refrigerator.
Buttoning and zipping.	*Pour juice in glass.*	Pour juice in glass.
	Carry to seat at table.	Carry to seat at table.
Goals for 1st Grade	*Eat cereal prepared by mother.*	Eat cereal prepared by mother.
CWP on training bathing skills.	*Wipe mouth with napkin.*	Wipe mouth with napkin.
CWP on training washing hair, IST on combing wet hair and hanging up towel.	4. Go to bathroom for brushing teeth, *washing face,* washing hands.	Carry dishes to sink after finished.
*CWP on training independent nighttime toileting.**	5. *Getting dressed.*	4. Go to bathroom for brushing teeth, washing face and hands, combing hair, and putting materials away.
IST on dressing independently.	6. *Picking up packed lunch for school.*	5. Getting dressed.
	7. *Leaving for bus stop.*	6. Picking up packed lunch for school.
Goals for 2nd Grade		*Build Evening Routine*
Build a Morning Routine	**Goals for 4th Grade**	1. Select outfit for next day.
1. CWP waking to alarm.	Maintaining 1, 2, 3 above and adding into 4):	2. Packing a lunch.
2. Independent toileting	*Combing hair.*	3. Taking bath.
3. GTH eating breakfast using a fork. *IST on putting dishes in sink.*	*Putting materials away— toothbrush; cap on toothpaste tube; washcloth on hook; comb in drawer; soap in soap dish*	4. Dressing for bed.
4. GTH go to bathroom for brushing teeth, washing hands.	5. *Getting dressed.*	5. Brushing teeth.
(Mother will assist with tasks for remainder of morning routine)	6. *Picking up packed lunch for school.*	6. Going to the bathroom.
5. *Getting dressed.*	7. *Leaving for bus stop.*	7. Getting into bed.
6. *Picking up packed lunch for school.*		
7. *Leaving for bus stop.*		

Note. PP = partial participation; IST = in-school training; GTH = generalize to home; CWP = consultation with parent; *italicized print* = new skills.

*See references Azrin, Sneed, and Foxx (1973); Baller (1975).

for developing a morning routine for Sharice (Table 12.3) and Michael (Table 12.4), including provisions for in-school training (IST), followed by a process to generalize the skills to the home setting (GTH) and notations about when a consultation with parent (CWP) might be needed for training and generalization to be successful.

Transferring skills learned in school to home and community settings is a generalization issue, in most cases stimulus generalization (i.e., the need for skills to be performed in other settings and under different conditions) and maintenance (i.e., the need for skills to be maintained over time even after training conditions have been discontinued). For some students, the transfer of skills to home and community may occur without any special intervention. Other students may require very specific strategies, several of which are discussed later in this chapter. In this section, we will discuss some practical ideas to facilitate the generalization of personal care and hygiene skills from the school to home and community settings.

Transferring skills from school to home presents a challenge to teachers for several reasons. The setting and antecedent stimuli found in the home will differ from those in the school. Specifically, the appearance of the setting and the equipment and materials may be different. For example, the family bathroom may have a medicine cabinet with a mirror or a vanity with drawers where toiletry supplies are stored, whereas the school bathroom does not. The washing machine in the home economics classroom may be different from the one in the student's home and even more dissimilar than that at the neighborhood coin-operated Laundromat. Changes in the setting and the way the materials are accessed may cause some differences in the sequence of steps in a training task analysis. In addition, the way a teacher sets up a task, starts a task, or prompts the student within a task may differ from the way a parent presents the task to the student in the home setting. Although these differences may not cause problems for some students, they may be the determining factors that prevent other students from generalizing skills. There are several ways that generalization of personal care and hygiene skills have been addressed that have proven effective.

Train Personal Care and Hygiene Skills in Routines

Arranging a stream of skills into a consistent sequence keeps the student from knowing how to do several different activities, but being unsure about which to do first, second, and so on. By arranging the different morning "get ready for school" activities into a consistent routine, the teacher creates a higher likelihood that the end of one activity will cue the student to start the next one. If training is successful, the student will be more capable of completing the various activities independently (e.g., student will not need to be prompted after completion of each task to start the next task and will be more likely to maintain the skills over time; Alberto & Troutman, 1995; Lucyshyn, Albin, & Nixon, 1997). In this regard, students with disabilities may be able to maintain their level of independence following an entire routine more successfully than he or she might be able to do with separate and disconnected skills.

Include Students and Parents in Planning the Instruction

If parents and student are involved in *selecting* specific skills for instruction, they will be more likely to become actively involved in supporting the student's progress on the skills. Further, it makes sense to include the parent when developing IEP goals and objectives so that they can collaborate on how to plan for the skills' transference to the home setting. When the parent is involved in planning, it is useful to write a specific objective about transferring the skills to the home setting with the parent responsible for some degree of instruction or skill assessment.

Include Students in Implementing the Instruction

Self-management techniques can be used to promote generalization. Students can be taught to use a pictorial task analysis to help them remember the sequence of certain tasks or tasks steps (Wacker & Berg, 1983). The home setting might be used for the pictures (e.g., the student brushing her teeth, washing her face, and brushing her hair in the bathroom at her house; the student getting dressed in her room at her house) in the pictorial task list. The home pictures can be used to signal the task in both home and school settings. The student can make a checkmark next to the picture to indicate task completion.

Plan Instruction To Facilitate Generalization

Ecological assessment or functional assessment techniques can be used for gathering information on student personal care and hygiene needs. When conducting an ecological assessment of a student's home setting, the teacher should include a careful analysis of the family routine and a description of the student's home setting (e.g., materials used) and gather information on how the parent interacts with the student in the context of the personal care and hygiene tasks that are targeted for instruction. The instructional design should incorporate as much of this information as possible.

Train in Natural Settings

Teachers should try to plan a home visit so the student can practice the skills in the real setting. Such a visit helps the teacher incorporate details into the instruction that might facilitate generalization and offers parents an opportunity to see how the teacher interacts with the student for training. For skills with applications to additional settings, such as hand washing and toileting, the teacher can plan practice sessions in other appropriate places, such as public restrooms.

Train Parents on Instructional Techniques

Teachers who are using a task analysis to teach the steps of a task should share the task analysis with the parents when communicating with them about the student's ability to do the task. If a teacher writes the steps in the task analysis in the form of verbal prompts, he or she can demonstrate or explain this strategy to the parents. If the student will be following a pictorial task list or task analysis, the teacher can inform the parents about what is expected of the student. A teacher can work with parents so that they present the activities or tasks in ways that are similar to how he or she has presented them at school. Some parents may need help to fade their prompts or to give less direct prompts.

Use a General Case Programming Strategy

Teachers should look for commonalities across settings and materials when devising instructional strategies. For example, a teacher could analyze similarities and differences among various washing machines and dryers and organize teaching around those features that are most common between machines. In an early study, Sprague and Horner (1984) looked at various types of vending machines and determined which of the features were the most typical across the different machines. They then designed their instruction to teach those features that were most typical. Students trained using these common features were able to operate a variety of vending machines across different settings.

Program Common Stimuli

Another teaching strategy is to plan to use similar supplies and equipment across settings, such as using a plastic box to keep toiletry supplies like a toothbrush, toothpaste, mouthwash, floss, and washcloth together in both the school and home settings. Likewise, when teaching students to set and wake up with an alarm clock, the teacher should make sure the clocks used for instruction in the classroom are the same as the clocks the students will use at home.

Send Video Postcards Home to Parents

Short video clips of students performing tasks in school can be sent home to show parents how their son or daughter performs the tasks or sequence of tasks in the school setting. The teacher might want to include with the videotape a list of pointers to help parents present the task in similar fashion (e.g., how to prompt the child to begin the task, how to set up the task, how to allow a reasonable wait time for the student to perform the task before giving a prompt). Obvious first steps for implementing this idea include finding out how many households have a VCR available and getting parent and student permission before doing any taping. There are some personal care and hygiene tasks that would not be appropriate for taping under any circumstances because of their need for privacy (e.g., dressing, toileting, bathing). Other tasks such as brushing teeth, brushing hair, and washing face and hands can be easily videotaped for parents to see. The videotape can share student successes with parents or caregivers, offer demonstration of how the task is set up for the student, serve as a reinforcer for students, and serve as a self-model for students.

Researchers and practitioners have been working on ways to improve the link between school instruction and home practice. Sowers and Powers (1995) conducted a study in which the parents of two students and the group home assistant of one student were trained to increase their students' independence and participation in home and community settings through the activity of eating in a fast-food restaurant. In-school training of the parents, group home assistant, and the students was held in a conference room in the school. Training also consisted of practice in fast-food restaurants in the community. After training was provided, all three students demonstrated higher levels of participation and independence in the community restaurant settings. In another study, the authors used video self-modeling to improve parents' interactions with children with developmental disabilities (Reamer, Brady, & Hawkins, 1998). The videotaping was used to alter parental assistance patterns during self-care and social play activities. The results indicated that the video intervention package did help parents provide less directive prompts. Additionally, the authors observed that parents' newly trained interaction patterns generalized to other tasks and into new settings. Garff and Storey (1998) taught three individuals to use self-management techniques in supported employment settings to help them take care of some important hygiene activities. The intervention involved the development and use of a checklist (i.e., task analysis) for each individual's particular hygiene issue, instruction on the steps for each individual, use of positive reinforcement and feedback, and instruction for the individuals in delivering their own reinforcement. The results demonstrated that the self-management strategies helped each individual improve his or her performance of personal hygiene skills in the job setting.

Finally, in an example of a child having trouble completing personal care and hygiene tasks because of interfering behaviors, Clarke, Dunlap, and Vaughn (1999) used a positive behavior support intervention to improve a child with Asperger syndrome's willingness and ability to complete a daily morning routine. The researchers first conducted a functional assessment that included observations of the student and family in the home setting and interviews with selected family members and the student. The functional assessment procedure delineated the sequence and events in the family's morning routine; the places, times, and conditions in which problems occurred; and the activities that the student enjoyed that could be used as reinforcers. The morning routine consisted of (a) getting out of bed; (b) going to the bathroom; (c) changing from pajamas to underwear; (d) putting on pants, shirt, socks, and shoes; (e) brushing hair; and (f) walking to the breakfast table in the kitchen. The intervention involved the use of a visual task chart with pictures and words to indicate the tasks in the sequence; some accommodations were made to the clothing and dressing tasks, and a reinforcement strategy was implemented. The researchers conducted the assessment and then trained the mother to act as the primary intervention agent in this study.

It is important to remember that with regard to personal care and hygiene skills, generalization is important to consider from the beginning of the instruction; for some students, it will need to be specifically targeted. Finally, teachers are reminded that although it may entail more work to communicate and collaborate with parents, in the long run such collaboration may be the most important factor for a student to become independent enough to live in the community with a minimum level of outside support.

Planning for Middle School Years

In middle school, Sharice and Michael have a new set of personal care and hygiene needs. With adolescence comes puberty and a host of changes in students' interests and bodies. If one were to examine a group of competent adolescent peers, one would find students dealing with changes such as breast development and the onset of menstruation for girls, facial and chest hair on boys, underarm and pubic hair, skin problems, more active sweat glands, a developing interest in sex, and the emotional upheaval that accompanies all of this change. Social relationships with peers become the dominant focus of adolescents' universe. Personal care and hygiene skills become critical for a student to be successful in developing secure social relationships with age peers. The biological changes and needs for students with disabilities are no different from those for students without disabilities.

Physical attractiveness becomes very important (near life or death) for adolescents, increasing the importance of exercise and nutrition. For students with physical impairments, weight gain may become an issue because their ability to burn calories may be hindered by their impaired mobility. Weight gain can further hinder mobility for students with physical disabilities, thereby impeding their ability to be independent at various personal care and hygiene tasks. Students with physical disabilities need to develop patterns early in life (during elementary school) that include practicing good nutrition and regular exercise to avoid complicating their physical limitations with weight gain. Table 12.5 delineates what

TABLE 12.5

Personal Care and Hygiene Skills To Be Addressed During Sharice's Middle School Years

Skill Area	Subskills or Related Skills	Training (T), Maintenance (M), and Generalization (G) Concerns
Menstrual care	1. Feeling dampness in pants or recognizing menstrual soiling 2. Pulling pants down and up 3. Transferring to and from toilet 4. Wiping 5. Using sanitary napkin	1. (T) Selection of a menstrual care product best suited for Sharice 2. (T, M) Gross motor range of motion for reaching 3. (T, M) Fine motor skills for manipulating sanitary napkins or tampons 4. (G) Consistency of menstrual care product used 5. (G) Physical placement of materials in home setting 6. (G) Access to materials in community settings
Use of deodorant	Removing a lid from deodorant container (a certain container type, such as round screw-off top or oval pull-off top, may facilitate Sharice's independence with this task)	1. (T) Selection of product for Sharice 2. (T, M) Fine motor skills for manipulating deodorant container 3. (T, M) Gross motor range of motion for reaching and holding applicator under both arms 4. (G) Physical placement of materials in home setting
Nutrition and weight control	1. Selecting nutritious, low-calorie foods 2. Independent eating 3. Physical exercise	1. (T, M) Best if patterns are started and maintained early 2. (T) Will require developing a controlled repetoire of food choices 3. (T, M) Will depend on close collaboration with parents from beginning throughout program
Developing and maintaining a personal look	1. Selecting clothes (fit, style, season, laundering instructions, cost, maintenance) 2. Independent dressing 3. Using accessories if desired 4. Applying makeup if desired	1. (T, M) Will depend on close collaboration with parents 2. (T, M) Fine motor skills for manipulating deodorant container 3. (T, M) Gross motor range of motion for reaching 4. (G) School staff will need to inform parents of how Sharice can make clothing selections *Note.* If by middle school, Sharice is unable to make clothing selections, it may be beneficial to work with her parents on selecting clothes and accessories for her that are compatible with her competent age peers.
Shaving legs and underarms	—	1. (T, M) Fine motor skills for manipulating electric shaver 2. (T, M) Gross motor range of motion for reaching all areas of both legs and underarms

personal care and hygiene skills might be included for Sharice as she moves through her middle school years. All skills should be taught within the context of expanding and maintaining morning and evening routines.

Planning for Michael's middle school years will involve adding a few activities into his morning and evening routines. Considering recent information about preventing gum disease (American Dental Association, 2001), adding mouthwash use to the morning bathroom routine immediately following toothbrushing would be valuable. Using deodorant fits logically in the morning bathroom sequence right after washing face and hands (see Table 12.4, 5th grade, number 4). After completing the task, Michael would return the deodorant top to the deodorant container and then put this and his other morning bathroom materials (e.g., toothbrush, toothpaste, comb) away. When training these skills and routines in the classroom, teachers should plan ahead for generalization by using materials that are the same or similar to what students have at home. In addition, generalization will be more efficient if the storage and retrieval of materials can be similar to that in the home. For example, because it is unlikely that the school bathroom setting can be remodeled to approximate the home bathroom settings for all students, the transference of the skill sequence to home could be facilitated if students are taught to return all of their materials to a shoe box or plastic storage box to then be put in one specific place. A similar box can be incorporated into the home routine, thereby keeping an important antecedent stimulus consistent in both settings, thereby improving the likelihood of the students' skills generalizing to the home setting.

Accommodating Personal Style and Cultural Diversity

When given an opportunity, people like to have choices about how they look. To a large degree, style decisions for individuals with disabilities have often been made according to the convenience and style preference of the caregiver, not the individual who would be wearing the style. The personal style of a student with disabilities should not be overlooked for the preference or convenience of the caregiver but rather accommodated as much as possible. Clothing selection, clothing fit, color preference, hairstyle, accessories or jewelry use, and makeup use (for girls) are all matters of personal style that should be accommodated for people with disabilities. A certain look may enhance a student's acceptance and inclusion with his or her valued age peers, or it may be a way for the student to express his or her individuality.

Students usually begin to make style choices during their middle school years. Many of their selections are inevitably influenced by styles put forth in the media and by trends that develop among peers. Parents of adolescents and preadolescents with disabilities can monitor style trends so that they can assist their child in choosing more age-appropriate clothes and accessories by watching competent age peers in the schools and teenagers portrayed in the media.

Attention to style is very important to students' fitting in with their age peers. For this reason, attending to personal style preferences of students with disabilities is just as important, perhaps even more so, as it is for students without disabilities. Issues such as affordability and the ability of the student to maintain the look independently are fair considerations, just as they would be for anyone.

In addition to personal choice, many students have preferences that are related to their cultural or ethnic background. America offers a rich diversity of different races, cultures, and ethnic backgrounds, and over the past 10 to 20 years, there has been a renewed interest in cultural heritage and dress that should be considered and even encouraged when supporting a student's desire to develop a personal look.

Facilitating Age-Appropriate Dress

In cases where students are not interested in making personal choices or if their choices are grossly out of sync with their competent age peers, it may be necessary for the teacher to offer some guidance to parents so that they might assist their teenage sons and daughters in making more appropriate clothing selections. Many special education professionals have had teenage students with disabilities come to school dressed in clothing or equipped with accessories that are more appropriate for students in their early elementary school years (e.g., Barney lunch boxes, Barbie doll sweatshirts, Mickey Mouse notebooks, immature hairstyles). Some parents (and some professionals) tend to treat their sons and daughters as if they are much younger than they are. As services move toward inclusive education, it is critical that teachers help students with disabilities and their parents recognize the importance of chronologically age-appropriate dress. Teachers often struggle with the awkwardness of how to tell parents that they are dressing their teenager in baby clothes. A possible way to address this is to prepare one-page flyers to go home to parents monthly or every other month to address various issues pertaining to growing up. Figure 12.2 offers an example of a flyer that teachers might use to communicate one of these potentially awkward issues to parents. The flyer is designed to be proactive (i.e., giving information to all of the parents of the students in a class hoping to avoid fashion mistakes from occurring). Other topics that may be addressed with a send-home flyer include use of deodorant, "Down with Baby Talk, Up with Teen Talk," and conversational topics for teens (e.g., movies, sports, music). Sending home a flyer gets the message across while avoiding an uncomfortable confrontation with parents who might react defensively if approached directly.

Planning for Adulthood: Transition from School to Adult Life

Personal care and hygiene skills that would be desirable to address in high school for Sharice (or other female students at this age) might include learning to dress in clothes appropriate for work, revising morning and evening routines to accommodate work schedules, preparing simple meals (e.g., frozen waffles, instant oatmeal, cereal with milk, lunchmeat sandwich, microwave entrees, frozen vegetables, warming up leftovers) and storing different food types, cleaning up after meals, and so on. However, teachers will need to devote some time to the maintainance and generalization of the skills learned during elementary and middle school years.

Looking toward Sharice's long-term needs (and those of other students with the most severe disabilities), it seems likely that she will need support on a daily basis for some of the tasks for which she may only achieve a level of partial participation (e.g., medication management, first aid, grocery shopping, banking, house cleaning, clothes shopping, laundry). In addition, she will inevitably undergo changes during her life that may cause disruptions to her daily living routines. These disruptions might be caused by changes in her environment (e.g., moving to a new setting with different conditions), changes in her schedule (e.g., a supported employment opportunity that necessitates a different time to leave and return to her home or apartment), emotional upheaval (e.g., death of a parent), or changes in support personnel involving a caregiver (e.g., parent or relative, group home, personal care provider). For each of these changes in her life, Sharice will need for her

Hey Mommy and Daddy
(Ooops!! No more baby talk)
Hey, Mom and Dad

Your son or daughter is growing up.
Help him or her to blend in to the scene
here at middle school.
As a middle school student, your son or daughter
needs to wear clothes that teenagers wear.

No more Barney!

No more Barbie!

No more Mickey Mouse!

If you need help knowing what kinds of clothes
teenagers are wearing,
watch their classmates, watch MTV, or
ask a teenager in your neighborhood.

FIGURE 12.2. Sample flyer to keep parents informed of their children's growing up.

support systems (e.g., family, friends, or public community service system) to assist her in adjusting to the change or disruption. Sharice's particular supports and services will be designed based on a personal futures plan (Mount, 1987; Vandercook & York, 1990) that will be initiated before Sharice graduates, in conjunction with her individual transition plan (ITP), and will continue for as long as needed to support Sharice's personal goals as an adult in the community.

Looking toward Michael's adulthood, it seems that, given his abilities and anticipated improvements in community support services, by the time Michael graduates, he could participate in a community support service system to help him set up house in a shared apartment for which he will choose his roommate. Given this situation for Michael, supported living personnel will work with supported employment staff, Michael's friends, and his family to help him adjust his morning and evening routines to fit his new independent life and job in the community. Between family, friends, and community support services, Michael will have ongoing support to ensure that he meets all of his responsibilities and that his needs and desires are achieved. As for Michael's preparation for adulthood, his ITP team, again using a personal futures planning approach, should examine some or all of the following skills to be addressed during Michael's final years in school. To live as independently as possible, Michael will need to learn to shave, dress for work, shop for clothes, perform basic first aid (e.g., caring for minor cuts, abrasions, fever), manage any medications that may be prescribed, do his laundry, prepare simple meals, clean up after meals, store food safely, and other tasks. In addition, he will need to expand, maintain, and generalize his daily and weekly routines to new settings, new conditions, and schedule changes. If he develops a healthy social life, he may meet and fall in love with someone, necessitating his learning and practicing safe and responsible sex.

By addressing personal care and hygiene skills early in a student's life, educators and parents increase the likelihood that the student will be able to live independently as an adult in the community. Training students to carry out these tasks within a logical daily routine, thereby chaining one task with another early in life, provides for a block of daily living skills that can be efficiently transferred from the family home setting to another setting when the time comes. The more independent a student is with personal care and hygiene skills, the less restrictive his or her adult living and community participation arrangements can be. Adults who smell clean and have clean hair and breath will be more likely to gain and maintain paid employment in integrated community employment settings. Individuals who can toilet themselves with little or no assistance and who can eat independently will not have to depend on others to assist them with these essential daily activities. For these reasons, educational programs serving very young children have a real responsibility to address these issues early so that behavioral and physical patterns can be established as soon as possible. Looking at personal care and hygiene skills development as a long-term process that starts at the earliest point in public education and continues to build over time helps educators ensure maximum independence for adulthood.

In this section we have identified the scope and sequence of personal care and hygiene skills, identified the students who are most likely to need significant systematic and longitudinal intervention, discussed the curriculum that is based on personal care and hygiene skills needed in subsequent environments and by competent peers, provided longitudinal examples with Sharice and Michael, and addressed the issue of diversity and personal choice in appearance and clothing selection. In the next section we discuss the implementation of instructional strategies for training personal care and hygiene skills to persons with special needs.

INSTRUCTIONAL STRATEGIES

The underlying approach to teaching new behavior, skills that are not in the behavioral repertoire of the learner, or skills that the learner may, in part, be able to perform is a technology of manipulating environmental stimuli commonly called applied behavior analysis. Applications of using behavior analysis to teach basic domestic skills such as toothbrushing and more advanced skills such as clothing selection to people with special needs are prevalent in the literature (e.g., for toothbrushing, see Horner & Keilitz, 1975; Snell, Lewis, & Houghton, 1989; Wolber, Carne, Collins-Montgomery, & Nelson, 1987; for toileting, see Azrin & Foxx, 1971; for dressing, see Day & Horner, 1986; Diorio & Konarski, 1984; for washing clothes, see Cuvo, Jacobi, & Sipko, 1981; for mending clothes, see Cronin & Cuvo, 1979; for selecting clothes, see Nutter & Reid, 1978). Implementation of applied behavior analysis for teaching persons with severe disabilities is also prevalent in texts devoted to instructional strategies for this population (Cipani & Spooner, 1994; Ryndak & Alper, 1995; Snell, 1993). Additionally, there are numerous documented success stories about teaching persons with special needs personal care and hygiene (for menstrual care, see Epps, Prescott, & Horner, 1990; Richman, Ponticas, Page, & Epps, 1986; Richman, Reiss, Bauman, & Bailey, 1984; for use of roll-on deodorant, see Elium & McCarver, 1980; for grooming, see Brown, Evans, Weed, & Owen, 1987; Doleys, Stacy, & Knowles, 1981; Thinesen & Bryan, 1981).

Over the years, as instructional applications for persons with special needs have matured, we have found collectively that there is more to teaching skills than acquisition alone. If a skill is to be valuable to an individual, the learner must not only acquire the skill but also must be fluent in using the skill, be able to generalize the newly acquired skill to other environments, be likely to perform the skill for other people (other than the original trainer), and be able to maintain the skill across time (e.g., Billingsley, Liberty, & White, 1994; Haring, Liberty, & White, 1980). Consider an example of an individual who acquired the skill of making an appropriate clothing selection (i.e., picking out a color-coordinated outfit to wear to work the next day). The individual mastered the accuracy criterion that was set (i.e., 5 consecutive trials without error or assistance) and demonstrated that she was appropriately dressed on the job, day after day, with clothing selections that were socially validated by chronologically aged peers without disabilities. Yet, data indicated that it took the individual 1 hour each evening to make the selection. Most people do not spend an hour deciding what they will wear to work the next day. Some may not even make the decision until they begin to get dressed for the day's activities. Many people know what is clean, what combinations work together, and where various articles of clothing are stored. An individual picks out each clothing, based on the coordinated outfit, puts these items together, and gets dressed. Total time to make the decisions of what to wear and to lay out the items should take 15 minutes or less.

Taking 1 hour each evening to select an outfit does not show fluency in selecting clothes, even though the individual has met an accuracy criterion. There may be any number at reasons why this individual is not fluent in this skill. If she has a living arrangement in which support staff assist her, perhaps the support staff become impatient with the amount of time she takes to pick out an outfit and begin to supply prompts to assist the her in the selection process, but these additional cues may detract from her independent performance. The individual may have been trained by a particular staff person but now may be required to perform the skill without assistance or with minor assistance provided by other staff who were not part of the original training. What is the degree to which the individual can generalize the original training to these new, somewhat different conditions? For the skill to be useful, the individual will need to perform the skill within a reasonable amount of time and will need to generalize her performance across staff members.

Snell (1988) has offered nine important points for consideration in the development of any instructional application: (a) teaching partial participation, (b) promoting generalization, (c) improving attitudes toward people with disabilities, (d) allowing daily interactions with peers without disabilities, (e) teaching academics, (f) integrating instruction into natural routines, (g) integrating therapy, (h) making instructional decisions to improve teaching, and (i) analyzing functions of maladaptive behavior. In addition to following current best practices, which are the foundation of designing instructional strategies, educators must integrate other important components into the overall planning of instructional strategies, including (a) considerations prior to starting instruction, (b) considerations about the instructional context, and (c) the use of systematic strategies for teaching personal care and hygiene skills.

Considerations Prior to Starting Instruction

If instruction is to be successful, several pieces of information need to be considered before actual training begins, including the goals of the overall instructional process, the student's skill level as determined through assessment, the specific steps required for the student to successfully perform the task, and the way in which the skill will be taught (Billingsley et al., 1994). This section examines each of these preinstruction considerations individually.

Determining Goals of the Instructional Process

The overall goal of any instructional application is to produce a student who can not only perform the skill accurately but who can also execute the skill fluently, maintain the skill across time, and generalize the skill to new situations. Skills that are not transferable to other environments, skills that are performed too slowly, and skills that are forgotten in a short period of time will not be useful to the student. Planners and trainers must consider more than mere acquisition of the skill; they must plan for the additional phases of learning fluency, maintenance, and generalization. The goal of the instructional process should also be developed with three additional considerations: personal choice, immediate use of skill, and chronological age appropriateness (Test & Spooner, 1996).

Making Initial Assessments of the Student's Skill Level

An assessment of the student's current functioning level is necessary to determine what skills need to be taught. Analyzing skills that the student will need in the immediate environment as well as those skills that he or she will need in subsequent environments is a process that Brown et al. (1979) and Falvey (1986, 1995) call an ecological inventory. An ecological inventory assists the instructor in determining what skills are most functional for the student. Once the student's current functioning level has been determined, the assessment process is not over. Assessment should continue as an ongoing process for determining how both curriculum and methods should be modified to keep pace with changing student performance (Billingsley et al., 1994; Browder, 1991; Falvey, 1995).

Analyzing the Number of Steps for Instructional Tasks

In most cases, many personal hygiene tasks (e.g., toothbrushing, dressing, toileting) will comprise a series of steps. The process of delineating the sequence and order in which steps will be performed is called *task analysis*. Task analyses serve three basic functions. First, they identify the teachable components of a task. Second, the steps developed in a task analysis serve as the basis for data collection and measurement in the evaluation of the student's progress to mastering the skill sequence. Third, the steps of the task set the occasion for the way the task will be taught (e.g., application of a chaining procedure). This third function becomes the link between curriculum (content, the steps in the task) and methods (the way the task will be taught). Each step of the task should be delineated in the form of a verbal prompt with parenthetical information as needed to describe the steps of the task. Table 12.6 is an example of a task analysis for teaching toothbrushing.

Although there is no magic number of steps that a task analysis should contain, the literature does provide some guidelines. Crist, Walls, and Haught (1984) indicate that task analyses with smaller increments of learning and more steps produced fewer errors by students with severe disabilities. Sailor and Guess (1983) and Neel and Billingsley (1989) suggest that task analyses that contain long chains of behavior in excess of 20 or so steps should be avoided. Ultimately, the number of steps that are delineated to be learned is based on a relationship between the level of the student and the complexity of the task (Bellamy, Horner, & Inman, 1979). Test and Spooner (1996) suggest that there are three steps in developing task analyses: (a) determining critical steps in the instructional process, (b) considering partial participation and other adaptations, and (c) field-testing the task analysis.

TABLE 12.6
Task Analysis for Brushing Teeth

1. Get your toothbrush case.
2. Unzip the case.
3. Take out toothpaste.
4. Unscrew toothpaste cap.
5. Lay cap on countertop.
6. Turn on cold water.
7. Take out your toothbrush.
8. Wet bristles of toothbrush.
9. Put toothpaste on toothbrush.
10. Lay toothpaste tube on countertop.
11. Bring toothbrush with paste up to mouth.
12. Begin brushing teeth:
    left back: top—outside then inside
    left back: bottom—outside then inside
    then front: top—outside then inside
    then front: bottom—outside then inside
    then right back: top—outside then inside
    then right back: bottom—outside then inside
13. Spit toothpaste into sink.
14. Rinse toothbrush under water stream.
15. Shake water out of brush.
16. Put toothbrush into toothbrush case.
17. Get drinking cup from case.
18. Fill cup with cold water.
19. Rinse mouth with water.
20. Spit water into sink.
21. Rinse cup with water.
22. Wipe cup dry.
23. Put cup back into toothbrush case.
24. Put toothpaste cap on tube.
25. Put toothpaste into toothbrush case.

Note. For Sharice or other students with physical limitations, the trainer might want to add steps for approaching and positioning next to or up under the sink at the beginning of this task analysis. Sharice may need the handle of her toothbrush adapted to facilitate her grasping and moving it through the motions of brushing her teeth. It may also be helpful to have a stand-up pump-style toothpaste dispenser for Sharice rather than the squeeze-style tube. In some cases, it may be helpful to stabilize the toothpaste tube or pump by devising some kind of jig to hold it in place while squeezing or pumping to extract the toothpaste. For any of the above alterations, the task analysis would need to be written to accommodate the specific details for the particular learner.

As the task at hand is being considered and the steps to completion are being developed, there are usually a number of steps that are absolutely essential to the effective performance of the task. These steps are called *critical steps* (Wright & Schuster, 1994). For example, consider toothbrushing. The actual brushing of the teeth is an important component of the toothbrushing task, but equally critical is the use of toothpaste. Only a portion of the task is effectively accomplished if toothpaste is not applied to the toothbrush. Therefore, applying toothpaste to the toothbrush and brushing would be viewed as critical steps for toothbrushing.

Although the purpose of training personal hygiene skills is to make the student as independent as possible—in most cases totally independent—some students have physical limitations that may prohibit them from performing the skill completely independently. *Partial participation* (Baumgart et al., 1982; Ferguson & Baumgart, 1991) is an excellent way to allow a student to perform the parts of the task that he or she physically can and receive assistance from another person, perhaps a roommate or a staff person, to complete the task. Partial participation can be used in working with a student with an extreme physical disability who does not have the necessary finger dexterity to button or snap. This finger dexterity limitation should not preclude the student from receiving training in dressing. Through the use of partial participation, personal assistance could be provided by a caregiver or roommate when the steps of dressing require buttoning or fastening. The person should be trained to perform the steps that he or she is capable of doing and receive assistance for the steps that he or she cannot physically perform. Another solution would be for the student to wear clothing that does not require buttoning, like pullover shirts. For students with physical limitations, decisions should be made early in life to use adaptive devices and modifications of material. Often the use of adaptive devices and modified material will allow a student to participate in many daily living tasks that otherwise would not be possible.

Once a task analysis has been developed and partial participation has been taken into consideration for those individuals who may have physical limitations, the task analysis must be *field-tested*. Due to the private nature of many personal hygiene tasks, testing the steps to see if the finished product is achieved is different than with many community-based tasks. In such cases, a task analysis can still be field-tested if it is given to another staff member, roommate, or spouse who can follow the steps exactly as written. The person field-testing can evaluate the task analysis. Do the steps make sense? Are the steps sequenced in a logical order? This process is discussed in the literature as the "stranger test" (Test & Spooner, 1996). Of course, it still may be necessary to make adjustments to the task analysis to accommodate the particular style or abilities of the student.

Deciding How the Skill Will Be Taught

Many, if not all, personal hygiene skills are skills that have multiple steps. In the case of grooming hair, even for a student with a mild disability, grooming instruments need to be chosen (e.g., comb or brush, hair clips, spray or mousse), and the instrument needs to be oriented (e.g., on a comb, the finer teeth are at one end). The student will place the comb either to the right or left of the head (depending on the part) and point the comb teeth or brush bristles into hair, or perhaps place the comb at the front and move toward the back of the head. The hair-combing process continues until the student is satisfied with his or her hair. The steps of this grooming process become the task analysis as discussed above. After the steps have been determined, the way in which they will be taught is decided, based on the particular student and usually the application of a chaining procedure. Chaining is a way to teach tasks that have several steps. A chain is a specified series of steps, each associated with a unique stimulus condition. Each behavior, except for the first and the last steps, reinforces the previous step. Consider the example of a student following a set of directions to put on a pair of jeans. The steps of the task analysis for putting on jeans can vary depending on the abilities of the student for which the steps have been delineated. For example, some students with adequate foot and leg dexterity may be able to stand and remain standing while putting on a pair of jeans. Other people may start out sitting and then stand, whereas others may prefer to remain seated through the whole process.

The directions for putting on jeans have been written in a series of steps, a portion of which will be used for the purposes of illustrating how a chain works. The directions read as follows: (a) find the zipper; (b) lay pants against legs with zipper facing out; (c) move hands to waistband of pants; (d) put left hand on waistband above left pocket; (e) put right hand on waistband above right pocket; (f) with both hands, grasp waistband tightly with a pincher-type grasp; and (g) lower pants toward floor while at same time lifting left leg. (This is only part of the entire task analysis.) The second step in the sequence, "lay pants against legs with zipper facing out," gives the student a "landmark" as to where to place the jeans. The student picks up the jeans, finds the zipper, and places the jeans with the zipper facing out on his or her legs. When the student has the jeans on his or her legs, he or she begins to look for the next step in the sequence. The placement of the jeans on the legs indicates the completion of one step and signals the beginning of the next step in the sequence. The remainder of the steps also work in the same way, with the completion of the previous step indicating the next step in the sequence. The diagram in Figure 12.3 illustrates the relationship between the cue, the response, and the reinforcer. Placing pants on legs with zipper out functions both as a reinforcer for "finding the zipper" and as a cue for the next response, "placing hands." As such, steps in a task analysis serve the dual function

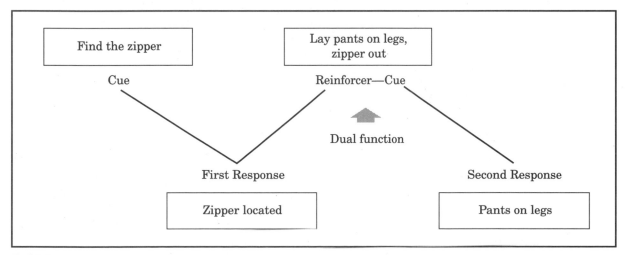

FIGURE 12.3. How chaining works in the context of putting on jeans.

as both a reinforcer for the previous step in the chain and a cue for the next step in the chain. It is this dual function that holds the sequence of steps together in a task analysis.

There are three basic chaining procedures—forward chaining, backward chaining, and total task presentation—that researchers and practitioners have used to teach learners who function at all levels of the special needs continuum tasks that have multiple steps. In *forward chaining* (FC), the instructor starts with the first step of the task analysis and teaches one step at a time, each to a predetermined criterion (e.g., five correct performances of Step 1 without error or assistance). After the student has met the criterion for Step 1 of the task analysis, the instructor moves on to Step 2. Training continues in a forward direction, with the student mastering each step before moving on to the next step, until the student can perform all of the steps in the task analysis without error or assistance.

In *backward chaining* (BC), the instructor begins on the last step in the task analysis. Similar to FC, only one step is trained at a time, but in BC, the first step trained is actually the last step of the task. The last step in the task analysis is trained to criterion before moving to the next-to-last step. When a new step is added, the student receives training on this new step and the last step, which has already been learned to criterion and should be executed independently without error. Training follows this backward sequence, with training progressing from the final step of the task analysis to the first step of the task analysis. Because both FC and BC introduce steps in a cumulative fashion over successive training trials, McDonnell and McFarland (1988) and Billingsley et al. (1994) suggest that FC and BC are sometimes discussed in the literature as serial or part training methods.

In the third chaining procedure, *total task presentation* (TT), the instructor begins with the first step of the task, but unlike FC, each step of the task analysis is performed during every training trial. Assistance is provided to the student as needed, and corrective feedback is given on only those steps of the task on which the student needs some help. The total (or entire) task, not each individual step as with FC and BC, is trained to a predetermined criterion level (e.g., three complete sequences without error or assistance).

Chaining procedures have been used to train a variety personal hygiene skills (e.g., for dressing, see Azrin, Schaeffer, & Wesolowski, 1976; Bensberg, Colwell, & Cassel, 1965; Breland, 1965; for toothbrushing, see Horner & Keilitz, 1975; for toileting, see Azrin & Foxx, 1971) to persons with special needs. Additionally, McDonnell and McFarland (1988) have indicated that all three chaining procedures have been successfully employed in teaching these skills. Although there would appear to be a theoretical advantage for using BC, because of the readily available conditioned reinforcer to strengthen the new response, comparisons of FC to BC have shown no differential effects (McDonnell & Laughlin, 1989). Recently, several investigators whose work has primarily focused on training persons with severe disabilities (e.g., Kayser, Billingsley, & Neel, 1986; Martin, Koop, Turner, & Hanel, 1981; Spooner, 1984; Test, Spooner, Keul, & Grossi, 1990) have suggested the relative effectiveness of TT when compared to BC. There appear to be some advantages to using the TT procedure. First, every step of the task analysis or chain is practiced each time the skill is taught. Second, the steps are presented in the order in which they naturally occur, so the steps have a logical relationship to one another. Third, a student does not have to continuously repeat a single step (e.g., having to do Step 1 three times without error and assistance before moving to Step 2). Multiple trial instruction on the same step can bore the student. Fourth, students can make the most efficient use of instructional time by practicing the whole task, rather than part of the task. Thus, each time training occurs, the task is completed (e.g., dressing is finished, the student gets a bite of food, hair is combed), rather than only the beginning or end of the task.

Considerations About Instructional Context

Decisions about instructional context may include the following: Where will instruction take place? Who will teach the skill? Will the skill be taught in multiple environments? When will instruction occur? Judgments about where the skill is taught and if the skill is to ultimately be performed in some other environment (other than the environment where the skill was originally taught) are likely to affect the degree to which the skill is maintained and, perhaps, generalized to other settings.

Where Will Instruction Take Place?

Personal care and hygiene skills, to a certain extent, differ from skills in other curriculum domains in that personal care and hygiene skills are likely to be performed in multiple environments, whereas other skills (e.g., vocational job skills) may only be performed in one environment (e.g., work setting). For example, a student may only take a shower at home, but he or she may go to the restroom at home, at school, or at a friend's house. Major grooming tasks such as washing, drying, and combing hair may be done at home, yet there are other times during the day when appearance needs to be checked. If upon the appearance check, hair is untidy, then hair will likely need to be fixed. Some individuals may get dressed two or three times a day (e.g., changing from work clothes, to leisure clothes, to pajamas), but there are additional times during the day when portions of the dressing task need to be executed (e.g., after one has used the restroom). The instructor needs to estimate probable multiple environments when training personal care and hygiene skills. He or she should determine the primary environment where the skill will take place (e.g., home, school) and identify any other environments where the skill will likely be used. Because of the likelihood that personal hygiene and grooming skills will be needed in multiple environments, *generalization is a key feature* in successfully transferring skills (e.g., hand washing) from home to school to a friend's house to a public restroom.

Generalization may be described as an expansion of an individual's performance beyond the initial conditions under which a skill was taught (Alberto & Troutman, 1995; Stokes & Baer, 1977). Learner performance may be expanded in one of three ways or in multiple combinations: (a) *across stimuli* (called stimulus generalization), (b) *across time* (called maintenance), and (c) *across responses* (called response generalization). When performance is extended across stimuli, the student may perform the skill with new or different cues, materials, trainers, or in new environments. In the case of *stimulus generalization,* applying soap when taking a shower or applying soap when washing hands shows how "lathering up" will take place in separate parts of the bathroom (e.g., the shower for washing the total body and a public restroom sink for washing hands). The ability to *maintain* personal hygiene skills across time is also important. Once a student learns to brush teeth, the act shold occur, it is hoped, two times a day across several environments (e.g., at home, at grandparents' home for an overnight visit) 7 days a week, 365 days a year. The skills that are practiced the most are usually the skills that will transcend the passage of time (Horner, Williams, & Knobbe, 1985). When the response is different from the original response that was trained, it is called *response generalization*. From a personal hygiene perspective, some of the same steps that are used in putting on and buttoning a shirt are similar to putting on and buttoning a coat, yet the response outcomes are different. Buttoning and putting arms in sleeves are similar maneuvers that should transfer from putting on a shirt to putting on a coat.

In an effort to facilitate the transfer of skills from one environment to another and to have those skills be maintained across time, Stokes and Baer (1977) suggested a number of strategies effective for training generalization. Numerous researchers have discussed and applied Stokes and Baer's strategies (e.g., for introductory textbooks in behavior analysis, see Alberto & Troutman, 1995; Cooper, Heron, & Heward, 1987; for lifestyle changes, see Horner, Dunlap, & Koegel, 1988; for investigating strategies and solutions for skill generalization, see Haring, 1988; Haring et al., 1985; Stokes & Osnes, 1988; for decision rules for generalization, see Liberty, Haring, White, & Billingsley, 1988; for training domestic and community living skills, see Spooner & Test, 1994; Thompson, Braam, & Fuqua, 1982; for training community skills, see Test & Spooner, 1996). Because these sources and numerous others are available, we will not provide a detailed discussion of these generalization strategies here. Instead, we will briefly discuss three generalization strategies that are readily understood. One strategy is *sequential modification*. To use this strategy, an instructor finds a procedure, including antecedent prompts and reinforcement strategies, for a skill that has been effective at school and encourages the use of those same strategies at home by family members. The instructor would demonstrate to the parent that the procedure was effective at school and then encourage its use at home. For example, if the teacher taught Sharice the toothbrushing task sequence with the student's toothbrush and toothpaste in a cup next to the sink and started Sharice on the task by giving her the terminal cue "Let's brush your teeth," it would be helpful for the instructor to demonstrate these same setting conditions (antecedents) and task start-up cue for Sharice's mother so she could use them with Sharice at home.

Another generalization strategy is to *train loosely*. When training a skill, the instructor emphasizes different antecedent cues across environments and across persons. For example, it is highly likely that Sharice's grandmother does not ask Sharice to brush her teeth the same way Sharice's mother does. Instead of asking the grandmother to change her mode of request, the instructor views this difference as acceptable and uses the different cues as tools that will increase the likelihood of Sharice responding to different prompts from different people that are said in different ways but that basically mean the same thing.

A third simple generalization strategy is to use *common stimuli* across settings. Considering the toothbrushing example, it is unlikely that the instructor will be able to make the school bathroom sink or the classroom sink look like the sink in Sharice's home bathroom. For example, it is unlikely that the instructor can mount a toothbrush holder next to the sink at school, and it would be unsanitary to put student toothbrushes standing up in a cup or glass next to the sink like you might find in some home bathrooms. Therefore, to teach the task in the school setting and, at the same time, to plan ahead for generalization to the home setting, the instructor might ask Sharice's mother to buy Sharice two identical zippered travel cases for storing her toothbrush and toothpaste, one for school and the other for home. The toothbrushing task analysis that the instructor writes to guide his or her teaching of the skill should include the zippered travel case. Then, when Sharice learns the task in the classroom setting, with the travel case being part of the beginning and end of the task analysis, the fact that she has the same travel case at home will facilitate generalization because the travel case will serve as a common cue between the two settings. The zippered travel case would also help to transfer Sharice's successful toothbrushing skill to her grandmother's house as well.

Personal care and hygiene skills are no different than any other skill area; these skills will not automatically transfer to a new environment or to new people. If personal care and hygiene skills are to generalize, specific training strategies must be implemented to increase the likelihood of the skills being transferred across environments, across time, and across people. The three generalization strategies described above can be helpful in facilitating this transfer process.

When Will Instruction Take Place?

Decisions about when instruction will take place affect the scheduling and frequency of training. Personal care and hygiene skills should be taught in relation to other temporal events that suggest that the hygiene skill needs to be performed as a consequence of the preceding event. For example, hand washing should take place after one has gone to the restroom and at other times when hand washing would naturally occur. Natural opportunities for instruction are also described as naturally distributed training trials. These natural opportunities provide the contextual sequence for the skill and will be the discriminitive stimuli and consequences present in the environment after instruction is concluded. As such, scheduling instruction at natural times when the skill would likely take place can improve acquisition and generalization (Bambara, Warren, & Komisar, 1988; Mulligan, Guess, Holvoet, & Brown, 1980; Neel & Billingsley, 1989).

Based on the relationship between some naturally occurring events throughout the day and personal hygiene, personal hygiene skills should be taught in a temporal sequence to those events. Instruction for skills such as dressing, washing hands, combing hair, and toileting should not be scheduled at arbitrary times during the day (e.g., dressing training at 10:00 A.M. for Melba, Fred, and Jason), but rather during the times of the day when these events would naturally occur (Billingsley et al., 1994; Gaylord-Ross & Holvoet, 1985). Gaylord-Ross and Holvoet (1985) have suggested that the training of skills in their naturally occurring sequences addresses the when and why of instruction. Most people do not put on a coat just after taking off the coat. Yet in many cases, instructors have given people with severe disabilities multiple trials of dressing (e.g., putting on a coat) in a discrete trial format training sequence.

Instructional Ratio

Although data are beginning to accumulate that may suggest that group instruction is not only feasible for individuals with more limited cognitive abilities but also an effective and efficient way to conduct instruction (e.g., Billingsley et al., 1994; Cosden & Haring, 1992; Reid & Favell, 1984), many personal care and hygiene skills, due to their nature (e.g., toileting, dressing), will likely lend themselves to one-to-one instruction. Additional instructional support in a school, group home, or other residential setting may be drawn from volunteers, peers without disabilities (Haring & Breen, 1992), and peers with disabilities who may have already mastered the skill and have been found to be good helpers. At home, parents and siblings can all be part of the instructional team.

Using Systematic Instructional Strategies: Starting a Morning Routine

In the case examples in this chapter, various personal care and hygiene skills are suggested for instruction according to Sharice's and Michael's unique needs. We have discussed breaking down each task into a sequence of discrete steps called a task analysis and teaching the skill using this sequence in a consistent and systematic fashion. We have also suggested that the daily personal care and hygiene skills be built into a consistent routine for the morning and the evening to maximize the degree to which each student will ultimately be able to perform a sequence of personal care and hygiene activities independently. Much like a supported employment specialist would analyze a specific job, organizing the various daily job duties into a logical sequence and then forming a task analysis for each specific duty (Moon, Inge, Wehman, Brooke, & Barcus, 1990), a teacher can work with parents to help structure a series of personal care and hygiene activities into a logical routine that can facilitate a student's ability to function within and across tasks more independently. We have discussed in general terms various instructional strategies that have been demonstrated to be effective with students with mild and severe disabilities. In this section, we take a slice out of the morning routines of both Sharice and Michael and illustrate how, when, and where some of these instructional strategies might be used.

To make the best of natural conditions for training some tasks in the school setting, it helps to plan ahead—in some cases, way ahead. For example, most working Americans wake up every morning to an alarm clock that sets into motion a stream of activities designed to get them ready for the day's activities, either a work day or a weekend leisure activity. Using an alarm clock is one of many steps to independence that youth begin to take during middle or high school. The alarm clock takes over the role of the parent for waking the student up at the necessary time of day. Given that kindergarten is usually the last year that schoolchildren take naps during school hours, it offers a naturally occurring time for the teacher to have children learn to wake to an alarm clock. Thus in Tables 12.3 and 12.4, earlier in this chapter, "waking to alarm" is listed as a goal for both Sharice and Michael. It will be the starting point for a morning routine for both of these students and is initially linked to going to the bathroom as the logical first activity of the morning.

By asking parents to donate several inexpensive battery-operated alarm clocks, the teacher can set the alarm clocks around the classroom in proximity to the students and set them to go off at the scheduled conclusion of nap time. When the alarms ring, the teacher should prompt students to get up and go to the bathroom. The teacher will want to plan to fade the prompts over time. Using a prompt-fading procedure called decreasing assistance, the teacher might initially prompt the students with something like, "Time to get up, let's all go to the bathroom," then fade to "Okay, we're awake, what do we do first?" (indirect verbal prompt) to "What's first?" (indirect verbal prompt) to no prompt. Some students may still need some gentle nudging (physical prompting) to get them stirred to wakefulness. The alarm clock ringing (in addition to a full bladder) will eventually act as a cue for the next step in the chain, which is going to the bathroom. After waking and going to the bathroom, if the child is then consistently prompted to go to the kitchen for breakfast, a pattern is established. Finishing in the bathroom becomes a cue for going to the kitchen and taking a seat at the table or breakfast bar. The point of arranging for this consistency in routine is to eventually have each completed activity cue the child for the next activity instead of the parent, teacher, or other caregiver having to provide each cue. The alarm clock can then be used to transfer (generalization using common stimuli) this sequence to the child's home.

For Michael, establishing a consistent behavioral chain of activities in a morning routine (i.e., prompting him to move from one morning activity to another in the same sequence every morning) will eventually establish the completion of one task to act as a cue for the next task in the sequence. This is the same concept as successful completion of one step in a task analysis serving as a reinforcer for the completed step and a cue for the next step in the sequence (refer back to Figure 12.3).

For students with severe cognitive or physical disabilities, the skill of waking to an alarm clock will take more intensive and extensive instruction. In Sharice's case, before she can respond to the alarm clock by going to the bathroom independently, she will need intensive intervention from the occupational therapist or physical therapist to help her develop a strategy and the skill to transfer from the bed, cot, or floor pad to her chair, so that she can then be encouraged to wheel herself from her bedroom (or the nap area) to the bathroom where she is learning to transfer from her chair to the toilet.

Sharice's independent toileting must be treated as a complex task with a full task analysis. She will need physical guidance while learning to get up from her prone position and move her body from her bed to her chair. The teacher should identify positive reinforcers for Sharice to receive for correctly completing parts of this task. She will initially require a continuous schedule of reinforcement with gradual fading to a fixed or variable ratio of reinforcement.

As stated above, Sharice will need assistance from the occupational therapist or physical therapist to help her devise the best method for transferring from her bed to her wheelchair. *One possible* strategy for Sharice to independently transfer from her bed to her wheelchair is as follows:

1. She rolls herself onto her side so that she is facing the outside of the bed. (If necessary, sidebars can be added to her bed to give her places to grasp to roll herself on her side.)

2. Once on her side, she rolls her legs and hips out of bed first, so that she slides out of bed on her stomach with her feet landing on the floor.

3. Steadying herself with both hands on the side of the bed, she will then need to lower her body backward into the chair.

4. Placing both of her arms on top of the armrests of the wheelchair, she pushes herself up to a straight position in the chair.

5. Put the foot pedals down on the chair.

6. Unlock the brakes on the chair.
7. Back away from the bed.
8. Turn the chair in the direction of the door.
9. Wheel to the bathroom.

This sequence is written as a task analysis in Figure 12.4.

Sharice will need to practice this task numerous times using a total task presentation before she will be able to perform it correctly without assistance and at a level of fluency that allows her to complete it within a comfortable time frame. This task could also be taught using backward chaining.

Even though Sharice is practicing the two actions together (waking to the alarm and going to the bathroom), it may be a long time before she is able to perform the second task in the chain (independent toileting) independently. However, even if she is performing a task at some level of partial participation, it still makes sense to arrange the various tasks in a consistent sequence so that she can begin to move from one activity to another with some degree of independence. Therefore, when Sharice completes the toileting task with partial participation, she should be consistently prompted to go to the kitchen for breakfast, followed by prompting to go back to the bathroom to brush teeth, wash face and hands, and comb hair. While the special education teacher and other school staff work on Sharice learning the specific steps of each complex task, Sharice's parents can begin to build the sequence of morning routine tasks so that when Sharice achieves independence with any one task, her acquired skill can be transferred to the home setting, with minor adjustments to accommodate setting

1. Roll onto your side.																			
2. Roll your legs out of bed.																			
3. Hold onto the side of the bed.																			
4. Come back into the chair.																			
5. Pull yourself up straight.																			
6. Put your foot pedals down.																			
7. Unlock the brakes.																			
8. Back away from the bed.																			
9. Turn the chair toward the door.																			
10. Wheel to the bathroom.																			
Number of steps correct																			
Percentage of task correct																			

FIGURE 12.4. A task analysis for transferring from the bed to wheelchair.

and structural variations, and can become another link in the chain of daily personal care and hygiene activities that Sharice will need to be able to perform as independently as possible.

Of course there are numerous times during the day that a student will need to use the bathroom other than during the morning routine. These times are important in their own right and will have their own settings and cues to which Sharice will need to be able to respond. Therefore, Sharice's parents and the school staff should take steps to generalize her ability to transfer from her wheelchair to the toilet in several different locations (i.e., stimulus generalization). Each time Sharice is required to go through the steps to toilet herself independently, she is strengthening her muscles in ways that will facilitate her ability to toilet herself the next time.

CONCLUSION

Personal care and hygiene skills are just one component of a total longitudinal independent living curriculum for persons with special needs. Of the skill training areas in this longitudinal sequence (e.g., recreation and leisure skills, health and safety, financial planning and money management), personal care and hygiene would likely be the skill area that is most often taken for granted. Not only is being able to handle one's personal needs taken for granted in our culture, but it is also a highly valued basic component of self-sufficiency and personal independence. With personal independence comes the ability to make choices and more opportunity to participate in community living.

Many Americans naturally assume that practically everyone will be able to take a shower, get dressed, and eat something for breakfast. However, as we have indicated, many people with special needs, especially those with severe intellectual disabilities, will need systematic and longitudinal training in personal care and hygiene skills. The ability to manage one's personal needs is one of the skill hierarchies that usually sets apart those who function on an independent level from those who do not.

The professional literature that has accumulated over the past 25 years in the field of developmental disabilities is quite clear about the fact that people at all levels of disability and retardation can learn to perform many personal care and hygiene skills independently. The success of teaching curricular skills such as personal care and hygiene to persons with severe disabilities is so well documented, it could partly be one of the reasons why researchers have recently begun to focus on other areas.

Over the course of the past 25 years, an effective, efficient, and validated technology for training numerous skills to persons of all walks of life and levels of functioning has emerged. We encourage trainers, developmental care technicians, and teachers to use this technology to not only train skill sequences but to also validate the progress of their learners. The behavior approach is one of the few approaches that allows for switching training tactics midstream when the learner is not acquiring the skill at the level that was anticipated. We have attempted to show a longitudinal sequence of these skills and the application of instructional strategies through the case studies of Sharice and Michael.

REFERENCES

ABT Associates. (1974). *Assessment of selected resources for severely handicapped children and youth* (Vol. 1). Cambridge, MA: Author.

Alberto, P. A., & Troutman, A. C. (1995). *Applied behavior analysis for teachers* (4th ed.). Columbus, OH: Merrill.

American Dental Association. (2001, July 19). *Oral health topic: Gum disease (periodontal disease).* Retrieved September 3, 2001, from http://www.ada.org/public/topics/gum.html

Azrin, N. H., & Foxx, R. M. (1971). A rapid method of toilet training the institutionalized retarded. *Journal of Applied Behavior Analysis, 4,* 89–99.

Azrin, N. H., Schaeffer, R. M., & Wesolowski, M. D. (1976). A rapid method of teaching profoundly retarded persons to dress by a reinforcement–guidance method. *Mental Retardation, 14*(6), 26–33.

Azrin, N. H., Sneed, T. J., & Fox, R. M. (1973). Drybed: A method of eliminating bedwetting (enuresis) of the retarded. *Behavior Research and Therapy, 11,* 427–434.

Baller, W. R. (1975). *Bed wetting: Origins and treatment.* New York: Pergamon Press.

Bambara, L. M., Warren, S. F., & Komisar, S. (1988). The individualized curriculum sequencing model: Effects on skill acquisition and generalization. *Journal of the Association for Persons with Severe Handicaps, 13,* 8–19.

Baumgart, D., Brown, L., Pumpian, I., Nisbet, J., Ford, A., Sweet, M., et al. (1982). Principle of partial participation and individualized adaptation in educational programs for severely handicapped students. *Journal of the Association for Persons with Severe Handicaps, 7*(2), 17–27.

Bellamy, G. T., Horner, R. H., & Inman, D. P. (1979). *Habilitation of severely and profoundly retarded adults: A direct service technology.* Baltimore: University Park Press.

Bensberg, G. J., Colwell, C. N., & Cassel, R. H. (1965). Teaching the profoundly retarded self-help activities by behavior shaping techniques. *American Journal of Mental Deficiency, 69,* 674–679.

Billingsley, F. F., Liberty, K., & White, O. (1994). Instructional technology. In E. Cipani & F. Spooner (Eds.), *Curricular and instructional approaches for persons with severe disabilities* (pp. 81–116). Needham Heights, MA: Allyn & Bacon.

Breland, M. (1965). Application of method. In G. J. Bensberg (Ed.), *Teaching the mentally retarded: A handbook for ward personnel.* Atlanta, GA: Southern Regional Education Board.

Brimer, R. W. (1990). *Students with severe disabilities: Current perspectives and practices.* Mountain View, CA: Mayfield.

Browder, D. M. (Ed.). (1991). *Assessment of individuals with severe disabilities: An applied behavioral approach to life skills assessment* (2nd ed.). Baltimore: Brookes.

Brown, F., Evans, I., Weed, K., & Owen, V. (1987). Delineating functional competencies: A competent model. *Journal of the Association for Persons with Severe Handicaps, 12,* 117–124.

Brown, L., Branston, M. B., Hamre-Nietupski, S., Pumpian, I., Certo, N., & Gruenwald, L. (1979). A strategy for developing chronological-age-appropriate and functional curricular content for severely handicapped adolescents and young adults. *Journal of Special Education, 13*(1), 81–90.

Brown, L., Nietupski, J., & Hamre-Nietupski, S. (1976). Criterion of ultimate functioning. In M. A. Thomas (Ed.), *Hey, don't forget about me!* (pp. 2–15). Reston, VA: Council for Exceptional Children.

Cipani, E. C., & Spooner, F. (1994). *Curricular and instructional approaches for persons with severe disabilities.* Needham Heights, MA: Allyn & Bacon.

Clarke, S., Dunlap, G., & Vaughn, B. (1999). Family-centered, assessment-based intervention to improve behavior during an early morning routine. *Journal of Positive Behavior Interventions, 1,* 235–241.

Cooper, J. O., Heron, T. E., & Heward, W. L. (1987). *Applied behavior analysis.* Columbus, OH: Merrill.

Cosden, M. A., & Haring, T. G. (1992). Cooperative learning in the classroom: Contingencies, group instruction, and students with special needs. *Journal of Behavioral Education, 2,* 53–71.

Crist, K., Walls, R. T., & Haught, P. A. (1984). Degrees of specificity in task analysis. *American Journal of Mental Deficiency, 89,* 67–74.

Cronin, K. A., & Cuvo, A. J. (1979). Teaching mending skills to mentally retarded adolescents. *Journal of Applied Behavior Analysis, 12,* 401–406.

Cuvo, A. J., Jacobi, L., & Sipko, R. (1981). Teaching laundry skills to mentally retarded students. *Education and Training of the Mentally Retarded, 16,* 54–64.

Day, H. M., & Horner, R. H. (1986). Response variation and the generalization of a dressing skill: Comparison of single instance and general case instruction. *Applied Research in Mental Retardation, 7*(2), 189–202.

Diorio, M. S., & Konarski, E. A. (1984). Evaluation of a method for teaching dressing skills to profoundly mentally retarded persons. *American Journal of Mental Deficiency, 89,* 307–309.

Doleys, D. M., Stacy, D., & Knowles, S. (1981). Modification of grooming behavior in adult retarded: Token reinforcement in a community-based program. *Behavior Modification, 5,* 119–128.

Elium, M. D., & McCarver, R. B. (1980). *Group vs. individual training on a self-help skill with the profoundly retarded* (EC150366). Tuscaloosa, AL: Partlow State School and Hospital. (ERIC Document Reproduction Service No. ED223060)

Epps, S., & Myers, C. L. (1989). Priority domains for instruction, satisfaction with school teaching, and postschool living and employment: An analysis of perceptions of parents of students with severe and profound disabilities. *Education and Training of the Mentally Retarded, 24,* 157–167.

Epps, S., Prescott, A. L., & Horner, R. H. (1990). Social acceptability of menstrual-care methods for young women with developmental disabilities. *Education and Training in Mental Retardation, 25,* 33–44.

Evans, I. M., Salisbury, C. L., Palombaro, M. M., & Goldberg, J. S. (1994). Children's perceptions of fairness in classroom and interpersonal situations involving peers with severe disabilities. *Journal of the Association for Persons with Severe Handicaps, 19,* 326–332.

Falvey, M. A. (1986). *Community-based curriculum: Instructional strategies for students with severe handicaps.* Baltimore: Brookes.

Falvey, M. A. (1995). *Inclusive and heterogeneous schooling: Assessment, curriculum, and instruction.* Baltimore: Brookes.

Ferguson, D. L., & Baumgart, D. (1991). Partial participation revisited. *Journal of the Association for Persons with Severe Handicaps, 16,* 218–227.

Fredericks, H. D., & Brodsky, M. (1994). Functional assessment. In E. Cipani & F. Spooner (Eds.), *Curricular and instructional approaches for persons with severe disabilities* (pp. 31–49). Needham Heights, MA: Allyn & Bacon.

Garff, J. T., & Storey, K. (1998). The use of self-management strategies for increasing the appropriate hygiene of persons with disabilities in supported employment settings. *Education and Training in Mental Retardation and Developmental Disabilities, 33,* 179–188.

Gaylord-Ross, R., & Holvoet, J. (1985). *Strategies for educating students with severe handicaps.* Boston: Little, Brown.

Haring, N. G. (1988). *Generalization for students with severe handicaps: Strategies and solutions.* Seattle: University of Washington Press.

Haring, N. G., Liberty, K., Billingsley, F., White, O., Lynch, V., Kayser, J., et al. (Eds.). (1985). *Investigating the problem of skill generalization* (3rd ed.). Seattle: Washington Research Organization.

Haring, N. G., Liberty, K. A., & White, O. R. (1980). Rules for data-based strategy decision in instructional programs: Current research and instructional implications. In W. Sailor, B. Wilcox, & L. Brown (Eds.), *Methods of instruction for severely handicapped students* (pp. 159–192). Baltimore: Brookes.

Haring, T. G. (1991). Social relationships. In L. H. Meyer, C. A. Peck, & L. Brown (Eds.), *Critical issues in the lives of people with severe disabilities.* Baltimore: Brookes.

Haring, T. G., & Breen, C. (1992). A peer-mediated social network intervention to enhance the social integration of persons with moderate and severe disabilities. *Journal of Applied Behavior Analysis, 25,* 319–333.

Haring, T. G., Roger, B., Lee, M., Breen, C., & Gaylord-Ross, R. J. (1986). Teaching social language to moderately handicapped students. *Journal of Applied Behavior Analysis, 19,* 159–171.

Helmstetter, E., Peck, C. A., & Giangreco, M. F. (1994). Outcomes of interactions with peers with moderate or severe disabilities: A statewide survey of high school students. *Journal of the Association for Persons with Severe Handicaps, 19,* 263–276.

Horner, R. D., & Keilitz, I. (1975). Training retarded adolescents to brush their teeth. *Journal of Applied Behavior Analysis, 8,* 301–309.

Horner, R. H., Dunlap, G., & Koegel, R. L. (1988). *Generalization and maintenance.* Baltimore: Brookes.

Horner, R. H., Williams, J. A., & Knobbe, C. A. (1985). The effect of "opportunity to perform" on the maintenance of skills learned by high school students with severe handicaps. *Journal of the Association for Persons with Severe Handicaps, 10,* 172–175.

Justin, J. E. (1976). Who are the severely handicapped? A problem in definition. *AAESPH Review, 1*(5), 1–12.

Kayser, J. E., Billingsley, F. F., & Neel, R. S. (1986). A comparison of in-context and traditional instructional approaches: Total task, single trial versus backward chaining, multiple trials. *Journal of the Association of Persons with Severe Handicaps, 11,* 28–38.

Liberty, K. A., Haring, N. G., White, O. R., & Billingsley, F. (1988). A technology for the future: Decision rules for generalization. *Education and Training in Mental Retardation, 23,* 315–326.

Lucyshyn, J. M., Albin, R. W., & Nixon, C. D. (1997). Embedding comprehensive behavioral support in family ecology: An experimental, single-case analysis. *Journal of Consulting and Clinical Psychology, 65,* 241–251.

Martin, G., Koop, S., Turner, G., & Hanel, F. (1981). Backward chaining versus total task presentation to teach assembly tasks to severely retarded persons. *Behavior Research of Severe Disabilities, 2,* 91–112.

McDonnell, J. J., Hardman, M. L., McDonnell, A. P., & Keifer-O'Donnell, R. (1995). *An introduction to persons with severe disabilities: Educational and social issues.* Boston: Allyn & Bacon.

McDonnell, J. J., & Laughlin, B. (1989). A comparison of backward and concurrent chaining strategies in teaching community skills. *Education and Training in Mental Retardation, 24,* 230–238.

McDonnell, J., & McFarland, S. (1988). A comparison of forward and concurrent chaining strategies in teaching laundromat skills to students with severe handicaps. *Research in Developmental Disabilities, 9,* 177–194.

Meyer, L. H., Peck, C. A., & Brown, L. (Eds.). (1991). *Critical issues in the lives of people with severe disabilities.* Baltimore: Brookes.

Moon, M. S., Inge, K., Wehman, P., Brooke, V., & Barcus, J. M. (1990). *Helping persons with severe mental retardation get and keep employment.* Baltimore: Brookes.

Mount, B. (1987). *Personal futures planning: Finding directions for change* (Doctoral dissertation, University of Georgia). Ann Arbor, MI: UMI Dissertation Information Service.

Mulligan, M., Guess, D., Holvoet, J., & Brown, F. (1980). The individualized curriculum sequencing model (I): Implications from research on massed, distributed, or spaced trial training. *Journal of the Association for the Severely Handicapped, 5,* 325–336.

Neel, R. S., & Billingsley, F. F. (1989). *Impact: A functional curriculum handbook for students with moderate to severe disabilities.* Baltimore: Brookes.

Nietupski, J., Hamre-Nietupski, S., Curtin, S., & Shrikanth, K. (1997). A review of curricular research in severe disabilities from 1976 to 1995 in six selected journals. *Journal of Special Education, 31,* 36–55.

Nutter, D., & Reid, D. H. (1978). Teaching retarded women a clothing selection skill using community norms. *Journal of Applied Behavior Analysis, 11,* 475–487.

Pierce, K. L., & Schreibman, L. (1994). Teaching dialy living skills to children with autism in unsupervised settings through pictorial self-management. *Journal of Applied Behavior Analysis, 27,* 471–481.

Polloway, E. A., Patton, J. R., Smith, J. D., & Roderique, T. W. (1991). Issues in program design for elementary students with mild retardation: Emphasis on curriculum development. *Education and Training in Mental Retardation, 26,* 142–150.

Reamer, R. B., Brady, M. P., & Hawkins, J. (1998). The effects of video self-modeling on parents' interactions with children with developmental disabilities. *Education and Training in Mental Retardation and Developmental Disabilities, 33,* 131–143.

Reid, D. H., & Favell, J. E. (1984). Group instruction with persons who have severe disabilities: A critical review. *Journal of the Association of Persons with Severe Handicaps, 9,* 167–177.

Richman, G. S., Ponticas, Y., Page, T. J., & Epps, S. (1986). Simulation procedures for teaching independent menstrual care to mentally retarded persons. *Applied Research in Mental Retardation, 7,* 21–35.

Richman, G. S., Reiss, M. L., Bauman, K. E., & Bailey, J. S. (1984). Teaching menstrual care to mentally retarded women: Acquisition, generalization, and maintenance. *Journal of Applied Behavior Analysis, 17,* 441–451.

Ryndak, D. L., & Alper, S. (1995). *Curriculum content for students with moderate and severe disabilities in inclusive settings.* Boston: Allyn & Bacon.

Sailor, W., & Guess, D. (1983). *Severely handicapped students: An instructional design.* Boston: Houghton Mifflin.

Sailor, W., & Haring, N. G. (1977). Some current directions in education of the severely/profoundly handicapped. *AAESPH Review, 2*(2), 3–24.

Sewell, T. J., Collins, B. C., Hemmeter, J. L., & Schuster, J. W. (1998). Using simultaneous prompting within an activity-based format to teach dressing skills to preschoolers with developmental delays. *Journal of Early Intervention, 21,* 132–145.

Snell, M. E. (1987). *Systematic instruction of persons with severe handicaps* (3rd ed.). Columbus, OH: Merrill.

Snell, M. E. (1988). Curriculum and methodology for individuals with severe disabilities. *Education and Training in Mental Retardation, 23,* 302–314.

Snell, M. E. (1991). Foreword: Sad voices from the twentieth century. In L. H. Meyer, C. A. Peck, & L. Brown (Eds.), *Critical issues in the lives of people with severe disabilities* (pp. xv–xix). Baltimore: Brookes.

Snell, M. E. (1993). *Instruction of students with severe disabilities* (4th ed.). New York: Merrill/Macmillan.

Snell, M. E., Lewis, A. P., & Houghton, A. (1989). Acquisition and maintenance of toothbrushing skills by students with cerebral palsy and mental retardation. *Journal of the Association for Persons with Severe Handicaps, 14,* 216–226.

Sowers, J., & Powers, L. (1995). Enhancing the participation and independence of students with severe physical and multiple disabilities in performing community activities. *Mental Retardation, 33,* 209–220.

Spooner, F. (1984). Comparisons of backward chaining and total task presentation in training severely handicapped persons. *Education and Training in Mental Retardation, 19,* 15–22.

Spooner, F., & Test, D. W. (1994). Domestic and community living skills. In E. C. Cipani & F. Spooner (Eds.), *Curricular and instructional approaches for persons with severe disabilities* (pp. 149–183). Needham Heights, MA: Allyn & Bacon.

Sprague, J., & Horner, R. (1984). The effects of single instance, multiple instance, and general case training on generalized vending machine use by moderately and severely handicapped students. *Journal of Applied Behavior Analysis, 17,* 273–278.

Stokes, T. F., & Baer, D. (1977). An implicit technology of generalization. *Journal of Applied Behavior Analysis, 10,* 349–367.

Stokes, T. F., & Osnes, P. G. (1988). The developing applied technology of generalization and maintenance. In R. H. Horner, G. Dunlap, & R. L. Koegel (Eds.), *Generalization and maintenance: Life-style changes in applied settings* (pp. 5–19). Baltimore: Brookes.

Test, D. W., & Spooner, F. (1996). *Innovations: Community-based training as an instructional support.* Washington, DC: American Association on Mental Retardation.

Test, D. W., Spooner, F., Keul, P. K., & Grossi, T. (1990). Teaching adolescents with severe disabilities to use the public telephone. *Behavior Modification, 14,* 157–171.

Thinesen, P. J., & Bryan, A. J. (1981). The use of sequential pictorial cues in the initiation and maintenance of grooming behaviors in mentally retarded adults. *Mental Retardation, 19,* 247–250.

Thompson, T. J., Braam, S. J., & Fuqua, R. W. (1982). Training and generalization of laundry skills: A multiple probe evaluation with handicapped persons. *Journal of Applied Behavior Analysis, 15,* 177–182.

Vandercook, T., & York, J. (1990). A team approach to program development and support. In W.

Stainback & S. Stainback (Eds.), *Support networks for inclusive education: Interdependent integrated education* (pp. 95–120). Baltimore: Brookes.

Vincent, L. J., Salisbury, C., Walter, G., Gruenwald, L. J., & Powers, M. (1980). Program evaluation and curriculum development in early childhood special education: Criteria of the next environment. In W. Sailor, B. Wilcox, & L. Brown (Eds.), *Methods of instruction for severely handicapped students* (pp. 303–328). Baltimore: Brookes.

Wacker, D., & Berg, W. (1983). Effects of picture prompts on acquisition of complex vocational tasks by mentally retarded adolescents. *Journal of Applied Behavior Analysis, 16,* 417–434.

Westling, D. L. (1996). What do parents of children with moderate and severe mental disabilities want? *Education and Training in Mental Retardation and Developmental Disabilities, 31,* 86–114.

Wolber, G., Carne, W., Collins-Montgomery, & Nelson, A. (1987). Tangible reinforcement plus social reinforcement versus social reinforcement alone in acquisition of toothbrushing skills. *Mental Retardation, 25,* 275–279.

Wolf, M. M. (1978). Social validity: The case for subjective measurement or how applied behavior analysis is finding its heart. *Journal of Applied Behavior Analysis, 11,* 203–214.

Wright, C. W., & Schuster, J. (1994). Accepting specific versus functional student responses when training chained tasks. *Education and Training in Mental Retardation and Developmental Disabilities, 29,* 43–56.

Ysseldyke, J. E., Christenson, S., & Kovaleski, J. F. (1994). Identifying students' instructional needs in the context of classroom and home environments. *Teaching Exceptional Children, 26*(3), 37–41.

CHAPTER 13

Health and Safety

Martin Agran

MALINDA

Malinda is 16 years old and attends 11th grade at West Bench High School. Except for one period committed to intensive academic instruction (reading and math) in the resource room, Malinda is in regular content area classes. She functions in the moderate to severe range of cognitive impairments. Also, she is given medication to control seizures that occur once or twice a week. She can accomplish most basic living skills independently and adapts easily to routines. She does not know how to use various appliances at home but has expressed an interest in learning how to operate them, especially the microwave and coffeemaker. She is generally friendly and social and is concerned about dressing nicely for school. She enjoys going shopping with friends for clothing. Although she has enjoyed attending several dances and parties, Malinda appears to have little interest at this time in dating or interacting with boys during social situations. Once a week, she and a number of other students with disabilities clean the recreational center of a local church. Also, she works 1 hour a day at the school store selling snacks, supplies, and souvenirs.

Her parents have strongly expressed an interest in having her work in a part-time job in the community after graduation, and Malinda has indicated that she would like to live in an apartment with roommates and work in a grocery store one day. Her parents have indicated to Malinda's homeroom teacher that it is critical that Malinda be taught a variety of safety skills, such as crime prevention, fire safety, first aid, and relevant work safety skills, so that she can handle situations more independently when she is an adult. As educators strive to ensure that individuals with disabilities—particularly those with severe disabilities—participate as fully as possible in the many work, living, recreational, and civic activities available in their communities, it is becoming increasingly clear that these individuals may be exposed to potential risk situations they either do not know how to identify or to respond to. If Malinda were in a crisis situation, such as a stranger inviting her into a car or a fire in the house, her parents wonder if she would know what to do.

Throughout her life, Malinda will participate in varied settings where any number of risks may be present. To ensure her well-being and good health, Malinda needs to learn how to use public transportation; to acquire a variety of home, community, and fire safety skills; and to learn numerous work safety skills and crime prevention skills. The consequences of not teaching her these skills are far too serious to ignore. Educators cannot assume that their students have a basic set of safety skills. All too frequently, there are reports of, for example, the death of several individuals who were trapped in a group home due to a fire or the rape of a woman with a disability. These stories are sad reminders that many individuals with disabilities do not have basic safety skills in their adaptive repertoires.

NEED FOR SAFETY SKILLS INSTRUCTION

Safety from harm is a basic entitlement to all people (Halpern, 1993). There is no question that both the public and private sectors of our country have made committed efforts to ensure the safety of all citizens. Potential risks in the community, at home, in schools, and even in remote areas (e.g., national parks, national forests) have been identified (e.g., signs are posted, protective barriers are installed). Unsafe products are recalled and redesigned. There is no question that personal safety is a highly valued expectation in our society. As Maslow (1954) suggested, we cannot have higher motives toward self-development until our most basic ones are satisfied, and safety is clearly one of them. That said, this is a regrettably imperfect world, and insults and injuries occur despite concentrated efforts to prevent them. Consequently, members of society have learned to trust and rely on protective resources that have been provided but to also safeguard themselves with a full repertoire of preventive skills, from avoiding dark alleys to wearing sturdier shoes when mowing the lawn.

Educators have realized, too, that as they prepare students with disabilities to become independent and competent, educators also need to teach these students a full array of safety skills. Nevertheless, a number of researchers have suggested that teaching students safety skills has been largely ignored as a curricular domain (Agran, Marchand-Martella, & Martella, 1994; Gast, Wellons, & Collins, 1994; Juracek, 1994), and when these skills have been taught, fragmented and unsystematic procedures have often been used. Despite some alarming information that suggests that many students with disabilities—particularly those with more significant disabilities—have minimal knowledge to respond to potentially risky situations (see Agran et al., 1994), few curricula for these students contain much information about these skills, and little has appeared in the special education research literature.

There are several reasons for this oversight. First, many teachers and parents may assume that students already possess basic health and safety skills and that time could be better spent teaching students other adaptive skills. For many teachers and others, safety skills were acquired coincidentally, without formal instruction. Teachers may assume the same for students with disabilities, despite data to suggest otherwise. Second, teachers and parents may have low expectations of students with disabilities and think it unrealistic to teach them skills routinely performed by service providers. Professionals and parents may assume that safety skills involve complex discriminations that students will have difficulty making (e.g., appropriately identifying dangerous situations, assessing the seriousness of an injury). Nevertheless, many of the basic safety skills we will discuss in this chapter can be systematically acquired by students with mild through severe disabilities. Third, although injuries may be serious, the likelihood of sustaining one is small. Because the selection of instructional targets is largely based on the frequency of occurrence of target skills (i.e., functional skills that occur more frequently are prioritized), both parents and professionals may question why a safety skill that is needed infrequently should be taught at all. They reason that even if there is a possibility of an accident occuring, a teacher or other service provider usually will be present to intervene if needed. Last, many persons continue to equate safety or good health with having a positive attitude. Awareness of risks comes with such attitudes. That is, an awareness of potential risks will by itself produce safe work behavior. Because safety is associated to a large extent by what one does not do (e.g., not having an accident or sustaining an injury), some professionals may think that there is not really much to teach and that periodic counseling should be sufficient. In summary, many teachers and parents may believe that students should not be intentionally exposed to risks and that learning is difficult enough for students with special needs without adding the challenge of teaching them to deal with risks.

It is safe to say that virtually any community can be dangerous for individuals unable to identify and respond appropriately to risk stimuli, and accidents remain the leading cause of death for nondisabled children (Haller, 1970; Peterson, 1984). Because most individuals can identify and potentially respond to unsafe stimuli automatically, they do not attend to these stimuli and do not take them seriously. Nevertheless, a critical analysis of most work and community environments would reveal certain risks. Additionally, there is sufficient evidence to suggest that persons with disabilities are at a particular risk for accidents and emergency situations due to such characteristics as "poor judgment; lack of awareness of danger; impulsiveness and restlessness; inability or difficulties in communicating; low pain threshold; abnormal muscle functioning causing difficulties in chewing, swallowing, standing, walking; and impaired vision and/or hearing" (Bryan, Warden, Berg, & Hauck, 1978, p. 8). Also, such health problems as seizures, vulnerability to infection (Blackman, 1984; Bryan et al., 1978), and other chronic health-related conditions (Lorr & Rotatori, 1985) may increase the risk of emergencies and accidents for individuals with disabilities. Furthermore, as Khemka (2000) noted, to avoid potentially abusive situations, individuals with disabilities need to acquire decision-making and assertiveness skills, which are skill areas that may be limited for persons with mental retardation. With teachers' increased efforts to prepare students for fuller participation in community settings, there is no question that there is a higher likelihood that an accident may occur. Also, injury rates for persons with disabilities may be as high, if not higher, than for nondisabled persons.

Although accident or victimization data for persons with disabilities are limited, the available reported data are indeed sobering. For example, Stimpson and Best (1991) reported that 73% of women with disabilities have been victims of violence. Chotiner and Lehr (1976) indicated that 70% of abused children had disabilities, and Muccigrosso (1991) stated that at least 90% of children with developmental disabilities have been sexually exploited. According to Lumley and Miltenberger (1997), estimates of sexual abuse of persons with disabilities range from 25% to 83%. Jaskulski and Mason (1992) noted that in a sample of 108 rehabilitation facilities, approximately 30% of the consumers were HIV-positive. Last, Agran and Madison (1995) stated that, in a sample of 11,000 individuals served by 800 vocational rehabilitation facilities, there were more than 4,000 injuries for these individuals reported. These data underscore the need for safety skills instruction.

As noted previously, students are often denied access to settings where risks may be present. Denying students the opportunity to respond to potentially risky situations endangers their dignity and prevents them from experiencing the risk taking of ordinary life (Wolfensberger, 1972). Perske (1972) stressed the importance of risk taking for persons with disabilities and indicated that "there can be such a thing as human dignity in risk. And there can be a dehumanizing indignity in safety" (p. 200). Students must be allowed to experience the consequences of their decisions and to realize that there will not always be someone to offer guidance when they need help (Vogelsberg & Rusch, 1979). Failure to teach students safety skills may lead parents and school boards to restrict students' access to community environments. Worse still, it may result in a student's total inability to avert a serious accident or assault.

The purpose of this chapter is to describe a health and safety curriculum for students with disabilities. Additionally, procedures to assess and teach health and safety skill performance are suggested, and selected IEP objectives for elementary, middle, and secondary school students are presented. As Sobsey (1994) indicated, although steps can be taken to reduce individual risk, no amount of preventive behavior can eliminate risk entirely. It is not the purpose of this chapter to teach individuals skills that will keep them totally out of harm's way. But the health and safety skills addressed in this chapter comprise a repertoire of skills that will allow students to respond appropriately to many risks and dangers they may be exposed to at work, in their homes, and in their communities.

OVERVIEW OF CURRICULUM

Agran et al. (1994) noted,

> Given the exigencies of these times and rapidly evolving sociological, cultural, and medical changes in our society, the curricular domains we have formerly taught remain important, but, ultimately, inadequate. There is no question that an individual unprepared to take responsibility for his or her health and safety represents an individual ill-equipped for contemporary living. (p. xii)

As indicated in this book, independent and functional living skills encompass a broad range of activities, including, but not limited to, work, community, home living, academic, recreational and leisure, mobility, financial management, personal care, social, and a number of self-advocacy and self-determination skills. Participation in these varied functional activities allows individuals with disabilities to have normalized and valued life experiences, but as indicated previously, it expands the range of environments individuals will participate in and, as a result, may expose them to numerous environmental risks. Many potential dangers are present in most home, work, and community settings for unknowledgeable persons or persons who do not behave safely. Failure to teach safety skills leaves individuals vulnerable to injury, limits their competence, and further promotes their dependence on caregivers or service providers.

Although the type of health and safety skills instruction provided depends on a student's instructional needs and circumstances (e.g., the settings in which he or she participates, the medical needs of the student), critical skill areas include the following: home and community living, work, fire and crime prevention,

HIV/AIDS prevention, substance use, and self-medication and health care. In each of these skills areas, students need to be taught to recognize potentially dangerous or abusive conditions or stimuli, to act to correct or modify them on either a short- or long-term basis, and to report the situation to a relevant person (e.g., supervisor, parent, police officer).

The following section presents justification for each of the preceding critical skill areas. Additionally, important instructional targets are identified and recommended assessment and teaching procedures are presented.

Home and Community Living

Identifying Skills

Accidents occur at home and in the community frequently. Foege (1988) reported, "Injury is the principal public health problem in America today. . . . It will touch one of every three Americans this year" (p. 1). One person in 11 has incurred an injury at home that required medical attention or resulted in a half day or more of restricted activity (National Safety Council, 1988), and 1% of the population suffers serious burn injuries each year (Tarnowski, Rasnake, & Drabman, 1987). Risks abound in every setting, and persons unaware of these dangers may be in potential danger. It is essential that students be taught to identify these risks and be able to complete a task that has an element of fear in a safe manner (Gast et al., 1994).

Table 13.1 presents selected safety skills areas identified by a sample of parents as skills their children needed to learn (Collins, Wolery, & Gast, 1992). The respondents identified a diverse repertoire of skills across several key areas: safe appliance use, mobility skills, interacting with animals, and responding to fire, to name a few. Although this is an extensive list, it does not include a number of problems in other environments a student may frequent. For example, there are other specific risks present in homes with working fireplaces or staircases, at Christmas and other holiday times (e.g., fireworks on July 4th), and with varied

TABLE 13.1
Safety Skills Areas Identified by Parents

Home safety
    Kitchen
    Bathroom
    General home areas

Community safety
    Yards and playgrounds
    Responding to strange animals
    Bicycle use
    Community mobility

Fire safety

First aid

Responding to strangers

Sex education

Note. Adapted from "A National Survey of Safety Concerns for Students with Special Needs," by B. C. Collins, M. Wolery, and D. L. Gast, 1992, *Journal of Developmental and Physical Disabilities, 4,* pp. 263–276.

recreational equipment (e.g., swimming pools, volleyball nets). In a sense, the list of potential risks is unending. The threat of injury from stimuli in the physical environment is an inherent part of our society (Bevill & Gast, 1998), and all students with disabilities need to be aware of them.

Ideally, students should acquire all the safety skills they may need, but available resources and circumstances warrant that skill selection will need to be prioritized. Gast et al. (1994) suggest the following procedure for prioritizing skills. First, teachers need to identify the environments at home and in the community in which the student currently participates or is expected to participate. This information can be obtained from the student, parents, siblings, the student's friends, and informal observations by the teacher. Once this information is obtained, the teacher can identify the types of accidents that may occur and the likelihood of occurrence in each environment. Thus, the teacher can determine in which environments the likelihood of an accident occurring are the highest and prioritize instruction based on the student's frequency of participation in environments where risks are present. Another consideration in prioritization is the severity of a potential injury. A cut from a kitchen knife is more likely to occur than a burn from a fire; nevertheless, the latter is far more serious than the former and a critical preventive skill to acquire. Consequently, frequency of participation and seriousness or severity of consequences must be weighed against each other when determing which skills to teach.

Second, priority must be given to teaching skills that will prevent *immediate danger* (e.g., using a power tool or an appliance, crossing the street). This is not to suggest that risks that may have a delayed effect (e.g., HIV/AIDS, hypothermia) are not important to teach, but only that more immediate dangers should be addressed first. Once immediate risks are addressed, teachers can teach responses to other potential threats and risks.

Last, teachers need to give priority to the particular concerns of students, parents, and significant others. Because of the importance of student-directed learning—that is, active student involvement in both educational planning and delivery, particularly in transition-age youth—it is essential that professionals obtain the input of students and their parents regarding personal safety instructional goals. Failure to do so will discourage collaborative planning and problem solving.

Teaching Safety Skills

It is generally recommended that the teaching of functional skills be conducted in the natural settings in which skills are typically performed. Instruction in such environments promotes generalized responding and helps to establish stimulus control. However, instruction in community settings may not be practical because of logistical or scheduling difficulties. Furthermore, for the curricular area of health and safety, community-based instruction may subject students to unnecessary risks. In such cases, we recommend using simulations for instruction. Simulations allow for frequent, repeated trials, in contrast to the limited number of instructional trials that may be provided in community settings. And they permit students to acquire and practice a variety of safety skills that would otherwise expose them to great danger or harm. When feasible, instruction should be provided in natural settings, but simulation instruction is an acceptable alternative. When using simulation instruction, teachers should use natural, community settings frequently (at least once a week) to assess target skills.

Additionally, Gast et al. (1994) recommend that safety skills be taught in the context of a natural routine (e.g., practice safe use of appliances during meal preparation), not at an arbitrary time convenient for the teacher. Contextual instruction allows the student to learn what to do if an accident occurs during the execution of a task (e.g., liquid spills on floor during a work task), when it would typically occur. Also, to minimize risk, instructional materials may need to be modified (e.g., knife blades dulled, match tips removed). These adaptations allow for instruction that would otherwise be too difficult to conduct. In all, systematic, data-based instructional procedures should be used to teach students the variety of home living and community skills needed to promote their well-being and independence. Safety skills, like other discrete behaviors, need to be systematically shaped and reinforced.

Work Safety

Virtually every work environment can potentially be dangerous (Agran & Martella, 1994). A sample of employers rated safe work behavior and safety awareness as the most important skill for the job survival of all employees (Mueller, Wilgosh, & Dennis, 1989). However, according to Heath (1983), "Not only are workers entering the work-force with a minimum of job safety and health knowledge and skills, many of them receive little or no instruction on job risks upon entering the work force" (p. 22). Without assurance that students with disabilities can work safely, both employers and employment specialists may restrict placements and work opportunities. Martella and Marchand-Martella (1995) indicated that employers would be hesitant to employ individuals if the employers knew the individuals either had no safety awareness or had a history of on-the-job injuries. Regrettably, although data are limited on the prevalence of work injuries for persons with disabilities, reported data suggest that individuals with disabilities sustain injuries due to work accidents at levels comparable, if not higher, than workers without disabilities (Martella & Agran, 1994). For example, as mentioned previously, in a nationwide study from 20 randomly selected states, respondents representing 800 vocational rehabilitation facilities (e.g., supported employment programs) indicated that of the 11,000 individuals served by the agencies contacted, 4,338 injuries were reported. The actual number of accidents is probably higher because minor injuries and near misses are rarely reported (Duenk & Burke, 1991). Not surprisingly, the types of injuries (e.g., lacerations, strains) sustained by employees with disabilities were the same as employees without disabilities (U.S. Department of Labor, 1988).

Despite the reported data on the high level of work injuries sustained by persons with disabilities, Agran, Swaner, and Snow (1998) found that only a minority of secondary-level special education personnel in their sample provided ongoing work safety skills instruction to their students. Even though 85% of the respondents indicated that work safety skills was a high priority area, only one third of them provided ongoing safety skills instruction. The reasons for this disparity are unknown, but it may be due to the assumption that students have these skills, or it may be that teachers believe it is not their responsibility to teach these skills. Nevertheless, the fact that only a minority of students receives ongoing work safety instruction underscores the need to provide it. Failure to do so potentially limits the employability of these students and may put them in potentially dangerous situations.

Accident Causes

Work injuries are caused by either behavioral or environmental factors. Behavioral causes refer to the inappropriate or unsafe actions of employees or their lack of an appropriate response to an injury-causing situation (e.g., using wrong tool, not wearing goggles). Environmental causes include physical stimuli at a job site that may cause an injury (e.g., exposed electrical wiring, spilled food on floor).

Agran and Madison (1995) identified primary causes of work accidents (see a sample of causes in Table 13.2) and classified them as either behavioral or environmental. Behavioral causes were reported to occur at a significantly higher level than environmental causes. The most frequently reported cause was general carelessness, followed by improper positioning, failure to adhere to safety procedures, and not wearing protective equipment. The most frequently reported environmental causes were objects on floor, wet floors, and flammables near a heat source. What is compelling about these data (and potentially motivating to educators) is that most of these accidents are preventable because they are caused by the inappropriate actions of the employees. Teaching individuals to not engage in the behaviors listed in Table 13.2 and to discriminate hazardous environmental stimuli suggests a potentially useful curriculum. At minimum, students should be taught to respond to all of these situations or conditions.

Identifying Skills

Work safety skills include both generic and job-specific skills. The generic skills include the skills needed to avoid the accident causes listed in Table 13.2, such as knowing how to lift a heavy box, attending to what you are doing, and not engaging in horseplay while working. In addition, many jobs may present specific risks. To identify these risks, several procedures are recommended. First, employers, supervisors, and coworkers should be asked about potential risks in the work setting

TABLE 13.2
Causes of Work Accidents

Environmental Hazards

Wet floors
Objects on floor
Flammables near heat source
Exposed electrical wires
Sharp objects

Behavioral Causes

General carelessness
Fighting
Improper positioning (lifting heavy objects inappropriately)
Not wearing protective equipment
Running/horseplay
Inappropriate tool use
Not following safety procedures

Note. Adapted from "Prevalence of Injuries Among Supported Employees," by M. Agran and D. Madison, 1995, *Journal of Vocational Rehabilitation, 5,* pp. 5–13.

and how best to respond to them. Second, a job safety analysis should be conducted (see Figure 13.1 for a sample format). A safety analysis includes the work task steps and the related environmental cues. Next, a potential hazard for each of these steps is identified. Last, an appropriate safe procedure is suggested. For example, if the work task was to clean a campsite in a national forest campground, then the response sequence consists of all the steps needed to complete this task, from cleaning the litter at the site to cleaning the fire area. The related environmental cues include such stimuli as the drive-in area and the stoned fire area. Potential hazards may include broken glass or a still-smoldering fire. Safe responses to these potential hazards may include wearing thick work gloves and extinguishing the fire.

With the information gathered in a job safety analysis, employees can be taught to respond appropriately to the work hazards at their jobs. Further, a job safety analysis helps trainers to nest safety instruction into ongoing work training. The contextual nature of a job safety analysis also allows students to have a better idea of the situations in which an accident may happen, instead of viewing it an event that occurs independent of the work routine.

Last, specific skills taught may depend on the individual student's needs. A student with a sensory impairment or a physical challenge may need instruction adapted to his or her needs on how to respond to potential risks (e.g., operating

Task Steps	Environmental Cue	Potential Safety Hazard	Safe Procedure

FIGURE 13.1. Sample format for a job safety analysis.

machinery, using tools, maneuvering through the work setting). For a student with a severe cognitive disability, partial participation may be recommended. That is, if it is not feasible to teach the student to identify a potential risk, correct the situation, and then report it to a supervisor, it may be appropriate to only teach the student to tell the supervisor or a coworker about a suspected hazard. Such instruction is critical to the student's physical well-being and work performance.

Martella and Agran (1994) suggest that the assessment of a student's work safety skills should be an integral part of any work performance evaluation. Without having information on students' command of safety skills, educators may be sending ill-prepared students into many work settings. Students should either be asked to describe or demonstrate how they would respond when presented with various risk stimuli.

Teaching Work Safety

Teaching work safety needs to be directed to changing behaviors, not attitudes as is commonly thought. Work safety involves teaching students a set of specific and observable safe work skills that are identified through the procedures discussed earlier.

Instruction in work safety involves two major components: identifying safety hazards and determining appropriate responses. Safety skills are best taught using a systematic behavior-analytic approach, in which the work behaviors of students are systematically modified (see Chapter 2). This allows teachers to shape behaviors over time and to motivate students by rewarding safe work behavior. In particular, a problem-solving strategy can be an effective way to teach safety skills (Martella & Agran, 1994). First, using the job safety analysis previously described, students can identify the hazards specific to their environments. Second, students are taught to determine how an accident can be prevented. Specifically, they learn to ask and respond to the following questions:

- How would an accident happen?
- When would an accident be prevented?
- Who would you talk to?
- What would you do or say?
        or
- What is dangerous?
- Why is it unsafe?
- What can I do to make it safe?

Initially, students are taught to state that a problem exists (e.g., heavy box near workbench) and to devise a solution (e.g., ask coworker to help move it). Immediately after, they are asked to direct themselves to perform the planned response.

Instruction can be implemented in either one-on-one or group formats. In one-on-one instruction, the student is asked to respond to the question after a risk stimulus is presented (either verbally or actually); in a group format, participants take turns suggesting solutions to problem situations. Next, students are taught how to respond appropriately to risk stimuli, then are observed responding to staged assessments (e.g., teacher spills a glass of water intentionally on the floor) or to naturally occurring risks in their work settings (e.g., a customer's spilled beverage on the floor of a fast-food restaurant). Also, teachers may want to teach their students to politely inform coworkers about risks. Thus, teachers may want to ask coworkers to serve as confederates (i.e., intentionally engage in unsafe work behavior such as running around), and the students' response to these situations can be observed.

Students need to be able to evaluate the safety of their work settings and the safety of their own work behavior (Martella & Agran, 1994). Without these skills, their own safety, employability, and future job success are greatly in peril.

Fire Safety

Home fires result in tragic deaths for many people and millions of dollars in property loss each year. To compound the problem, learning how to respond during a fire emergency is a demanding task, and various case studies have demonstrated that many persons, whether they have disabilities or not, have difficulty responding appropriately (Juracek, 1994). Although teaching students with disabilities fire safety skills is challenging, there is sufficient evidence to suggest that students with disabilities (mild to severe) can learn a variety of fire safety skills (see Bannerman, Sheldon, & Sherman, 1991; Haney & Jones, 1982; Katz & Singh, 1986). It goes without saying that the survival of individuals with disabilities during a fire may depend on their ability to perform these skills.

Identifying Skills

As indicated in Table 13.3, students need to acquire five major fire safety skills. Specifically, based on available data on home fires, students need to know how to respond appropriately to nighttime emergencies (most fire emergencies occur at night), how to respond to cooking fires (a large percentage of fires occur in the kitchen, and many of these can be extinguished), and how to use smoking materials appropriately (appropriate lighting and disposal of cigarettes and ashes; Juracek, 1994). A difficulty in assessing and teaching fire safety skills is that fires, fortunately, occur infrequently. The infrequency prevents students from practicing fire safety skills on a consistent basis, and assessment and instruction in these skills must rely extensively on simulations.

Assessment of fire safety skills involves two dimensions. First, parents (or, ideally, professionals) need to analyze the fire safety features of the student's home and determine the projected fire emergencies that may occur there (see Juracek, 1994, for detailed information that should be provided to teachers). Second, the

TABLE 13.3
Selected Fire Safety Skills

Exit from home at the sound of an alarm.
Respond appropriately to smoke, hot door.
Extinguish contained fires.
Practice fire prevention skills (e.g., safe lighting, safe disposal of ashes).
Use assistive fire safety devices (e.g., appliance timer, sensitive smoke alarms, auditory monitoring devices [devices that produce a sound]).

cognitive and physical capabilities of the student need to be assessed; this will indicate the student's ability to discriminate the type and seriousness of a fire and to safely escape it.

Teaching Fire Safety Skills

All fire safety skills require that students follow a specified sequence. In teaching these sequences, Juracek (1994) recommends that strategies include direct instruction, provision of rationale, repeated practice, modeling, feedback, and self-evaluation (i.e., Did I follow each step of the sequence?). If possible, training should take place in the student's home, and training probes should be scheduled in the home at various times, especially nighttime. To accomplish this, the teacher will need to coordinate the program with the parents. Also, to promote maintenance, teachers will need to conduct occasional probes periodically, at least once a month for an extended period. If home-based training is not feasible, simulated situations can be set up in the classroom (e.g., a teacher shouting "fire," even though one is not present), but, admittedly, the transferability of these skills to a home setting may be restricted.

Last, a critical skills area that should be addressed is preventive safety skills. It must strongly be emphasized to students that they must do everything possible to ensure that a fire does not start. For example, appliances should be used appropriately, flammable objects should be stored safely, cigarette use should be discouraged (but if used, cigarettes should be extinguished properly), lit candles or fires in fireplaces should be carefully monitored, and space heaters should only be used following manufacturer recommendations. All of these skills must become an integral part of the student's repertoire. One cannot assume that students have these skills unless their knowledge and execution is assessed.

Crime Prevention

Although precise statistics about the number of persons with disabilities who have been criminally or sexually abused are not available, the available data suggest that people with disabilities are particularly vulnerable, more so than nondisabled persons (Chotiner & Lehr, 1976; Lumley & Miltenberger, 1997; Sobsey, 1994; Stimpson & Best, 1991; West, Richardson, LeConte, Crimi, & Stuart, 1992). There are several reasons for this: They may be perceived by criminals as "easy prey"; they may be involved in dysfunctional familial and social relationships, isolated from supportive and protective communities; they may be unable to recognize a potentially dangerous situation or to extricate themselves from a criminal attack; and they may not know what is appropriate (e.g., when and how they can be touched). Regardless of the reason, individuals with disabilities, particularly women, are more likely to be victimized than other individuals (Sobsey, 1994); therefore, crime prevention should be recognized as an essential safety skills area.

Identifying Skills

There is widespread agreement that individuals with disabilities can reduce the likelihood of being victimized by acquiring skills in the following areas: decision making, assertiveness, sex education, personal rights and safety, social and communication skills, property management, and response to crimes (Sobsey, 1994). A brief discussion of each follows.

Decision Making. Although not all abusive situations can be prevented, certain situations that could potentially become abusive can be deescalated if students use a decision-making procedure that helps them identify problematic situations (Khemka & Hickson, 2000). Khemka and Hickson (2000) indicated that abuse takes several forms—sexual, physical, and psychological—and that students with disabilities need to be taught how to identify each. Similar to the problem-solving procedure discussed in the work safety section of this chapter, students learn to ask four questions by viewing a potentially abusive situation in a taped vignette. First, is (person in videotape) faced with a problem? Second, what is (person in videotape)'s problem? Third, what is the best thing for (person in videotape) to do in this situation? Fourth, why is this the best choice for (person in videotape)? It is crucial that these skills are taught.

Assertiveness. Students need to learn to be assertive, to express their preferences, and to protect their rights (e.g., control of one's own money, freedom from unwanted interventions or medications, freedom from coercion and abuse). Sobsey (1994) suggested that educators have spent excessive time teaching students to be compliant rather than to be assertive; by doing so, students have become more vulnerable to crime. Teaching students assertiveness skills may reduce considerably the likelihood of them becoming crime victims. For example, students should be taught to respond appropriately to teasing. By doing so, they may be able to defuse a potentially explosive situation and present themselves as being less vulnerable.

Sex Education. The incidence of sexual abuse or sexual assaults may be greatly reduced by the student's knowledge of sexuality and sexual relationships. Ignorance about sexuality appears to be a major factor in increasing a student's risk for abuse (Muccigrosso, 1991). Students may not know appropriate behavior for social interaction. Therefore, comprehensive and accurate sex education curriculum is essential. Students need to know about birth control, sexually transmitted diseases, hetero- and homosexual behavior, responsibility for sexual behavior, preventing abuse, hygiene, responding to harassment, and choice making pertaining to sexual behavior (Sobsey, 1994). Sex education should also include the decision-making skills discussed previously (Khemka, 2000).

Personal Safety. Although the issue of teaching self-defense skills to students with disabilities is somewhat controversial (i.e., opponents believe it will further jeopardize students), there is a growing opinion that these skills should be taught (Pava, Bateman, Appleton, & Glasscock, 1991). Such instruction will enable students to determine if, when, and how to fight back if attacked. Also, as Sobsey (1994) suggested, such instruction may increase the student's self-esteem and help the student overcome feelings associated with learned helplessness. Generally, such training involves teaching students strategies for breaking free of or temporarily disabling an offender (Bodnar & Hodge, 1989). The use of self-defense strategies will vary across students, depending on their instructional needs. If classes are available, parents and students may elect to include self-defense or martial arts instruction as an IEP goal.

Social and Communication Skills. People who are isolated because of social or communication deficits are more often victims of crime. Individuals who are unable to report abuse or seek help are more likely to be perceived as vulnerable (Lang & Frenzel, 1988). Conversely, individuals who have active friendships and community relationships are less likely to be victimized (Sobsey, 1994). Therefore, students need to learn how to establish friendships, date, and develop leisure and recreational skills that provide opportunities for social interactions. Furthermore, students need to learn practical communication skills related to crimes (e.g., stating that they were abused).

Property Management. People with disabilities are typically not provided instruction in protecting personal possessions or money. Students need to know that they have the right to possess and secure money and personal property. Skills as securing the home (e.g., safely securing doors and windows), securing valuables, discouraging others from taking possessions, using checks and credit cards, and hiding money are routinely performed by parents or caregivers, with scant attention directed to teaching them to students.

Response to Crimes. Students need to learn how to report a crime and to whom it should be reported. They need to be taught how to communicate this information to the police and whom in their community they can trust. In particular, they need to learn how to provide testimony and how to respond to questions from court officials. Watson (1994) also has suggested teaching students what to do if they were threatened or bribed to keep a "secret" and not tell.

Teaching Crime Prevention Skills. Crime prevention skills can be taught using the same instructional procedures as for other functional skills. Like the other safety skills, the crime prevention skills taught should be based on the specific student's instructional needs. Generally speaking, students need to know how to identify potentially dangerous or abusive situations, how to respond to them (from walking or running away to saying "no"), how to respond in dangerous situations if they occur (from screaming to fighting back), and how to report them. Most, if not all, of this instruction needs to involve simulation training with individual and small-group instruction, discussion, role playing, modeling, repeated practice, and the use of pictures and audiovisual instructional materials. Students should also be provided opportunities to practice skills in natural community environments. For example, to assess how well a student responds to strangers, a teacher may want to recruit a confederate to approach a student in a selected site in the community (with parental permission). Additionally, Gast et al. (1994) suggest that, although it is inappropriate to have students experience aversive consequences, they should be exposed to consequences that may occur if they do not behave safely; newspaper articles or television programs can serve this purpose. Although some people believe that such prevention programs may cause fear or anxiety in students, the research literature refutes this claim (Lumley & Miltenberger, 1997). Given the seriousness of this issue, it is critical that we teach students to protect themselves as best as possible.

HIV and AIDS Prevention

Health Concern

Because of inadequate sex education and HIV prevention training, ignorance about safe-sex practices, engagement in high-risk sexual behavior, and vulnerability to sexual abuse (Mason & Jaskulski, 1994), individuals with disabilities may be at great risk of becoming infected with HIV. It is unclear how many persons with disabilities are infected, but in a study involving member agencies of the National Association of Rehabilitation Facilities (NARF), 23% to 30% of the respondents reported that they were serving consumers who were HIV-positive (Jaskulski & Mason, 1992). In an additional study (NARF, 1989), more than 75% of member agencies indicated that they provided little or no prevention training to consumers. It is safe to say that the number of individuals with disabilities who are infected with HIV is growing, and the seriousness of this health problem for this population cannot be underestimated.

Effective Education Programs

The need to include HIV prevention training in a sex education program is critical for ensuring the safety of students with disabilities. Indeed, Mason and Jaskulski (1994) suggest that teaching objectives relating to HIV prevention need to be included in students' IEPs. Despite teachers' possible discomfort with this subject matter, students need to be provided frank and comprehensive information on sexuality, infectious diseases, and the need for hygienic measures. Scotti et al. (1997) recommended an instructional program that includes seven components. First, students learn about HIV and AIDS and about how they differ. Next, information on what happens if one "catches" HIV is discussed. Following, students learn who can become infected. After this, procedures to protect oneself are presented, followed by specific instruction on using condoms. Last, instruction on how to assertively refuse unwanted sex is presented. Prior to providing instruction, teachers need to assess students' knowledge in these areas. As with other safety skills, critical instructional targets can be determined based on assessment findings and the students' instructional needs. In particular, teachers need to determine if a student is engaging in high-risk behavior (e.g., multiple partners, needle use) so that appropriate target skills can be identified. To do so, teachers must make every effort to establish open and candid communication exchanges with students, their parents, and their friends.

In all, AIDS prevention involves many skills (for more detailed information, see Mason & Jaskulski, 1994; Scotti et al., 1997). At a minimum, students need to know that AIDS is a very serious disease that can result in death, it is transmitted via unsafe sexual activity or sharing intravenous needles, and it can be prevented through safe-sex practices, abstinence, and not sharing needles or syringes.

Instruction can be provided to individuals or groups, and students should practice target skills repeatedly. For example, students can practice unrolling condoms several times during an instructional session. Also, students may discuss ways to appropriately refuse sexual advances or drug or alcohol use. Role playing is strongly encouraged and, if possible, target skills should be practiced in natural environments in the community (e.g., a car).

Substance Use

Although prevalence figures regarding alcohol and drug use vary across disability groups, there is growing evidence that students with disabilities may be consuming substances at appreciable levels (Morgan, 1994). With more individuals with mental retardation and developmental disabilities living in integrated community settings, it is safe to assume that substance abuse will be a growing problem (Christian & Poling, 1997). Although the available data suggest a somewhat lower level of use among individuals with disabilities than the general population, prevalence is likely to increase. The negative effects of this include work suspension, health problems, dysfunctional family and social relations, arrests (Krishef, 1986), and negative interactions with prescribed medications (e.g., psychotropic and anticonvulsant drugs; Gadow & Poling, 1988). Additionally, several risk factors have been identified for predicting substance use among youth with disabilities, including a family history of substance abuse, lack of self-regulation skills, and desire for attention (Christian & Poling, 1997). As Morgan (1994) noted, substance use among youth with disabilities represents a largely undocumented yet serious problem. This situation is compounded because few prevention programs are designed for students with disabilities.

Effective Prevention Approaches

When teaching substance use prevention skills, instructors should use the following practices (Morgan, 1994).

- *Teach students specific skills* (e.g., problem solving, stress management) rather than attempting to change their attitudes, self-concepts, or self-esteem; changes in the latter may not produce changes in the former.

- *Address both the short- and long-term consequences* of substance use, and discuss ways to respond to pressure to indulge in substance use (from peers and from oneself).

- *Conduct instructional programs on a continuous, long-term basis.* A one-time discussion will produce little or no benefit.

- *Encourage active parent involvement.* Parents need to be persuaded to have a strong interest in this curricular area and to serve as appropriate models. Additionally, parents can be taught skills that may help prevent or ameliorate a substance use problem, including listening, behavior management, and identification of their child's drug use.

- *Use peers.* Youth with disabilities may be greatly influenced by positive peer interactions. Therefore, discussion about drugs between students with disabilities and peers is strongly encouraged.

- *Ensure that instructional activities are appropriate.* Teachers should present concepts in a concrete manner, build sufficient practice and reviews into lessons, and use instructional materials at the students' reading levels.

Prevention Skills

Prevention curricula include a diverse set of skills. Such instruction should start as early as possible (e.g., kindergarten) and continue through secondary school. The U.S. Department of Education (1990) recommends the fourth through ninth grades as the best times to provide instruction. Major skills areas include stress reduction, assertiveness training, problem solving, decision making, and communication.

The curriculum should teach students that substance use is an illegal and harmful activity. Also, in addition to learning about the harmful effects of drugs, students need to learn strategies to resist peer pressure and to learn that drugs do not solve problems and that there are better ways to get attention and make friends. Recommended teaching procedures include role playing, behavioral rehearsal, peer tutoring, cooperative learning experiences, and verbal instruction. Morgan (1994) suggests that students be actively engaged in instructional activities (e.g., role playing) rather than doing passive seatwork (e.g., responding to worksheets). Also, teachers may want to use a system in which students receive points or other reinforcers for acquiring and performing desired target behaviors and completing homework assignments as motivation. Last, the information that teachers present must be accurate, candid, and complete. Ultimately, as with the other safety skill areas discussed in this chapter, students need to learn decision-making skills—to determine what is in their best interest and how to regulate their own behavior. Prevention programs must present students with sufficient information and experiences so that they can conclude unequivocally that the risks of substance use far outweigh its benefits. This is indeed a serious challenge to educators, but one that certainly needs to be addressed.

Self-Medication and Health Care

An increasing number of students with special health care needs are being served in public schools. These students may require highly specialized treatments that trained medical and school staff need to provide (e.g., tracheostomy care, gastrostomy care). Additionally, taking medication may be a routine part of the day for many persons with disabilities (Harchik, 1994). In both cases, students with disabilities may have little or no involvement in their own health care or medication regimens. As Lehr and Macurdy (1994) suggested, health care procedures are typically done *to* students, rather than *with* or *taught to* students. This is unfortunate because it limits the autonomy and competence of students, and there are a number of skills students can perform to promote their participation, partially or fully, in their own health care. There is increasing evidence that students with disabilities can execute several procedures that have been routinely performed by caregivers. Given the current interest in ensuring that students have a more active involvement in their own learning and development, teaching students to participate in delivering their own health care is receiving increased attention.

Self-Medication

Students with disabilities need to be taught to assume as much responsibility as possible for their medication regimens. Prior to the implementation of such a program, students need to demonstrate that they will consistently take the medication (i.e., not be resistant to its use), have the necessary administrative behaviors (e.g., consume pills with water), and have sufficient emotional stability.

Harchik (1994) suggests that a self-medication curriculum has three components: recognizing and understanding one's medication, learning self-medication skills, and learning to respond to problems that may occur. First, although there appears to be no strong evidence that the student's knowledge of the medication will aid in the self-medication procedure, such knowledge may be helpful because it will allow students to learn why they need to take medication. Second, self-medication skills involve being able to locate the medicine, remove it from its container, consume or apply it correctly, and monitor one's own quality of performance. To facilitate this, students can be taught to chart their own medication behavior by responding to a checklist or a sequence of pictures illustrating the regimen. Last, students need to respond appropriately to problems that may occur in the medication regimen (e.g., what to do if too little or too much medication is taken, or if medication is lost) and learn to correct them or to notify an appropriate individual (e.g., teacher, parent).

Teaching Self-Medication Skills

Instruction may involve individual or group instructional formats and should coincide with the times of the day the student normally receives medication (Harchik, 1994). In teaching sessions, simulated medicines should be used (e.g., candies). Additionally, teachers may find it necessary to use adaptations (e.g., color-coded medication containers, picture schedules) for a self-medication program. Last, self-medication programs must be monitored to ensure that the student is appropriately following the regimen. Harchik indicated that students can learn to monitor their own self-medication behavior as described above or provide information about their drug regimen via interviews; additionally, teachers or service providers may want to observe students at designated drug consumption times.

Health Care

Students with special health care needs can also be taught to have a critical role in the administration of their own health care. Lehr and Macurdy (1994) suggest that students can be taught to assist in varying degrees in tube feeding, tracheostomy suctioning, and catheterization, among a number of procedures. At a minimum, they should be instructed in performing appropriate toileting, hand washing, and oral and nasal hygiene. Ideally, students with health care needs should be taught to assume full responsibility for their own health care. However, the decision to teach self-administration of health care procedures needs to be carefully made by the student's IEP team, with the approval of the student's physician. As with the other skills discussed in this chapter, specific objectives should be determined based on the student's medical, cognitive, and physical needs and abilities.

CURRICULUM DESIGN

Table 13.4 presents selected IEP objectives across different health and safety skills areas. They are organized across elementary, middle, and high school levels. With coordinated efforts by educators and parents, students can learn and practice these skills in school, home, and community settings.

Figure 13.2 lists selected IEP goals established for Malinda, the 16-year-old student with moderate to severe cognitive impairment who was introduced at the beginning of this chapter. Malinda's goals are in the following skill areas: home and community safety, work safety, and crime prevention and personal safety. These skills will strongly promote Malinda's independence and safety in the community, both at work and in the home.

TABLE 13.4
Selected Individualized Education Plan Objectives

	Grade Level		
Skill Area	**Elementary School Student**	**Middle School Student**	**High School Student**
Home and Community Safety[1]	Will not climb into a refrigerator or freezer	Will use knives safely	Will discriminate spoiled meat and other food
	Will not touch a hot stove or oven	Will use shower and bathtub safely	Will use hair dryer appropriately
	Will recognize marked poisons	Will use tools and appliances safely	Will change lightbulb appropriately
	Will pick up toys on stairs	Will lock and unlock doors in his or her house	Will safely use gym equipment
	Will not play with matches	When outdoors, will know what to do in a thunderstorm	Will know how to respond to aggressive animals
	Will stay away from power sources outdoors	Will know how to enter and exit a public bus	Will treat burns appropriately
	Will use bicycle safety	Will select lighted streets in the evening	Will recognize hypothermia or frostbite signs
	Will walk on sidewalks	Will know how to treat minor injuries	Will call the humane society about stray animals
	Will not feed strange animals	Will clean up broken items appropriately	Will identify overloaded wall outlets
	Will use utensils properly		Will aid a drowning swimmer
Work Safety[2]	Will not play while engaged in a task	Will move safely on slippery floors	Will identify exposed wires
	Will not throw objects while engaged in a task	Will move safely around objects on the floor	Will use power tools appropriately
	Will attend to relevant stimuli for specified period	Will not place flammable objects near fire	Will lift heavy objects safely
	Will follow safety rules at school	Will use tools appropriately	Will wear appropriate clothing at work
	Will exit school building when alarm is heard	Will place and store work materials appropriately	Will follow company safety policies while working
	Will show care with sharp objects	Will not fight while working	Will keep work area clean
	Will clean up desk	Will identify safety symbols	Will ask for instruction on how to use equipment
	Will report an emergency to a teacher or other school representative	Will understand the function of protective devices	Will operate equipment at appropriate speed
	Will identify tools and their intended functions		Will use protective equipment
			Will identify dangerous conditions at work
Fire Safety[3]	Will respond to fire and smoke alarms	Will identify flammable materials	Will use matches and lighters safely
	Will call fire department	Will use a fire extinguisher appropriately	Will respond appropriately to person on fire
	Will leave burning building	Will extinguish an electrical fire	Will respond appropriately to nighttime fires
	Will identify emergency exits	Will extinguish a grease fire	Will dipose of ashes safely
	Will feel doors for heat		

(continues)

TABLE 13.4 *Continued.*

Skill Area	Grade Level		
	Elementary School Student	**Middle School Student**	**High School Student**
	Will go to window to call for help if door is hot	Will use a stove properly Will keep flammables away from a fire or stove Will extinguish a fire in a wastebasket	Will know how to check whether a home fire alarm is operating correctly
Crime Prevention[4]	Will not talk to strangers Will say no to physical approaches Will attract attention when attacked Will demonstrate proper care of body Will demonstrate how to build friendships Will learn when to dial 911	Will identify dangerous areas Will exercise caution in public restrooms Will identify body parts Will demonstrate knowledge of maturation Will learn how to lock and unlock the doors in his or her house Will demonstrate how to secure and protect private property	Will learn about his or her rights as a citizen Will demonstrate knowledge of responsible sexual behavior Will demonstrate how to provide police with a statement after an attack Will identify who in the neighborhood can be trusted Will know how to behave appropriately when questioned in court
HIV/AIDS Prevention[5]	Will describe how diseases are transmitted Will identify what HIV infection is Will describe different emotions and feelings Will describe functions of body parts Will identify various situations to avoid (e.g., playing with needles, talking to strangers)	Will identify AIDS as a sexually transmitted disease Will identify the risks of drug and alcohol use Will describe how blood can be contaminated Will describe the function of a condom and its limitations Will describe the dangers of sharing needles and syringes	Will demonstrate knowledge of safe sex Will identify resources in the local community for AIDS prevention Will describe how HIV and AIDS affect relationships, families, and society Will describe the function of testing for HIV infection Will describe his or her responsibility to sexual partner
Substance Use Prevention[6]	Will indicate that alcohol and drugs are harmful Will state that most individuals do not use drugs Will state various drugs individuals use	Will discuss the specific risks of drug use Will describe how drugs are sold Will describe the seriousness of the drug problem Will describe the legal and criminal consequences of drug use Will describe how drugs and AIDS are related	Will describe how drug use is related to various disabilities Will describe how drug use can be fatal Will describe how drug use can affect a fetus Will describe the negative effects of drug use and driving and other physical tasks Will describe how drug use can negatively affect his or her education and professional development Will describe treatment and intervention resources

(continues)

TABLE 13.4 *Continued.*

Skill Area	Grade Level		
	Elementary School Student	**Middle School Student**	**High School Student**
Self-Medication and Health Care[7]	Will identify function of medication prescribed Will identify medication prescribed Will swallow pills Will follow proper toileting procedures Will wash hands properly Will demonstrate proper nasal and oral hygiene practices Will state reason for alternative eating method, suctioning, or catheterization Will turn on suctioning machine Will identify need to be catheterized	Will identify side effects of medication Will monitor his or her self-medication Will identify administration of medication Will measure feeding liquid into feeding bag or syringe Will feed self independently using feeding equipment Will describe steps necessary to suction Will self-catheterize	Will seek appropriate attention or assistance in the event of an injury or illness Will consume appropriate medications as needed (e.g., aspirins, antacids) Will respond appropriately if too little or too much medication is taken Will clean feeding equipment Will wash and assemble catheterization materials

[1] Adapted from "Home and Community Safety Skills," by D. L. Gast, J. Wellons, and B. Collins, in *Promoting Health and Safety: Skills for Independent Living* (pp. 11–32), edited by M. Agran, N. E. Marchand-Martella, and R. C. Martella, 1994, Baltimore: Brookes.

[2] Adapted from "Prevalence of Injuries Among Supported Employees," by M. Agran and D. Madison, 1995, *Journal of Vocational Rehabilitation, 5,* pp. 5–13.

[3] Adapted from "Teaching Adults with Severe and Profound Retardation to Exit Their Homes Upon Hearing the Fire Alarm," by D. J. Bannerman, J. B. Sheldon, and J. A. Sherman, 1991, *Journal of Applied Behavior Analysis, 24,* pp. 571–578; also adapted from "Fire Safety Skills," by D. B. Juracek, in *Promoting Health and Safety: Skills for Independent Living* (pp. 103–119), edited by M. Agran, N. E. Marchand-Martella, and R. C. Martella, 1994, Baltimore: Brookes.

[4] Adapted from "Crime Prevention and Personal Safety," by D. Sobsey, in *Promoting Health and Safety: Skills for Independent Living* (pp. 193–213), edited by M. Agran, N. E. Marchand-Martella, and R. C. Martella, 1994, Baltimore: Brookes.

[5] Adapted from "HIV/AIDS Prevention and Education," by C. Y. Mason and T. Jaskulski, in *Promoting Health and Safety: Skills for Independent Living* (pp. 161–191), edited by M. Agran, N. E. Marchand-Martella, and R. C. Martella, 1994, Baltimore: Brookes.

[6] Adapted from "Preventing Substance Use," by D. P. Morgan, in *Promoting Health and Safety: Skills for Independent Living* (pp. 135–159), edited by M. Agran, N. E. Marchand-Martella, and R. C. Martella, 1994, Baltimore: Brookes.

[7] Adapted from "Self-Medication Skills," by A. E. Harchik (pp. 55–69) and from "Meeting Special Health Care Needs of Students" by D. H. Lehr and S. Macurdy (pp. 71–84), both in *Promoting Health and Safety: Skills for Independent Living,* edited by M. Agran, N. E. Marchand-Martella, and R. C. Martella, 1994, Baltimore: Brookes.

Annual Goal: Malinda will increase her home and community safety skills.

Objectives/Activities	Person Responsible	Evaluation Criteria	Learning Environment S = School C = Community H = Home W = Work	Date Initiated	Date Completed	Quarterly Program
With assistance from mother, Malinda will operate microwave.	Mother, home economics teacher	100% correct performance	S, H			
With assistance from mother, Malinda will use coffeemaker.	Mother, home economics teacher	100% correct performance	S, H			
Malinda will exit safely during simulated fire emergencies.	Malinda, father	100% performance, parent evaluation	H			
Malinda will treat cuts and abrasions, sprains, and burns.	Health education teacher, parents	90% correct performance	S, H			
When presented with different emergency situations (e.g., fire, severe injury), Malinda will call 911.	Special education teacher, parents	100% correct performance	S, H			
Malinda will recognize marked poisons.	Home economics teacher, special education teacher, parents	100% correct performance	S, H			
Malinda will identify spoiled food.	Home economics teacher, parents	100% correct performance	S, H			
Malinda will respond appropriately to cooking fires.	Home economics teacher, special education teacher, parents	100% correct performance	S, H			

FIGURE 13.2. Goals for Malinda's IEP.

Objectives/Activities	Person Responsible	Evaluation Criteria	Learning Environment S = School C = Community H = Home W = Work	Date Initiated	Date Completed	Quarterly Program
Annual Goal: Malinda will demonstrate critical work safety skills.						
While working at a grocery store, Malinda will lift boxes appropriately.	Job coach, employer	80% correct performance, employer's rating	S, W			
While working at a grocery store, Malinda will walk safely around objects on the floor or slippery floors.	Job coach, employer	80% correct performance, employer's rating	S, W			
While assigned to clean areas of a grocery store, Malinda will safely use cleaning agents and materials.	Job coach, employer	80% correct performance, employer's rating	S, W			

FIGURE 13.2. *Continued.*

Objectives/Activities	Person Responsible	Evaluation Criteria	Learning Environment S = School C = Community H = Home W = Work	Date Initiated	Date Completed	Quarterly Program			
Annual Goal: Malinda will demonstrate crime prevention and personal safety skills.									
Malinda will initiate social interactions with peers at school and in the community.	Special education teacher, parents	Self-report data, parents' satisfaction	S, C						
Malinda will lock and unlock the doors in her home.	Parents	Parents' satisfaction	H						
Malinda will state what the HIV/AIDS virus is and how it is transmitted.	Health education teacher	100% correct performance	S						
Malinda will respond appropriately to strangers.	Special education teacher, parents	100% correct performance, self-report data, parents' satisfaction							
Malinda will say no to physical approaches.	Special education teacher, parents	100% correct performance, parents' satisfaction	S, C, H						
Malinda will say no when offered alcohol or drugs.	Health education teacher, parents	100% correct performance, parents' satisfaction	S, C, H						

FIGURE 13.2. *Continued.*

REFERENCES

Agran, M., & Madison, D. (1995). Prevalence of injuries among supported employees. *Journal of Vocational Rehabilitation, 5,* 5–13.

Agran, M., Marchand-Martella, N. E., & Martella, R. C. (Eds.). (1994). *Promoting health and safety: Skills for independent living.* Baltimore: Brookes.

Agran, M., & Martella, R. C. (1994). Safety skills on the job. In M. Agran, N. E. Marchand-Martella, & R. C. Martella (Eds.), *Promoting health and safety: Skills for independent living* (pp. 121–134). Baltimore: Brookes.

Agran, M., Swaner, J., & Snow, K. C. (1998). Work safety skills: A neglected curricular area. *Career Development for Exceptional Individuals, 21,* 33–44.

Bannerman, D. J., Sheldon, J. B., & Sherman, J. A. (1991). Teaching adults with severe and profound retardation to exit their homes upon hearing the fire alarm. *Journal of Applied Behavior Analysis, 24,* 571–578.

Bevill, A. R., & Gast, D. L. (1998). Social safety for young children: A review of the literature on safety skills instruction. *Topics in Early Childhood Special Education, 18,* 222–234.

Blackman, J. (1984). *Medical aspects of developmental disabilities in children: Birth to three.* Rockville, MD: Aspen.

Bodnar, M., & Hodge, M. (1989). *Personal security.* Wellington, New Zealand: GP Books.

Bryan, E., Warden, M. G., Berg, B., & Hauck, G. R. (1978). Medical consideration for multiple handicapped children in the public schools. *Journal of School Health, 48,* 84–89.

Chotiner, N., & Lehr, W. (1976). *Child abuse and developmental disabilities: A report from the New England regional conference.* Boston: New England Developmental Disabilities Communication Center.

Christian, L., & Poling, A. (1997). Drug abuse in persons with mental retardation: A review. *American Journal on Mental Retardation, 102,* 126–136.

Collins, B. C., Wolery, M., & Gast, D. L. (1992). A national survey of safety concerns for students with special needs. *Journal of Developmental and Physical Disabilities, 4,* 263–276.

Duenk, L. G., & Burke, S. R. (1991). Greater accident awareness can prevent injuries. *School Shop/Tech Directions, 50,* 13–14.

Foege, W. H. (1988, November). *Newsletter of the Family Health Services Division, Utah Department of Health* (Available from Stephen McDonald, 288 North 1460 West, Salt Lake City, UT 84116–0650).

Gadow, K., & Poling, A. (1988). *Pharmacotherapy and mental retardation.* Boston: College Hill.

Gast, D. L., Wellons, J., & Collins, B. (1994). Home and community safety skills. In M. Agran, N. E. Marchand-Martella, & R. C. Martella (Eds.), *Promoting health and safety: Skills for independent living* (pp. 11–32). Baltimore: Brookes.

Haller, J. A. (1970). Problems in children's trauma. *Journal of Trauma, 10,* 269–271.

Halpern, A. (1993). Quality of life as a conceptual framework for evaluating transition outcomes. *Exceptional Children, 59,* 486–498.

Haney, J. I., & Jones, R. T. (1982). Programming maintenance as a major component of a community-centered preventative effort: Escape from the fire. *Behavior Therapy, 13,* 47–62.

Harchik, A. E. (1994). Self-medication skills. In M. Agran, N. E. Marchand-Martella, & R. C. Martella (Eds.), *Promoting health and safety: Skills for independent living* (pp. 55–69). Baltimore: Brookes.

Heath, E. D. (1983). Youth and safety for the world of work. *Vocational Evaluation, 58,* 23–24.

Jaskulski, T., & Mason, C. (1992). AIDS policies and education: What are vocational and residential rehabilitation providers doing? *American Rehabilitation, 19*(3), 12–19.

Juracek, D. B. (1994). Fire safety skills. In M. Agran, N. E. Marchand-Martella, & R. C. Martella (Eds.), *Promoting health and safety: Skills for independent living* (pp. 103–119). Baltimore: Brookes.

Katz, R. C., & Singh, N. N. (1986). Comprehensive fire-safety training for adult mentally retarded persons. *Journal of Mental Deficiency Research, 30,* 59–69.

Khemka, I. (2000). Increasing independent decision-making skills of women with mental retardation in simulated interpersonal situations of abuse. *American Journal on Mental Retardation, 105,* 387–401.

Khemka, I., & Hickson, L. C. (2000). Decision-making by adults with mental retardation in simulated situations of abuse. *Mental Retardation, 38,* 15–26.

Krishef, C. H. (1986). Do the mentally retarded drink? A study of their alcohol usage. *Journal of Alcohol and Drug Education, 31,* 64–70.

Lang, R. A., & Frenzel, R. R. (1988). How sex offenders lure children. *Annals of Sex Research, 1,* 303–317.

Lehr, D. H., & Macurdy, S. (1994). Meeting special health care needs of students. In M. Agran, N. E. Marchand-Martella, & R. C. Martella (Eds.), *Promoting health and safety: Skills for independent living* (pp. 71–84). Baltimore: Brookes.

Lorr, C., & Rotatori, A. F. (1985). Who are the severely and profoundly handicapped? In A. F. Rotatori, J. O. Schween, & R. A. Fox (Eds.), *Assessing severely and profoundly handicapped individuals* (pp. 38–48). Springfield, IL: Charles C Thomas.

Lumley, V. A., & Miltenberger, R. G. (1997). Sexual abuse prevention for persons with mental retardation. *American Journal on Mental Retardation, 101,* 459–472.

Martella, R. C., & Agran, M. (1994). Safety skills on the job. In M. Agran, N. E. Marchand-Martella, & R. C. Martella (Eds.), *Promoting health and safety: Skills for independent living* (pp. 121–134). Baltimore: Brookes.

Martella, R. C., & Marchand-Martella, N. E. (1995). Safety skills in vocational rehabilitation: A qualitative analysis. *Journal of Vocational Rehabilitation, 5,* 25–31.

Maslow, A. (1954). *Motivation and personality.* New York: Harper & Row.

Mason, C. Y., & Jaskulski, T. (1994). HIV/AIDS prevention and education. In M. Agran, N. E. Marchand-Martella, & R. C. Martella (Eds.), *Promoting health and safety: Skills for independent living* (pp. 161–191). Baltimore: Brookes.

Morgan, D. P. (1994). Preventing substance use. In M. Agran, N. E. Marchand-Martella, & R. C. Martella (Eds.), *Promoting health and safety: Skills for independent living* (pp. 135–159). Baltimore: Brookes.

Muccigrosso, L. (1991). Sexual abuse prevention strategies and programs for persons with developmental disabilities. *Journal of Sexuality and Disability, 9*(3), 261–272.

Mueller, H. H., Wilgosh, L., & Dennis, S. (1989). Employment survival skills for entry-level occupations. *Canadian Journal of Rehabilitation, 2,* 203–221.

National Association of Rehabilitation Facilities (NARF). (1989). *1989 NARF Education Needs Analysis Survey.* Washington, DC: Author.

National Safety Council. (1988). *Accident facts.* Chicago: Author.

Pava, W. S., Bateman, P., Appleton, M. K., & Glasscock, J. (1991, December). Self-defense training for visually impaired women. *Journal of Visual Impairment and Blindness,* pp. 397–401.

Perske, R. (1972). The dignity of risk and the mentally retarded. *Mental Retardation, 10*(1), 24–26.

Peterson, L. (1984). Teaching home safety and survival skills to latch-key children: A comparison of two manuals and methods. *Journal of Applied Behavior Analysis, 17,* 279–293.

Scotti, J. R., Nangle, D. W., Masia, C. L., Ellis, J. T., Vjcich, K. J., Giacoletti, A. M., et al. (1997). Providing an AIDS education and skills training program to persons with mild developmental disabilities. *Education and Training in Mental Retardation and Developmental Disabilities, 32,* 113–128.

Sobsey, D. (1994). Crime prevention and personal safety. In M. Agran, N. E. Marchand-Martella, & R. C. Martella (Eds.), *Promoting health and safety: Skills for independent living* (pp. 193–213). Baltimore: Brookes.

Stimpson, L., & Best, M. C. (1991). *Courage above all: Sexual assault against people with disabilities.* Toronto, Ontario, Canada: DisAbled Women's Network.

Tarnowski, K. J., Rasnake, L. K., & Drabman, R. S. (1987). Behavioral assessment and treatment of pediatric burn injuries: A review. *Behavior Therapy, 18,* 417–441.

U.S. Department of Education. (1990). *Drug prevention curricula: A guide to selection and implementation.* Washington, DC: Office of Educational Research and Improvement.

U.S. Department of Labor. (1988). *Annual survey of occupational injuries and illnesses.* Washington, DC: Author.

Vogelsberg, R. T., & Rusch, F. R. (1979). Training severely handicapped students to cross partially controlled intersections. *AAESPH Review, 4,* 264–273.

Watson, J. D. (1994). Talking about the best-kept secret: Sexual abuse and children with disabilities. *Exceptional Parent, 14,* 15–20.

West, M. A., Richardson, M., LeConte, J., Crimi, C., & Stuart, S. (1992). Identification of developmental disabilities and health problems among individuals under child protective services. *Mental Retardation, 30,* 221–225.

Wolfensberger, W. (1972). *The principle of normalization in human services.* Toronto, Canada: National Institute on Mental Retardation.

Index

About the Editors and Authors

Paul Wehman, PhD, is professor of physical medicine and rehabilitation at Virginia Commonwealth University (VCU), with joint appointments in the Department of Curriculum and Instruction and the Department of Rehabilitation Counseling. He pioneered the development of supported employment at VCU in the early 1980s and has been heavily involved in the use of supported employment with people who have severe disabilities, such as those with severe mental retardation, brain injury, spinal cord injury, or autism. Dr. Wehman is also director of the VCU Rehabilitation Research and Training Center on Workplace Supports and chairman of the Division of Rehabilitation Research. Dr. Wehman has written extensively on issues related to transition from school to adulthood and special education as it relates to young adulthood. He has published more than 150 articles, 24 book chapters, and has authored or edited 33 books. He is a recipient of the Joseph P. Kennedy, Jr. Foundation International Awards in Mental Retardation, was a Mary Switzer fellow for the National Rehabilitation Association in 1985, and received the Distinguished Service Award from the President's Committee on Employment for Persons with Disabilities in 1992. Dr. Wehman was recognized as one of the 50 most influential special educators of the millenium by a national survey coordinated by the *Remedial and Special Education* journal in 2000, and he received the VCU Distinguished Service Award in 2001. He is also editor-in-chief of the *Journal of Vocational Rehabilitation*.

John Kregel, EdD, is professor of special education at Virginia Commonwealth University (VCU) and is associate director and research director of the VCU Rehabilitation Research and Training Center on Workplace Supports. He also coordinates the Urban Services Leadership track in the School of Education doctoral program. His professional interests include supported employment and transition from school to work for individuals with disabilities. He is the author of more than 75 articles, chapters, monographs, and books on the employment of individuals with disabilities. He also serves as coeditor of the journal *Focus on Autism and Other Developmental Disabilities.*

Martin Agran, PhD, is a professor in the Department of Special Education at the University of Northern Iowa. Dr. Agran's research interests include the education of students with severe disabilities, self-determination and self-regulation, transition, and personnel preparation. He has authored or coauthored nine books and has been published extensively in professional journals. He is the coeditor of the Innovations Research-to-Practice series published by the American Association on Mental Retardation and serves on the editorial board of five refereed journals. His research has been supported by the U.S. Office of Special Education and Rehabilitative Services and the National Institute on Disability and Rehabilitation Research. Dr. Agran served as a Fulbright Scholar in the Czech Republic.

Kathryn Banks, EdS, currently serves as a due process specialist and interrelated special education teacher for the Savannah/Chatham County Public School System in Savannah, Georgia. She teaches in the inclusion setting at Savannah High School and assists the special education department and new teachers with due process requirements. She is a second-year doctoral candidate at Berne University and expects to complete her doctoral studies in administration and special education soon. Her research involves documentation of the impact of high-stakes testing on students with limited academic potential. She began her teaching career in 1975 as a teacher of students with mild cognitive impairment and emotional disturbance. Beginning in 1981, she served for 17 years as a transition specialist where she was responsible for placing students with disabilities on job sites in the community and coordinating their transition from high school to the adult environment. She has presented at four annual international conventions of the Council for Exceptional Children on the topics of transition, parental involvement, and the interagency transition team process. Ms. Banks gives Millie Kitchens credit for the teaching concept of "one dollar at a time." Ms. Kitchens shared this with Ms. Banks as a method Ms. Kitchens used frequently to assist her adult clients at the Coastal Center for Developmental Services with learning how to manage their money.

Teri L. Burcroff, PhD, is an associate professor and graduate coordinator in the Department of Special Education and Rehabilitation at East Stroudsburg University in Pennsylvania. In her current position, she teaches graduate and undergraduate courses in special education. She received her doctorate in special education at the State University of New York–Buffalo. Prior to that, she was a public school special education teacher. Dr. Burcroff has consulted extensively to public schools regarding the development of inclusive educational practices. Her professional interests include the provision of quality services to individuals with severe disabilities, development of inclusive practices, and positive behavioral support strategies.

Shirley K. Chandler, PhD, is the chair of the Division of Human Services and the director of the rehabilitation counseling graduate program at Thomas University in Thomasville, Georgia. Dr. Chandler is also a partner with the counseling and evaluation center, Opportunities & Solutions, where her primary focus is the assessment and evaluation of children who have been physically, emotionally, and sexually abused. Prior to her current position, she was director of Florida's state systems change project, The Florida Blueprint for School to Community Transition, and served on the faculty of Florida State University where she taught a transition course for the Special Education Department. She has also worked as a research associate at The University of Texas Southwestern Medical Center at Dallas, where she directed a national study on partnership building within the rehabilitation process, as well as a study to identify and provide vocational services to individuals with traumatic brain injuries. Dr. Chandler has taught numerous courses in special education and rehabilitation counseling. She was a special education teacher and transition counselor in the public schools in New York State and is a certified rehabilitation counselor. Dr. Chandler has published an assessment instrument on vocational decision making and numerous book chapters, journal articles, and training materials. She was the recipient of the 1999 Georgia Service to Rehabilitation Award. Her research interests include the long-term effects of child abuse on adult functioning, transition issues for students with severe disabilities, and employment outcomes in the welfare-to-work system. Dr. Chandler holds master's degrees in rehabilitation counseling and special education from Syracuse University and a PhD from Virginia Commonwealth University. She has more than 25 years in the field of rehabilitation working with individuals with disabilities, employers, attorneys, and educators.

Lana Collet-Klingenberg, PhD, is an associate lecturer for the Department of Rehabilitation Psychology and Special Education at the University of Wisconsin–Madison. She is also an associate researcher for the Research Institute on Secondary Education Reform (RISER) for youth with disabilities in the Wisconsin Center on Educational Research. She has published work and obtained grants related to transition, career development, and vocational preparation of youth with disabilities. Her background also includes teaching students with moderate and severe disabilities, conducting research in the areas of social skills and communication, and providing training and support to educators in implementing transition services. Her research interests include enhancing transitional services for youth with disabilities, family and student participation in the transitional processes, and best practices in transition.

Victoria Dowdy, MEd, is currently a consulting teacher for exceptional education serving the high school programs in Henrico County, Virginia. Beginning in 1990, she served as a classroom teacher working with adolescents at Virginia Randolph Special Education Center in Hentico County, and prior to that she taught at the Eastern State Hospital education program in Williamsburg, Virginia. She earned her master's degree in special education from Virginia Commonwealth University.

Stacy K. Dymond, PhD, is an assistant professor of special education at the University of Illinois at Urbana–Champaign. Her primary interests, background, and experience relate to serving children and youth with severe disabilities in inclusive school and community settings. She has served as a special education teacher, an employment specialist, and a statewide technical assistance provider. She has also directed and coordinated a number of grant-funded projects, including a supported employment demonstration project, a severe disabilities technical assistance center for school personnel, two personnel preparation programs in severe disabilities, the development of Virginia's Alternate Assessment Program, and a legislative study on the services available for children with autism. Her primary research interest is in the area of evaluating inclusive school programs using a participatory action research approach. In addition, she has a strong interest in exploring curriculum and instructional issues for students with severe disabilities, particularly with regard to teaching functional skills in inclusive settings, alternate assessment, and the use of instruction in the community for both students with and without disabilities.

Cheryl Hanley-Maxwell, PhD, is a professor in the Department of Rehabilitation, Psychology, and Special Education at the University of Wisconsin–Madison. Currently, she is the director of the Research Institute on Secondary Education Reform (RISER) for youth with disabilities. The purpose of RISER is to identify and describe educational policies and practices that enhance inclusive and challenging secondary education for all students. She has published numerous articles and chapters related to supported employment and to transition. She also has extensive experience in preparing professionals and paraprofessionals to work with students as they move from school to their adult lives and to provide employees with disabilities employment-related services. Additionally, she has provided technical assistance in the development of innovative transition services and supported employment programs. Her research interests include career development, enhancing family and student participation and power in educational processes, and postschool life planning.

Richard M. Kubina Jr., PhD, is an assistant professor at Pennsylvania State University. He received his doctorate in special education at The Ohio State University. His current interests include measurably effective teaching methods such as Direct Instruction and Precision Teaching. Dr. Kubina's recent research has explored how measurably effective teaching methods can benefit students with autism.

Kelly Ligon, MEd, has worked for several years with students with moderate and significant disabilities at the elementary, middle, and high school levels. She earned her BS in mental retardation from James Madison University, Endorsement in severe disabilities from Virginia Commonwealth University, and her MEd in special education/assistive technology from George Mason University. Mrs. Ligon's interests are inclusion, assistive technology, augmentative communication, and transition. She is currently a program specialist with the Training and Technical Assistance Center at Virginia Commonwealth University.

James E. Martin, PhD, is director of the Zarrow Center for Learning Enrichment at the University of Oklahoma. Dr. Martin has extensive expertise in transition, self-determination, and student-centered curriculum planning. As director of the Zarrow Center, Dr. Martin directs research and teaching toward improving the lives of individuals with disabilities.

Sara C. Pankaskie, PhD, is an assistant professor at the University of Central Florida. Prior to coming to Orlando, she was a program specialist for the Florida Department of Education in the areas of transition and mental retardation. Her background includes more than 30 years of special education experience in institutional, community, and academic settings with individuals across the spectrum of mild to profound disabilities. Dr. Pankaskie is the author of numerous book chapters, journal articles, and position papers on special education and persons with disabilities.

Paul Sale, EdD, is a professor and dean of the College of Education and Human Development at Radford University in Radford, Virginia. His experiences and research interests focus on the education of students with severe disabilities, transition of youth with disabilities to adult life, and leadership issues in education.

Fred Spooner, PhD, is a professor in the Department of Counseling, Special Education, and Child Development in the College of Education at the University of North Carolina at Charlotte. He coordinates the graduate-level personnel preparation program in severe disabilities. From 1988 to 1996, he served as the coeditor of the Council for Exceptional Children's practitioner-oriented journal, *Teaching Exceptional Children.* His research interests have focused on instructional applications for persons with severe disabilities, evaluations of distance learning delivery, and practitioner-oriented writing. At present, he is directing a 5-year federally funded personnel preparation project in the area of severe disabilities that will collaborate with other institutions of higher education in North Carolina and deliver its content over a satellite network via a distance learning model.

Daniel E. Steere, PhD, has worked in the field of special education and rehabilitation since 1973. He has worked as a special education teacher, a manager of a community residence, a consultant to schools and rehabilitation agencies, and as a professor at two universities (Montana State University–Billings and East Stroudsburg University in Pennsylvania). In his current position at East Stroudsburg University, Dr. Steere teaches courses in special education and in rehabilitation. He has coauthored numerous journal articles and book chapters on topics related to the employment of people with disabilities, transition from school to adulthood, and systematic instruction. He has served on the editorial board of the journal *Career Development for Exceptional Individuals,* as a field reviewer for *Teaching Exceptional Children,* and as a guest editor of the *Journal of Vocational Rehabilitation.* Dr. Steere is past president of the Vocational Rehabilitation Division of the American Association on Mental Retardation. His professional interests include supported employment and transition from school to adulthood.

Pam Sherron Targett, MEd, is a collateral faculty member at the School of Education at Virginia Commonwealth University (VCU) and program manager for the Employment Services Division at the VCU Rehabilitation Research and Training Center on Workplace Supports, which provides supported employment services to people with severe disabilities. Over the years, she has overseen a number of employment demonstration projects, has authored or coauthored journal articles and book chapters, and has served as guest editor for the *Journal of Vocational Rehabilitation.*

Colleen A. Thoma, PhD, is an assistant professor in the Division of Teacher Education and is the coordinator of the undergraduate and graduate programs that prepare special educators to teach students with cognitive disabilities/mental retardation at Virginia Commonwealth University. She teaches courses in methods/strategies, transition planning, assistive technology, characteristics of students with cognitive disabilities, and assessment. She has conducted research in the areas of assessment, self-determination in transition planning, positive behavior supports, and teacher education. Dr. Thoma has published articles, book chapters, and made presentations on self-determined transition planning, alternative assessment, person-centered planning, assistive technology, and teacher education.

Michael D. West, PhD, is an assistant professor at Virginia Commonwealth University (VCU) and is also a research associate with the VCU Rehabilitation Research and Training Center on Workplace Supports. Dr. West's research projects have included national surveys of supported employment policies and practices, a study of students with disabilities in higher education in Virginia, and states' use of Medicaid home- and community-based waivers to fund employment services. Dr. West also is involved in research and demonstration efforts related to Social Security disability reform.

Katherine Wittig, MEd, is a program specialist for Secondary Transition at the Virginia Commonwealth University Training and Technical Assistance Center in Richmond, Virginia. She has more than 20 years of experience in the fields of special education and supported employment.

Pamela S. Wolfe, PhD, is an associate professor of special education at Pennsylvania State University where she teaches and conducts research related to transition and students with severe disabilities. Specific research interests include instructional methodologies, transition planning, sexuality training, and applied behavior analysis. She is currently codirector of a grant to train graduate students for work with students who have autism. Dr. Wolfe has a strong interest in fostering self-advocacy for persons with severe disabilities in integrated community settings.

Wendy M. Wood, PhD, is an associate professor in the Department of Counseling, Special Education, and Child Development in the College of Education at the University of North Carolina at Charlotte. She teaches special education coursework concentrating in supported employment, transition from school to adult life, and behavior management. She is also involved in research activities in the areas of transition and self-determination.